Ancient China: Studies in Early Civilization

Ancient China:
Studies in
Early Civilization

Edited by
David T. Roy and Tsuen-hsuin Tsien

The Chinese University Press

Typesetting by the Chinese University Press, Hong Kong

Printing by Wing Tai Cheung Printing Co. Ltd., Hong Kong

Dedicated to

HERRLEE GLESSNER CREEL

Martin A. Ryerson Distinguished Service Professor Emeritus
Department of Far Eastern Languages and Civilizations
and of History
The University of Chicago

Contents

Preface

This volume of essays on various aspects of Chinese civilization from its beginnings through the Han dynasty has been brought together in honor of Herrlee Glessner Creel, who celebrated his seventieth birthday in 1975. It has been a pleasure for all of the scholars associated with this undertaking to have an opportunity to give tangible expression to their admiration for his accomplishments. It is not given to many men in any generation to have the impact on a significant area of scholarship that Herrlee Creel has had on our understanding of early Chinese civilization.

From the appearance of his first book in 1929 until the present time he has been in the forefront of sinological scholarship. Some indication of the lasting value of his work may be seen in the fact that though he has been publishing in this field for half a century all of his major books remain in print. This fact is due not only to the quality of his scholarship but also, in no small part, to that of his prose style which consistently exemplifies standards of cogency, lucidity, and grace rarely to be found in academic writing. In his ability to explore the frontiers of knowledge, no matter how esoteric or complex his subject matter, and report his findings with a degree of clarity and elegance that makes them readily accesible not only to specialists but to every interested layman, he has set standards to which the rest of us can only aspire.

We did not ask the contributors to write on specific topics so long as their subjects were relevant to the early period of Chinese civilization which ended in the third century A.D. This restriction was made by the editors in the hope of producing a volume which would have greater coherence than the usual festschrift. Despite the heterogeneous nature of the contents, which reflects the differing areas of specialization of the contributors, we feel that this aim has been largely achieved. Since many of the articles cross disciplinary boundary lines, we have chosen to arrange them, in so far as possible, in chronological rather than topical order. The reader will find that the individual articles have something significant to say, from one disciplinary point of view or another, about every important period from pre-historic archaeology through the abdication of the last Han emperor in A.D. 220. A glance at the table of contents will indicate that the disciplinary approaches represented include archaeology and anthropology; epigraphy, philology, and linguistics intellectual, cultural, economic, and institutional history; and philosophy, art and literature. Such catholicity of approach is only appropriate in a volume which is inspired by the work of a scholar who has made significant contributions to every one of these fields.

The editors would like to take this opportunity to express our thanks to the many people who have helped to bring this project to fruition. The individual contributors, without whose cooperation this book could not exist deserve our thanks for the promptness with which they responded to our original letters of inquiry and the patience with which they have awaited the outcome. June Work compiled the bibliography of Herrlee Creel's publications in the appendix and also assisted with some of the editorial work. Gail Oman, Diane Perushek, and John Grobowski helped in the compilation and typing of the index. Marvin Waschke played a significant role in the launching of this project and rendered material assistance during its early stages. Others who have helped in important ways include Ma Tai-loi and Lois Fusek. The editorial work could not have been done without the excellent facilities provided by the Far Eastern Library of the University of Chicago and its staff. We are especially grateful for the expert assistance rendered by the staff of the Chinese University Press. Finally we wish to acknowledge our gratitude to the Center for Far Eastern Studies at the University of Chicago, and to its director Tetsuo Najita, for their willingness to offer the financial assistance which made this publication possible.

June, 1978   David T. Roy
Chicago   Tsuen-hsuin Tsien

List of contributors

NOEL BARNARD
Senior Fellow, Department of Far Eastern History, Australian National University.

DERK BODDE
Professor Emeritus, Department of Oriental Studies, University of Pennsylvania.

CHANG KWANG-CHIH
Professor, Department of Anthropology, Harvard University.

CHENG TE-K'UN
Visiting Professor and Pro-Vice-Chancellor, The Chinese University of Hong Kong; and Reader Emeritus in Chinese Archaeology, University of Cambridge.

CHOW TSE-TSUNG
Professor and Chairman, Department of East Asian Languages and Literature and Professor, Department of History, University of Wisconsin, Madison.

A. C. GRAHAM
Professor, Department of Chinese, School of Oriental and African Studies, University of London.

HSÜ CHO-YÜN
Professor, Department of History, University of Pittsburgh.

DAVID R. KNECHTGES
Associate Professor, Department of Asian Languages and Literature, University of Washington.

LAO KAN
Professor Emeritus, Department of Oriental Languages, University of California at Los Angeles.

CARL LEBAN

Associate Professor, Department of Oriental Languages and Literatures University of Kansas.

GÖRAN MALMQVIST

Professor, Department of Chinese Studies, Institute of Oriental Languages University of Stockholm.

EDWIN G. PULLEYBLANK

Professor, Department of Asian Studies, University of British Columbia

SYDNEY ROSEN

Former Assistant Professor, Department of History and Government Colby College.

RICHARD C. RUDOLPH

Professor Emeritus, Department of Oriental Languages, University of California at Los Angeles; and Director, University of California Study Centre, The Chinese University of Hong Kong.

KENNETH STARR

Director, Milwaukee Public Museum.

BENJAMIN E. WALLACKER

Professor, Department of Oriental Languages, University of California at Davis.

Some new discoveries in Prehistoric and Shang China

Cheng Te-k'un

In giving an account of some new discoveries in Prehistoric and Shang China, the recent exhibition of archaeological finds of the People's Republic of China may be taken as the starting point. The exhibition which was held at the Burlington House in London in the winter of 1973-74, presents a total of 385 objects, all archaeological materials which were unearthed under scientific control in recent years, especially during the Great Cultural Revolution. They are selected from a great exhibition which had been on show in Peking in 1972.[1] The collection went first to Paris[2] before coming to London[3] and other cities in Europe and America.[4] Supported with many maps, charts, ink-rubbings and photographs, and a series of explanatory notes, it covers the entire range of cultural development in ancient China from the Lan-t'ien Man 藍田人, 600,000 years ago to the Yüan dynasty in the 14th century when modern history began.

The exhibition is by itself an excellent academic exercise, a beautiful display of art objects supported with archaeology. Arranged in 12 well-defined sections, it covers the development of ancient China in three stages: the

---

[1] See *Historical relics unearthed in new China* (Peking: Foreign Languages Press, 1972); *Wen-hua ta-ko-ming ch'i-chien ch'u-t'u wen-wu* 文化大革命期間出土文物, Part I (Peking: Wen wu, 1972); and *Chung-hua Jen-min Kung-ho-kuo ch'u-t'u wen-wu chan-lan chan-p'in hsüan-chi* 中華人民共和國出土文物展覽展品選集 (Peking: Wen wu, 1973).

[2] Vadime Elisséeff and others, *Tresors d'Art Chinois* (Paris, 1973); and Hsia Nai, "600,000 years of labor and struggle—exhibition of archaeological finds in new China," *China Reconstructs*, 1973.6, 20-27; 1973.7, 30-37.

[3] William Watson, *The genius of China* (London: Times Newspaper, 1973).

[4] National Gallery of Art and Nelson Gallery—Atkins Museum, *The Chinese exhibition: an illustrated handlist of the exhibition of archaeological finds of the People's Republic of China* (Washington, D. C. and Kansas City, 1975); similar catalogs were also published in San Francisco, Toronto and other cities, where the exhibition was held.

Primitive Society in Paleolithic and Neolithic times, the Slave Society in the Shang and Chou dynasties, and the Feudal Society beginning from the 5th century B.C. The exhibition presents in a most concrete fashion a summary of the contributions made by the Chinese archaeological workers in the last few decades and demonstrates how archaeology in China now serves not only as a handmaiden of Chinese history but also as a foundation for the study of Chinese art.

In a way the exhibition is limited in scope and highly selective in nature. It contains only a very small part of the entire corpus of archaeological materials up to the end of 1971. They include, of course, the best and well-preserved specimens which are of interest to specialists as well as to ordinary spectators. This paper aims at reviewing some important discoveries which are not included in the exhibition in order to present a more detailed picture of the archaeology of ancient China up to the end of 1973. It covers the three early periods namely the Paleolithic, the Neolithic, and the Shang, the early historical period, as shown in the table accompanying.

PALEOLITHIC PERIOD—600,000-10,000 YEARS AGO

Evidence for Man in the Lower Pleistocene in China is still lacking. In 1946, Franz Weidenreich came up with a theory that *Gigantopithecus*, a giant ape from south China, may be directly ancestral to Man. But the investigation of the early caves in Kwangsi in recent years has recovered enough fossils to reconstruct the lower mandible of the giant ape, giving definite proof that *Gigantopithecus*, though widely distributed in south China, is not a hominid and has no connection with the evolution of Man.

By the Middle Pleistocene, around 600,000-400,000 years ago, China was populated by a human type of *Homo erectus*. The exhibition presents two distinct sub-species, the *Lantienensis* along the river and lake marshes of Shensi and the *Pekinensis* in the limestone caves in Hopei. To these we may add now a third, the *Yuanmouensis* in the forest regions of Yunnan. The early man is represented by two teeth discovered in the red loam of the Shang-pang-wei 上邦煒 region in Yuan-mou 元謀.[5] They are two upper medial incisors, ash-white and deeply fossilized. The depressions on the back of the teeth constitute a prominent feature; such teeth are called shovel-shaped and are noticeable not only in the Lan-t'ien Man and Peking Man but also in most of the later inhabitants including the majority of the modern Chinese. The new discoveries show that the *Homo erectus* in China were able to adapt themselves to the widely different environments in the various parts of the

[5]Cheng Te-k'un, "Metallurgy in Shang China," *T'oung Pao*, 64 (1973), 1-3.

MAN AND CULTURE IN ANCIENT CHINA

eological period	Man	Culture	Proposed dating (years ago)
	Shang Chinese	**HISTORIC** An-yang Cheng-chou Yen-shih (City and dynastic)	3,100
	Proto-Chinese	**NEOLITHIC** Upper: Lung-shan Ch'ing-lien-kang Ch'ü-chia-ling Yang-shao (Village and agriculture, Gobi microlithic)	4,000
		Lower: (Polished stone industry, corded ware, cord industry, transitory settlement, Gobi microlithic)	7,000
			10,000
Upper:	*Homo sapiens* Upper Cave Man Ting-ts'un Man Ordos Man Lai-pin Man Tzu-yang Man Liu-chiang Man	**PALEOLITHIC** Upper: (Neolithic element, bone industry, Gobi microlithic, chopping-tool tradition)	100,000
	Homo neanderthalensis Ordos Man Ch'ang-yang Man Ma-pa Man	Middle: (Primary microlithic, chopping-tool tradition)	200,000
Middle:	*Homo erectus* Pekinensis Lantianensis Yuanmouensis	Lower: (Chopping-tool industry)	600,000
Lower:	Ape Gigantopithecus		1,000,000

HOLOCENE

PLEISTOCENE

country. Their culture, characterized by the chopping-tool industry and the use of fire, is recognized as Lower Paleolithic. A few specimens are on display in the Burlington House.

The lack of Middle and Upper Paleolithic and Lower Neolithic culture in the exhibition does not mean that China was depopulated during this prolonged period, which ended around 7,000 years ago. In fact the early population continued to evolve and increase in number. The Middle Paleolithic Man is now represented by three groups of fossils in the three main river basins in China. They are the Ordos Man 河套人 in Inner Mongolia at the northern bend of the Huangho, the Ch'ang-yang Man 長陽人 in Hupei in the middle Yangtse, and the Ma-pa Man 馬壩人 in Kwangtung in the Sikiang valley. Morphologically they are all recognizable as Neanderthal Man, but they have transitional features between the typical Neanderthal Man and *Homo sapiens*. An upper incisor of the Ordos Man is clearly shovel-shaped. The stone industry of these peoples is basically in the chopping-tool tradition of the *Homo erectus*, but because of geographical differences and the supply of raw materials, new techniques were evolved. In Inner Mongolia, for instance, the Ordos Man began to make small flakes with neat secondary trimming at the cutting edge. These are described as "Gobi microliths," but evidence seems to show that the tradition was evolved from the advanced chopping-tool industry at this stage. It was destined to become a dominant trait in the semi-arid north, playing an important role in the shaping of Chinese culture.

Archaeological evidence of Man in China during the Upper Pleistocene is even more abundant and has been recorded in several areas in various sorts of environment. So far six groups of Upper Paleolithic Man, all *Homo sapiens*, have been found, three in south China and three in the north. The three southern fossils were in various stages of development, with Liu-chiang Man 柳江人 from Kwangsi as the oldest, followed by Tzu-yang Man 資陽人 from Szechwan and Lai-pin Man 來賓人 also in Kwangsi in chronological order. They all bear primitive mongoloid features which seem to suggest that they were in an evolutionary stage towards racial specialization, and it has been suggested that the Mongoloid race might have its cradle in south China.

The cultures of the three Upper Paleolithic men in north China are quite different from one another. The Ting-ts'un Man 丁村人, who lived in the watersheds of southern Shansi, continued to use pebble and flake chopping-tools. The industry may be regarded as a Middle Paleolithic survival into the Upper Pleistocene. The upper incisors of the Ting-ts'un Man are also shovel-shaped. The Ordos Man, who occupied the oasis in Inner Mongolia, practiced the microlithic type of industry which began to flourish in the steppe and desert north, stretching southward into the Central Plain and

tward into Tibet.[6] The human fossils found in the Upper Cave 上洞 at
ou-k'ou-tien comprise several types of *Homo sapiens*, which had been
viously classified into three races, but now, with the new materials from
th China for comparison, it seems clear that they are all fundamentally
ngoloid, but in various degrees of specialization. The skeletal remains
resent no less than ten individuals, including three complete skulls, who
e the weaker members of the group—an old male, a middle-aged and a
ng woman. Among these skulls, two had been perforated by a violent
w on the side while a third suffered a fatal blow on the neck. They seem
ave belonged to a primitive familial social unit and were attacked by their
mies. They led, to some degree, a sedentary way of life and practiced a
ognizable burial rite. Besides, among the artifacts, there are polished stone
bone, including a needle for tailoring, and the bow and arrows were
sumably in use. All these neolithic elements evolved right at the very
inning of the Holocene without a transitional Mesolithic stage. With these
ations in view, the Upper Cave culture may now be dated to about 10,000
rs ago, marking the end of the Paleolithic period in China.[7]

✓ LOWER NEOLITHIC PERIOD—10,000-7,000 YEARS AGO

The inhabitants of Holocene China were no doubt Mongoloid, but we
w very little about their life at the beginning of the period. Most of the
s consist of the remains of impermanent settlements along rivers, around
es, and by the sea, apparently with economies based on fishing. It may
presumed that they were linked to one another through the numerous
erways throughout the land. Their ways of life varied from region to
on according to the respective environments. In the southwest, where the
ography was mainly covered by dense vegetation and forests, the early
abitants continued to use pebble and flake implements in the chopping-
tradition. In its later development, pecking and polishing were intro-
ed, but never replaced the paleolithic techniques completely. Along the
coast, the stone implements consist of both chipped and polished artifacts
ether with fragments of bone arrowheads and awls. The semi-arid steppe
on in the north was populated by people with the Gobi microlithic
ustry. Their settlements are usually found in the consolidated sand dunes
ancient oases. In the loess region of the middle Huangho basin, some Gobi
rolithic remains were found scattered among a large number of pebble-
e-using settlements. These facts seem to indicate that some cultural mixing

[6]"New finds in archaeology and palaeontology," *China Reconstructs*, 1972.8, 40-41.
[7]Cheng Te-k'un, "The beginning of Chinese civilization," *Antiquity*, 47 (1973),
-209.

had taken place here in the Central Plain, destining it to become the cradl
Chinese civilization.

The most common finds in the Lower Neolithic deposits were fragm
of pottery, a coarse gritty ware fired at a low temperature and decor
mainly with cord marks, and occasionally with mat impressions and inc
patterns. We do not know yet where, when and how pottery making was
invented, but the useful industry spread fast and wide. By this time it
already a wide distribution in East Asia, covering not only China, but also
neighboring areas, from Siberia and Japan in the north to Assam and Ir
China in the south. The tradition served as a foundation for the cera
industry in these regions throughout the ages. No carbon dates for Lo
Neolithic China are available at present, but for Japan, the corded w
known in the island world as the Jōmon phase, is dated as 9,000 years agc
it seems reasonable to presume that the industry was in service on the m
land right at the beginning of the Holocene around 10,000 years ago.[8]

UPPER NEOLITHIC PERIOD—7,000-4,000 YEARS AGO

Around 5000 B.C. China was teeming with busy life, especially in
Huangho basin. There was already a large population of agriculturists
lived in villages with a subsistence economy based on cereal cultivation
plemented by animal husbandry, though hunting and fishing were
practiced. Thousands of Upper Neolithic sites have been recorded an
number of the more important ones thoroughly excavated. Some of tl
are surprisingly extensive and must imply large social units. In the exhibi
this stage is represented by 45 specimens from three different phases in n
China, namely, the Yang-shao 仰韶 in Shensi and Kansu, the Ch'ing-lien-k
青蓮崗 in northern Kiangsu, and the Lung-shan 龍山 in Shantung. In the
they had been regarded as three different cultures, but later discove
revealed that they were basically similar, though in various stages of deve
ment. They can easily be distinguished from one another by the typ
ceramic wares which they produced: the painted red pottery of Yang-sl
the black burnished pottery of Lung-shan, and another type of pai
pottery of Ch'ing-lien-kang.

The stratigraphical sequences gathered from hundreds of these U
Neolithic sites give concrete evidence of the fact that the development of
new way of life may be traced to the Central Plain in the Huangho valle
is a small basin where the Huangho is joined by its two great tributaries,
Fen-shui from Shansi and the Wei-shui from Shensi. Being the most eas

[8]*Ibid.*

nsion of the loess highland, it is bounded by the Shansi plateau in the
n and the Ch'in-ling 秦嶺 mountains in the south, but opens into the flood
 in the east. It constitutes a borderland between the semi-arid highland to
vest and the swampy lowland to the east, a favored natural region less sus-
ible than any other areas to the hazards of drought and flood. As a result
·came a center of human settlement where peoples of various cultures
peted for occupation as we have noted in the Upper Paleolithic days.

This small basin, known in historical times as Chung-yuan 中原, the
ral Plain, served as a fertile ground for the continuous mixing of cultures,
ugh the Neolithic into historical times. Because of the distribution of
g-shao and Lung-shan in north China it was presumed in the early
)s that Yang-shao originated in the western loess highland while Lung-
emerged in the eastern flood plain. Their contact in the Central Plain
rise to the Hsiao-t'un 小屯 culture which was ancestral to the Shang
sty. This was the three-culture theory advanced by the members of the
lemia Sinica.[9] But the excavation of Pan-p'o-ts'un 半坡村 in Shensi[10] and
·ti kou 廟底溝 in Honan[11] in 1954-57 yielded enough evidence to prove
 the neolithic culture in China was directly ancestral to the historical
ese civilization and that the Central Plain was not the meeting place of
three cultures, but their original home. Yang-shao, Lung-shan, and Hsiao-
constituted actually a continuous development of the same culture in
e stages.[12] The Central Plain was indeed the cradle of Chinese civilization
 from the very beginning. In its development Yang-shao moved westward,
hing its height in Kansu. Another branch moved east to become the
ng-lien-kang phase in the east. Then came the newly evolved Lung-shan
:h expanded eastward and dominated finally a large territory along the
 from the Liao-tung peninsula to Taiwan in the South China Sea. It was
ne Hsiao-t'un stage that a rudimentary form of central government was
blished. This became in time the Shang dynasty which held sway over the
ngho basin from the eastern part of the loess highland to the sea.

But this picture of Upper Neolithic China is far from being final. In
1 another important site was investigated at Hsia-wang-kang 下王崗, in
ch'uan 淅川, at the southern edge of the Central Plain. Two seasons of
 work revealed a cultural deposit in four distinctive levels in successive

Shih Chang-ju, "Hsin shih-ch'i shih-tai ti Chung-yüan" 新石器時代的中原, Ta-lu tsa-
, 4 (1952), 65-73.
[0]Institute of Archaeology, Hsi-an Pan-p'o 西安半坡 (Peking: Wen wu, 1963).
[1]Institute of Archaeology, Miao-ti-kou yü San-li-ch'iao 廟底溝與三里橋 (Peking: K'o-
h ch'u-pan-she, 1959).
[2]An Chih-min, "Lüeh-lun wo-kuo hsin shih-ch'i shih-tai ti nien-tai wen-t'i" 略論我國
器時代的年代問題, Kaogu 考古, 1972.6, 35-44, 47; and Institute of Archaeology,
aeology in new China (Peking: Wen wu, 1962).

order: Yang-shao in the bottom, overlaid by a new stage known as Ch'ü-d
ling屈家嶺, then came Lung-shan and finally a Shang level on top. The re
was published in October 1972.[13] It became clear immediately that the
stage of Ch'ü-chia-ling can be linked with a phase which had been establi:
at Ta-ssu 大寺 in Yün-hsien郇縣, Hupei, in the middle Yangtse a few y
earlier.[14] From the ceramic point of view, the Ch'ü-chia-ling wares furni
transitional stage between Yang-shao and Lung-shan, with an advanced pai:
pottery in close association with a rudimentary form of black pottery. Th
fore, it becomes evident that the Upper Neolithic culture in China had a n
complex development than we know so far. While Ch'ü-chia-ling serves
transitional stage between Yang-shao and Lung-shan in the Central Plai
took another direction in its expansion, that was to the south. The key sit
Ch'ü-chia-ling is located at Ching-shan京山, Hupei, and the culture enjoy
wide distribution in the lake districts in the middle Yangtse.[15] Future e
vation in the Yangtse valley may show that the neolithic culture of the Ce:
Plain might have expanded through the waterways of the river eastwar
the coast. In this way Ch'ü-chia-ling may be linked up with Ch'ing-lien-I
where the painted designs degenerated into a less imaginative static sch
as shown by the examples in the exhibition.[16]

The process of mixing and amalgamation of cultures in Upper Neoli
China was long and complicated. The ancient sites in different parts of
Huangho and Yangtse regions show almost always a mixture in various :
portions of the known cultures including some paleolithic survivals. The s:
has been observed also in other parts of China, stretching from Heilungk:
on the Siberian frontier to Yunnan on the Burma-Thailand border and f
Sinkiang in central Asia to Taiwan in the South China Sea.

In the past a few radio-carbon dates have been acquired from the
historic sites in Taiwan, but beginning from 1972 the Institute of Archaeo!
in Peking have been publishing in *Kaogu* others which have been derived f
well-excavated sites in various parts of China. They seem to indicate
Yang-shao might have begun around 5000 B.C., Ch'ü-chia-ling, around 4
B.C., Ch'ing-lien-kang, around 3500 B.C., and Lung-shan, around 3000 l
The earliest date of Lung-shan in Taiwan is 2500 B.C. This is roughly
chronological sequence we have for the present, and it is followed by

[13]Honan Provincial Museum and others, "Ho-nan Hsi-ch'uan Hsia-wang-kang yi-
ti shih-chüeh"河南淅川下王崗遺址的試掘, *Wen wu* 文物, 1972.10, 6-19.

[14]Institute of Archaeology, *Ching-shan Ch'ü-chia-ling* 京山屈家嶺 (Peking: K'o-h
ch'u-pan-she, 1965).

[15]*Ibid.*

[16]See also "Tui Chiang-su ku-tai li-shih ti hsin t'an-t'au" 對江蘇古代歷史的新:
Kaogu, 1962.3, 146.

to-Shang Hsiao-t'un in around 2000 B.C.[17] The Shang dynasty was
blished around 1750 B.C.

SHANG PERIOD—2000-1100 B.C.

The Shang period is well documented in Chinese history and ever since
beginning of the excavation of the Shang ruins at An-yang 安陽, the
ient historical accounts have been verified and enriched at various stages
1 archaeological finds. In the last few decades hundreds of other Shang
s have been investigated. We know now that the domain of the Shang
asty stretched far beyond the Huangho basin to the Great Wall regions in
north and the Yangtse valley in the south. The Shang capitals were not
y political centers but also flourishing industrial towns. The majority of
people were essentially Mongoloid, just as the inhabitants of the prehis-
c days had been and as the Chinese of the later historical times are. The
letal remains show invariably that their upper incisors are shovel-shaped.

For this period, 33 fine specimens are on display in the exhibition. They
drawn from the Shang sites in various provinces, including two capitals,
at Cheng-chou 鄭州 and the other at An-yang. China entered now into
Bronze Age with a highly developed metallurgy. The Shang section in the
ibition is dominated by some magnificient bronze vessels which are unique
hapes as well as in decoration.

All the Shang bronze vessels were cast in one piece with a composite
tery mold which could only be used in one casting, and as a result, no two
els are exactly identical. It is generally agreed that the best living craftsmen
d by all the resources of modern science and technology can do no better
n the bronze masters of the Shang period.

In the exhibition a section is devoted to the ancient technologies. It is
resting to note that apart from the mining, smelting, and refining of the
als, the mixing of the alloy and the retouching of the cast, the entire
cess of bronze manufacture in Shang times was in the hands of the
ter. The basic technique was casting, a unique method in the Chinese
amic tradition. From the beginning, the Shang bronze master was proficient
casting, especially by the piece-mold method. The absence of methods,
h as sheet metal working, riveting, annealing, tracing, engraving, stamping,
ousse, and the *cire perdue* lost wax process in Shang bronze technology
s clear evidence that the industry had indigenous origins. Its close relations
h the ceramic art may be illustrated also by the similar types of vessels

[17]Cheng Te-k'un, "The beginning of Chinese civilization," *Antiquity*, 47 (1973),
-209.

and decorative designs inherited by the bronze industry.[18]

The Shang potter made another spectacular break-through in his c field. In the exhibition there is a glazed pottery wine vase which was excava from the ruins of the Middle Shang capital at Cheng-chou in 1965, datable the 16th century B.C. It is a hard stoneware, covered with a high-fired f spathic glaze, representing the beginning of the porcelain known in the W as Chinese celadon. The making of such a hard glazed ware requires a l capable of reaching a temperature of no less than 1,200°C and the product of the celadon glaze shows that the kiln was under expert control for fi in a reducing atmosphere. The industry was destined to make "china product synonymous with its country of origin.

It is interesting to note that the two excavated Shang capitals w originally prehistoric settlements. Under the Shang occupation they w rapidly developed in several stages into great cities. After the fall of the cap parts of the sites were reinhabited at various intervals in later dynasties. / whole the Shang deposits covered a very wide territory, some four squ kilometers for the city at Cheng-chou and much more at An-yang. Apart fi a large assemblage of architectural foundations, there were remains of bro foundries, refuse heaps of pottery kilns, and workshop ruins of bone and h industries at various levels. Huge royal tombs were scattered beyond the (limits. The same situation has been observed in many other sites within Shang domain. As a result a number of chronological sequences tabula with the stratigraphy from various sites have been proposed and continu be discussed. However, the main deposit at Cheng-chou has been gener taken to represent Middle Shang and that of An-yang, Late Shang.

The absence of the Early Shang stage in the exhibition does not m that it is still a blank in Shang archaeology. On the contrary, a number of earlier levels at Cheng-chou and other sites are clearly Pre-Middle Shan stratigraphy. Some of the finds could even be confidently ascribed to l dynastic or Proto-Shang in date. The most important site for the early st may now be represented by the ruins of another Shang capital at Erh-li-t 二里頭 in Yen-shih 偃師, Honan. According to ancient accounts the cap was established by King T'ang 湯, the founder of the dynasty who reig from 1751 to 1739 B.C. The ruins covered a large territory. The excava continued for eight seasons in 1960-64 and the report was published in 1 before the Cultural Revolution.[19] Besides the palace foundations, the dep has been found to consist of three distinct levels. The lowest one can be lin to the prehistoric Lung-shan stage in various respects, especially in pott

[18]Cheng Te-k'un, "Metallurgy in Shang China," T'oung Pao, 64 (1973), 1-3.

[19]Institute of Archaeology, "Ho-nan Yen-shih Erh-li-t'ou yi-chih fa-chüeh chien- 河南偃師二里頭遺址發掘簡報, Kaogu, 1965.5, 215-24.

e the later stratum had been intruded by a storage pit of the Cheng-chou
od.

Among the miscellaneous objects found at Erh-li-t'ou are several simple
ze articles: an awl, a rod, an arrowhead and a bell. All these were manu-
ured by casting, the simple articles in open hearths or valve molds and
bell in the multi-mold process. The beginning of bronze casting in China
now be traced back to the middle of the 18th century B.C.

The excavation furnishes additional evidence that the Erh-li-t'ou stage
ved directly from the prehistoric Lung-shan on the one hand and marked
beginning of the Bronze Age on the other. The Shang period, which
red some 900 years, may now be represented by three capital cities, Yen-
for the Early, Cheng-chou for the Middle, and An-yang for the Late stage.

Finally, another spectacular discovery has been made at the Shang site
'ai-hsi-ts'un 台西村 in Kao-ch'eng 藁城, Hopei, more than 230 kilometers
h of An-yang. The ancient deposit covers an area of no less than 10,000
re meters. It was discovered in 1965, excavated by the members of the
incial Museum in October 1972, and the report published in May 1973.[20]
most ancient dwelling sites, it continued to be occupied throughout the
at various intervals. The main deposit, however, was of the Shang period,
prising an assortment of building foundations, dwelling floors, storage
kiln sites, and burial tombs. In one of the burials, a group of bronze
els and implements, a musical stone, and two jade pendants were recovered.
bronzes are consistently similar to those reported from the lower levels
n-yang, so they may be dated from the pre-capital days before 1384 B.C.
the most interesting find at T'ai-hsi-ts'un was a bronze tang of a damaged
a 鉞 axe. The blade had broken off and disintegrated, but the remaining
left in the tang was made of iron. The metal has been subjected to a
ber of scientific investigations by the Institute of Metallurgy. Apart from
nical analysis, a variety of instrumental techniques such as X-radiography,
y diffraction, and electron-beam micro-spectrometry have been employed.
concluded that the blade was made of wrought iron which was beaten
the required shape and then joined to the bronze tang by the casting-on
hod. The remaining part inside the bronze tang measures about one
imeter deep. It is indeed fascinating to find that the Shang technology
another break-through in metallurgy.[21] The invention of wrought iron
hina may now be dated to at least the 14th century B.C.[22]

[0]Hopei Provincial Museum, "Ho-pei Kao-ch'eng T'ai-hsi-ts'un ti Shang-tai yi-chih"
藁城台西村的商代遺址 , *Kaogu*, 1973.5, 266-71.

[1]Rutherford John Gettens and others, *Two early Chinese bronze weapons with
oritic iron blades* (Washington, D. C.: Freer Gallery of Art, 1971).

[2]Cheng Te-k'un, "New light on Shang China," *Antiquity*, 49 (1975), 25-32.

Archaeology in China is young. We are far from reaching the point w
a truly valid synthesis for the ancient periods can be firmly established.
picture sketched in this article takes us up to the end of 1973. It may
to be readjusted, perhaps quite drastically with the announcement of
discoveries in the future.

T'ien kan: a key to the history of the Shang*

Chang Kwang-chih

ten *t'ien kan* 天干 ("heavenly or celestial stems" or denary cyclical
—*chia, i, ping, ting, wu, chi, keng, hsin, jen, kuei* (Figure 1)—are said
ve been invented by one of the Yellow Emperor's officials, and they are
n use today. The real origin of this set of signs is as yet unknown, but

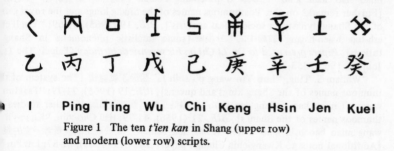

| | I | Ping | Ting | Wu | Chi | Keng | Hsin | Jen | Kuei |

Figure 1 The ten *t'ien kan* in Shang (upper row)
and modern (lower row) scripts.

bly it began as a system of numbers.[1] At the time of the Shang (*c.* 1850-
B.C.), *t'ien kan* (not a Shang term) had two prominent uses: to combine
he twelve *ti chih* 地支 ("earthly or terrestrial branches" or duodenary
al signs, again not a Shang term) to produce the 60-day calendrical
and to be employed to designate deceased ancestors. The latter custom,
f posthumously referring to a relative as Father Chia, Mother I, Elder

ie first draft of this paper was presented at a meeting of the University Seminar on
onal China, Columbia University, on April 16, 1974.
o Mo-jo, "Shih chih kan" 釋支干 [An interpretation of *chih* and *kan*], in his
wen-tzu yen-chiu 甲骨文字研究 [Studies of oracle bone inscriptions] (Peking:
Press, 1952).

Brother Ping, and so forth, declined with the fall of the Shang dynasty it became virtually extinct after the subsequent Chou period (1100-220 E But the other use of the *t'ien kan*, for the 60-day cycle, continued int modern period. At the Shang time, *t'ien kan* alone formed a shorter, te cycle, called *hsün* 旬. *Hsün* ("week") actually had greater ritual signific than the longer, 60-day cycle.

Here we are concerned only with the use of the *t'ien kan* for thumous names. By a careful study of the interrelationships of the bearing names of the Shang we are able to uncover important but hit completely hidden aspects of Shang history and social and political sys This was first brought to light in 1963[2] and was the subject of man ditional studies.[3] In this paper I present my current thinking on the su taking into account my own additional research in recent years. Since t also the first detailed presentation of the issue in English, I will repeat

[2] Chang Kwang-chih, "Shang wang miao hao hsin k'ao" 商王廟號新考 [posthu names of the Shang kings and the royal genealogy of the Shang dynasty: a sociol analysis], *Bulletin of the Institute of Ethnology, Academia Sinica* (Taipei; her abbreviated as *BIE*), 15 (1963), 65-94. See also his "Some dualistic phenomena in society," *The Journal of Asian Studies*, XXIV (1964), 45-61; "Kuan-yü 'Shang miao hao hsin k'ao' i wen ti pu-ch'ung i-chien" 關於商王廟號新考一文的補 [Further remarks on the 'Posthumous names of the Shang kings and the royal gen of the Shang dynasty: a sociological analysis'], *BIE*, 19 (1965), 53-69; "Yin li ch erh-fen hsien-hsiang" 殷禮中的二分現象 [some dualistic phenomena in Shang tutions], *Papers presented to Dr. Li Chi on his seventieth birthday* (Taipei: The Ts Journal, 1965), 353-70.

[3] William S. Ting, "Lun Yin wang p'i shih fa" 論殷王妣諡法 [The system of th thumous names of the Shang kings and queens], *BIE*, 19 (1965), 71-79; "Tsai lun wang p'i miao hao ti liang tsu shuo" 再論商王廟號的兩組說 [Further studies thumous names of the Shangs], *BIE*, 21 (1966), 41-79; Hsü Cho-yün, "Kuan-yü wang miao hao hsin k'ao' i wen ti chi tien i-chien" 關於商王廟號新考一文的幾 [Additional notes to Kwang-chih Chang's paper], *BIE*, 19 (1965), 81-87; Liu Pin-l "Yin Shang wang-shih shih fen tsu chih shih lun" 殷商王室十分組制試論 [An int ation on the kinship system of the royal house of the Shang dynasty], *BIE*, 19 (89-114; Lin Heng-li, "P'ing Chang Kwang-chih 'Shang wang miao hao hsin k'ao' c lun cheng fa" 評張光直商王廟號新考中的論證法 [Review of Chang Kwang-chih's p *BIE*, 19 (1965), 115-19; Hsü Chin-hsiung, "Tuei Chang Kwang-chih hsien-sheng ti wang miao hao hsin k'ao' ti chi tien i-chien" 對張光直先生的商王廟號新考的幾 [Comments on Dr. K. C. Chang's paper], *BIE*, 19 (1965), 121-37; Yang Hsi-mei, ming chih yü pu-tz'u Shang wang miao hao wen-t'i" 聯名制與卜辭商王廟號問題 [logical linkage naming system and the interpretation of the posthumous names Shang dynasty], *BIE*, 21 (1966), 17-39; Itō Michiharu, *Kodai Inōchō no nazo* 古 朝のなぞ [The riddle of the ancient Yin dynasty] (Tokyo: Kadokawa Shoten, Hayashi Minao, "Inshū jidai no zushōkigō" 殷周時代の圖象記號 [The pictographi of the Yin and Chou periods], *Tōhōgakuhō (Kyoto), 39 (1968),* 1-117; Mats Michio, "Inshūkokka no kōzō" 殷周國家の構造 [The state structure of the Yin an dynasties], in *Iwanami Kōza Sekaichi*, 4 (1970).

the more essential arguments first set forth in my 1963 paper (hereafter
reviated as the *New studies*). But for detailed documentation of many
inical points the reader must be referred to this earlier work.

POSTHUMOUS *T'IEN KAN* NAMES AND TRADITIONAL INTERPRETATION

Ssu-ma Ch'ien in his *Shih chi* (compiled *c.* 100 B.C.) presented the
owing account of the dynastic succession of the Shang kings:

The mother of Ch'i, of Yin, was named Chien Ti, a daughter of the Yu
Jung Shih, second consort of Ti K'u. At a bath with two companions,
Chien Ti saw a black bird let fall an egg, and she picked it up and
swallowed it. Thus impregnated, she then gave birth to Ch'i. . . . Ch'i
died, and his son Chao Ming ascended the throne. [Then, in succession],
Chao Ming's son Hsiang T'u, . . . Hsiang T'u's son Ch'ang Jo, . . . Ch'ang
Jo's son Ts'ao Yü, . . . Ts'ao Yü's son Ming, . . . Ming's son Chen, . . .
Chen's son Wei, . . . Wei's son Pao Ting, . . . Pao Ting's son Pao I, . . .
Pao I's son Pao Ping, . . . Pao Ping's son Chu Jen, . . . Chu Jen's son Chu
Kuei, . . . Chu Kuei's son T'ien I, known as Ch'eng T'ang. . . . T'ang
died. Crown Prince T'ai Ting died before ascendance, and T'ai Ting's
younger brother Wai Ping was enthroned. . . . [Then], Wai Ping's
younger brother, Chung Jen, was enthroned, . . . Chung Jen died in four
years, and I Yin [the Prime Minister] placed T'ai Ting's son T'ai Chia on
the throne. . . . [The subsequent rulers were, in succession], T'ai Chia's
son Wo Ting, . . . Wo Ting's younger brother T'ai Keng, . . . T'ai Keng's
son King Hsiao Chia, . . . Hsiao Chia's younger brother Yung Chi, . . .
Yung Chi's younger brother T'ai Wu, . . . T'ai Wu's son King Chung
Ting, . . . Chung Ting's younger brother Wai Jen, . . . Wai Jen's younger
brother Ho Tan Chia, . . . Ho Tan Chia's son King Tsu I, . . . Tsu I's
son King Tsu Hsin, . . . Tsu Hsin's younger brother Wo Chia, . . . Tsu
Ting (son of Wo Chia's elder brother, Tsu Hsin), . . . Nan Keng (son of
younger brother Wo Chia), . . . Yang Chia, son of King Tsu Ting, . . .
Yang Chia's younger brother P'an Keng, . . . P'an Keng's younger
brother Hsiao Hsin, . . . Hsiao Hsin's younger brother Hsiao I, . . . Hsiao
I's son King Wu Ting, . . . Wu Ting's son King Tsu Keng, . . . Tsu Keng's
younger brother Tsu Chia, . . . Tsu Chia's son King Lin Hsin, . . . Lin
Hsin's younger brother Keng Ting, . . . Keng Ting's son King Wu I, . . .
Wu I's son King T'ai Ting, . . . T'ai Ting's son King I, . . . I's son Hsin. . . .
Chou Wu Wang [defeated Hsin, toppled the Shang dynasty, and] gave
land to [Hsin's] son Wu Keng Lu Fu where he could carry on Yin's
rites. (*Shih chi*, Vol. III, K'ai-ming Edition, 1935.)

Later we will discuss some of the historical issues contained in this accou
Here, let us note only that the Shang kings after Wei all had a *kan* sign as
of their names: T'ai *Chia*, Pao *I*, Pao *Ping*, Pao *Ting*, T'ai *Wu*, Yung *Chi*,
Keng, Tsu *Hsin*, Chu *Jen*, Chu *Kuei*, and so forth. Wei, Pao Ting's fathe
known in other texts ("Lu yü" and Kuo P'u's annotation to *Shan hai ch*
as Shang Chia Wei or Chu Chia Wei, which also includes a *kan*. Thus, from
to Wu Keng, all the Shang rulers had in their names one or another of the
t'ien kan. After the discovery of the Shang oracle bone inscriptions in 18
students of Shang history have found in the oracle records almost all of
kings' names, essentially validating the *Shih chi* account.[4] In addition, in
oracle records we have learned that the names of the wives of the kings w
also made up of *t'ien kan* signs.[5]

The royal couples were not the only ones to have names so constitu
Many Shang and early Chou bronze artifacts (especially ritual vessels)
inscriptions, often indicating an ancestral name to which the object
dedicated. Many of these names again contain a *t'ien kan*: Tsu (Ancesto
Fu (Father) Ting, Mu (Mother) Kuei, and the like. In a catalogue of 4,
inscribed Shang and Chou bronzes my associates and I have compiled,[6]
find that 1,295 of them, or almost a third, were inscribed with a *t'ien*
name.[7] All of them were obviously not kings and kings' wives. Was ev
Shang Chinese so named? This is perhaps unanswerable, but Tung Tso-p
believed that this practice was largely confined to members of the royal ho

What is the origin of, and explanation for, this practice? The earl
recorded explanation is in *Pai hu t'ung* 白虎通 , a book said to have been c
piled in A.D. 79, in which it is stated that the Shang royal family named t
children according to their birthdays. T'ien I, the dynasty's founder, accor
to this theory, was born on a *i* day during the *hsün* week, and his Cr
Prince, T'ai Ting, born on a *ting* day. This has been the traditional interpr
tion throughout Chinese history. Another old explanation, not much noti

[4] Lo Chen-yü, *Yin hsü shu ch'i k'ao shih* 殷墟書契考釋 [A study of Yin hsü ins
tions], 1914; Wang Kuo-wei, *Yin Pu-tz'u chung so chien hsien kung hsien wang k*
殷卜辭中所見先公先王考; *Hsü k'ao* 續考 [A study of the predynastic ancestors and k
from the Yin oracle bone inscriptions; A further study], 1917.

[5] Lo Chen-yü, *Yin hsü shu ch'i k'ao shih.*

[6] Chang Kwang-chih, *et al.*, *Shang Chou ch'ing-t'ung ch'i yü ming-wen ti tsun
yen-chiu* 商周青銅器與銘文的綜合研究 [Inscribed Shang and Chou bronzes: a com
hensive study] (Taipei: Institute of History and Philology, Academia Sinica, 1973).

[7] See also Li Chi, *Yin hsü ch'u-t'u ch'ing-t'ung chüeh-hsing ch'i chih yen-chiu* 殷
土青銅爵形器之研究 [Studies of the bronze *chüeh*-cup] (Taipei: Institute of His
and Philology, 1966), 85.

[8] Tung Tso-pin, "Lun Shang jen i shih jih wei ming" 論商人以十日爲名 [A discus
of the Shang custom of naming after the ten days], *Ta-lu Tsa-chih*, Vol. 2, No. 3 (19
6-10.

e referred to later. In recent years, scholars have advanced a few other theses, attributing the *t'ien kan* part of the names to the days of death,[9] rder of birth, enthronement, and death,[10] and decision by oracles,[11] but has been widely accepted.

Naming by day or date of birth is a common enough practice among eoples of the world for it to be regarded as a reasonable explanation for ihang names. However, it is now clear, first of all, that the *t'ien kan* s were not in fact the names given to the children during their lifetimes, dicated in *Pai hu t'ung*. Every Shang king was known by one or more nal names during his lifetime, and the *t'ien kan* appellations were assigned m only after death.[12] It could be said that a name was conferred on a n after death according to his birthday. But this is still insufficient to ınt for some very interesting patterns of the distribution of these names ecific populations. I refer in particular to the Shang king list and to the e inscriptions.

Of the 1,295 bronzes that contain *kan* names, the breakdown with l to their estimated age is as follows: 1,102 are estimated to be of Shang 191 of Western Chou, and 2 impossible to judge. Of the 191 Western artifacts, only 19 are considered to date from later than the reign of K'ang, approximately 1000 B.C. Insofar as the bronzes are concerned, it ıs plain that the practice of *kan* names is largely a Shang and initial ern Chou custom.

The ten *kan* do not occur with equal frequency within this significant lation of 1,295. The distribution of the various *kan* is shown in Figure 2, It may be noted that each occurrence may not in every case represent ndividual, because a set of vessels was sometimes made to be dedicated e same ancestor and all would bear his name. This, of course, would be for each of the ten signs. One would not hesitate to say that the distri- n pattern of these ten *t'ien kan* among the 1,295 names is not random, hat in no way can they represent birthdays. One would imagine that : the same number of births would occur on any particular day of the —whether it be a ten-day week or a seven-day week. A random distri- n of birthdays of 3,995 births during the year 1973 at the Yale-New

id.

Ch'en Meng-chia, *Yin hsü pu-tz'u tsung shu* 殷墟卜辭綜述 [A comprehensive ɔtion of the oracle inscriptions from Yin hsü] (Peking: Science Press, 1956).
Li Hsüeh-ch'in, "P'ing Ch'en Meng-chia *Yin hsü pu-tz'u tsung shu*" [Review of Meng-chia's *Yin hsü pu-tz'u tsung shu*], *K'ao-ku Hsüeh-pao*, 1957.3, 119-30.
Wang Kuo-wei, *Yin li cheng wen* 殷禮徵文 [Documentation of Yin customs], Ch'ü Wan-li, "Shih fa lan-shang yü Yin tai lun" 諡法濫觴於殷代論 [The beginning ıorific posthumous names in the Yin period], *Bulletin of the Institute of History ılology, Academia Sinica*, 13 (1948), 219-26.

Haven Memorial Hospital in New Haven, Connecticut, demonstrates t
Figure 2, *right*. The fact alone that disproportionately large numbe
persons had names of all the even numbered days of the *hsün* week durin
Shang and initial Chou periods would render the birthday explanation u
able. In terms of probability theory, there is practically no chance tha
figures shown in Figure 2, *left* could reflect the distribution pattern of na
birthdays.

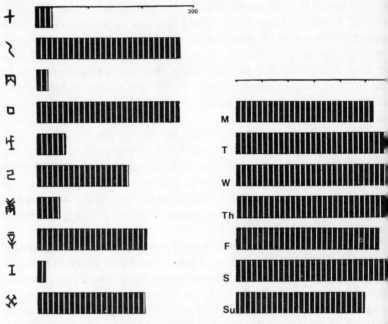

Figure 2 *Left* Numbers of bronze artifacts with *kan* names (total: 1,295)
Right Yale-New Haven Memorial Hospital 1973 births by days of week (total
3,995).

The birthday explanation fails even more miserably to explai
pattern of occurrence of the *kan* names in the royal genealogy of the S
kings and their official spouses. Figure 3 shows the names in the best g
logical interrelationship that we can now work out on the basis of ava
data. Most of it is based on *Shih chi*, as a comparison of Figure 3 wit
above *Shih chi* quotation will quickly make clear. The individual names
been changed, wherever necessary, to accord with the oracle records o
last two kings, which also provide most of the names of wives. The A
numerals indicate order of enthronement. At a few places, the genera

r and sequence of *Shih chi* had to be changed in accordance with either
;putable oracle records data or my best judgment. This, in short, is a

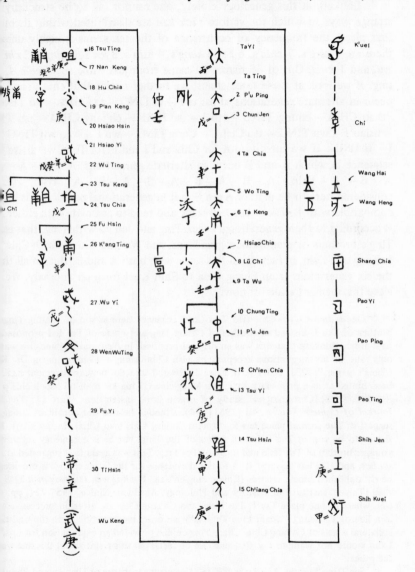

Figure 3 Genealogical chart of Shang kings and official wives (based on Tung
Tso-pin's *Chia ku hsüeh liu-shih nien* [Sixty years of oracle bone inscription
studies], Taipei: I-Wen Press, 1965; but see n. 13).

genealogy that, except for two places,[13] can be basically accepted by alm
all oracle record specialists.[14]

Looking at this genealogy closely, one cannot fail to be struck by
strange ways in which the various *t'ien kan* are distributed within it. In
first place, the frequency of occurrence of the ten stems is highly une
there are 8 *ting*'s, 7 *chia*'s, 6 *I*'s, 4 *keng*'s, 4 *hsin*'s, 3 *jen*'s, 2 *ping*'s, 2 *chi*
wu, and 1 *kuei*. Out of 38 names 21 came from just three signs, *chia*, *I*,
ting. If we look at these three stems, we further notice that *chia*, *I*, and
occur in alternate generations, thus: ta I – ta TING – ta CHIA – wo TIN
hsiao CHIA – chung TING – tsu I – tsu HSIN – ch'iang CHIA – tsu T
– hsiao I – wu TING – tsu CHIA – k'ang TING – wu I – wen wu TING
I – ti HSIN. If we substitute A for Chia and I and B for Ting, we arrive
sequence in which A and B occur in alternate generations: A – B – A –
A – B – A – Hsin – A – B – A – B – A – B – A – B – A – Hsin. Hsi
considered here to be neither A nor B, but in generational position it is lar
compatible with B. The other *kan* signs also tend to associate with either
B according to their generational order. Ping and Jen go with Ting, that is.
Ting's brothers or grandfathers-grandsons, and Wu and Chi go with Chia
I. Keng and Hsin, in fact, go in this sense with both A and B. But, in all th
the six generations from Shang Chia to Shih Kuei form an anomaly. We
leave this segment aside for now.

[13] One is that Ch'ien Chia (Ho Tan Chia) is placed here as son of Chung Ting
brother of Tsu I, instead of brother of Chung Ting and uncle of Tsu I. I proposec
new order, thinking that this was an original proposal, in *New studies*, and this wa
only one of my suggestions accepted by Hsü Chin-hsiung ("Comments on Dr. I
Chang's paper," 123). But I have since discovered that the new arrangement had
been hinted at as a possibility by Ch'en Meng-chia ("Chia ku tuan tai hsüeh chia p
甲骨斷代學甲編 [Chronological study of oracle bone inscriptions, Part 1], Yenc
Journal of Chinese Studies, 40 [1951], 14), although he was not confident enoug
suggest it. The second place has to do with Ch'iang Chia (Wo Chia). In my chart,
shown to be son of Tsu Hsin and father of Tsu Ting, but he is commonly regarde
younger brother of Tsu Hsin and uncle of Tsu Ting. This was again first suggested in
studies, and Hsü has rejected it. Additional evidence for the latter change is provide
newly published oracle records (Chang Ping-ch'üan, *Yin hsü wen tzu ping pien* 殷墟
丙編 [Taipei: Institute of History and Philology, Academia Sinica, 1957-72], pp.
62), where at one place Tsu I, Tsu Hsin, and Ch'iang Chia are given in successive c
as a line of Ta Tsung ("Main Line Tablets"), an order incompatible with the traditi
collateral status of Ch'iang Chia. Chang Ping-ch'üan provided an explanation for this
I too would not want to say that one can be certain at this point about this one wa
the other.

[14] See Tung Tso-pin, *Yin li p'u* 殷曆譜 (Li-chuang: Institute of History and Philol
Academia Sinica, 1945); *idem*, *Chia ku hsüeh liu-shih nien* 甲骨學六十年 [Sixty yea
oracle bone inscription studies] (Taipei: I-wen Press, 1965); Ch'en Meng-chia, "ch
tuan tai hsüeh chia pien" (1951), and *Yin hsü pu-tz'u tsung shu* (1956).

Another interesting phenomenon is that the royal couples never had
ntical *t'ien kan*. In fact, although I and Ting are among the most common
n signs among the kings, they do not occur in the names of their official
ves at all. This was pointed out by Yang Shu-ta,[15] who speculated that the
ang royal family may have observed a marriage taboo between men and
omen with identical birthday signs.

If the matter of the wives' names were the only issue, the marriage
oo hypothesis could have sufficed. But the above patterns all taken
gether constitute to me powerful—in fact, conclusive—evidence that the
ming could not have been made according to the natural days of birth.

WHAT DID THEY REALLY STAND FOR?

There is another old explanation for the Shang naming practice, but the
xtual reference to it is so brief (all of four characters) and obscure that it in
ct explains little. In a T'ang annotation to *Shih chi*, a certain Ch'iao Chou
周 (210-270) was quoted as saying, in his book *Ku shih k'ao* 古史考 (no
nger extant), that "[He was] named Chia because after death one is referred
by his tablet in the [family, lineage, or clan] temple."

Let us try to expand and elaborate on this explanation a bit. Presumably
thin the ancestral temple the tablets were grouped and numbered *chia, i,*
ng, ting, and so on. After death, a person was perhaps given a new tablet, or
new entry onto an existing tablet, and assigned to one of the ten possible
its. These units were probably also arranged according to generational and
xual order: Elder Brother's generation; Father's; Ancestor's; Mother's;
male Ancestor's. A tablet was referrable to as one in the FATHER'S
neration, TING unit, for example, which could easily be abbreviated as
ATHER TING. But since there were only ten *t'ien kan* and there could be a
r larger number of individuals per temple unit, one can only conclude that
mes such as Fu Ting may have two meanings: a generational group within a
eage or clan, and an individual member of that group. For kings, especially
ose of the more remote past, individual identity was important, and specific,
efix-like compounds, such as Ta ("Great"), Chung ("Middle"), Hsiao
Small"), and Wu ("Martial"), were added.

The assignment of an individual's tablet to one of the ten units within
e temple could have been entirely arbitrary; in that event nothing could
er be made of it. Far more likely there was some objective basis. The
rthday explanation is attractive for its simplicity, and Wang Kuo-wei[16]

---

[15] Yang Shu-ta, *Nai-lin-ch'ing chia wen shuo* 耐林廎甲文說 [Studies of turtle shell
scriptions] (Shanghai: Ch'ün-lien Press, 1954).

[16] Wang Kuo-wei, *Yin li cheng wen.*

in fact combined the *Pai hu t'ung* and the Ch'iao Chou explanations by say
that, when the deceased ancestor was born on a *chia* day, he would be nam
Chia after death, so named on his tablet, and given sacrifice to on a *chia* d
But in that event we should not obtain the kind of patterns that we h.
discussed above. An alternative explanation to the birthday hypothesis is tl
the assignment of the tablet had some basis in his or her position in
within the family, lineage, or clan. If this is so, then the posthumous *t'ien k*
names would assume extraordinary importance because they may give
important and otherwise unavailable clues to the social classification of in
viduals. We may make an effort to generate sociological models to fit the da
i.e., the pattern of distribution of the *kan* names within the structu
population. If we are able to design models that make sense in terms of
empirical data, then the two following premises may be regarded as hav
been validated: that the names came from tablet assignment, and that
tablet assignment was based on a prior arrangement meaningful with reg.
to the person's social and ritual status during his or her lifetime.

Before we proceed with the model, let us first take a look at th
premises themselves and see if they can stand on their own. There is
question that the name Tsu Hsin, for example, in the genealogical chart of
Shang kings stands for an individual person. But in the hundreds of Sh;
bronzes that each bears a name such as Tsu Hsin, do these names also sta
for individual, deceased persons? That is what they have been always belie
to be, but this should not be taken for granted. The ancients believed thi:
view of the Shang kings' names. Could the kings' names have been exc
tions? Could it be that Tsu Hsin was actually, as described before, at leas
some cases, a ritual unit of a particular generation and lineage position?

The inscribed Shang bronzes referred to above offer some good evide
for an affirmative answer to these questions. The inscriptions are of two ty
according to complexity. The first consists of simple, straightforward sig
There is usually one or more emblems, often realistic ideographs that oc
also in oracle bone inscriptions and, from their oracle bone context, proba
designated clans, lineages, and/or clan- or lineage-based settlements.
addition, in some cases there is a *t'ien kan* sign, often but not invaria
accompanied by a kin term, i.e., *fu, mu, tsu, p'i*, or *hsiung* (Fig. 4). The sec
type consists of messages, mostly brief but occasionally long. These may
may not have an emblem. Sometimes they describe an event of importan
in the context of which the bronze object was made. But the most essen
line is: "So-and-so made (or had made) [this] Father Chia [or Mother Kt
et cetera] vessel" (Fig. 5). Since Sung times, when bronze vessels were f
described in scholarly treatises, the "Father Chia" in the message has b
regarded as denoting a specific individual, the father (born on a *chia* day)

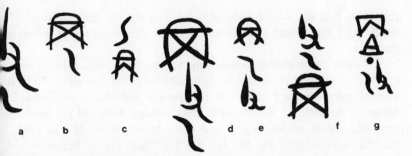

Figure 4 "Signs" on Shang bronzes. a. Fu+I; b. Emblem Chü+I; c. I+Chü;
d. Chü+Fu+I; e. Chü+I+Fu; f. Fu+I+Chü; g. Chü (?)+Tsu+Ting+Fu+I.
(From Lo Chen-yü, *San tai chi chin wen ts'un*, 1937.) Chü is probably a clan
or lineage of considerable antiquity (see Chang Kwang-chih, "Preliminary
remarks on a comprehensive study of form, decoration and inscription of
Shang and Chou bronzes," *Bulletin of the Institute of Ethnology*, 30 [1972],
264, 269).

Figure 5 "Messages" on Shang Bronzes. These two inscriptions were probably cast at the same time on the occasion of a single event. Left is on a *chiao*;
right a *yu*. From Lo Chen-yü, *San tai chi chin wen ts'un*, 1937, Chap. 13:34
and Chap. 16:47. The message at left is more complete: "On the day *chia-yin*,
the Prince gave [name of a person] a gift of cowrie shells. These were used to
cast a Father Kuei ritual vessel. Emblem."

the maker (the one who bought or ordered it, not the manufacturer) of t
vessel. And the "sign" type inscriptions are thus regarded as abbreviat
messages.

I offer an alternative explanation. Any explanation must begin with t
question as to what these vessels were made for in the first place. To be su
a vessel was made for Father Chia, for example. But what could Father Chi
deceased, do with it? Vessels with these messages have not yet been fou
from the graves at An-yang,[17] and those bearing signs of *Tsu* Chia, a
the like, were often made too late for Tsu Chia's burial. The most logic
and common, explanation is that the vessels were used for rituals at t
lineage or clan temples.[18] What can be more logical and simpler than to rega
the signs as place markers?—Vessels for this or that clan or lineage, *chia* un
father's generation. Once in a while a vessel is dedicated to two generatio
(e.g., Tsu Ting Fu I in Fig. 4, g), in which case the two generations never h
identical signs. The "message" type inscriptions in no way contradict t
explanation—the "signs" were merely incorporated in the messages. Anoth
fact may also bear on this point, i.e., that the *kan* designations are seldom
ever found on weapons. Perhaps weapons were not part of the standa
paraphernalia on the ancestral temple's sacrificial altars.[19]

Thus, the evidence from the bronzes alone seems to suggest that the
Chia's and the Mu I's in the bronze inscriptions referred to ritual categories
persons but not to individuals, and that when and if an individual was th
referred to he was referred to by his ritual label. For example, I can be simp
called Chang, and people would know who Chang is in the proper contex
even though there are millions of Changs in China.

But what is the nature of this ritual unit during a person's lifetime?
person surely belonged to some social group that corresponded in son
fashion to a temple or tablet unit. But what was such a group, and what w
its term? Was there an exact equation between a social unit (lineage, linea
segment, subsegment, or their clusters) and a ritual *kan* unit? I cannot as y
answer these questions. The Chinese did not describe or even talk about the
own institutions, at least not in the existing record, until late Chou, and

[17]Li Chi, *Yin hsü ch'u-t'u ch'ing-t'ung chüeh-hsing ch'i chih yen-chiu*, 85.

[18]Jung Keng, *Shang Chou i ch'i t'ung k'ao* 商周彝器通考 [A general study of Sha
and Chou ritual vessels] (Peking: Harvard-Yenching Institute, 1941), 1.

[19]The best-known exceptions to these rules are the famous Three Shang *Ko*-halber
said to have been found in Pao-ting, Hopei (Lo Chen-yü, *Meng-wei-ts'ao-t'ang chi ch
t'u* 濛邸草堂吉全圖, 1917). Not only do we find *kan* names on these weapons; names
three generations (*tsu, fu, hsiung*) share identical *kan* signs. Many scholars regard the
weapons, or at least the inscriptions, as fakes, for very good reasons. One could rega
them as fakes on this ground alone.

n the *t'ien kan* names had all but disappeared. The inscription of signs on
sels to mark their place, such as those cast in the bronzes, is apparently a
tom of considerable antiquity in China. Numeral-like signs have been
nd on pottery vessels at several early Chinese dwelling sites, including the
ag-shao Culture site at Pan-p'o, in Shensi,[20] the Lung-shan Culture site at
eng-tzu-yai, in Shantung,[21] the Lungshanoid site at Feng-pi-t'ou, in
wan,[22] and the Shang ruins at An-yang[23] (Fig. 6). These signs (other than
se at Feng-pi-t'ou, which have escaped general notice) have recently spurred
ne enthusiastic discussion about the origin of Chinese writing.[24] Some
n kan signs are found on Shang pottery, which included ritual vessels, but
ae has been identified on the Neolithic utilitarian wares. At least some of
se numerals and other signs probably designated familial or lineage units to
ich the pottery vessels belonged. This is strengthened by the occurrence of
te a few clan or lineage emblems on Shang pottery. But the data are still
» scarce to inform us of any detailed social categorization that may corres-
nd to the *t'ien kan* ritual units shown in the bronzes.

Perhaps people were classed by *t'ien kan* units in life as well as in death,
t they were never referred to by them until after death. There is one single
ce of evidence for this, which will be discussed at the end of the paper. It
also possible that the earliest concept of *hsing* 姓 in China included a
rson's precise placement in his group by virtue of birth (*sheng* 生, earliest-
own version of *hsing*) into a generational or other subdivision of a clan as
ll as a clan itself. In *Tso chuan*, under the 25th year of Hsiang Kung (546
C.), we find this interesting passage:

[20] Shih Hsing-pang, *et al.*, *Hsi-an Pan-p'o* 西安半坡 (Peking: Science Press, 1963), 196.

[21] Li Chi, *et al.*, *Ch'eng-tzu-yai* 城子崖 (Nanking: Institute of History and Philology,
ademia Sinica, 1934), 53-54.

[22] Chang Kwang-chih, *et al.*, *Fengpitou, Tapenkeng, and the prehistory of Taiwan*
ew Haven: Yale University Publications in Anthropology No. 73, 1969), 95.

[23] Li Chi, *Hsiao-t'un t'ao-ch'i* 小屯陶器 [Hsiao-t'un pottery] (Taipei: Institute of
story and Philology, Academia Sinica, 1956), 129-47.

[24] T'ang Lan, "Tsai chia ku chin wen chung so chien ti i-chung i-ching i-shih ti Chung-
o ku-tai wen-tzu" 在甲骨金文中所見的一種已經遺失的中國古代文字 [A lost script in
cient China as seen from oracle bone and bronze inscriptions], *K'ao-ku Hsüeh-pao*,
57.2, 33-36; Li Hsiao-ting, "Ts'ung chi-chung shih-ch'ien ho yu-shih tsao-ch'i t'ao wen
kuan-ch'a li-ts'e Chung-kuo wen-tzu ti ch'i-yüan" 從幾種史前和有史早期陶文的觀察蠡
中國文字的起源 [The origin of Chinese writing as hypothesized on the basis of obser-
tions of some prehistoric and early historic pottery inscriptions], *Bulletin of Nanyang
niversity*, 3 (1969), 1-28; Kuo Mo-jo, "Ku-tai wen-tzu chih pien-cheng ti fa-chan" 古代
字之辯證的發展 [The dialectic development of ancient writings], *Kaogu Xuebao
'ao-ku Hsüeh-pao*), 1972. 1, 1-13; Cheng Te-k'un, "Chung-kuo shang ku shu ming ti
n-pien chi ch'i ying-yüng" 中國上古數名的演變及其應用 [Numerals of ancient China],
urnal of The Chinese University of Hong Kong, I (1973), 41-58; Ho Ping-ti, *The Cradle
the East* (Hong Kong: The Chinese University of Hong Kong, 1975).

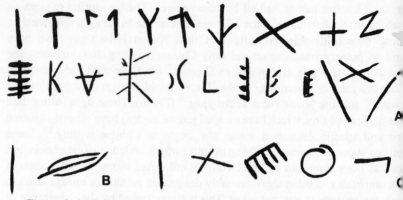

Figure 6   Incised signs on Neolithic pottery (A. Pan-p'o; B. Ch'eng-tzu-yai; C. Feng-pi-t'ou).

The wife of T'ang Kung of Ch'i was Tung-kuo Yen's elder sister. Tung-kuo Yen was a family official of Ts'ui Wu Tzu. When T'ang Kung died, Yen drove Wu Tzu to his funeral. [Ts'ui Wu Tzu] saw T'ang Kung's widow and admired her beauty, and he asked Yen to go and ask her for marriage. Yen said, "Men and women [in a union] must have different *hsing*. Now you descended from Ting and I from Huan. It cannot be done."

The last statement is rather puzzling. Why did Yen not simply say, "You and I are both members of the Chiang *hsing*, which rules out such a union?" It was as if the sharing of the Chiang *hsing* was not in itself sufficient grounds for prohibiting the union, and that the marriage was undesirable only because Yen was a descendant of Huan Kung and Wu Tzu a descendant of Ting Kung. From the genealogy of the Ch'i dukes, we find that Ting Kung and Huan Kung were separated by 9 generations, which makes Ting (!) Kung and Huan Kung members of the same generational group, in opposition to the generational group represented by I (!) Kung, Ting Kung's son. One is tempted to read what Yen said to mean that, should one of them have descended from I Kung or one of I Kung's generational group, the marriage would have been all right. If this reading of the text is permitted, then the generational subdivision within the Chiang as well as the larger group, Chiang itself, was covered by the general rule of "Men and women [in a union] must have different *hsing*." Perhaps even in the late Ch'un-ch'iu period some of the old taboos were still good, and so was this unusual meaning of the word *hsing*, even though the practice of using the *t'ien kan* for posthumous names had all but gone out.

A NEW EXPLANATORY MODEL

Since the most intricate set of data pertaining to the whole problem of
n names has to do with the distribution of kingship among the ten *kan*
its, the most relevant model must be the one that explains the system of
ccession to the throne. To design this model one must think in comparative
rms and familiarize himself with the known blueprints according to which
e fragmented pieces of the original design could be fitted together. Since
roughout most of Chinese history the pattern of an agnatic stem dynasty
as the rule, it is tempting for us to project it back into the time of the Shang
ad interpret the Shang data first of all in that light. But it would be well to
me into this issue without prejudice but equipped with knowledge of a
ide range of what is possible. Ethnographic facts and models are useful only
cause they tell us what is realistic and what is not, and our own models for
ie Shang data must be responsible to the Shang data itself. Both Yang Hsi-
ei and Hsü Chin-hsiung[25] criticized the *New studies* as an attempt to "fit
ie Shang data to ethnographical theory." This represents a serious misunder-
anding and is simply and plainly not true.

What, for a society at the level of development of the Shang, are some
ossible succession systems consistent with the evidence? In a general study
f the rules of succession to high office, Jack Goody[26] distinguishes four
pes of dynastic institutions: the "royal descent group" of the Basuto, the
uthern Bantu generally, and of many other societies; the "dynasty" which
onstitutes the only significant descent unit in the society, as is the case
mong the Gonja, Lozi, Hausa, Nupe, and in some of the Mossi states; the
narrow lineal dynasty" of the Baganda in the nineteenth century, and more
specially of the Ottoman Turks; and the "bilateral or familial dynasty" of
ie kind found in modern Europe (Fig. 7).

Since the Shang kings belonged to no fewer than ten tablet units, and in
iew of the fact that in the royal genealogy the kingship shifts between tablet
nits and never continues within a single unit, plainly the Shang system is not
onsistent with the characteristics of the stem or the familial dynasty systems.
'or the two other systems there is a very common practice of what Goody
as called the "circulating succession." This is found widely in Africa, Europe,
\sia, and the Pacific, and although it has many variations its general under-
ying principles are not complex. In the societies with such systems, kingship
s confined to a ruling class, and within this class it circulates among its

[25] Yang Hsi-mei, "Genealogical linkage naming system and the interpretation of the
osthumous names of the Shang dynasty"; Hsü Chin-hsiung, "Comments on Dr. K. C.
*]hang's paper."
[26] Jack Goody, *Succession to high office* (Cambridge: Cambridge University Press,
1966), 26.

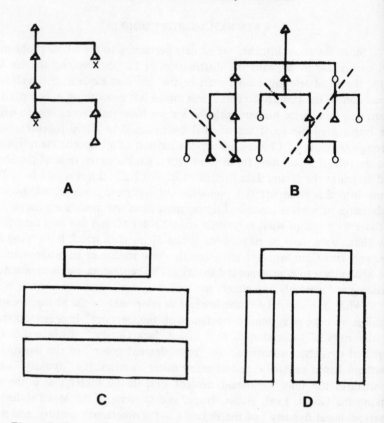

Figure 7 Four types of dynastic structure. A. Stem dynasty (agnatic succession over time). B. Familial dynasty (English pattern, exclusion of children of non-succeeding daughters and grand-children of non-succeeding sons). C. Dynastic descent group. The short rectangle on top represents a hereditary dynasty, segmented in circulating systems, and the longer rectangles represent other estates. D. Royal descent group. Each rectangle represents a uni-lineal descent group. X, no children. Broken lines are lines of exclusion. (From Jack Goody, *Succession to high office* [Cambridge University Press, 1966], 27.)

various sections or segments. These segments may be several unrelated descen groups (the "royal descent group"), or they may be subdivisions of a sing kin-based ruling unit ("the dynasty" or "the dynastic descent group"). In man cases there is a tendency toward a dualistic grouping of these segments, wi the throne being assumed by members of the two parties in turn in alterna generations. In the case of alternate succession among two or more lines, th

chiefs of the groups not currently in power often serve as assistant or
ndary chiefs or prime ministers. Among the lines of royal descent there
ally are elaborate marrage ties. When these lines constitute segments of a
le dynasty, the dynasty is often endogamous.

The Shang situation looks suspiciously like such a system, a "dynastic
ent group" in particular. Historians think forward, not backward, and
should remember that the Chinese agnatic stem dynasties developed out
he Shang system, not the other way around. Serious students of Shang
ory with open minds will profit from reading the anthropological accounts
uch circulating succession systems, especially those in Malaya[27] and in the
afuni of the Ellis Islands,[28] the Fakaofo in the Union Group,[29] and in
uma[30] in the Pacific Islands, societies that may even claim some historical
liation with the ancient Chinese. Yang Hsi-mei,[31] in his critique of the
studies, asks how anybody can formulate a Shang social system only
n a genealogical chart and not on the basis of fieldwork. I fully agree that
l research among the Shang would have been desirable, but under the
umstances we must be satisfied with mere ethnographic analogies. But
lick's account of the succession rules of the western Malaya Sultans is
e capable of giving one the illusion of reading an ethnographical account
he Shang kings!

Despite these illusions, the value of these accounts is only heuristic. We
st attempt to write a set of rules that can account for the empirical data
n the Shang society, even though ethnographical analogy may give us the
ial inspiration. The following are the rules that I have worked out to
ount for the genealogy of the Shang kings (Fig. 8).

(1) The Shang society was ruled by a hereditary ruling class, of a single
sanguineal origin (the Tzu clan). Members of the clan that were actively
olved with the kingship were ritually classed into ten segments: Chia, I,
g, Ting, Wu, Chi, Keng, Hsin, Jen, Kuei. Let us call them *kan* units. These
al *kan* units were also political entities, and they figured importantly in
riage alliances. We do not know their other characteristics, but the ten
ts were probably not equals. Some were politically more powerful, more

[27] J. M. Gullick, *Indigenous political systems of western Malaya* (London: L.S.E.
ographs on Social Anthropology, No. 17, 1958).
[28] Robert W. Williamson, *The social and political systems of Central Polynesia*, I
nbridge University Press, 1924), 378-79.
[29] A. M. Hocart, "Chieftainship and the sister's son in the Pacific," *American Anthro-
gist*, 17 (1915), 631-46.
[30] F.L.S. Bell, "A functional interpretation of inheritance and succession in Central
nesia," *Oceania*, 3 (1932), 167-206.
[31] Yang Hsi-mei, "Genealogical linkage naming system . . . ."

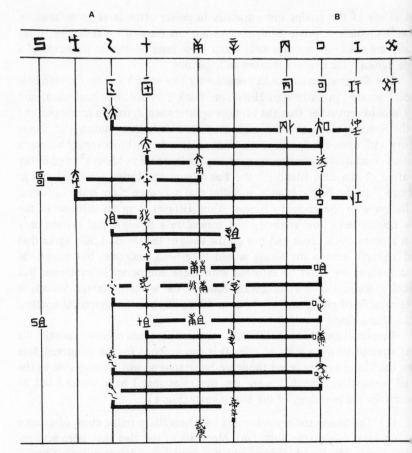

Figure 8 A model of ten ritual units (in two major divisions) in the royal
house of the Shang dynasty and their circulating succession to kingship.
Vertical, thin lines are descent lines within the ritual unit. Broad lines indicate
the passage of kingship.

populous, and/or more ritually prominent than others. Chia, I, and Ti
were three such units.

(2) The ten *kan* units were affiliated with one another to form tw
major divisions, A and B. Chia and I were undoubtedly fellow members of
and Ting a member of B. These were the most politically powerful. The oth
kan units aligned themselves similarly: Ping was a member of division B; V
and Chi undoubtedly were units of A; and Jen and Kuei were perhaps
Keng and Hsin were non-aligned, or formed a separate segment a level abo

parallel to both A and B, although Hsin at least probably sided more often
in not with B.

(3) Succession did not follow automatic rules except for two: that it
not stay within the same *kan* unit, and that when the kingship stayed
thin division A or B, it must be assumed by an heir, from another *kan* unit,
m within the same generation as the former king, but if it went over to the
er division it must go to an heir of the next generation. To phrase this
ferently: when the kingship passed over to the next generation, it must
ve to the opposite division. Keng and Hsin counted as either division, but
same cross-divisional and generational rules applied.

(4) The king was assisted by a (formal or loosely informal) council of
portant officials,[32] the prime official being, not invariably, the chief of a
n unit from the opposite division. The heir was probably chosen when the
g was still alive, although after his demise a new successor could emerge.
e choice of the successor was determined by, first, the availability of
gible heirs and, then, their capability and political following. There could
bloody or bloodless struggles. The prime minister could play key roles in
transition of power, and he would be likely to favor a cross-divisional and
ss-generational succession, because it would enthrone a member of his own
ision, conceivably his own son or at least one of his younger affiliates. He
y or may not lose his job as a result.

(5) A male member of the dynastic descent group was eligible to
come an heir if he was physically and mentally capable of assuming the
iduous task of political, military, and religious leadership. He must be of
right generation: the same generation as the reigning monarch if he (the
narch) was in the same A or B division, or the next generation if he was of
opposite division. He (the heir) must also have a mother who was a
mber of one or more of the ten *kan* units. In the event of two or more
gible heirs, military power and political following may determine the actual
oice, but those more capable than others and those whose mothers came
m the politically or ritually higher ranking *kan* units may have been more
ored than the others.

(6) The ten *kan* units were probably engaged in an endogamous network
some order. Names of some daughters-in-law in oracle bone inscriptions
ggest that royal princes took some of their mates from outside the Tzu
n,[33] but there is no evidence that the official wives were anything but the

---

[32] Li Tsung-t'ung, *Chung-kuo ku-tai she-huei hsin yen* 中國古代社會新研 [A new
dy of the ancient society of China] (Shanghai: K'ai-ming Book Co., 1948), 228.

[33] Hu Hou-hsüan, "Yin tai hun-yin chia-tsu tsung-fa sheng-yü chih-tu k'ao" 殷代婚姻
族宗法生育制度考 [A study of the marriage, family, lineage, and birth institutions of
Yin dynasty], in his *Chia ku hsüeh Shang shih lun ts'ung* 甲骨學商史論叢 (Ch'eng-tu:

kings' clan co-members. Particular *kan* units may be regarded as the m
desirable source of a mate, but the marriage traffic does not seem to fol
the same A-B division. The kings at least were polygynous. The status of s
as eligible heirs might be determined in large measure by the ranking of tl
mother's *kan* units. In the *New studies* I relied solely upon the patrilat
cross-cousin marriage as the mechanism for the kingship to be passed c
from one division to the other. I still think it was one of such mechanis
perhaps the most important, but would allow for a greater degree of flexibi
and additional variations.

HISTORY OF SHANG KINGSHIP IN THE NEW PERSPECTIVE

Aspects of Shang history are clearly known, but others are obscı
The above model has been formulated on the basis of the known aspects
the historical reality of the Shang, and its aim is to help explain both
known and the obscure. If it is capable of doing so, then the model n
approximate the reality, and it would additionally help throw new light oı
Let us go over the history of the Shang kingship in the perspective of
above model. We will do this in four segments.

1. K'uei (Ti K'u) to Wang Hai (Chen)

A few names occur in the oracle records to match the *Shih chi* acco
of this segment, but the entire era before Shang Chia must still be regardec
more legendary than historical. Nevertheless, a few of these remote ancest
are singled out both in early texts and in the oracle records as being of ı
ticular import. In the latter, only three ancestors were designated by
honorific title Kao Tsu ("High Ancestor"); these were Kao Tsu K'uei, l
Tsu Wang Hai, and Kao Tsu I.[34] K'uei was Shang's supreme ancestor-god, ;
Ta I the dynastic founder, and they properly deserved to be so revered. ı
why Wang Hai? Since Wang Kuo-wei's[35] pioneer study of this man, it
been generally accepted that Wang Hai and Chen, in *Shih chi*'s account, w
one and the same. In the poems called "T'ien wen," in the anthology *C
tz'u*, perhaps fourth century B.C., a short section was devoted to Shı
history, and only a very few Shang rulers were important enough to

University of Shantung, 1944), 12; but see Ting Shan, *Chia ku wen so chien shih-tsu
ch'i chih-tu* 甲骨文所見世族及其制度 [Clans and their institutions as seen from the orɑ
bone inscriptions] (Peking: Science Press, 1956), 55-56.

[34] Hu Hou-hsüan, "Chia ku wen Shang tsu niao t'u-t'eng ti i-chi" 甲骨文商族鳥圖ⵏ
遺跡 [Relics of the bird totem of the Shang people in the oracle bone inscriptions]
shih lun ts'ung, I (Peking: Chung-hua Book Co., 1964), 150-51.

[35] Wang Kuo-wei, *Yin pu-tz'u chung so chien hsien kung hsien wang k'ao.*

entioned: K'u, Chi, Kai, Heng, Hun Wei, and Ch'eng T'ang, or, in oracle
ne parlance, K'uei; Chi, his two sons Wang Hai and Wang Heng, and grand-
n Shang Chia; and T'ang or Ta I. The special importance of these ancestors
again underscored by the following paragraphs in *Li chi* ("Chi fa"):

The Yin people *ti* K'u and *chiao* Ming, and they *tsu* Ch'i and *tsung*
T'ang.

d in *Kuo yü* ("Lu yü"):

The Shang people *ti* Shun and *tsu* Ch'i, and they *chiao* Ming and *tsung*
T'ang.

he italicized terms are kinds of rituals performed for the different ancestors.
ere again K'u (Shun), Ch'i, and T'ang are understandable, but why Ming (the
racle records' Chi)? It appears that the three generations from Chi, through
ang Hai and Wang Heng, to Shang Chia Wei, are of some crucial importance.
o understand this, Wang Hai is a key figure.

Wang Hai has been the subject of much discussion by Shang historians.[36]
here is no need to repeat here all the known facts about him of which there
e not very many to begin with. But the question of the *kan* day for sacrificial
tes to Wang Hai is an issue of importance and must be raised.

In the traditional view about the use of *kan* for posthumous names, it is
sually thought that it began with Shang Chia, and that it was limited to the
yal family.[37] But I believe that, in the case of at least some ancestors before
hang Chia and some high officials, even though they were not recorded as
aving been given posthumous names with *t'ien kan* signs, they were sacrificed
only on some *kan* days but not on others, just like the *kan*-named fore-
ears. In other words, they also participated in the *t'ien kan* system of temple
nd tablet units. For Wang Hai, his ceremonial day is, normally, Hsin.

In discussing the date of sacrifices to Wang Hai, Hu Hou-hsüan[38] stated
at "from the oracle records cited here one finds that sacrifices to Wang Hai
ere made on the following days [of the 60-day cycle]: *hsin-wei*, *chia-hsü*,
sin-ssu*, *chia-shen*, *ping-hsü*, *hsin-mau*, *jen-ch'en*, *i-wei*, *kuei-mau*, *i-ssu*,
ng-ssu*, *hsin-yu*." In other words, they were performed on *chia*, *i*, *ping*, *ting*,
sin*, *jen*, and *kuei* days. But when we take a closer look at the oracle records

[36]*Ibid.*; Wu Ch'i-ch'ang, "P'u-tz'u so chien hsien kung hsien wang san hsü k'ao"
三續考 [A still further study of the pre-dynastic ancestors and kings as seen from the
racle bone inscriptions], *Yenching Journal of Chinese Studies*, 14 (1933), 1-58; Hu
lou-hsüan, "Chia ku wen Shang tsu niao t'u-t'eng ti i-chi"; Naitō Torajirō, "Ōgai 王亥"
nd "Zoku Ōgai 續王亥," in *Naitō Konan zenshū*, Vol. 7 (Tokyo: Chikuma Shobō,
970), 469-500 (originally published 1916, 1917, 1921).

[37]Tung Tso-pin, "Lun Shang jen i shih jih wei ming," 8-9.

[38]Hu Hou-hsüan, "Chia ku wen Shang tsu niao t'u-t'eng ti i-chi," 149.

Hu cited, most of these days actually turn out to be the days on which t
oracles were taken to inquire about the sacrifices that were being anticipate
but not the days on which they were actually performed. This distinction
readily apparent in the following example:

The day *keng-hsü*, cracked. Asked: Perform this sacrifice to Tsu Hsin?

The day *keng-hsü*, cracked. The King asked: Perform the *yu* ceremo
to Tsu Hsin on the following day *hsin-hai*?"[40]

The ritual was *yu*. The object of sacrifice was Tsu Hsin. The intended day
the ritual was *hsin-hai*, which was the right (*hsin*) day for the right (Hs
person. The divination took place the day before (*keng-hsü*). Sometimes t
divination would be performed several days beforehand, or it could also ta
place on the day of the ritual. Therefore, unless the day of the ritual w
specifically mentioned in the query, there is no way to know for sure t
intended day of the ritual. This point was recognized by Wang Kuo-wei
early as in 1917, but perhaps inadvertently missed by Hu in 1964. In t
oracle records, there are over a hundred references to Wang Hai,[41] but on
eleven are associated with data on the day of the ritual:

1. "[. . . ,] cracked. Cheng asked: The following day *hsin-ssu*, go to
   place] . Perform the *chiu* and *ch'ai* ceremonies to [Wang] Hai?"[42]
2. "Asked: Perform the *yu* ceremony to Wang Hai, 40 sheep, on t
   day *hsin-hai*?"[43]
3. "The day *chia-ch'ou*, cracked. Ku asked: On the coming day *hs*
   hai, perform the *ch'ai* ceremony to Wang Hai, 30 cattle?"[44]
4. "On the following day *hsin-hai*, perform the *chiu* ceremony
   Wang Hai, 9 ch'iang [captives]?"[45]
5. "The coming day *hsin-yu*, perform the *chiu* ceremony to Wa
   Hai?"[46]

[39] Sun Hai-po, *Chia ku wen lu* 甲骨文錄 (K'ai-feng: Ho-nan T'ung-chih Kuan, 193
#295.

[40] Sun Hai-po, *Chia ku wen lu*, #297.

[41] Shima Kunio, *Inkyo bokuji sōrui* 殷墟卜辭綜類 [A comprehensive classification
the oracle records from Yin hsü] (Tokyo: Daian, 1967), 479; Chang Ping-ch'uan, Y
hsü wen tzu ping pien.

[42] Liu E, *T'ieh-yün ts'ang kuei* 鐵雲藏龜 (Peking: Pao-ts'an-shou-ch'üeh Chai, 190
#114.3.

[43] Lo Chen-yü, *Yin hsü shu ch'i* (1911), #4.8.3.

[44] Lo Chen-yü, *Yin hsü shu ch'i hou pien* (1916), #I.23.16.

[45] Hayashi Taisuke, *Kikkō jūkotsu monji* 龜甲獸骨文字 (Tokyo: Nihonshōshūibunk
1921), #1.9.1.

[46] Kuo Mo-jo, *Yin ch'i ts'ui pien* 殷契萃編 (Tokyo: Bunkyūdō, 1937), #76.

6. "On the following day *hsin-mau*, perform the *ch'ai* ceremony to Wang Hai, 3 cattle?"[47]

7. "The day *i-ssu*, cracked. Ku . . . asked: Perform the *chiu* ceremony to Wang Hai? On the following day *hsin-hai*, perform the *yu* ceremony to Wang Hai, 40 cattle?"[48]

8. "On the following day *hsin-wei*, perform the *chiu* and *ch'ai* ceremonies to Wang Hai?"[49]

9. "The day *chia-hsü*, perform the *chiu* ceremony to Wang Hai?"[50]

10. "The day *chia-wu*, asked: The day *i-wei*, perform the *chiu* ceremony to Kao Tsu Hai, [with . . .], to Ta I, with 5 Ch'iang and 3 cattle, to Tsu I with [. . .] Ch'iang [and cattle], to Hsiao I, with 3 Ch'iang and 3 cattle, and to Fu Ting, with 5 Ch'iang and 3 cattle?"[51]

11. "The day *kuei-ssu*, asked: On the day *i-wei*, perform the *chiu* ceremony to Kao Tsu Hai?"[52]

these, eight refer to ceremonies performed on a *hsin* day, one on a *chia* y, and the other two on an *i* day. The ratio for *hsin* is overwhelming enough place Wang Hai on a par with the other Shang kings with *kan* names, who re also sacrificed to, but not exclusively, on their particular *kan* days of the *in* week.[53] The passage above in (10) refers to sacrifices to Wang Hai, Ta I, u I, Hsiao I, and Fu Ting on an *i* day, indicating that you didn't have to be an o be sacrificed to on an *i* day. Another example is:

On the day *chia-shen*, perform the *chiu* ceremony to Hsiao Ting?"[54]

sides, since these were oracles to find out whether it was all right *or not all* *ht* to perform these ceremonies on certain days in certain ways, one must ow for a small number of queries that must solicit negative responses; this

[47]Ch'en Pang-huai, *Chia ku wen ling shih* 甲骨文零拾 (Tientsin: Jenmin Press, 1959), 8.

[48]Chang Ping-ch'üan, *Yin hsü wen tzu ping pien*, #117.

[49]Itō Michiharu, "Fujii Yūrin Kan shozō kōkotsu monji" 藤井有鄰館所藏甲骨文字 racle bone inscriptions in the collections of the Fujii Yūrin Kan], *Tōhōgakuhō*, 42 971), 66.

[50]Chang Ping-ch'üan, *Yin hsü wen tzu ping pien*, #116.

[51]Hu Hou-hsüan, *Chan hou nan pei so chien chia ku lu* 戰後南北所見甲骨錄 (Peking d Shanghai: Lai-hsün Ko, 1951), #II.477; also James M. Menzies and Hsü Chin-hsiung, n hsü pu-tz'u hou pien 殷墟卜辭後編 (Taipei: I-wen Press, 1972), #B2459.

[52]Hu Hou-hsüan, *Chan hou nan pei so chien chia ku lu* . . . , #478; also Menzies and ü, *Yin hsü pu-tz'u hou pien*, #B2466.

[53]Chou Hung-hsiang, *Shang Yin ti-wang pen chi* 商殷帝王本紀 [*Biographies of Shang n kings*] (Hong Kong: Privately printed, 1958), 44.

[54]Tung Tso-pin, *Yin hsü wen tzu chia pien* [Hsiao-t'un Inscriptions Fasc. 1] (Shang-i: Commercial Press, 1948), #841.

would be especially true in the oracle records of Tung Tso-pin's "Old School
In short, were Wang Hai to be named by a *kan* sign, he would have been calle
Kao Tsu Hsin. This immediately calls to one's mind the name Kao Hsin Shi
which is another appellation for Ti K'u, the supreme ancestor-god of tl
Shang. We will come back to this below.

If Wang Hai is a Hsin, he is in the right generational order. He was fath
of Shang Chia. His descendant Tsu Hsin was father of Ch'iang Chia; Lin Hsi
son of Tsu Chia; Ti Hsin, son of Ti I. I would have grouped Hsin with Ting
division B were it not for Hsiao Hsin, who was of the same generation as H
Chia and Hsiao I, and I have, therefore, with reluctance, placed Hsin, togeth
with Keng, in a category outside the man I-Ting opposition. But very probab
Hsin was in fact a member of the B division, and Hsiao Hsin was just a
anomalous exception under some special circumstances of which we are n
longer aware.

I am very curious about Wang Hai's brother (or his generational c
member) Wang Heng. How was it that at this crucial juncture in Shang histo
"T'ien wen" saw fit to mention both brothers? Is it possible that Wang H
and Wang Heng initiated the two main lines of succession? If Wang Hai w
initiator of division B, could it be that Wang Heng began division A? Wu Ch'
ch'ang,[55] on the basis of "T'ien wen," long ago raised the possibility th
Shang Chia Wei was in fact Wang Heng's son, not Wang Hai's. Unfortunatel
we know next to nothing about Wang Heng. Shima[56] lists only 11 entri
under Wang Heng, compared with about a hundred under Wang Hai. None c
these contain information on the day of rituals for him. I will wait mo
anxiously for additional records to see whether Wang Heng's day of ritu
would put him in generational alignment with, or place him in oppositic
to, Wang Hai. The fact itself, that there are more references to Wang H
than to Wang Heng, is significant. Most rites performed to the forebears befo
Shang Chia were performed during the reigns of Wu Ting and Wen Wu Ting,[5]
both from division B.

In fact, I have a strong suspicion that until Shang Chia and Ta I, powe
ful figures from division A, the Shang's most prominent personalities ofte
came from division B, or from the division's most prominent unit at the tim
Hsin. Just above I mentioned the interesting coincidence of Ti K'u's othe
name being Kao Hsin Shih; that, of course, puts him with Wang Hai's divisio
When my attention was directed to this, I became curious and looked up th
oracle records of sacrifices to K'uei, the oracle record name for Ti K'u.

[55]Wu Ch'i-ch'ang, "Pu-tz'u so chien hsien kung hsien wang san hsü k'ao," 45.
[56]Shima Kunio, *Inkyo bokuji sōrui*, 479.
[57]*cf.* Hu Hou-hsüan, "Chia ku wen Shang tsu niao t'u-t'eng i-chi," 144.

nd four places where the days of such sacrifices were mentioned, and, sure
ugh, three out of the four days are Hsin! They are:

1. "The day *chia-yin*. Asked: on the day *hsin-hai*, perform the *chiu*
   and *ch'ai* ceremonies to K'uei, 3 cattle?"[58]
2. "The day *chi-ssu*, cracked. To make request of K'uei. Perform the
   hui ceremony on the day *hsin-yu*?"[59]
3. "Asked: On the following day *hsin-mau*, [at a certain place,]
   request rain of K'uei? . . . it rained."[60]
4. "The day *ping-wu*, cracked. Lü asked: On the following day *ting-
   wei* for K'uei to perform ceremonies *ch'ai* . . . ?"[61]

this point one could only become more and more curious about the sacri-
al days of all the other Shang ancestors before Shang Chia, and Shima's
alogue of oracle records[62] proved its worth. The only other ancestral god
t has yielded enough sacrificial day data is Kao (or Yüeh). There are six
ries with such information, and their days are: *chia-yin*,[63] *i-ssu*,[64] *hsin-
i*,[65] *hsin-wei*,[66] *hsin-hai*,[67] and *hsin-hai*.[68] Four *hsin* out of six is certainly an
pressive enough percentage, and this further supports the hypothesis that
in was politically and ritually the most important unit before Shang Chia-
I took over. But this segment of Shang history is the most chaotic, and
above merely points up the need for further research.

Shang Chia to Shih Kuei

Shang Chia initiates the annual ritual cycle performed during the reigns
Tsu Chia and Ti I, and Ta I was the founder of the Shang dynasty. Both
pivotal personalities. But the five generations between them could have

[58] Hu Hou-hsüan, *Chan hou nan pei so chien chia ku lu*, #II.481; also Menzies and
i, *Yin hsü shu ch'i hou pien*, #B2429.
[59] Hu Hou-hsüan, *Chan hou nan pei so chien chia ku lu*, #II.485; also Menzies and
i, *Yin hsü shu ch'i hou pien*, #B2171.
[60] Shang Ch'eng-tso, *Yin ch'i i ts'un* 殷契佚存 (Nanking: University of Nanking,
33), #519.
[61] Hu Hou-hsüan, *Chia ku hsü ts'un* 甲骨續存 (Shanghai: Ch'ün-lien Press, 1955),
.599.
[62] Shima Kunio, *Inkyo bokuji sōrui*.
[63] Hu Hou-hsüan, *Chia ku hsü ts'un*, #1.395.
[64] Kuo Mo-jo, *Yin ch'i ts'ui pien*, #26.
[65] Kuo Mo-jo, *Yin ch'i ts'ui pien*, #34.
[66] Hu Hou-hsüan, *Chia ku hsü ts'un*, #2.49.
[67] Roswell S. Britton, *The Couling-Chalfant Collection of inscribed oracle bone*
langhai: The Commercial Press, 1935), #714.
[68] Kuo Jo-yü, *Yin ch'i shih cho* 殷契拾綴 (Shanghai: Lai-hsün Ko, 1951), #1.411.

been symbolic in nature, representing all the major ritual *kan* units in t
royal house; or they may actually have been rulers whose chronological orc
happened to coincide with the first four and the last two of the ten *kan* sig
If there is a code in this somewhere, it has defied all my efforts to crack it.

3. Ta I to P'an Keng

This is the segment from the founding of the dynasty by Ta I (T'ang)
1766 B.C., or thereabouts, to the removal, under P'an Keng, of the capital
An-yang, where almost all of the oracle records are found. The major issue
this segment of Shang history has to do with the relationship between T:
and his prime minister I Yin, and the succession to the throne from Ta I
Ta Chia.

I Yin was certainly a most important person in Shang history. Ancie
texts depict him as a loyal and able prime minister under Ta I. The sto
becomes complicated after Ta I's death, however.[69] The orthodoxy has
that after Ta I died, his Crown Prince Ta Ting having predeceased him, I Y
enthroned Ta Ting's brother Wai Ping. Wai Ping died in two years. I Yin th
put Wai Ping's brother Chung Jen on the throne. Chung Jen succumbed
four years. By then, Ta Ting's son Ta Chia had come of age, and he ascend
the throne. But after three years of rule Ta Chia began to misbehave himse
and I Yin exiled him and assumed the power of Regent. Three years lat
repentant and reformed, Ta Chia resumed the rule. I Yin finally passed aw
during the reign of Wo Ting, Ta Chia's son, who gave him a fitting burial.
this view, I Yin was the ideal prime minister—loyal, selfless, but righteo
But in other texts, I Yin was less than perfect, and the succession from T
to Ta Chia was more violent than peaceful. In one text (*The bamboo annal*
Ta Chia is even said to have killed I Yin after escaping from imprisonment.

This story takes on a quite different light when viewed in terms of t
succession model presented in the preceding section. One finds that when T:
was king, from division A, I Yin was his secondary chief or prime minister
virtue of his being the head of division B. By the rule of circulating successic
Ta Ting, of division B and of the succeeding generation, became heir a
Crown Prince. But he died before Ta I's death. After Ta I's death, I Yin,
head of division B, put up two temporary replacements (Wai Ping, Chung Je
from his own division, before, finally, yielding to Ta Chia, a member of Ta
division and from the generation of his grandsons. Throughout these ye:
there must have been power struggles and palace intrigues. Perhaps I Y
exiled Ta Chia simply to grab power, and perhaps Ta Chia did kill hi
Interestingly, his burial was performed by another king of his own B divisic

[69] See Ch'en Meng-chia, "Chia ku tuan tai hsüeh chia pien," 22-25.

Ting.

This new twist of the I Yin story would be little more than historical ssip were it not for this amazing piece of new evidence: I Yin's day of rifice was Ting! I Yin's sacrificial rites, like Wang Hai's, are given (or least recorded) in the oracle archives left from the reigns of Wu Ting d Wen Wu Ting. During the Wu Ting interval he is referred to as Huang n, but the I Yin name appears in Wen Wu Ting's records. I have found two erences to Huang Yin and three to I Yin, all associated with information the day of rites:

1. "Asked: The coming day *ting-yu*, perform the *yu* ceremony to Huang Yin?"[70]
2. "On the day [*ting-*]*mau*, perform the *chiu* ceremony to Huang Yin?"[71]
3. "The day *yu-ssu*, [. . .]: Perform the [. . .] ceremony to I Yin on the day *ting-wei*?"[72]
4. "The day *chia-tzu*, cracked. Perform the *yu* ceremony to I Yin on the day *ting-mau*?"[73]
5. "Perform the [. . .] ceremony to I on the day *ting-yu*?"[74]

of them were done on a *ting* day. This is probably the most important ece of evidence for the entire *kan*-name issue, highly informative with gard to I Yin's place in Shang history and to the succession model as a ole.

The subsequent successions pose few problems with regard to the odel if the two corrections (with reference to Ch'ien Chia and Ch'iang Chia) e accepted. If not, they were perhaps the results of power politics and bitrary shifts of rules. Ssu-ma Ch'ien mentioned "chaos during the reigns of ne kings."

P'an Keng to Ti Hsin

The successions in this segment conform to the model best. There is nother point of interest: *Shih chi* states that "Ti I's eldest son was Wei Tzu h'i. Ch'i's mother was of inferior origin, and he was consequently not eligible

[70] Wang Hsiang, *Fu-shih Yin ch'i cheng wen* 簠室殷契徵文 (Tientsin: Tientsin Mu- um, 1925), #18.

[71] Liu E, *T'ieh-yün ts'ang kuei*, #242.4.

[72] Tung Tso-pin, *Yin hsü wen tzu chia pien*, #564.

[73] Chin Tsu-t'ung, *Yin ch'i i chu* 殷契遺珠 (Shanghai: Chinese-French Cultural ublications Commission, 1939), #638.

[74] Hu Hou-hsüan, *Chan hou nan pei so chien chia ku lu*, #II.503; Menzies and Hsü, in hsü pu-tz'u hou pien, #B2512.

to be heir." This helps explain aspects of the mechanisms for heir selecti
mentioned in the previous section under Rule 6. We may recall that none
the kings' official wives were I or Ting. Perhaps these two units were so p
tigious that kings could not afford to marry from them. Mere nobles cou
and their progenies were, thus, likely to become heirs.

A very important point concerning this segment is the fact that An-ya
served as capital city during it. I have pointed out before[75] that the num
of Shang kings at An-yang (11, plus Ti Hsin, who was burned to death a
was perhaps beheaded, and presumably not buried in the same grandi
manner in An-yang by his victors) and the number of large graves at the
called Royal Cemetery at Hsi-pei-kang (11) are identical. Furthermore, of
11 kings, 7 (P'an Keng, Hsiao Hsin, Hsiao I, Tsu Chia, Tsu Keng, Wu I, T
were of division A, generationally speaking, and 4 (Wu Ting, Lin Hsin, K'a
Ting, Wen Wu Ting) of division B. Seven of the 11 royal tombs found at
yang are located in a single cluster in the western sector of the cemetery, a
the other four in another cluster in the eastern sector.[76] According to
chao-mu 昭穆 rules of temple-tablet arrangement in the early Chou peri
the tablets of the chao generation are placed in a row on the eastern side
the hall, and those of the mu generation on the western side. Was division
mu, and division B chao?

DISCUSSION

In *New studies* I have discussed the question of the continuation
both the circulating succession system and the use of *t'ien kan* for ritual un
and ritual names into the Chou, and I have nothing new to add. With
greater degree of power and wealth concentration, in the latter half of
Chou period, the circulating system of succession to high office gave way
the stem system at all political levels. With this, political office beca
a permanent holding of single familial or lineage lines, the need to ke
track of the multiple lines in the temples was no longer compelling, and
custom of using *t'ien kan* for posthumous names died out. Aristocra
endogamy, perhaps another reason for keeping track by way of the *kan* uni
became overtaken by clan exogamy at high levels, and this could be anoth
factor in the disappearance of the *kan* names. If this was the way it happen
some historical puzzles could receive more satisfactory explanations than
now given them. The episode of the Chou Kung Regency and the custom
Twin Capitals, for example, are interesting to look at this way. Chou Kung,

[75] Chang Kwang-chih, "Some dualistic phenomena in Shang society," 52-53.

[76] Chang Kwang-chih, *The archaeology of ancient China* (rev. ed.; New Haven a
London: Yale University Press, 1968), 221.

t, looks like another I Yin, with whom he was often mentioned together in cient texts.

At the earlier end, if this speculation is right, one would expect that the *n*-naming custom was perhaps invented or at least perfected *after* the circu- ing succession system itself had become an established and elaborate insti- tion at several governmental levels. Li Tsung-t'ung long ago speculated at in earliest historical China chiefs were elected,[77] and the circulating ccession had its elective elements. The fact that Wang Hai had a fixed place the ritual calendar, but not yet a *t'ien kan* name, would tend to lend pport to the priority of circulating succession over the use of *kan* names. u-ma Ch'ien placed Shang Chia Wei at the approximate time of the three 'angs of the Hsia dynasty (T'ai K'ang, Chung K'ang, and Shao K'ang), and ese happened to be the first Hsia rulers to use *kan* names (=Keng).

We may conclude this discussion with another Hsia problem. In "Kao ao Mo," of *Shu ching*, there is this strange clause:

I, [Yü declared,] married the daughter of T'u Shan, Hsin Jen Kuei Chia.

e usual explanation is that the wedding took place on a *hsin* day, and Yü ok off three days later, on a *chia* day, to continue his famed toil in trying control the flood.[78] But if we look at this clause in its context, we find at Yü was enumerating his appropriate, dignified behavior, in comparison ith Tan Chu's style of self-indulgence, and he was saying that "I married this oman from T'u Shan, and [it was a marriage of the proper and ideal kind, e marriages between] Hsin and Jen [or between] Kuei and Chia." Proper arriages in ancient China were often prescribed between the right *hsing* oups. In *Shih ching*, we read ("Heng Men," translated by Waley[79]):

"Must the fish one sups off   "Must the fish one sups on
Needs be bream from the river?   Needs be carp from the river
Must the girl one weds   Must the girl one weds
Needs be a Chiang from Ch'i?   Needs be a Tzu from Sung?"

bviously the answer was that they were supposed to. A Chiang or a Tzu ould be a proper mate for a Chi of Ch'en, just like, within an endogamous ling dynasty, a Jen would be for a Hsin, a Chia for a Kuei, or a T'u Shan girl r a Great Yü. In fact, exactly such unions did take place in the Shang royal ouse itself. The wife of the only Kuei in the Shang house, Shih Kuei, is

[77] Li Tsung-t'ung, *Chung-kuo ku-tai she-hui shih* 中國古代社會史 [History of ancient hinese society] (Taipei: Chinese Culture Publications Commission, 1954).

[78] As explained in Ch'ü Wan-li, *Shang shu shih i* 尚書釋義 (Taipei: Chinese Culture ublications Commission, 1956), 24-25.

[79] Translated by Arthur Waley, *The book of songs* (New York: Grove Press, 1960).

known to have been a Chia, and of three known mates for Tsu Hsin, one wa
Jen.[80] This does not mean that the *t'ien kan* naming system began with Y
the Hsia dynasty's founder, because "Kao T'ao Mo" was probably not writt
until late Chou. But this is further corroborating evidence for our Shang mod
not to mention the fact that this reading makes better sense of the baffli
sentence. It also suggests that perhaps the *t'ien kan* units were for livi
people as well as for the dead.

[80]Ch'en Meng-chia, *Yin hsü pu-tz'u tsung shu*, 452.

The childbirth myth and ancient Chinese medicine

A study of aspects of the *wu* tradition

Chow Tse-tsung

my article, "The early history of the Chinese word *shih* (poetry)," published
Wen-lin: Studies in the Chinese humanities, for which Professor H. G. Creel
o contributed a very inspiring article,[1] I pointed out how in ancient Chinese
 word for foot (or toe or footprint) was often confused with the word for
ıss (hence life or birth), and related this phenomenon to the birth myth
mmon to the ancestor of the Chou royal house and the legendary king Fu
i, a myth suggesting that treading on a footprint could cause childbirth.
e origins of both the confusion and the myth must be sought in the social
d cultural backgrounds of the time. I believe this phenomenon and myth
ıy be understood better in the light of pre-Ch'in Chinese thought and
titutions, particularly the ancient Chinese concept of sex, wedding customs,
d the early development of medicine.

I would like to begin the discussion by citing a poem from the *Book of
etry,* "South Mount" (Nan-shan).[2]

> *South Mount high and steep,*
> *Male fox walks slyly.*
> *The Road to Lu was easy and wide,*
> *As the young lady of Ch'i went as a bride.*
> *Since she has gone as a bride,*
> *Why does she still long for the wild?*

[1]Professor Creel's article is entitled "The great clod: A Taoist conception of the uni-
se," in Chow Tse-tsung (ed.), *Wen-lin* (Madison: University of Wisconsin Press, 1968),
7-68.
[2]See *Mao shih yin-te* 毛詩引得 (Harvard-Yenching Sinological Index Series), poem
. 101; all numbers for poems used hereafter refer to those in this edition. All trans-
ions are my own unless noted otherwise.

> Ko-*vine sandals, five pairs;*
> *Cap ribbons, a couple.*
> *The Road to Lu is easy and wide,*
> *For the young lady of Ch'i to travel.*
> *Since she has traveled it,*
> *Why does she still follow it?*
>
> *How do we plant hemp?*
> *Across and along plough the field.*
> *How does a man take a wife?*
> *He must tell her father and mother.*
> *Since he has told them,*
> *Why does he still question her?*
>
> *How do we split firewood?*
> *Without an axe we cannot do it.*
> *How does a man take a wife?*
> *Without a go-between he cannot win her.*
> *Since he has won her,*
> *Why does he still thwart her?*

I have translated the whole poem anew, as I believe it has not been accurately translated and sufficiently understood before.[3] Both the "Minor preface" (*Hsiao hsü*), possibly of the 5th century B.C., and the "Mao commentary" (*Mao Shih ku-hsün chuan*), of the 5th century B.C. or later, assert that the poem is a satire on the alleged incestuous affair of Lady Wen-chiang, wife Duke Huan of Lu (r. 711-694 B.C.), with her elder brother Duke Hsiang Ch'i (r. 697-686 B.C.).

[3]I have consulted the English translations by James Legge (1871), Arthur Wale (1937), Bernhard Karlgren (1944-1945), and Ezra Pound (1954). The last two lines each stanza have bothered all scholars and seem to have been misunderstood. I think t main verbs in the two lines of each stanza are parallel words with similar or contrasti meanings. The word *kuei* 歸 (to return, to go as a bride) is coupled with *huai* 懷 (to lo for, cherish), as *huai kuei* (long for returning home) is a popular phrase frequently us in the *Book of poetry* (see poems Nos. 162, 168, 207) and *huai* is also often related to girl's longing for marriage as in the phrases *huai-ch'un* 懷春 (cherish the spring) (No. 2 and *huai hun-yin* 懷昏姻 (longing for marriage) (No. 51). In stanza 2, as Ma Jui-ch' (1782-1853) has pointed out, *yung* 庸 (to use) is identified with *yu* 由 (to travel throug by the "Mao commentary" (No. 67), and *yu* is identified with *ts'ung* 從 (to follo through) in the *Erh-ya* ("Shih ku"). In stanza 3, *kao* 告 (to tell) is identified with *chü* (to examine and investigate in a criminal case, to kick) by the "Mao commentary (No. 178), also in Cheng Hsüan's commentary to *Li chi* ("Wen-wang shih-tzu") and oth works. In stanza 4, *te* 得 (to get) seems to contrast with *chi* 極 which carries the meani *ch'iung* 窮 or *k'un* 困 (to thwart, to limit), *chin* 盡 or *chung* 終 (to end) in vario sources of the Chou and Han dynasties.

According to the *Spring and autumn annals* and the *Tso commentary*, rly in 709 B.C. Duke Huan of Lu secured the approval of Lady Wen-chiang's ther to marry her, and the wedding took place in the 9th month in the nar calendar of the same year. The wedding appeared to be excessively borate; her father went beyond the limits of propriety by personally ac- mpanying her to the border of Lu where Duke Huan met them. After her other took over the rulership of the Ch'i state when their father died in 7 B.C., the relationship between Ch'i and Lu gradually deteriorated. Even ough Duke Huan of Lu went to meet his brother-in-law several times, a war oke out between them in 695 B.C. and Lu was defeated. A year later, parently persuaded by his wife, Duke Huan went with her to Ch'i to meet r brother again. There they stayed for about three months, and during that ne he discovered, as recorded in the *Tso commentary* and the *Shih chi*, his fe's incestuous relations with her brother. He immediately reproached her, d as a result was murdered in Ch'i probably by the order of his brother-in- v. Lady Wen-chiang did not return to Lu until a few months later, after her a succeeded to the dukedom of Lu. Subsequently, she went against the stoms governing the conduct of married women and widows by traveling tside her home town. On a number of occasions she went to see her brother Ch'i. Concerning the personality of this lady we know very little, except t she seemed to be quite attractive and unconventionally active, and parently played a significant role in diplomacy and politics. Before her ath in 673 B.C. she seems to have nearly succeeded in helping her son make a respectable ally and rival of Ch'i.

It is not my intention here to speculate as to whether the allegation out Lady Wen-chiang's affair with her brother is based on facts or gossip. any rate, she and her brother have been unanimously condemned by inese historians and commentators. Chinese scholars almost without excep- n agree with the "Minor preface" that the "South Mount" poem is intended censure this affair. Among Western scholars, James Legge seems to accept s view of the poem, whereas Arthur Waley and Bernhard Karlgren do not. rlgren explicates the poem as follows: "A lady of Ts'i [Ch'i] has gone to Lu l been married. A lover who has lost her is grieved, but is admonished: he uld not be desperate and continue to think of her or try to follow her. All proper rites required have been duly carried out, and the fact is irrevo- le." Karlgren further suggests that the people involved in the poem are y common folk.[4] I think Karlgren's interpretation is less convincing than traditional one. In the same book two other poems also have the lines

---

[4]*The book of odes* (Stockholm: The Museum of Far Eastern Antiquities, 1950), 65; also his *Glosses on the Book of Odes* (1964), 189-90.

"The young lady of Ch'i went as a bride" and "The Road to Lu was easy a wide" (Nos. 104 and 105). The "Minor preface" and the "Mao commenta also regard them, and I think quite reasonably, as referring to the same aff particularly to Wen-chiang's wedding procession and travels. These poems that "her escort is like a trail of clouds" and "like a river," and her carri decorated with "bamboo mat and red leather awning," drawn by "four bl. horses well-groomed, dangling reins are numerous." All these things show t the woman could not be anyone but a noblewoman. At the time such in state marriages must have been quite unusual. And most of all, an affair wh gave rise to so many well-composed poems or songs is not likely to have b an insignificant event in the life of a commoner. Furthermore, at the tim Li Tao-yüan (d. A.D. 527), the "Road of Lu" and a "Wen-chiang's Terrac still existed along the old border of Ch'i and Lu (modern T'ai-an of Shantu

If we accept the poem "South Mount" as a satire on the Wen-chi episode, we might also point out several sex symbols in it which have esca notice. Traditional and contemporary scholars have already pointed out t firewood is an often used term in the *Book of poetry* which always stands woman.[6] In this poem "split firewood" with an axe seems even furthe symbolize sexual action. As a matter of fact, the *Book of poetry* cont. sufficient evidence that firewood was probably a common ceremonial ob in weddings in ancient China.[7] In the same vein as "split firewood" we read "plant hemp" and "plough the field" in stanza 3. This last metap prevailed in many other civilizations. The Latin poet Lucretius (*c.* 96-*c.* B.C.) has the famous saying, "plough the fields of woman (*muliebria arv* Other Latin and English writers use "tillage," "husbandry" and the I Shakespeare for one employed this metaphor quite often, for instance *Antony and Cleopatra,* "He plough'd her and she cropt" (II, ii, 240-42); in *Pericles,* "An if she were a thornier piece of ground than she is, she shal plough'd." (IV, v, 145-46). He also uses such a term as "poll-axe" (*Lo labour's lost,* V, ii, 571-72).

In the first stanza, the use of a fox to represent a licentious pe is possibly the earliest example of a practice that later became a comm place in Chinese fiction. But the line "Male fox (*hsiung hu*) walks s (*sui-sui*)" needs some explanation. The "Mao commentary" and glosses by Cheng Hsüan (127-200) and Chu Hsi (1130-1200) all note

---

[5]*Shui-ching chu* 水經注 (*Yung-lo ta-tien* ed., Peking: Wen-hsüeh ku-chi k'an-i she, 1955 reprint), 457; Wang Hsien-ch'ien's commentary in *SPPY* ed., 24/20b.

[6]See Wen I-to, "Shih ching t'ung-i: K'ai-feng" 詩經通義：凱風, in *Wen I-to ch chi* 聞一多全集 (Shanghai: K'ai-ming shu-tien, 1948), II, 174-81.

[7]*The book of poetry,* poems Nos. 9, 156, 218. For an axe used as a metaphor go-between see also poem No. 158.

-sui indicates the manner of walking slyly alone to seek a mate. The
racter sui 綏 (archaic sniwər, according to Karlgren) is often defined in
classics as an 安 (sit or live at ease). The original character of sui must be
妥 (archaic t'nwâr), which is made with a hand above a woman, while an
ws a woman under a roof. Chinese philologists such as Tuan Yü-ts'ai
35-1815) and Chu Chün-sheng (1788-1858) have already pointed out that
th the characters an and t'o originally denoted sexual relations between
n and woman. Moreover, the Ch'i edition of the Book of poetry in the Han
nasty has the sui-sui in this poem written in the form 夊夊, which is defined
the Shuo-wen chieh-tzu as "prowl slowly." If we look at the various oracle
ne inscription forms, this last character sui 夊 seems to be a picture of a
t with a leg. But the Shuo-wen considers the two parallel lines to be two
nbones or legs which drag as if wearing straw sandals or slippers without
lbacks. The Shuo-wen also lists an entry chih 夂 with a shorter right line,
ich is defined as "to approach from behind the two legs." The two forms,
and chih, are so similar that contemporary scholars of oracle inscription
dies consider them to have been originally the same word. Several Chinese
racters made with this element in the oracle inscription form show a kind
human figure with a bare leg and a noticeable big foot. These characters
re often used as men's names, and one of them, Chi 稷 is the name of the
estor of the Chou royal house, whose birth was connected with the foot-
nt myth mentioned earlier. To this point I will come back later. Here I
y want to point out another related character, chün 峻 (variants 朘, 屦),
ich means the male organ as shown in the Tao te ching (Chapter 55). The
t that the characters 妥, 綏, 夋 (thus 夊) are interchangeable is attested
the fact that the medical herb chün 葰 also appears as 荾, 荽, or 綏.[8] It
pparent that the "South Mount" poem contains a number of symbols of
and marriage.

The poem, however, contains another puzzling line in stanza 2, that is,
"ko-vine sandals, five pairs." According to many records in the Book of
s, ko-vine shoes or sandals (ko chü 葛屦) were coarse and cheap apparel
ally worn in the summer, whereas in the late fall and winter leather shoes
uld be used.[9] Why then should such cheap straw sandals be presented in
well-prepared wedding of a noble couple late in the autumn?[10] Even if

[8] See Chu Chün-sheng, Shuo-wen t'ung-hsün ting-sheng 說文通訓定聲 (Taipei: Shih-
h shu-chu, 1956 reprint), 706.
[9] See Chou li 周禮, "T'ien kuan, chü-jen"; I li 儀禮, "Shih sang li"; and commentaries
heng Hsüan, K'ung Ying-ta, and Sun I-jang.
[10] The Spring and autumn annals records a solar eclipse on the first day of the seventh
nth in the same year, i.e. 709 B.C., that Wen-chiang's wedding took place. Shinjō
nzō figured out that this date was the Julian date 1,462,659.9, that is, about July 9

the line is merely a poetic formulaic device indicating an earlier or still p
vailing wedding custom rather than a description of an actual wedding, t
question still remains as to why such shoes or sandals should be used in su
a custom.

The *Spring and autumn annals* also records the wedding of Lady We
chiang's son, Duke Chuang of Lu (r. 693-662 B.C.) when he, like his fath
went to Ch'i in person to receive his bride, possibly the daughter of the ve
Duke Hsiang. The *Shuo-yüan*, a book edited by Liu Hsiang (c. 79-c. 8 B.
but written much earlier by another author, in connection with this eve
describes in detail the Chou dynasty nobility's "ceremony of receiving t
bride in person" (*ch'in-ying* 親迎). It says that the prospective bridegroc
presented to the bride's mother two (later scholars suggest that "two" is
error for "five") pairs of shoes or sandals (*chü*) plus jade. The mother accep
them, picked out a pair of the shoes or sandals and let the bride tread (*li*
in them. While adjusting her daughter's hairpins and dress, she made a spee
advising her to perform a good wife's duty. After the bride did obeisance, t
mother gave the bride's hands to the bridegroom by the door, then he led l
out of the room.[11] This description of the ceremony is quite similar to the
in other ritual works, but the latter do not mention shoes or sandals.[12] Ho
ever, the *Chung-hua ku-chin chu,* which is sometimes attributed to the Cl
dynasty (A.D. 265-420) but may belong to the tenth century, does say t
in popular custom the bridegroom's family must present a pair of silk
hemp sandals to the bride at a wedding.[13] It seems quite believable that
ancient China *ko*-vine sandals were presented at a wedding.

But what we need to explain is why the *ko*-vine material specifica
was used and why the bride was required to tread in such sandals. To do t
we must remember that marriage in ancient times in China as well as in ma
other places, besides being for the union of the sexes, was conducted w

at 2 p.m. See his *Tōyō tenmongaku-shi kenkyū* 東洋天文學史研究 (Tokyo, 19
Chinese tr. by Shen Chün (Shanghai, 1933). If we accept this calculation, Wen-chia
wedding must have taken place between September 10 and October 10. Tung Tso-
however, suggests in his *Chung-kuo nien-li tsung-p'u* 中國年曆總譜 (Hong Kong, 19
that the eclipse took place on July 17. Thus the ninth month would have been Au
16 to September 14. But Tung, in order to fit it into his calculation, had to amend
Annals' record of "the first day of the seventh month" to "the last day" of that mo
and that makes his suggestion doubtful.

[11]*Shuo-yüan* 說苑 (*SPPY*), "Hsiu-wen p'ien," 19/3b-4a; also Ma Jui-ch'en, *Mao S
chuan chien t'ung-shih* 毛詩傳箋通釋 (*SPPY*), 9/7a.

[12]See *I li* (*SPPY*), "Shih hun li," 2/1a-21b; and *Li chi* (*SPPY*), "Hun i," 20/2a-5a.

[13]This book in its description of early historical events may not be reliable, but
gift of sandals is mentioned therein as a contemporary popular custom and this se
quite believable.

at emphasis on ethnic, social, and economic purposes, particularly the
rease of population.

The ko-vine, known in English as ko-hemp, and also as kudzu vine
ough the Japanese pronunciation *kuzu,* is a kind of creeper similar to
ichos or arrowroot called in botanical terms *pueraria thunbergiana benth.*
pliable stems, which may extend to more than thirty feet, have often been
d for making sandals and its fiber for making cloth in China. Probably
ause of its long, narrow, many-seeded pods, and its long, durable stems,
vine is often mentioned in the *Book of poetry* as a symbol of marriage or
od relationship. For instance, in the poem "The creeping of the ko-vine"
). 2, "Ko t'an") the plant is employed to symbolize a new marriage as the
m depicts a girl's preparation for the ritual of her first visit to her parents
r marriage. In another poem, "The growth of the ko-vine" (No. 124, "Ko
ng"), which expresses a woman's longing for her deceased or departed
band, the ko-vine definitely alludes to a wife, as the "Mao commentary"
already pointed out, "The ko-vine which grows and climbs over thick
hes is a metaphor for a woman's marriage to another family."

In one case, however, the ko-vine metaphor seems to be unclear. The
t stanza of "The twisted bending tree" (No. 4, "Chiu mu") reads:

> *In the south is a twisted bending tree;*
> *The* ko-*vine and the* lei-*climbers bind it.*
> *How happy our lord is,*
> *Blessed union gives him ease.*

ave translated the last line, *fu li sui chih* 福履綏之, differently from all
vious interpretations. Although I realize *fu li* (or *lü*) might really be a
ferent way of writing *fu lu* 福祿 (happiness and prosperity) and *sui* merely
an "at peace" *(an),*[14] one cannot dismiss the curious interpretation by
h the "Minor preface" and the "Mao commentary" that the poem de-
bes the wife of a prince who treated her husband's concubines generously
hout jealousy and thus caused them all to serve him well in harmony and
sperity. Even if we have no way of telling how close this interpretation is
the truth, it must have been made for some reason by the commentators.
ce nothing else in the poem (the other two stanzas of the poem are quite
ilar in wording) indicates such a meaning, I suspect that besides ko-vine
l *lei*-climbers having been considered wife and concubines, and the tree
husband, the character *li* might still carry, even if only partly, its original
aning of "tread in the sandals" in a wedding, and *sui,* as I have explained
lier, denote union in matrimony. The *Chou li* says, "In the second month

[14] Poem No. 222, "Ts'ai shu," and No. 171, "Nan yu chia-yü."

of the spring, the order is given to unite men and women; during this peri
those who marry irregularly (elopement) will not be prohibited".[15] In
similar passage in the *Almanac of Hsia* (*Hsia hsiao cheng*) which is attribu
to the twenty-second, or at the latest the first, century B.C., it is said, "In
second month, many women and men are united in matrimony" (*sui to
shih* 綏多女士). The commentary attributed to Pu Shang of the fifth cent
B.C. or Tai Te of the first century B.C. says here, "*Sui* is *an* 安; it is the ti
for grown men to take wives."[16] This is a testimony that the characters
and *an* are viewed as meaning to take a woman into a house, and thus th
have the connotation "satisfaction" and "at ease." If this is correct, the
vine in the "twisting, bending tree" poem seems also reasonably to im
marriage.

Other relevant imagery involving the *ko*-vine is found in the poem "1
ko-vine and the *lei*-climber" (No. 71, "*Ko lei*"), in which the two plants
used to imply blood relationship, and in "Gathering the *ko*" (No. 72, "T
ko"), in which a girl's gathering *ko* is mentioned as a means of arousing
longing for her lover.

A further example of the metaphoric use of the *ko*-vine can be found
ancient Chinese rituals. The *Li chi* says that in mourning "women shall
wear *ko*-vine girdles."[17] I believe this was so because such material imp
the joyful experience or symbolic meaning of a wedding.

In a popular belief and custom this vine is also associated with won
and weddings. According to Wu Ch'i-chün (1790-1847), in certain locali
in China the *ko*-fiber cloth was made only by wives for their own husba
and not for sale. Only women would gather this vine, and there were cert
ko stems which only maidens (and not even betrothed girls) were allowed
gather.[18] Moreover, the *ko*-vine is so significantly related to marriage
fertility that this plant has been used since ancient times in China as a me
cine for women in childbirth. Its roots are used for curing certain illnes
during pregnancy and post-childbirth, and also for hastening childbirth
abortion. Its stems are used for curing the lack of breast milk.[19]

[15]*Chou li* (*Kuo-hsüeh chi-pen ts'ung-shu* ed.), "Ti-kuan," 90; also Sun I-jang, C
li cheng-i (*Kuo-hsüeh chi-pen ts'ung-shu* ed.), 68-71.

[16]Masuda Kō (ed.), *Kashōsei kōchū* 夏小正校注 (Tokyo: Sūbun-in, 1927), I, 13b-1

[17]Sun Hsi-tan (ed.), *Li-chi chi-chieh* 禮記集解 (*Wan-yu wen-k'u* ed.), 114-15. 1
same chapter says "Caps for mourning must have no ribbons" (*sang kuan pu wei* 喪冠
綏), *ibid.*, 62. This may also take into consideration the lines in the "South Moun
"Cap ribbons, a couple."

[18]Wu Ch'i-chün, *Chih-wu ming shih t'u k'ao* 植物名實圖考 (Peking: Chung-hua
chü, 1963 reprint), 540-43.

[19]For curing illness during pregnancy the *Cheng chih chun-sheng* 證治準繩 by W
K'en-t'ang (*fl.* 1573-1619) lists a prescription *ko-ken san* 葛根散 for after childbir

As for the *ko*-vine sandal, it is also mentioned in another poem in the *ok of poetry* entitled "The *ko*-vine sandals" (No. 107, "Ko chü"):

> *Tangled, tangled are the strands of the* ko-*vine sandals;*
> *They are good for treading on hoarfrost.*
> *Long and slender are a girl's fingers;*
> *They are good for sewing clothes.*
> *Shape the waist, hem the collar.*
> *The good bride wears them.*
>
> *The good bride is beautiful and at ease.*
> *Speciously she retires to the left.*
> *From her girdle hangs her ivory comb-pin.*
> *But she is narrow-minded and mean.*
> *So I make this stab.*

ave interpreted this poem as the complaint of a poor working girl who kes bridal clothes for others. One recalls the well-known verse-proverb, o make bridal clothes for others" (*wei t'a-jen tso chia i-shang*), which lies to do work for another's advantage. I also take the term *hao-jen* 好人 the 6th and 7th lines to mean a bride or mate, as *hao* has been used in this se in the *Book of poetry*.[20] The character may also have had the extended aning "good," but in the context, it must have been used in a satirical way. first two lines of this poem also appear in the second stanza of another m, "The great east" (No. 203, "Ta tung"). I believe this stanza also refers a man's lack of opportunities to be married.

From these records it seems quite reasonable to assert that in ancient na treading in *ko*-vine sandals symbolized marriage and sexual relations. As atter of fact, the action of stepping in a shoe or socks, as Carl G. Jung and ny other Western scholars have pointed out, has symbolic sexual meanings many contemporary primitive societies.[21] Also, in an anthology of Chinese ksongs collected in about 1609, there is a song "The sandal," in which the dal alludes to a coquettish girl, and putting on socks is compared to flir-

en t'ang 湯. For the use of the *ko*-vine roots for abortion see Hsieh Kuan (comp.), ng-kuo i-hsüeh ta tz'u-tien 中國醫學大辭典 (Shanghai: Commerical Press, 1921), 5.

[20] See "Chün-tzu hao-ch'iu" in poem No. 1, "Kuan chü" and "Ch'i tzu hao ho" in 164. Wen I-to points out that *hao* was originally the same word as *fei* 妃 (a wife); his "Shih-ching hsin-i" 詩經新義, in *Wen I-to Ch'üan-chi*, II, 69-70.

[21] See Carl G. Jung, *Symbols of transformation: An analysis of the prelude to a case chizophrenia*, tr. by R.F.C. Hull, in *The collected works of C. G. Jung* (New York: theon Books, 1956), V, 209, 250, 277, 314-15, 352, 506-7, 517, 556. See also J. E. ot, *A dictionary of symbols*, tr. by Jack Sage (New York: Philosophical Library, 2), 282.

tation. One of the lines reads, "Even a foot-dragging grass sandal is better t
a woman married to the left." "A woman married to the left," noted F
Meng-lung (1574-1646), meant in the Wu dialect, a re-married widow.²
seems not irrelevant to compare this with the line in the "*Ko*-vine sand.
poem which says the bride "speciously retires to the left." "Left" in Chir
sometimes means "depraved, treacherous, or heretical."

The character *li* (step on or tread on or in) itself in the *Book of poe*
sometimes even carries the connotation of sexual relations. The poem ".
in the east" says:²³

> *Sun is in the east!*
> *This lovely girl*
> *Is in my house.*
> *Being in my house*
> *She treads in my footsteps and approaches me.*
>
> *Moon in the east!*
> *This lovely girl*
> *Is in my room.*
> *Being in my room*
> *She treads in my footsteps and stirs me.*

In interpreting this poem the "Minor preface" says, "It is a satire on de
The sovereign and the ministers missed the right principles. Men and wor
eloped and could not be civilized by ritual (*li*)." The "Mao commentary
explaining the character *li* 履 (to tread in footsteps) in the last line of
first stanza also says that "*li* 履 means ritual (*li* 禮)." And it defines
character *shu* 姝 (lovely) in the second line as "the appearance of a
bride." All these indicate that the earliest commentary interprets the scen
a girl's elopement in contrast to a wedding ceremony.

However, I feel the wording of the last lines of the two stanzas, *li*
chi hsi 履我即兮 and *li wo fa hsi* 履我發兮 may still need some further ex
nation. The Mao definition of "treads in footsteps" as ritual seems not
to have used a homophone but also implied that treading in footsteps w

----

²²Feng Meng-lung (ed.), *Shan-ke* 山歌 (Peking: Chung-hua shu-chü, 1962; base
the ed. *c.* 1627-28), 9/71a-73a.
²³Poem No. 99, "Tung-fang chih jih." I have followed the Chinese tradition in ur
standing the person mentioned in line 2 to be a woman. Waley and Karlgren unders
the passage to refer to a man. This line also appears in poem No. 53. Although the '
commentary" suggests there that the line refers to a gentleman, yet in ancient t
there was a custom of using a beautiful woman to allude to a virtuous gentleman. Or
other hand, the term *shu* 姝 as in poem No. 42 has usually been applied to fe
beauty rather than male.

dding ritual. This intriguing definition has much other evidence to support
and I will return to this point later. In addition, the character *chi* in the
e probably does not mean to approach or to advance in general, but
:ording to certain ancient usage has the meaning to approach for marriage
family life. To this we should compare the same character *chi* in the lines
chi wo mou 來即我謀 (come to approach and arrange about me) in poem
). 58, "The simple peasant" ("Mang") and *chi yu T'ai chia-shih* 即有邰家室
e made house and home in T'ai) in No. 245, "The birth of our people"
Sheng min"). The term *chi mou* also appears in the *Ku-liang commentary to
e Spring and Autumn Annals* under the year 703 B.C. in the sense of
rangement of a marriage. The early meaning of *chi* seems to be "to approach
r eating"; and "to eat" (*shih* 食) has been a pun for sexual activity in
inese since the Chou dynasty, as Wen I-to has pointed out. As for the
aracter *fa* 發 in the last line, Ma Jui-ch'en tries to establish its meaning as
otsteps. I think its general meaning "to stir, to set in, to rise, or to arouse"
ay be relevant. Cheng Hsüan notes on the term *wei fa* 未發 in the *Li chi*,
Vei fa* means the desire has not yet been aroused."[24] This sense of the
aracter is still present in such popular terms as *fa-ch'ing* 發情 and *fa-shen*
身 (puberty). The original meaning of *fa* is to shoot out an arrow. Such
. action might have been associated with sex and birth, as will be explained
ter. All of this is relevant to what the character *li* (tread in footsteps) may
ply in the poem as I have suggested.

Now let me go back to the "*Ko*-vine sandals" poem. First of all, one
ay ask why it should say such sandals are good for "treading on hoarfrost"
' *shuang* 履霜). I would venture to suggest that the term may have had the
nnotation of a formal marriage. The term also appears in the *Book of
anges*, in the second hexagram "K'un, the Lines, Six in the first place":
When treading on hoarfrost, solid ice is coming." This saying has been
aditionally interpreted as a forewarning of an immediate danger. While this
ight be the case in later usage, I think its original meaning may have been
kind of jest referring to an approaching marriage. It is well known that the
K'un" hexagram stands for female and marriage; so its "Decision" says that
is hexagram is "Good for inquiring in divination about the mare." It also
ys, "*an chen, chi*" 安貞, 吉. Recalling the structure of *an* as a woman under
roof, I interpret the original meaning of this sentence as "inquire through
ivination about settling in marriage: good fortune." The "treading on hoar-
ost" saying in the same hexagram should be read from this angle, since
eddings in ancient China, at least during a certain period, may have been
nducted, customarily, only in the season when hoarfrost first took form.

[24] *Li chi* (*SPPY*), "Hsüeh-chi," 11/1a-6b.

The question of the wedding period in ancient China has been a subje‹ of controversy among scholars and historians for centuries. In a Chine‹ article of mine to be published soon, I have tried to unravel all the maj‹ arguments and evidence. Without space to discuss the details here, I ha‹ to be content with merely stating my conclusion and citing the minimu‹ evidence. In remote antiquity when marriage started to be institutionalize‹ while a fixed period may not have been observed, spring may have bee‹ considered a natural, popular time for weddings. Later on, however, aft‹ agriculture became well developed and most people were engaged in farmin‹ they may have tried to avoid weddings during the busy farming season‹ Therefore, in most cases in the countryside, particularly among t‹ peasants, the seasons from harvest up to the spring planting time may ha‹ become a customary period for formal weddings. Several poems in the *Boo‹ of poetry* mention this custom. In the first stanza of "The simple peasan‹ (No. 58, "Mang"), the girl tells her lover about their possible wedding date:

> *It is not I who want to postpone it;*
> *But you do not have a good go-between.*
> *Please do not be angry;*
> *Autumn will be our fixed time.*

In another poem "The gourd has bitter leaves" (No. 34, "P'ao yu k'u-yeh‹ the young lady reminds her lover:

> *If a gentleman brings home his bride,*
> *He must do so before the ice melts.*

The "Mao commentary" on the poem "The willows of the east gate" (N‹ 140, "Tung-men chih yang"), which the "Minor preface" regards as a con‹ plaint of the loss of proper chances of marriage, says, "Men and women lo‹ their proper time of autumn and winter (for marriage)." In fact, Hsün-tz‹ even states this clearly when he discusses the wedding ritual. He says, "Whe‹ hoarfrost is formed, it starts the period of accepting brides; when the ic‹ starts to melt, this will be reduced and stopped."[25] The "Mao commentary,‹ the *Li-chi,* and other sources assert that the hoarfrost starts to form in the 9t‹ month of the year. These views have been accepted by many writers of th‹ Han dynasty, including Tung Chung-shu (176-104 B.C.).[26] The union of me‹ and women in the second month as mentioned in the *Chou li* and the *Almana‹ of Hsia* can be explained as the last effort of the wedding season and refers t‹

---

[25] Wang Hsien-ch'ien (ed.), *Hsün-tzu chi-shih* 荀子集釋 (Taipei: Shih-chieh shu-chü 1965 reprint), 327.

[26] *Ch'un-ch'iu fan-lu* 春秋繁露 (*SPPY*), "Hsün t'ien chih tao," 16/8a-13a; and "Yi‹ yang ch'u-ju shang-hsia," 12/2b-3b.

»pements only. While those who did not engage in farming may not have
ictly observed this wedding custom, it definitely existed among the peasants
ancient China, and was still observable even early in this century.

Since hoarfrost was sometimes associated with marriage, the Chinese
led and still call a widow *shuang-fu* 孀婦. This term appears in *Lieh-tzu,*
ai-nan-tzu, and other sources. The character 孀 in this term in the latter
ork often occurs simply as 霜 (hoarfrost), and a widow has also often been
led *shuang-fu* 霜婦, that is, a "hoarfrost woman."²⁷ According to tra-
ional Chinese morality, a widow was not supposed to remarry; "hoarfrost"
course could serve as a reminder of a formal, permanently binding marriage.
irthermore, the ancient Chinese believed hoarfrost was formed out of white
w as mentioned in the *Book of poetry* (No. 129). Therefore, whereas hoar-
ɔst was associated with formal marriage and everlasting love, dew has always
en a symbol of an illicit or pre-marital connection or unfaithful fragile
irriage.²⁸ These considerations lend support to the assumption that "tread-
ʒ on hoarfrost" could have the connotation of marriage.

The wedding ceremony of treading in sandals in its earliest development
iy have been carried out in an open field, and the earlier ceremony may not
ve involved treading in sandals but in footsteps, which indeed had been a
igious ritual in antiquity. In this connection we may consider the available
ɔords of the legendary birth of Hou Chi (Prince Millet) mentioned earlier.
ie famous poem No. 245, "The birth of our people" (Sheng-min) starts with:

> *In the beginning the birth of our people*
> *Was from Lady Yüan of Chiang.*
> *How did she give birth to our people?*
> *She was able to make sacrifices for purification and fertility,*
> *So that she might be rid of being childless.*
> *She trod on the big toe of God's footprint;*
> *Being elated, she was confined to a side building and rested,*²⁹
> *Then she conceived and was in awe;*
> *Then she gave birth, she bred;*
> *And this was Prince Chi.*

²⁷See Yang Po-chün (ed.), *Lieh-tzu chi-shih* 列子集釋 (Shanghai: Lung-men lien-ho
u-chü, 1958), 100; Liu Wen-tien (ed.), *Huai-nan hung-lieh chi-chieh* 淮南鴻烈集解
ʰanghai: Commercial Press, 1923), 1/2b.
²⁸See poems Nos. 94 and 17; also the popular terms "dew" (*lu-shui* 露水) and "husband
d wife of dew" (*lu-shui fu-ch'i* 夫妻) (man and woman living together without being
arried), in T'ang Hsien-tsu, *Mu-tan t'ing* 牡丹亭 "Ming shih" 冥誓, and *Chin-p'ing-mei*
ʼu-hua 金瓶梅詞話, Chapter 12 respectively. This last is also a contemporary phrase.
e also the term *lu-hui* 露會 (illicit connection).
²⁹I have separated "Being elated" from the previous line because, as Karlgren has

The poem here seems to indicate that Chiang Yüan's treading on God's fo⟨
print was either a part of the sacrifice for fertility or its aftereffect. The "M⟨
commentary" elaborates on this sacrifice here:

> In antiquity, to eliminate childlessness and to pray for children, t⟨
> Temple of Chiao-mei 郊禖 (Divine Matchmaker) was established. At t⟨
> time when the dark birds [swallows] arrive [in the second month
> the year], oxen, sheep, and pigs were sacrificed in such temples, a⟨
> the Son of Heaven attended the ceremony in person. His wife and all
> his concubines accompanied him and were favored there. Then rit⟨
> (*li*) was made to those the Son of Heaven had favored, quivers bei⟨
> hung on their girdles, and bows and arrows being presented to them,
> front of the Temple of Chiao-mei.

This note is essentially the same as a passage in the *Lü-shih ch'un-ch*⟨
and in the "Yüeh-ling" [Almanac of Chou] chapter of the *Li chi* under t⟨
second month of spring. Cheng Hsüan's note on this poem also explains th⟨
after Chiang Yüan conceived as a result of her treading on the footprint, s⟨
was in a state of awe in order to avoid being favored again right afterwar⟨

Similar customs existed in other cultures; Arthur Waley has pointed o⟨
that treading on a big toe can actually form part of the ritual of marria⟨
among the Arapesh in New Guinea, and for the bride to tread on the brid⟨
groom's toe used to be a sort of ritual joke at a German peasant wedding.
Nowadays in some parts of southeast China the bride tries to put her sho⟨
on top of the bridegroom's in the belief that then she won't be oppressed ⟨
her husband.

Except for the archery implements, probably symbolic of the birth⟨
sons, the ritual (*li*) mentioned in the "Mao commentary" is not furth⟨
explained. However, Kuei Fu (1733-1802) has pointed out that Ts'ai Yun⟨
(133?-192) *Li chi yüeh-ling chang-chü* quotes the character *li* 禮 (ritual) in t⟨
passage as *li* 醴 (a crude, weak, sweet wine made overnight), and Ts'ai not⟨
"This means that the *li* wine was given them to drink." Wines, and the *li* wi⟨
in particular, seem to have been used often in wedding and mating in ancie⟨

---

noticed, *hsin* 訢 does not rhyme with the rest. Early quotations of these lines such as
the *Erh-ya* ("Shih hsün" 釋訓, 3) also leave out this character. For *chieh* 介 (confin⟨
to a side building), I have followed Cheng Hsüan (poem No. 211) and Ma Jui-ch'e⟨
Karlgren thinks this interpretation "obscure" and "obviously impossible," see his *Gloss*
on the *Book of Odes* (1964), 141-42. Actually, the *Erh-ya* ("Shih-ku" 釋詁) also defin⟨
chieh as *liang* 亮, and *liang* as "the [buildings] to the left and the right." This is certain⟨
the original meaning of *liang*. This last character is a pictograph of a building, and ⟨
meaning as such has been lost in other sources.

[30]Waley (tr.), *The book of songs,* 239. Also Margaret Mead, *Sex and temperament*⟨
three primitive societies (1935), 95.

hina, as recorded in the chapter on the wedding ceremony for gentlemen "Shih hun-li") in the *Li chi* and as evidenced in the character *p'ei* 配 which means "to match, to mate" but originally meant *chiu-se* 酒色 (passion or the ush on the face caused by wine, or the color of wine) as defined in the *huo-wen*. The *li* wine was also used as medicine.

As for the footprint mentioned in the poem, Cheng Hsüan thinks it was od's, but the "Mao commentary" interprets it as that of the legendary King 'u of the Kao Hsin clan 高辛氏 or one of his offspring, since the character 帝 could mean either a supernatural or human ruler. The *Shih-pen*, the *Ta- ai li* ("Ti-hsi"), and the *Shih chi* ("Chou pen-chi") even assert that Lady üan's husband was King K'u. K'u was also born, according to the *Lu shih*, fter his mother trod on a giant's footprint. Wang Ch'ung (27-91) gives a omewhat different version of the legend of Hou Chi's birth: "Hou Chi's nother trod on a giant's footprint or, according to another source, wore King 'u's clothes, sat and rested in his place, and thus became pregnant."[31] All hese are, of course, just folk beliefs or stories which cannot be verified.

Moreover, the *Shih chi* version specifies that the event took place in a ield visited by Lady Yüan of Chiang. Lu Te-ming (556-627) in his *Ching-tien hih-wen* mentions an early version of a quotation in the *Erh-ya* ("Shih-hsün") rom the birth poem in which the character *min* in the line *li ti wu min* 履帝 武敏 (trod on the big toe of God's footprint) was given as *mou* 畝 (field), and herefore goes on to comment, "In antiquity Chiang Yüan trod on God's ootprint in a tilled field drained by ditches, and consequently gave birth to Iou Chi."[32] The textual variant here does not seem to be acceptable, but the nterpretation that the event in question took place in a tilled field may still)e correct. Wen I-to has suggested that according to the poem what Chiang Yüan experienced was really a sacrificial ceremony in which she danced ollowing the steps of a priest who impersonated God. Wearing the priest's :lothes, she then rested in the place he lived, had sexual relations with him, ind was impregnated. Wen also suggests that such a dance could be performed n the fields in imitation of tilling the land. In his opinion, before the invention of the plough the Chinese may have farmed by treading on the soil. Such tramping may have been called in Chinese *chün* 踆 and this way of farming may have been called *chün* 畯, which, sometimes written 俊, also meant a

[31] Huang Hui (ed.), *Lun-heng chiao-shih* 論衡校釋 (Taipei: Commercial Press, 1964 reprint), "Chi yen," 79; see also "An-shu," 1161.

[32] Lu actually makes the mistake of thinking the character in Cheng Hsüan's com- mentary is the same as the character in the line of the poem itself. Wen I-to is not aware of this mistake when he uses this as one of his arguments in his article cited in note 33 below. For this see Yen Yüan-chao, *Erh-ya k'uang-ming* 爾雅匡名 (Kuang-ya shu-chü, 1885), "Shih ch'iu," 10/3b.

bailiff in charge of farming. The original form of the name of Hou Chi 后禾
who was, as mentioned above, borne by Chiang Yüan after her treading, mu
have been *chi* 畟 which the *Shuo-wen* defines as a way of tilling the land. B
cause of the similarity of sound, form, and meaning this character could be th
same as *chün* 畯. The Chou royal house called its land god T'ien-chün 田畯
who was in fact Hou Chi. Furthermore, since Hou Chi was thought to be Kin
K'u's son, and K'u's other name is Chün 俊, it certainly can be inferred tha
K'u was related to the method of farming by tramping. Wen's reasoning seem
quite convincing, but he concludes without further evidence that this danc
ceremony did not in fact happen to Chiang Yüan, that she might have ha
instead, illicit intercourse with someone in the fields and was impregnate
when she farmed there, and that the treading on a footprint is just a fictitiou
story to cover up such a relationship.[33]

I feel that this conclusion, while not impossible, may not be as satis
factory as the assumption that Hou Chi's birth was really caused by or too
place after the treading ritual. The story that he was discarded by his mothe
after his birth, and was hence also named *Ch'i* 棄 (to discard, or discarded
can be explained by the fact that Hou Chi may have been delivered in a breec
birth as implied in his name *ch'i*, since according to an ancient Chinese custom
a child born in such a manner should be discarded. On the other hand, a
Arthur Waley has mentioned, the survival of an infant from attempted de
struction is a common legendary motif attributed to ancient heroes in man
cultures.[34] The discard and survival legend is not incompatible with th
assumption that the birth resulted from the ritual of sacrifice to the Divin
Matchmaker.

With regard to the institution of this sacrifice, besides the commentarie
to the birth poem cited above, the "Mao commentary" also mentions it in it
note to poem No. 303, "The dark bird" ("Hsüan niao"):

The dark bird is the swallow. During the time of the vernal equino
[approximately March 20] when the dark birds lighted, the ancestor o
King T'ang [of the Shang dynasty, *c.* 1751-*c.* 1111B.C.], Lady Chier
Ti, daughter of the Yu Sung clan, was mated to the king of the Kac
Hsin clan. The king brought her with him to pray at the Temple o
Chiao-mei, and consequently she gave birth to Hsieh (The Cutter). Thus
based on the order of Heaven, he was born when the dark birds arrived.

The term "Chiao-mei" does not appear in any earlier records. But, as ha
been mentioned above, the "Almanac of Chou" preserved in the *Lü-shih*

[33]Wen, "Chiang Yüan li ta-jen chi k'ao" 姜嫄履大人跡考, in *Wen I-to ch'üan-chi*,
I, 73-80.
[34]Waley (tr.), *The book of songs*, 239-40.

'un-ch'iu and the *Li chi* calls it *"kao-mei"* 高禖, which is unmistakably the
me as *"chiao-mei."* Cheng Hsüan, who comments on the dark birds and the
lo-mei appearing in this passage in the *Li chi*, gives a little more information
id interpretation about the institution:

> The dark bird was [the insignia and/or title of] the official in charge of
> matchmaking, for indicating the proper season. During the time of the
> Kao Hsin clan a dark bird left an egg which Lady Chien of the Sung
> clan 娀簡 swallowed. She then gave birth to Hsieh. The later kings
> regarded such a bird as [the symbol or god of] the official in charge of
> matchmaking. It did give a good omen for pregnancy, so sacrifice to it
> was established. The change of form of the character *mei* 媒 (match-
> maker) into *mei* 禖 [changing the root "woman" 女 into "sacrifice" 示]
> is to deify it.[35]

heng Hsüan goes on to explain that "during the ritual the Grand Invoker
a-chu 大祝) offered wine in the courtyard of the temple of *kao-mei* to the
.dies who had been favored by the Son of Heaven in order to manifest the
›d's blessings." Ts'ai Yung also quotes a fragment from the "Almanac of
hou" in the *Li chi* which says that in the second month of spring "oxen,
ieep, and pigs were sacrificed to the temple of *kao-mei*." He goes on to
xplain that "such sacrificial victims were used in praying for birth."[36]

Concerning the *kao-mei* institution, contemporary scholars such as Wen
to and Ch'en Meng-chia have made some preliminary studies, but Wen's
tudy, in spite of its broad implications, mainly centers on the legend of the
oddess of Kao-t'ang, and Ch'en's on illicit sexual relations and elopement.[37]
think that the symbolic meanings of sex, birth (prolonging life), and agri-
ultural production represented by the treading ritual may be a key for the
nderstanding of the *chiao-mei* or *kao-mei* institution and virtually all the
ther main sacrifices in Chinese antiquity.

Before tracing the ritual further back, we may take a look at some
ncient, albeit scarce, descriptions of the temple of *kao-mei* in the Chou
eriod, which was at least in one case also called Pi-kung (the Closed or Secret

[35]*Li-chi cheng-i* 禮記正義 (Shanghai: Shih-chieh shu-chü, 1935 reprint), 1361. I have
iterpreted the term *chia-hsiang* 嘉祥 with reference to pregnancy based on the text in
'T'ien-wen" of *Ch'u tz'u*, from which the word *hsi* 喜 is quoted as *chia* 嘉 in the "Li
üeh chih" of the *Han shu*. Both *hsi* and *chia* carry the implication of pregnancy.

[36]*Ts'ai Chung-lang chi* 蔡中郎集 (P'an-yü: T'ao-shih Ai-lu, 1890), "Yüeh-ling ta-wen,"
0/14a-b.

[37]See Wen, "Kao-t'ang shen-nü ch'uan-shuo chih fen-hsi" 高唐神女傳說之分析 ,
:h'ing-hua hsüeh-pao, 10:4 (1935) 837-66; also in *Wen I-to ch'üan-chi*, I, 81-116; and
:h'en, "Kao-mei chiao-she tsu-miao t'ung-k'ao" 高禖郊社祖廟通考 , *Ch'ing-hua hsüeh-pao*,
2:3 (1937), 445-72.

Temple) at the time. Poem No. 300 of the *Book of poetry* has this as its titl
It starts with:

> The Closed Temple is still;
> It is very solid, board upon board.
> Glorious was Chiang Yüan,
> Her virtue was without flaw.
> God on High possessed her body,
> Without misery, without harm.
> Fulfilling her months, but not late,
> Thus she bore Hou Chi.

The "Mao commentary" in annotating the poem quotes an earlier sourc
which regards the temple as that of the divine matchmaker:

> Pi means closed. This is the temple for ancestor Chiang Yüan, whicl
> was often closed in the Chou and little used. Meng Chung-tzu says, "I
> is the temple of the divine matchmaker (*mei-kung*)."

The *T'ai-p'ing yü-lan* (*chüan* 135) also cites an apocryphal work, the *Ch'un
ch'iu yüan-ming pao,* possibly of the first century B.C., to the same effect:

> Chiang Yüan, the ancestor of Chou, visited the Closed Temple in th
> place Fu-sang [The Supporting Mulberry, which I have identified a
> the banyan tree in another article], trod on a big footprint, and gav
> birth to Hou Chi.

The identification of the Closed Temple as the temple of the divine match
maker seems to be reasonable, as it was associated with Chiang Yüan and he
birth episode. Various sources define the name of the Closed Temple, *pi* 閟
as *mi* (also pronounced *pi*) 祕 or 宓 or 密 (secret, mystic), all of which orig
inally are the same word. The *Shuo-wen* also defines *mi* 宓 as *an* 安, whicl
gives the implication of mating. Ssu-ma Piao (240-306) gives the character *m*
宓 the meaning of "rid of disease" which I think may be a vestige of th
ancient tradition of worship for getting rid of childlessness.[38]

The Closed Temple described in poem No. 300, however, was a nev
building probably built in the seventh century B.C., as the poem itsel
mentions that it was built by Prince Hsi Ssu of Lu, whose name appears in the
Tso commentary under the year 660 B.C. While this new temple might have
preserved some form and tradition of the earlier ones, there are no extant
records directly describing such buildings.

---

[38]Quoted by Li Shan in his annotation of Ssu-ma Hsiang-ju's "Shang-lin fu" in the
Wen hsüan 文選 (*SPPY*), 8/2a.

But in my own independent study I have reached the same conclusion Wen I-to and Ch'en Meng-chia, that the *kao-mei* must be similar to the *kao-ang* 高唐 and *kao-mi* 高密; and the altar for sacrifice to Heaven, earth, and ods, i.e. the *chih* 時, must be a derived or related institution. The basic root f the character *chih*, as I have pointed out in my article in *Wen-lin*, is a foot mbol with a hand symbol added later. The *Shuo-wen* defines *chih* as an tar for worship of the place trodden on by gods.[39] Its relation to the *kao-ei* or Pi-kung is shown in various ways. The earlier place for divine match-aking must have been, as shown by many records, in a certain hidden hollow art of a high mountain, and place names such as Kao (high), Mi (hidden), d Kao-mi (high hidden) can be found in a number of locations in northern d central China.[40] I would suggest that when those hidden places were cated at the bottom or below the top of the mountains, they were called *sia-mi* 下密 (lower hidden). A place for sacrifice bearing this name existed the Ch'i State besides the Kao-mi and is recorded in the *Han shu* ("Chiao-u chih"). Later on when buildings were made for the purpose of performing milar functions of divine matchmaking, in place of performance in an open ace, they may have preserved this same tradition by establishing either an pper story or hall or a lower story or hall in the building as a place for erformance. The State of Ch'in built Shang-chih (upper altar) and Hsia-chih ower altar), which seem to parallel the Kao-mi and Hsia-mi of Ch'i. The *hih chi* ("Feng-shan shu") says that Duke Te of Ch'in (r. 667-676 B.C.) uilt the Fu-chih in 677 B.C. The character *fu* 伏 here certainly had the same eaning as *mi* 宓, since the name of the legendary king Fu-hsi 伏羲 who was so said to have been born after his mother trod on a giant's footprint, metimes was written as Mi-hsi 宓犧.[41] Then in 672 B.C. Duke Hsüan of h'in (r. 675-664 B.C.) built the Mi-chih 宓時, which seems definitely to have ollowed the Pi-kung tradition by name.

Further evidence may be found to support this assumption that the

---

[39]I have interpreted the term *chi-chih* 基止 in Hsü Shen's definition of *chih* 時 as tread and stop." The *Shuo-wen* says *chih* 阯 is *chi* 基 ; see note 41 below. This and e *kao-mei* may be compared with the divine physician's infirmary in Epidauria of ncient Greece, the *abaton* which means "a holy place not to be trodden."

[40]See those cited in Ch'en's article mentioned in note 37 above.

[41]See *Shih wei han shen wu* 詩緯含神霧 and *Hsiao-ching kou-ming chüeh* 孝經勾命訣 uoted in *T'ai-p'ing yü-lan, chüan* 78; the former gives the name as Mi Hsi. The *Ho t'u* 圖 quoted in Kuo P'u's annotation to *Shan hai ching* 山海經 (13, "Hai-nei tung ching") nd Wang Fu's *Ch'ien-fu lun* 潛夫論 ("Wu-te chih") give Fu Hsi; see also my article in *en-lin*, 202. The *Hsiao-ching kou-ming chüeh* quoted in the commentary to the *Yüeh hi* 樂記 says, "Fu-hsi's music is called *li-chi* 立基." Wen I-to interprets *li* as *ta* 大 (big) nd *chi* as *chi* 跡 (footsteps); see his article on Chiang Yüan, 78-79; also my interpretation note 39 above.

chih altar is similar to the *kao-mei*. The *Shih chi* records that in 756 B.
Duke Wen of Ch'in (r. 765-716 B.C.) dreamed of a yellow serpent suspend
in the sky with its mouth reaching the marshes (or valley) of Mount Fu (
Lu) 鄜. He was told by a scribe that this was an omen of God, then he bu
the Fu-chih 鄜畤 for making the *chiao* 郊 sacrifice to the White God. Ssu-m
Ch'ien says:

> Before the construction of the Fu-chih, there had been a Wu-chih 武畤
> in Wu-yang 吳陽 at one side of the Yung region and a Hao-chih 好畤
> east Yung. They had both been abandoned and no sacrifice was ar
> longer made there. Some say that since antiquity, as it was believed th
> the Yung region was a high land of caves of gods who had the power
> enlighten, so *chih* altars were established there for making the *chia*
> sacrifice to the Supreme God, and thus various worship shrines agglon
> erated in the region. For there had been worship here during the tin
> of the Yellow Emperor (r. *c.* 2674-*c.* 2575 B.C.), and even in late Cho
> times such *chiao* sacrifices were still made. This account of the alta
> has not been circulated widely and the officials have never talked abov
> it.[42]

I think the name Wu of the altar Wu-chih here may mean the same thing
the character appearing in the line *li ti wu min* in poem No. 245, that
"footprint" or "footstep." And the name Hao may refer to a fertile woma
or a woman soon expected to be pregnant (see note 20 above). Therefore, th
earliest known *chih* altars all implied in their names the hope for childbirth
fertility, and thus their function was similar to that of the Pi-kung and th
kao (*chiao*)-*mei* temples. In fact, the association of the name Hao with th
kao-mei may be found in the oracle bone inscriptions. One of the oracles say
"Ask in divination: To favor Lady Hao in Kao?"[43] Lady Hao's pregnancy an
childbirth appears in another oracle inscription.[44] The Kao mentioned here
the oracle might be the *kao-mei* or a place so-named because of the existenc
of such institutions there. Such a place sometimes was called Hao (鄗 or 鎬
which indeed was the name of the capital of the early Chou dynasty. The us
of *hao* as a woman's proper name may be expressive of a desire for childre
and thus be a custom, at the latest, already existing in the Shang dynasty.

Although we have no precise knowledge of the structure of the *chia*
mei or *kao-mei*, we may imagine its appearance from later descriptions of
few of its remnants. The performance of *kao-mei* worship was repeatedl
renewed from 129 B.C. of the Han dynasty on up to A.D. 1531 of the Min

[42]*Shih chi* (*Po-na* ed.), 28/3b-4a.

[43]Lo Chen-yü (ed.), *Yin hsü shu-ch'i hsü-pien* 殷虛書契續編 (1914), 4.30.3.

[44]Wang Hsiang, *Fu-shih Yin ch'i cheng-wen* 簠室殷契徵文 (1925), No. 115.

ynasty or later by the emperors to pray for heirs. Their reconstruction of
ae *kao-mei* altars was usually based on their understanding of the institution
escribed in the classical records and oral tradition. It is difficult to determine
ow close these reconstructed altars and ceremonies were to the ancient
rstem. But certain features may be noteworthy. On the top of the altar there
aight be a stone tablet (*shih chu*), on which was carved a figure swallowing
1 egg, and which was sometimes housed in a small building. In the ceremony
ae legendary kings Fu-hsi and K'u, and sometimes also Nü Kua, Lady Chiang
üan, or her son Hou Chi, were worshiped. Bulls and jade were offered in the
tual. The music of the *teng* songs (*teng ke*) was played. The participating
omen placed arrows into quivers, an action apparently symbolizing sexual
ction. The women also drank the blessing wine, as described in the classics.[45]

Besides the *chiao-mei* and the *chih* altars which were related or similar
o each other, there were other altars of various names. The *Mo-tzu* says, "The
tate of Yen has the Tsu[-tse] (Ancestor Marsh) just as the State of Ch'i has
ae She-chi, the State of Sung 宋 has the Sang-lin (Mulberry Forest), and the
tate of Ch'u has the Yün-meng (Cloudy Dream): these are all places
here men and women observe their mating."[46] Contemporary scholars have
lready identified all these altars with the *kao-mei*.[47] Some of them believe
hat the *chih* or the *kao-mei* was derived from the *chi* 稷, and the *chi* in turn
rom the *she* 社.[48] Others believe that the *kao-mei* is one kind of *she*.[49] We
re still not very sure whether the characters *she* and *t'u* 土 were phallic as
arlgren suggests.[50] The object above the ground shown in the character *t'u*
aight symbolize a plant or seed instead of a male organ. At any rate there
eems to be no doubt that the *she* must have originally been connected with
type of worship concerned with fecundity and fertility.

The *she*, however, might not, in my opinion, be the earliest major
hinese sacrifice for fecundity and fertility. In the poem "The birth of our
eople," I translate the character *ssu* 祀 as a "sacrifice for fertility." The
huo-wen actually defines this character as "to sacrifice (or a sacrifice) in case
f childlessness." This character was used in the Shang dynasty to mean "a
ear," probably because such a sacrifice was originally a yearly event. It has
lso been used in most of the classics to mean "sacrifice" in general. I believe

---

[45]For source materials on the *kao-mei*, see *Ku chin t'u-shu chi-ch'eng* 古今圖書集成
Shanghai: Chung-hua shu-chü, 1934), *ts'e* 722, *chüan* 241.

[46]Sun I-jang (ed.), *Mo-tzu chien-ku* 墨子閒詁 (1907), 8/6a-b.

[47]See Kuo Mo-jo, *Chia-ku wen yen-chiu* 甲骨文研究 (Rev. ed.; Peking: K'o-hsüeh
h'u-pan-she, 1962), "Shih tsu p'in," 51-60; *Wen I-to ch'üan-chi*, I, 97.

[48]Wen I-to, "Chiang Yüan li ta-jen chi k'ao," *ibid.*, 74.

[49]Chiang Liang-fu, *Ch'ü Yüan fu chiao-chu* 屈原賦校注 (Hong Kong: Commercial
ress, 1964), 369.

[50]Karlgren, "Some fecundity symbols in ancient China," *BMFEA*, II (1930), 17-21.

this generalization took place probably because this particular sacrifice ha
been one of the earliest, most common and significant sacrifices. In the *Boo*
of history ("Hung-fan") and other classics longevity, fertility, and health we
the greatest concerns of the ancient Chinese, often taking priority over wealt
sociopolitical power, and prestige, and *ssu* was used to represent all sacrifice
The main root *ssu* 巳 of the character *ssu* 祀 with a similar pronunciatio
definitely had relevant meanings. The *Shuo-wen* says that this root represen
the picture of a snake or serpent. I will show later that this animal ofte
symbolized birth in ancient China. According to the *Huai-nan-tzu* ("T'ie
wen hsün") *ssu* 巳 is the sixth of the twelve branches and determines birt
and growth. (I may also point out here that the fifth branch, *ch'en* 辰, si,
nifies pregnancy.) The "Mao commentary" to poem No. 189, "Ssu-kan," say
ssu (巳, 似) means "heirs" (*ssu* 嗣). The *Kuang-Ya* ("Shih yen") defines th
character *ssu* 巳 with *ssu* 似 which also means "descendant" and henc
"resembling."

Two other sacrifices which are related to, or similar to, the *ssu* 祀 an
the *she* are the *chiao* 郊 and the *t'i* 禘. The *Chou li* ("Ch'un kuan"),
describing the functions of the Minor Invoker (*hsiao chu*), says: "When th
enemy invades, [the Minor Invoker] will protect the *chiao ssu* at the *she*.
The *Tso commentary* quotes the saying of Meng Hsien-tzu under the ye
566 B.C. that "the *chiao ssu* is a worship of Hou Chi in prayer for agricu
tural affairs, so the *chiao* is conducted during the solar season Stirring
Hibernating Insects [approximately March 5]; and following the chiao, far
ing is performed." The *I Chou-shu* ("Tso Lo chieh") describes in detail ho
the Duke of Chou in the twelfth century B.C. built the *chiao she* for worshi
ing his ancestor Hou Chi and the Supreme God. While the character *chia*
usually means "open spaces beyond a city," its main root *chiao* 交 mea
"copulate," and its two roots *i-chiao* 邑交 (*cf. yeh-ho* 野合) could have th
meaning "copulate near the town." While this interpretation is very uncertai
the *Li chi* ("Chiao t'e sheng") particularly mentions that bulls should be offere
for the chiao sacrifices and that during such a ceremony the Son of Heave
should refrain from eating the meat of pregnant animals. The same book als
says that both the *chiao* and the *t'i* are for ancestor worship. The root *ti* 帝 o
the character *t'i*, as shown in the form of the oracle and bronze inscription
seems to be a picture of a footstalk of a flower or fruit, a symbol of fertilit
It is also curious that the *Li chi* in its chapter on the *chiao* sacrifice contain
several long passages on wedding ceremonies. Conceivably, almost all of th
major sacrifices in ancient China were originally for the purpose of fertilit
and reproduction, and many of them probably were related to the *chiao-mei.*

As for the exact ritual of the *chiao-mei,* a few additional points may b
made here. The tramping dance performed in the ritual seems to have been

nd of great *wu* dance (*ta-wu* 大武). Such a dance was performed in the *chiao* crifice, according to the *Li chi* ("Chiao t'e sheng") and the *Chou li* ("Ta ı-yüeh") with white bulls offered to the ancestors. The original meaning of *u* might be "march with a lance" or "dance with a lance." It also meant "a ·otstep or footprint" as shown in the poem concerning Chiang Yüan's preg- ıncy, and "to follow the steps" as shown in poem No. 243, "Hsia wu." A ınce to pray for or show virility and military prowess might be closely ıated. More specifically, the ceremony described in poem No. 209, "Ch'u 'u," participated in by the official craftsmen-invokers (*kung-chu*) and the ·iests who impersonated the spirits (*shih* 尸), the divine protectors (*pao* 保), ıd the noble wives, seems to be quite close to the ceremony of the *chiao-mei* a certain stage of its development. Such spiritual impersonators also appear poem No. 292 and the four poems following No. 245 concerning Chiang üan's pregnancy as well as in the *Li chi* ("Chiao t'e sheng").

These invokers, spiritual impersonators, and divine protectors mentioned ove may all be what were also known as *wu* (巫) or what some translators ıve called witches, shamans, or shamanists. As is mentioned above, the *kao- ei* is sometimes called *kao-t'ang*; according to Sung Yü's (*c.* 290-*c.* 223 B.C.) Kao-t'ang fu," the goddess of Kao-t'ang is also a woman from the Wu ountain (*wu-shan*).

Ample evidence shows that the earliest *wu* performed the functions of romoting fertility and reproduction accompanied by tramping dances and ›ngs. According to the chapters on sacrifices in both the *Shih chi* and the *an shu*, early in the Han dynasty the imperial court following the ancient ıstitutions built altars for worshiping "wu hsien"巫先. Yen Shih-ku (581- 45) in his commentary to the *Han shu* and Sun I-jang (1848-1908) in his *hou li cheng-i* ("ch'un-kuan: ssu-wu") identify *wu hsien* as the earliest *wu*. he ancient medical work, *The Yellow Emperor's classic of internal medicine Huang-ti nei-ching: Ling shu*) (Chapter 58), says that the *hsien wu* 先巫 was ›le to foretell diseases so that they might be stopped by invocation. The ıaracter *hsien* 先 is constructed with a footstep on the top of a man, which robably means a person who led with footsteps. In describing the wedding ›remony the *Li chi* and the *I li* repeatedly use the character *hsien* to describe ıe bridegroom's leading (*hsien*) the bride through her door and in the pro- ·ssion. The "Chao hun" in the *Ch'u tz'u* also uses this character to describe ıe craftsman invoker's leading the soul. A Han commentator mentions that ıe Kuei-chih altars built in the fourth century B.C. were located below a ·emple of Ancestors (*Jen-hsien tz'u*). Contemporary scholars believe "Jen- sien" here means Hou Chi.[51] I think it might mean Chiang Yüan or men's

[51] See *Shih chi,* "Feng-shan shu"; *Chi-chieh* quotes an early source, and Wen I-to's rticle on Chiang Yüan, 75, as cited in note 33.

ancestors in general. The *Lü-shih ch'un-ch'iu* relates that a woman of the Y
Shen clan 有侁氏 found an infant in a hollow mulberry tree. The tree was i
mother. The infant, I Yin, later the famous chief minister of King T'ang o
the Shang dynasty, was also related to the *wu*. It is noticeable that the nan
Shen 侁 consists of *jen hsien* 人先 (men's ancestor). The *Classic of mountai*
and seas (*Shan hai ching*, "Ta-huang hsi-ching") records a Country of tl
Hsien People (*Hsien-min chih kuo*). I believe the Hsien people might refer t
those who had the custom of praying for birth by leading a tramping danc
ceremony.

Cheng Hsüan identifies the Wu Heng 巫恒 listed in the *Chou li* ("Ch'u
kuan: ssu-wu") with the *hsien wu*, and Wang Chung (1744-1794) thinks W
Heng is the same person as Wu Hsien 巫咸 , the alleged creator of the professic
of the *wu*. I think *heng* refers to the nearly full moon, and the early *wu* migl
have performed a kind of "dance under the full moon" (*t'iao yüeh* 跳月) suc
as that done by the Miao tribes for choosing mates before marriage. Th
original meaning of the character *heng* is a moon which is nearly full. Thus tl
moon goddess is called Heng-o 恒娥 ; the regularity of the moon's chang
lends the character its meaning "perseverance" or "constancy" and this kin
of virtue is also attributed to the *wu* physician which I will refer to later.

Furthermore, many other ancient records show that the *wu* were pries
whose function was to pray for reproduction and fertility. Let me first quot
the definition given by the *Shuo-wen chieh-tzu*:

> *Wu* is a *chu* 祝 (invoker or priest), a woman [some versions do not hav
> this word] who is able to render [herself] invisible, and with dance t
> invoke gods to come down. The character symbolizes the appearance c
> a person dancing with two sleeves. It also means *kung* 工 (a craftsman
> In antiquity Wu Hsien 巫咸 created the profession of the *wu*.

Hsü Shen's identification of *wu* with *chu* is quite believable. The two coul
have meant the same thing in ancient times, and later *chu* became a broade
term. The main element of the character *chu* depicts a person kneeling wit
mouth open, possibly to make invocations. Hsü Shen mentions a theory tha
this element could have been simplified from *tui* (or *yüeh*) 兌, which th
Book of changes ("Shuo kua") defines as follows: "represents a *wu* as well a
the mouth and the tongue." According to some Ch'ing scholars, the characte
chu was interchangeable with 籌 and 禱 and similar to *ch'ou* 詶 and *yu* 訧
(由).[52] The *Shuo-wen* defines *ch'ou* (or *t'ao*) 犨 as "infertility of cattle an
sheep," and *tao* 禱 as "pray for *fu* 福 (blessings, prosperity, happiness)." Th
character *fu* usually implied in ancient times longevity, wealth, health, fer

[52] See Ch'en Shih-t'ing, *Tu Shuo-wen cheng i* 讀說文證疑, in *Shuo-wen chieh-tzu ku
lin* 說文解字詁林 (Taipei: Commercial Press, 1959 reprint), *ts'e* 1, p. 70a.

lity, and prosperity.[53] The character *tao* 禱 should also be read *ch'ou* and was sometimes written 禂 . The *Chou li* says that one of the land invoker's (*tien chu* 甸祝) functions was to make the *ch'ou* 禂 sacrifice for ridding cattle and horses of disease. The character *tao,* I may point out here, has "longevity" as its main root, and *ch'ou* has its main root *chou* with an early meaning of the "boundary of a tilled field," and hence the name of the dynasty founded by Hou Chi's offspring. The medical classic *Huang-ti nei-ching: Su wen* (Chapter 13) says that the ancient healers could cure ailments by way of *chu yu* 祝由. Ho Hsiu (129-182) in his annotation to a passage in the *Kung-yang commentary* under the year 719 B.C. says, "A *wu* is a person who worships spirits and gods, makes prayer (*tao* 禱) for curing disease and seeking *fu* 福 ."

Whether the ancient *wu* had to be a woman is uncertain. The *Kuo-yü* ("Ch'u-yü," *hsia*) quotes Kuan She-fu (*fl.* 515-489 B.C.) as saying that in antiquity men and gods did not mix with each other, that wise and enlightened people might be able to invoke and call gods to descend, and that "such men were called *hsi* 覡 and such women, *wu*"; that after the period of the legendary King Shao-hao (r. *c.* 2597-*c.* 2514 B.C.) when the Nine Li corrupted virtue, men and gods mixed, all things were confused, everybody made sacrifices, and each family performed the function of the *wu* and the scribe"; and that only when the legendary King Chuan Hsü (r. *c.* 2513-*c.* 2436 B.C.) came to power was the situation rectified by the appointment of a certain official to be in charge of the worship of gods and another to be in charge of the affairs of men. Later the descendants of the Nine Li, the Three Miao, again mixed men and gods (in Kao Shen shih's time) and again the situation was corrected by King Yao. Many later scholars, however, point out that, as is shown in the *Chou li* and other sources, either a man or a woman could serve as a *wu.* The *Yüeh tung pi-chi,* quoted in Juan Yüan's (1764-1849) *Kuang-tung t'ung-chih,* says that in south China even the role of a so-called "woman *wu*" (*nü wu*) was actually impersonated by a man. The profession of *wu* was still popular in recent times in south China and among many minority tribes in south-western China, such as the Miao 苗 , the Yao 猺 , and the Lo-lo 羅羅. The male *wu* was called *hsi-kung* 覡公, or *hsi-pa* 覡爸 (father *wu*). I think the term "father" may derive from the *kao-mei* tradition. A relationship between the

[53]The "five blessings" (*wu fu* 五福) listed in the *Book of history* ("Hung-fan") have usually been interpreted as (1) longevity, (2) wealth, (3) health, (4) virtue (*yu hao te* 攸好德), (5) finishing the allotted span of one's life (*k'ao chung ming* 考終命). But Huan T'an (*c.* 24 B.C.-*c.* A.D. 56) in listing the five gives "prosperity in government" (*kuei* 貴) as no. 3, and after (4) "health" is (5) "fertility" (*tzu-sun chung-tuo* 子孫衆多). I believe *tao* and *te* in the *Book of history* still carry the original meaning "fertility and fecundity" but not the later meaning "virtue," and *ming,* as more often in the bronze inscriptions, "allotment and mandate of one's share in government position and society," but not the later meaning "the span of life."

Miao and Yao tribes and the ancient Nine Li and Three Miao has bee
suggested by many contemporary scholars.

As for the statement that the *wu* is able to call gods to come down t
dance, it is also mentioned in many other ancient works. The *Chou li* ("Ch'u
kuan") says: "The *wu* supervisor (*ssu wu* 司巫) is in charge of commanding
of the *wu*: if there is serious drought in the country he will lead the *wu*
perform the 'dance for rain' (*wu-yü* 舞雩)." The same work also mentions tl
function of male and female *wu* as performing these and other dances an
using herbs and invocation of the gods to cure ailments. These practice
carried on from antiquity to the following centuries, are described
many other records. For example, in the "Biography of Hsia T'ung" of tl
History of the Chin dynasty (*Chin shu*) two female *wu* are described as "gre
beauties who wore fabulous clothes, were skillful in singing and dancing, an
were able to make themselves invisible." In the evening after they tolled be
and beat drums, and played pipes and strings, they drew swords to pierc
their own tongues and demonstrated sword-swallowing and fire-spittin;
"They talked and laughed like gods and spirits," and practiced healing th
sick. Although this happened in the third century A.D., it seems to hav
carried on the earlier tradition of the *wu*.

Another fact may be mentioned here. When they performed dance
the ancient *wu* often held jade in their hands in order to invoke gods for th
sake of birth or production, healing ailments, and consolation for death. Th
character *wu* 巫 appears in the oracle bone inscriptions in the form 中, th
meaning or reason for which has not been satisfactorily explained. I woul
like to suggest that it must have been originally written 中 as is shown in th
stone inscriptions "Curses on the State of Ch'u" (*Tsu Ch'u wen*) dated 32
311 B.C., that is, two lines added to the character *yü* 王 (玉) (jade). Suc
lines or long dots usually indicate that the object makes sound or movemen
as evidenced in many other characters such as *yin* 音, *hu* 乎, and *p'eng* 彭
The stone tablet *Hsiao Tan pei* (A.D. 522 or after) has *wu* written 巫, and th
T'ang copied version of the *Tso commentary* preserved in the Kanazaw
Library of Japan has the same form (see Hsi-kung, 17th year, or 643 B.C.
It shows that the main root of *wu* is the character for jade. The Gran
Secretary of Sacrificial Worship (*Ta tsung-po*), who was in charge of the *wu*
had the duty, says the *Chou li*, to make jade objects for the worship o
Heaven, earth, and the four directions. The same book also mentions that th
work of the male *wu* was "to invoke gods to descend by calling in all direction
with young branches of plants or ears of grain; in the winter to expel plague;
to dance with a square [kerchief of silk] and to dance with jade."[54] A furthe

[54]I have read the *wu* in *wu-fang wu-suan* 無方無筭 as 舞 (dance) instead of a negativ
particle. *Wu* 無 is the original form of the character for dance. The character *suan*

ce of evidence is found in the *Shuo-wen chieh-tzu* which defines another
m for the *wu* as follows:

> *Ling* 靈 is *wu* 巫. As the *wu* uses jade to worship gods, so the character
> is made with a root jade (*yü* 玉) and the phonetic *ling* 需. The character
> sometimes is written 靈 with *wu* as its root.

tually the so-called phonetic here consists of a "rain" element and three
iouths"; this must be a representation of one of the main functions of *wu*,
"call" for "rain." The character *ling* meaning *wu* is also well attested in the
line songs" and in the "Li-sao" of the *Songs of the south (Ch'u tz'u)*. Jade was
lieved to possess magic power both for promoting birth and protecting the
ad. This and the young branches held by the *wu* may symbolize, among other
ngs, reproduction and fertility. (Popular Taoism has jade symbolize sex.)

A further question may arise from the *Shuo-wen* definition of *wu* as
ntical to *kung* (craftsman or crafts) in meaning. One possible explanation
that the character *kung* in the oracle bone and bronze inscriptions, like *wu*,
ms also to depict jade. Such an explanation has been advocated by some
ntemporary scholars, but rejected by others.[55] In my opinion, during early
ies there may have been separate graphs depicting an axe and a craftsman's
iare, but later their simplified forms became so similar that they sometimes
re regarded as the same character *kung*. This does not exclude the possibility
at both these early tools were made with stone or jade. On the other hand,
 wu who served both as a priest and a healer in antiquity, certainly could
considered a kind of craftsman, and his profession, a kind of witchcraft.
ch craftsmanship was usually professed, as I have pointed out in another
ticle, within certain clans or tribes in ancient China.[56] The craftsman-
oker (*kung-chu*) mentioned in poem 209, "Ch'u tz'u," of the *Book of
etry* which has been cited earlier, may serve as an independent testimony
at *kung* and *wu* were closely related. The term *kung-chu* also appears in the
i ("Shao-lao kuei shih li") and *Ch'u tz'u* ("Chao hun"). Wang I (*fl.* A.D.
4-144) defines it in his annotation to the latter as "a skillful, eloquent male
u." Indeed, one may even wonder whether this term is the same as *wu-chu*

---

ually made with *lung* 弄 which depicts two hands playing with jade. I believe the
ments on the top of *suan* in its original form do not mean bamboo but also two hands.
is character *suan* might have been similar in its construction to *hsing* 興. Also, the
'u square silk uncovered in Changsha in 1942 seems to be such a square for the *wu*
nce referred to in this passage in the *Chou li* ("Ch'un kuan: nan-wu").

[55] Sun Hai-po interprets *kung* in this way, cited in Li Hsiao-ting, *Chia-ku wen-tzu chi-
h* 甲骨文字集釋 (Taipei: Academia Sinica, 1965), V, 1591.

[56] See my paper, "A new theory on the origins of Mohism," presented at the XXVII
ternational Congress of Orientalists, Ann Arbor, Michigan, Aug. 17, 1967, to be pub-
hed in *Wen-lin,* Vol. 2.

which appears in many sources such as the *Li chi* ("T'an-kung," *hsia*),
Han Fei-tzu ("Hsien hsüeh"), and the *Shih chi* ("Biographies of Mencius ;
Hsün-tzu"). At any rate, it is very believable that in early times the profes:
of the *wu* was regarded as a kind of craft. The *Shuo-wen* in defining *kung* ;
reconfirms this by saying, "*Kung* is skillful craftsmanship. It depicts a r
possessing norm (square and compass). It means the same as *wu*."

It is of course a well-known fact that the ancient *wu* was at the sa
time a healer or physician. The term *wu-i* (*wu*-healer or physician) f
appears in Chapter 39, "The great assembling" (*Ta chü*) of the *I Chou-shu*
which the Duke of Chou of the 12th century B.C. recalls the following st
ment by his father, King Wen, with regard to previous social institutions:
each village a *wu-i* was established and a hundred medicines were gathered
that it was always prepared for sickness and calamities."[57] As is well know
in the *Lun-yü* (13:22) Confucius quotes a saying of the southerners, "C
who lacks constancy (*heng*) cannot be a *wu-i*." The term *wu-i* in both ca
definitely must be understood as "*wu*-healer" or "witch-doctor" instead o
wu and a healer, although the *Tso chuan* records under the year 581 B.C. (
10th year of Duke Ch'eng) a case in which the two professions were perform
by different persons by that time. The *Kuan-tzu* (3, "Ch'üan hsiu") menti
wu-i also in the sense of a *wu*-healer. And even in the *History of the La
Han* (*chüan* 72, "Biography of Hsü Yang") *wu-i* is still used to refer to ;
person.

Many ancient Chinese records suggest that the healing craft or medic
was created by a *wu,* and the Chinese word for a healer or physician may
derived from the word for a *wu*. The *Shuo-wen chieh-tzu* defines *i* 醫 (heali
or medicine, or a healer) as follows:

> *I* is the healing craftsman or craft. Its root *i* 殹 depicts a foul appearan
> The nature of a healer is such [or "is to stir by fire"] that he [or sl
> must work with spirits [or alcohol, *chiu* 酒]; hence the characte:
> made of the radical *yu* 酉 [ancient character for *chiu*]. This is W;
> Yü's theory. Another theory says that the root *i* indicates the groan
> sound of the sick, and the spirits are for curing ailments. The *Choi
> mentions the "medicinal spirits" [that is, tincture, or "medicine
> draught," *i chiu*]. In antiquity Wu P'eng created medicine [or "for
> first time became the healer"].[58]

[57]Chu Yu-tseng (ed.), *I Chou-shu chi-hsün chiao-shih* 逸周書集訓校釋 (preface da
1842; Taipei: I-wen, n.d.), 4/12a. In this edition the chapter is renumbered as 40.

[58]*Shuo-wen chieh-tzu ku-lin, ts'e* 10, pp. 6681-83. How to read this definitio
quite a problem; for a detailed discussion see my forthcoming article in Chinese o
similar subject.

The thesaurus *Kuang-Ya* ("Shih ku") compiled during A.D. 227-233 by ang I even goes so far as to say that "*i* 醫 means *wu*." Actually this·charac- *i* which is commonly understood as meaning the healer or healing craft may ·e at first primarily denoted only tincture. The early word for the healer, ·healing art, or medicine may have been constructed with *wu* as a root. Lu -ming (556-627) mentions that the character *i* (tincture) in the passage ·cribing the function of the official in charge of spirits (*chiu-cheng*) in the ·ou li appears in some editions as 毉 with *wu* in the lower part. This charac- also appears in the *Shuo-yüan* (*chüan* 18, "Pien-wu") edited by Liu Hsiang ·the *Yen t'ieh lun* (Chapter 59) edited by Huan K'uan of the first century ·. It is also listed in the *I-ch'ieh ching yin i* by the Buddhist Monk Hsüan- ·g of the 7th century, the *Ch'ieh yün*, and the *Kuang yün*. Even one of Han ·'s (768-824) acquaintances had this character as his personal name, as is ·icated in Han's "Letter to Lü I Shan-jen."

Among the above quotations from the *Shuo-wen chieh-tzu* we may ·tice the saying that Wu Hsien created the profession of the *wu* and Wu ·ng created medicine. The names Hsien and P'eng are mentioned by many ·er ancient records. Confucius spoke of an Old P'eng (*Lun-yü*, 7:1). P'eng, ·en, and Wu Hsien appear quite often in *The songs of the south* ("Li-sao," ·hiu chang: 4, 6, 9"). While we may acknowledge that both Hsien and P'eng ·re ancient *wu*, we are not sure who really originated the profession of the ·and medicine in ancient China. Hsien seems to be the earliest and most ·minent of the *wu*. Although both the *Shih-pen*—as quoted by Kuo P'u's ·76-324) commentary to the "Hai-nei ching" of the *Classic of mountains* ·seas—and the *Lü-shih ch'un-ch'iu* ("Fu kung") say that Wu P'eng created ·dicine, yet the *Yü-hai* by Wang Ying-lin (1223-1296) quotes the *Shih-pen* saying that Wu Hsien created it. Some modern scholars consider this last ·ribution a mistake for Wu P'eng. But a number of other sources also ·ntion Wu Hsien as a healer. The *T'ai-p'ing yü-lan* (*chüan* 721) quotes the ·ih-pen: "Wu Hsien was King Yao's minister who served Yao as a physician ·th the 'great (or wild goose) technique' (*hung shu* 鴻術) [medicine]." Another ·rce quotes the same book alleging, "When Wu Hsien cursed [or invoked, ·u] a tree, the tree would wither; when he cursed a bird, the bird would ·l."[59] Wang Ch'ung in his *Lun heng* (Chapter 66) says much the same thing.

Whether Wu Hsien belonged to the time of King Yao (r. *c.* 2356-*c.* 2256 ·C.), as is stated above, is an open question. The so-called *Kuei-tsang*, alleged ·be an earlier version of the *Book of changes*, describes him as a diviner of ·Yellow Emperor (r. *c.* 2697-*c.* 2598 B.C.). But most sources of the late ·ou and the Han dynasty such as the "Prefaces" to the *Book of history* and

---

[59]This is quoted in Ch'en Pang-hsien, *Chung-kuo i-hsüeh shih* 中國醫學史 (Rev. ed.; ·anghai: Commercial Press, 1954), 9; I have not found the source yet.

Ma Jung (79-166) all recognize him as a wise minister of the Shang dynasty 1766-*c.* 1122 B.C.). The Taoist works *Chuang-tzu* and *Lieh-tzu,* howev describe him as a person of as late as the Ch'un-ch'iu period (722-481 B.C Some sources like the *Shih chi* say that he was the earliest astrologer a astronomer; others like the *Lü-shih ch'un-ch'iu* consider him the earli diviner; there is still one epigraphical source, the "Curses upon the State Ch'u," which calls him "a great and splendid god" (*p'i-hsien ta shen*).[60]

The temporal discrepancies need not constitute a serious problem, we recognize that names like Hsien and P'eng may have been only indicatic of the nature of a profession or craft and could possibly be used by persc of different times. Although we may never be able to ascertain who t earliest *wu* or *wu*-physician was, we may try to find out roughly the kind work practiced by such an early profession. For this I think the semi-mytl logical and semi-historical and geographical work, the *Classic of mounta* *and seas,* which Liu Hsiang attributed to the early Hsia period, i.e. *c.* 22(2198 B.C., but which certainly dates from much later, may provide us so clues. Chapter 11, "Hai-nei hsi ching," of the book lists six *wu:*

> To the east of K'ai-ming there were Wu P'eng, Wu Ti, Wu Yang, Wu 巫履, Wu Fan, and Wu Hsiang, all of whom, clasping under their ar the body of the wild dog Yeh-yü, held the medicine of immortality resist it [Kuo P'u comments here: "To resist the death spell and se rebirth"]. Yeh-yü, who had a snake's body and a human head, h been killed by Erh-fu's minister.

Kuo P'u's commentary on the six *wu* mentioned here says that "all are divi physicians." The mention of a monster with a snake's body in the text dc not seem accidental. The same book in Chapter 7, "Hai-wai hsi ching" says:

> The State of Wu Hsien (*Wu Hsien kuo*) is located in the north of N ch'ou. [Its residents] hold green snakes in their right hands and r snakes in their left hands. It is on Mount Teng-pao, from which all t *wu* travel up and down.

Such works as the *Han shu* ("Ti-li chih") and the *Shui-ching chu* (*SPPY* e 6/20b) identify the State of Wu Hsien with the Mountain of Wu Hsien (M *Hsien shan,* modern Chung-t'iao Mountain in Shansi Province). But Hao hsing (1757-1825) thought that it must be located far beyond the Sou China Sea. I would suggest that because of the frequent movement of t ancient *wu,* many places could bear names of a similar nature, and theref it would be impossible to pin down a single definite location.

[60]Ku Yen-wu (1613-1681) has made a good summary; see Huang Ju-ch'eng, *Jih c lu chi-shih* 日知錄集釋 (Taipei: Shih-chieh shu-chü, 1962 reprint), 578-79.

What interests me here is the mention of the mountain related to the
and snakes. In Chapter 15, "Ta-huang nan ching," the *Classic of moun-
s and seas* says:

There is a Wu Mountain (*Wu shan*) to the west of which exist the yellow
(or brown) birds and the eight doses (kinds) of god's medicine. The
yellow (brown) birds are in charge of the dark snakes in the Wu Mountain.

same book in Chapter 12, "Hai-nei pei ching," also records a Mountain
Snakes and Wu which I think could be the same as the above-mentioned
Mountain: "At the top of the Mountain of Snakes and Wu (*She wu chih
ì*) there is a man [or men] who holds a wooden staff and stands facing
he east."

The Wu Mountain here of course reminds us of the mountain of the
e name described in Sung Yü's "Kao-t'ang fu" mentioned earlier. There I
ited out that such a mountain might be relevant to the *kao-mei* altar, that
in institution for sex, fertility, and fecundity. The yellow (brown) birds
ted to the mountain, we may note further, symbolize death or marriage
as do those in the *Book of poetry*.

Moreover, the snake and the wooden staff as symbols of sex, birth, and
exist in many cultures, as we can see, for example, from the story of the
iction of Eve in the *Old testament*. The molt of the snake can be a symbol
rejuvenation, healing, and rebirth, while the wooden staff may be phallic
symbolic of vegetation and fecundity. It is also interesting to note the
ilarity between the ancient Chinese *wu*-physician holding both a wooden
f and snakes and the ancient Greek god of medicine Asclepius, who is
ally depicted holding a staff with a serpent coiled round it, a symbol
ch is still used by the modern medical profession. Asclepius was further
ociated with the sparrow and sacrificed to with a cock. This may also be
mpared with the yellow (brown) bird in the Chinese *wu* tradition. Moreover,
ause of the belief that he had been guarded and protected by a dog, rep-
entations of Asclepius often include a dog.[61] This is remarkably similar to
Chinese *wu*-physicians' "clasping under their arms the body of the wild dog
a-yü." Some of the contents of the *Classic of mountains and seas* originally
m to be, as has been suggested by Chu Hsi (1130-1200), copied from captions
paintings or, in my view, possibly descriptions of works of sculpture.[62]

[51]See Walter Addison Jayne, M.D., *The healing gods of ancient civilizations* (New
en: Yale University Press, 1925), 201-369, particularly 222-23, 229, 230-31, 246,
, 281, 283-85; also M. Oldfield Howey, *The encircled serpent: A study of serpent
bolism in all countries and ages* (New York: Arthur Richard Co., 1955), 253-66.
[52]See Chang Hsin-ch'eng, *Wei-shu t'ung-k'ao* 僞書通考 (Rev. ed.; Shanghai: Com-
cial Press, 1957), 691.

While healing may have been one aspect of the general work of
ancient *wu,* fertility and childbirth seem to have been one of their m
concerns in the early days. This can be seen from the relationships betw
Wu Mountain and *kao-mei* mentioned above. Furthermore, the name of
Mount Teng-pao 登葆山 which the *wu*-physicians climbed may provide s
information in this regard. The character *teng* here can easily be underst
as meaning "to ascend," because its early sense might have been "to step u
But it also had a special meaning when used in invocation. The *Kung-y
commentary to the Spring and Autumn Annals* comments under the year
B.C. (Yin-kung, fifth year) on a long distance trip made by Duke Yin of
to attend a fish-shooting ceremony for sacrifice, saying that the trip is
teng-lai 登來 (obtaining) expensive fish. "What does *teng-lai* mean?" contir
the *Commentary,* "It is a term of rhetorical exclamation." Ho Hsiu (129-1
notes here:

> *Teng* stands for *te* 得 (to obtain). To "*te-lai* it" was a dialect express
> of the people of the Ch'i State. The Ch'i people called "pray for obt
> ing" *te-lai.* The reason for the term's becoming *teng-lai* is that it
> spoken aloud and urgently, because it was expressed orally.

I believe that the character *teng* in the name of Mount Teng-pao may c
the sense of *teng-lai,* which seems to have been an exclamation employe
the habitual invocations of the *wu.* The *Chuang-tzu* (Chapter 14, "T
yün") says, "Wu Hsien beckoned (*chao* 招) and called, 'Come (*lai*)! I will
you.' " This seems to have preserved partly the traditional expression
invocation employed by the *wu.* The character *chao* used here with a s
radical indicates that beckoning is a religious action. It is well known, as
been mentioned earlier, that *wu* had great influence in the State of Ch'i.

As for the name Mount Teng-pao, the *Huai-nan-tzu* (Chapter 4, "
hsing hsün," Liu Wen-tien's ed., 4/13a) refers to it as the Mount of Teng-
(*Teng-pao chih shan* 登保之山). The character *chih* (of) here definitely i
cates that *teng* and *pao* carry meanings, and the character *pao* without a g
radical on top seems to be the original word used. This *pao,* according to
Shuo-wen and other sources, means childbirth (*yang* 養), to nourish or
for children, and hence protection. The right side of the character indeed
pictograph of a newborn infant. In poem No. 172, "Nan-shan yu t'ai," of
Book of poetry there is the line, "Protect and care for (*pao-ai* 保艾) your
spring." Ma Jui-ch'en has pointed out that the term *pao-ai* also appears in
"K'ang kao" of the *Book of history* where *ai* is written 乂 without the g
radical on top. In another chapter ("Chun Shih") of the same book the D
of Chou is quoted as saying that in the time of T'ai-wu (r. *c.* 1637-*c.* 156
C.) of the Shang dynasty "Wu Hsien cared for (*ai* 乂) the royal house."

艾 plant (artemisia) has been used since antiquity for moxibustion; the ss symbol in the character must be a sign used in divination, as it appears the *Book of changes*. According to one of the prefaces to the *Book of tory*, Wu Hsien wrote four treatises entitled *Hsien ai* 咸乂. The character 葆 means young mulberry leaves. The mulberry tree in ancient Chinese thology and literature often had the symbolic meaning of sex and childbirth was undoubtedly related to the *wu* tradition. I have mentioned earlier "divine protector" (*shen pao*) in the *Book of poetry* (poem No. 209). The ine songs" of the *Ch'u tz'u* actually calls a *wu* "ling-pao." The *Shih chi* eng-shan shu") also mentions the worship of a Wu Pao. The "Ta-huang ching" of the *Classic of mountains and seas* gives Mount Teng-pao as ng-pei 登備. The character *pei* not only has the same meaning as *hsien* 咸, name of the early *wu*, but also means, according to the *Li chi* ("Chi ng") and the *Shuo-wen*, *fu* 福, and *hu* 祜, which may have been related sense to child-birth in earlier times.

Besides Mount Teng-pao, other place names related to *wu* and names of ient *wu* reveal how their work was connected with medicine and fertility childbirth. The "Ta-huang hsi ching" of the *Classic of mountains and seas* lists ten *wu*:

> In the great wilderness there are mountains named Luxuriant Marshes (*Feng-chü*) and Jade Gate (*Yü-men*), where the sun and moon enter. There is a Ling Mountain (*Ling-shan*), from which the ten *wu*, Wu Hsien 咸, Wu Chi, Wu Pan, Wu P'eng, Wu Ku, Wu Chen, Wu Li 禮, Wu Ti, Wu Hsieh, and Wu Lo, all ascend and descend, and in which a hundred medicines exist.

Ling Mountain here is probably the same as the Wu Mountain, as I have eady pointed out that *ling* is similar to *wu* in meaning.

As for the ancient *wu*, the *Chou li* ("Ch'un-kuan: shih-jen") also lists nine:

> The names of the nine wu: (1) Wu Keng, (2) Wu Hsien 咸, (3) Wu Shih, (4) Wu Mu, (5) Wu I, (6) Wu Pi, (7) Wu Tz'u, (8) Wu Shen, (9) Wu Huan.

In the three lists of *wu* quoted above, with the exception of the *wu* en, P'eng, and Ti who are listed twice, there are altogether twenty-two ferent names. While allowing that there is no sure way to find out how se names were actually adopted, I still feel that almost all of them are evant to the work of the *wu*. First of all, Wu P'eng and Wu Hsiang may be cussed together. The character *p'eng* 彭 denotes "drum sound" as defined the *Shuo-wen*. This name may have referred to the fact, attested by many ords, that drums were used by the *wu* in their magical performances. The

same is true for *hsiang* 相, which consists of a drum and drumstick, and me
a kind of musical performance accompanied with drum songs, such as th
found in the "Ch'eng hsiang" chapter of the *Hsün-tzu*.[63] On the other ha
the *Chou li* has *feng hsiang shih* 馮相氏 ("Ch'un kuan") and *fang hsiang s*
方相氏 ("Hsia kuan"); both of these professions performed some *wu-*
function.

I have mentioned earlier the dance of the *wu* with a square of silk
other material and with jade. The name of Wu Huan 環 seems to refer to
jade ring, and that of Wu Fan, from our knowledge of the character *fan* 凡
oracle and bronze inscriptions, may have symbolized the square object u
in such a dance called *hsing* 興, which shows four hands holding a *fan* an
mouth added later, and which carries the meaning of "arouse" and "allusive."

The name of Wu Yang 陽 definitely refers to the sun. This name appe
in the "Chao hun" of the *Songs of the south* (*Ch'u-tz'u*). Some mod
scholars believe Wu I is the same as Wu Yang. But I think *i* 易 may h
meant the moon or the lunar eclipse and be related to the *I ching* traditio
believe early *wu* practice was heavily based on the moon cult. The names
Wu Pan and Wu Shen may belong to a similar category. The character *shen*
is a name for the stars in Orion. As for Wu Pan 肦, I think the chara
should be written 朌 with a radical at the left meaning either the moon
flesh, since the latter character appears elsewhere in the same book:

> There is the State of the Chih People (*Chih-min chih kuo*). King Sh
> begot Wu-yin 無淫 [I think this literally means "Lustful Dancer"; Ch
> Meng-chia seems to have good reasons for suggesting that the word
> for lewd is derived from the *kao-mei* and *wu* traditions] who descen
> to the Chih place and consequently he (or she) and his (her) offspr
> are called Wu Chih People. The Wu Chih People have Pan 肦 as th
> family name. They eat grain. They do not spin or weave, but are cloth
> they do not sow and harvest, but are fed. There are dancing and sing
> birds. Female phoenixes sing spontaneously and male phoenixes da
> spontaneously. A hundred kinds of animals gather and a hundred ki
> of grain grow in that place. ("Ta-huang nan ching")
>
> The State of Chih is to the east of [the State of the Three Mia
> The people of this state are yellow and are able to shoot snakes w
> bows. ("Hai-wai nan ching")

[63]Tu Kuo-hsiang, "Lun Hsün-tzu ti 'Ch'eng hsiang p'ien'," *Tu Kuo-hsiang wen*
杜國庠文集 (Peking: Jen-min ch'u-pan-she, 1962), 158-83.
[64]See my paper, "Ancient Chinese views on literature, the Tao, and their relati
ship," delivered at the Conference on Traditional Chinese Literary Criticism, St. Cr
the Virgin Islands, Dec. 6-10, 1970.

If *pan* has a root meaning moon, the name of Wu Pan might be similar
that of the *wu* Ling Fen 靈氛 mentioned in the "Li-sao," as *fen* means the
: which may obscure the sun or the moon. Some sources show that *pan* 朌
haic *pwan* or *piwən*) may be written *pan* 頒 or *fu* 賦 (archaic *piwo*), both
which may mean "bestow," just as *i* 易 (*tz'u* 賜) developed the same
ning. The character *fu* with *wu* (footstep, hence a name of dance and
ic) as its root denotes a kind of chanting, a form of poetic composition,
"narrative," and later a literary genre. The famous saying in the "Mao
mentary" to the *Book of poetry* (No. 50), the *Han-shih wai-chuan*, and
Han shu ("I-wen chih") that "those who climb to a high place (*teng kao*)
can *fu* may become a *ta-fu* (official or physician)" may have developed
1 the *wu*-physician tradition.

In this connection, the name of Wu Pi may be brought into consider-
n. The character *pi* 比 which is structured with one person standing behind
:her, is defined by the *Shuo-wen* as *mi* 密 (intimate, secret) which reminds
of the *kao-mi* altar discussed earlier. Quite a few words composed of this
acter or a part of it carry meanings related to sex or childbirth, for
ince, *pi* 妣 (a deceased mother), *p'i* 媲 (to pair, a concubine), *pi* 祂
rship of the god governing life), *p'in* 牝 (the female of animals or birds),
化 (to transform, to hatch; its root at right, *pi*, is usually considered a
: or a dagger, but Wu Ta-ch'eng (1835-1902) in his *Ku chou pu* suggests
this root is the ancient form of both *hua* and *pi* for the deceased mother),
ni 尼. This last character is defined by the *Shuo-wen* as "to approach
. behind" and by the *Kuang-Ya* ("Shih ku") as *an* 安 which may refer to
as has been pointed out earlier. In the light of all this, it may not be too
.tched to suggest that the name of Wu Pi may have connotations of sex and
lbirth. Since the term *pi* also has the meaning of "metaphorical," the
et of principles of poetic composition, i.e. narrative, metaphor, and
ion, mentioned in the "Great preface" to the *Book of poetry* may have
een derived from the practices of the *wu*.

The other triplet of poetic genres, *feng* (the winds), *ya* (the elegantiae),
sung (the lauds) which together with that mentioned above makes up the
ous "six principles" (*liu i*) in the "Great preface," perhaps also deserves
:cussion here, because it may have arisen from a similar tradition. As is
known, the so-called *feng* section in the *Book of poetry* contains local
songs, many of which are concerned with love, courtship, and marriage.
"Great preface" interprets *feng* in terms of *feng-hua* (transform or influ-
by wind, later meaning: public morals, particularly concerning sex) and
·*tz'u* (satirize). Actually, *feng* as used in the *Book of history* ("Pi shih")
the *Tso commentary* (Hsi-kung, 4th year, 656 B.C.), means "the attraction
.ch other between male and female animals" or "[animals] being in heat."

I think the character may have acquired this meaning because the anci
Chinese believed life was brought by the wind. *The Yellow Emperor's cla
of internal medicine* says, "The East gives birth to wind; wind gives birth
wood; wood gives birth to the sour flavor; the sour flavor gives birth to
liver; the liver gives birth to the muscles; the muscles give birth to the heart.
The *Hsiang commentary* of the *Book of changes* states, "When there is w
under heaven, it is suitable to mate." (Hexagram 44). The apocryphal wo
t'ung kua yen (*c.* 1st century B.C.) quoted in the *T'ai-p'ing yü-lan* (*chüar*
also says that "when the eight kinds of wind blow in time, then the *yin
yang* will accomplish their changes, and the myriad things will be able
procreate and grow." The original meaning of the character *ya* is the cr
The dark bird mentioned in the childbirth myth is usually interpreted as
swallow; but I wonder whether it might not also have referred to the crow,
any rate, according to the *Shuo-wen,* the ancient word for *ya* (the elegant
is 疋 which is a pictograph of a foot, and this latter character is also read
with the meaning "to mate." As for *sung* it is apparently the early word
jung 容 (appearance, manner, bearing). The right side of *sung* 頌 is a pict
of a human figure, and the left is the character *kung* which means a ma
duke, or the public. Whether the latter serves as a phonetic or indicates se
uncertain. Since all the lauds in the *Book of poetry* are songs proba
accompanied by dance mostly in praise of ancestors but a few in prais
harvest or production, I think a close relationship between the *sung* and
wu tradition is quite possible.

The concern with sex and fertility may be further illustrated by
other *wu* names. Wu Ku 姑 may refer to a female *wu*. The musical note *ku
姑洗*, which is keyed to a purification ceremony in the third month
nourishing life (*yang-sheng* 養生) or cleansing for growth (*hsi-sheng* 洗
may have been related to *shang-ssu* 上巳 and the Wu Ku tradition. The n
of Wu Chi 即 may have implied approaching for marriage; this can be suppo
by my earlier discussion on the poem "Sun in the east." As for Wu Tz'u,
name may have referred to a sacrifice made in the spring at which prayers w
offered for fecundity and production. Actually, several sources suggest
this character *tz'u* 祠 is interchangeable with *ssu* 祀, i.e. a sacrifice for ferti
The name Wu Li 履 (treading-on) listed in the "Hai-nei hsi ching" must h
been related to the myth of pregnancy by stepping in a footprint, or suc
ritual.

[65] *Huang-ti nei-ching su-wen* 黃帝內經素問 (Shanghai: Shang-hai k'o-hsüeh ch
ch'u-pan-she, 1959), 42; *Cf.* Ilza Veith (tr.), *The Yellow Emperor's classic of int
medicine* (Berkeley: University of California Press, 1966), 118. For the relatio
between *wu* and the wind one may consult *Mo-tzu*'s reference to *wu-feng,* which w
discussed later.

Closely related to the last name and providing an interesting problem is
ther name with the same pronunciation, Wu Li 禮 (ritual), listed in the
-huang hsi ching." Hao I-hsing (1757-1825) has already noticed that this
e was quoted in the *Shui-ching chu* as Wu K'ung 孔. In his opinion, as the
ent form of *li* 禮 is 礼 which closely resembles the form of *k'ung,* this
i.e. *k'ung,* must be an error. And since *li* (ritual) has often been defined
(tread on), he suggests that the two names, Wu Li (ritual) and Wu Li
ding-on) really refer to the same person. This may or may not be the
. However, I would like to point out that both *li* and *k'ung* may be valid
both are relevant to *wu* practices intended to ensure fertility. According
he *Shuo-wen* the root at the right in both characters, *ya* 乙, means the
: bird, or swallow, representing both its form and the sound of its cry.
fact that the character *li* for ritual was, in its ancient form, written with
root seems to indicate that such ritual originally involved praying for
lbirth. The *Shuo-wen* defines *li* 禮 as "worship gods and seek *fu* 福." The
ya identifies *fu* with *hsi* 禧 which has the connotation of marriage and
lbirth. The *Shuo-wen* defines *k'ung* as "a term used for praise" or "praise-
hy, magnificent" (*chia mei chih* 嘉美之), and goes on to explain:

It consists of *ya* and *tzu* (child). *Ya* is a migrant bird which is used for
seeking childbirth. As *ya* arrives, a child is born; so [*ya* and *tzu* are
combined to make *k'ung*] "to praise it." That is why ancient people
named Chia 嘉 often have Tzu-k'ung 子孔 as their courtesy names.

definition, which reminds us of the stork story in the West, seems
vable in view of the meanings of several other characters which include
element *ya* as a root, *such* as *ju* 乳 (parturition of man and bird; milk),
乩 (ancient form of 始; the pregnant womb, or first pregnancy), and
亂 (lewd conduct).[66] The characters *k'ung* and *chia* are often used
ther in the *Book of poetry* and the latter character, which in my opinion
similar to or related to *hsi* 喜 originally, does seem to imply a bride's
ntial of fertility.
Concerning the relationship between the names Chia and Tzu-k'ung,
e are at least three relevant cases in the *Tso commentary to the Spring
Autumn Annals.* Actually, one of Confucius' ancestors was named K'ung-
Chia 孔父嘉. This family, a remnant of the nobility from the Shang
asty, seems to have followed the *kao-mei* tradition for some time. The
graphy of Confucius" (*K'ung-tzu shih-chia*) of the *Shih chi* says:

Ho and a girl of the Yen family had relations in the field and gave birth

[6]For the definition of *ju,* see *Shuo-wen;* for *shih,* see *Yü-p'ien;* for *luan,* see the
or preface" to poem No. 89, *Book of poetry* and *Li chi,* "T'an-kung," *shang.*

to Confucius (K'ung-tzu). They [or she?] prayed in the Ni-mound
ch'iu 尼丘) and thus conceived Confucius. Confucius was born in
twenty-second year of Duke Hsiang of Lu [551 B.C.]. There was a
tuberance on the top of his head. Therefore, he was named Ch'iu (mou
His courtesy name was Ni the Second (Chung-ni), and family name, K'

A later source, the *K'ung-tzu chia-yü*, gives a slightly different version
saying that the girl after her marriage to Ho "fearing that she might no
able to have a son on time because of her husband's old age, prayed in
mountain of Ni-ch'iu for fertility, and therefore gave birth to Confucius."
character *ni* may originally have had a sexual connotation, as I have alre
pointed out in discussing Wu Pi's name. It is very possible that the Ni Mo
had a *kao-mei* altar. All these things help explain the suitability of both *li*
k'ung as names for *wu* in view of the childbirth legend.

The names of several other *wu* also reveal that their work invol
supernatural power. With regard to Wu Chen, I may quote the *Shuo-w*
definition of *chen* 眞 as "the immortal undergoes a metamorphosis
ascends to Heaven." This reminds us of the *Shuo-wen* definition of *wu*
the *Chin shu* statement, quoted earlier, to the effect that *wu* could re
themselves "invisible." They could communicate with gods and spirits.
name of Wu Mu, the second character of which means eye, perhaps indic
the part played by eyes in the rituals performed by *wu*. According to
Chou li ("Ch'un-kuan: nan-wu") male *wu* had the duty of climbing to a
place to survey the mountains and streams (*wang ssu* 望祀 and *wang yen* 望
in all directions for portents. The *Mo-tzu* (Chapter 68, "Ying ti tz'u")
specifies that, anticipating the enemy's attack, the defenders should le
"*wise wu*" (*chih wu*) look at the mists (*wang ch'i* 氣) for portents and
as to the outcome of the coming engagement. I feel that the character
itself might also mean to look at the full moon and dance in moonligh
for Wu Hsieh 謝 , the name could have the meaning of "thanksgiving," b
is more likely to mean "to fade" or "to die" as it does in "The summo
the soul" (*Chao hun*) and "The great summons" (*Ta chao*) of the *Songs o
south*. The *Chou li* says that in a funeral the leading *wu* should take char
the ritual of summoning down gods and spirits. The name Hsieh, of co
may also imply that the *wu* could cause death by invoking curses.

In addition, I believe that the names of three or four ancient *wu*
be indicative of their work as physicians. Thus far, the meaning of the n
Wu Hsien 巫咸, the most prominent of all the ancient *wu*, has never
explained. I believe that the character *hsien* 咸 , the archaic pronunciati
which is reconstructed by Karlgren as *g'ɛm*, may be the earlier word for
箴(箴) (a bamboo or wooden needle) or *chen* 鍼 (a metal needle), both

n in archaic Chinese. Cases in which the names Hsien and Chen appear to
variants can be found in ancient records. Both in the *Spring and autumn*
als and the *Tso commentary* under the year 549 B.C. (Hsiang-kung, 24th
r) there is a man named Chen I-chiu 鍼宜咎, but this person is recorded in
Kung-yang edition of the *Annals* under the same year as Hsien I-chiu 咸宜
Moreover, in the *Tso commentary* under 538 B.C. (Chao-kung, 4th year)
name of the same person is written Hsien I-chiu, yet other editions give
en as Chen 箴 or Chen 蔵. The same book has Chen Yin-ku 鍼尹固 under
B.C. (Ting-kung, 4th year), but under 479 B.C. (Ai-kung, 16th year) the
e name is written 箴.

The character *hsien*, as is shown on the oracle bone and bronze inscrip-
ns, consists of pictures of a halberd and a mouth. In early classics it had
meaning of "cut or pierce." The mouth root may have indicated "a cry"
at least some activity of the mouth. Later on, redundant radicals were
ed to explain its meaning of cry, hence *han* 諴 or its variant 喊. This last
racter seems also to be related to the functions of *wu*. Yang Hsiung (53
.-A.D. 18) says in his *Fa-yen*, "The blind musician K'uang could silence [his
ience], but could not unify the divergent [taste of] ears; Ti-ya could *han*
but could not unify the divergent [voice or taste of?] mouths [tongues?]
u 口)." Ti-ya is also known as I-ya, a favorite official under Duke Huan
Ch'i (r. 685-643 B.C.), and is famous for his cookery. It is also known that
a's formal name was Yung Wu. Whether "Wu" was merely his personal name
as some commentators suggest, indicated that he was a *wu* is still in
estion.[67] But even if it was a personal name, Yung Wu or his family may
e been part of a *wu* tradition. The character *han* may mean "to blend
ors, to season" or "to cry." Commentators usually prefer the former
se because of I-ya's culinary skill. Yet as a parallel to "silence" in the
tence quoted the fact that *han* also means "cry" may not be lightly
nissed.

In view of these considerations, if *hsien* is understood to have an archaic
aning of "lance or lancet" (or something like "needle" or "needling") as
l as a kind of "cry" related to such objects, it definitely suits the ancient
tradition. Loud summons and singing are distinctly among the activities
aged in by *wu*.

There seems also to be no question that one aspect of the ancient *wu*-
sician's work was acupuncture. In the *Tso commentary* under 662 B.C.
uang-kung, 32nd year) there is a story that Duke Chuang ordered a certain

[67] See Wang Jung-pao (1878-1933), *Fa-yen i-su* 法言義疏 (Taipei: I-wen yin-shu-kuan,
), *chüan* 8, "Wen shen," 244-46; Liu Wen-ch'i, *Ch'un-ch'iu Tso-shih chuan chiu-chu
heng* 春秋左氏傳舊注疏證 (Hong Kong: T'ai-p'ing shu-chü, 1966), Hsi-kung, 17th
r (643 B.C.), 337.

man to wait in the household of the Chen Wu family (*Chen wu shih* 鍼巫.
and then had Chen Chi 鍼季 kill him with poisonous wine made out of b
feathers. This indicates that the *wu* family with Needle (Chen) as its na
was familiar with poisonous medicine. Furthermore, the oldest Chinese w
on acupuncture extant is entitled *Ling shu* 靈樞 , a part of the *Yell*
Emperor's classic of internal medicine, which may mean "The wu pivot."]
"Bibliography" chapter of the *Sui-shu* also lists a book *Chiu ling* [The Nine
treatises, or the Nine *wu*'s classic] which is probably of the same nature. M
scholars believe that this work is identical with the book by Huang-fu
(215-282) called the *Needle [acupuncture] classic (Chen ching)* which
mentioned in his preface to the *Chia-i ching*.

Contemporary historians of Chinese medicine speculate that acupu
ture, particularly that kind used to produce anesthesia, probably was
covered by accident as a result of the experience of being wounded b
pointed object. While this theory is not verifiable, it seems quite plausil
Such a pointed object might have been either wooden, or stone, or me
Records show that all these materials have been used for acupuncture need
The *Shuo-wen* says, "*Pien* 砭 means needling with stone for the purpose
curing an ailment." Both the *Ling shu* (Chapter 60, "Yü-pan p'ien") and
Su wen (Chapter 12, "I fa fang i lun p'ien") of the *Yellow Emperor's cla*
of internal medicine mention the use of *pien-shih* (stone probe or needle)
medical treatment. The *Ling shu* says, "When bloody pus has formed
should be pierced with the sharp point of a stone needle." The *Su wen* speci
that the stone needle was particularly suitable for curing sores and ulc
which were often caused by eating too much fish and salt, as the people
China's east coast often did because fish and salt were abundant there. The
fore, it concludes, such stone needles were also produced on the east co
According to the *Classic of mountains and seas* ("Tung-shan ching"), "on
of the Mountain of the Kao clan (*Kao shih chih shan*) there is plenty of ja
and at its foot there is plenty of needle-stone (*chen-shih* 箴石)." Kuo
notes here, "It may be used for stone needles (*ti-chen* 砥針) for curing ulc
and swellings." Hao I-hsing suggests that *ti* is a mistake for *pien*. I do
think so. Kao Yu (3rd cent.) in annotating the needle-stone mentioned in
Huai-nan-tzu ("Shuo shan hsün") also says, "Stone needles are used to pie
and poke (*ti-tan* 砥彈) ulcers and boils in order to release bloody pus."]
character *ti* definitely has the meaning of "needling with a stone."]
character for the name of Wu Ti 抵, according to the *Fang-yen* (Chapter
by Yang Hsiung, has the meaning of "a thorn" or "to pierce." It also n
have been a variant of 砥 and referred to such needling. Or, it may be sim
to *ti* 柢 (the root of a plant). At any rate, the main element of all th
characters, *ti* 氏, means "a straight root of a plant." Accordingly, I think

name is definitely related to the *wu*-physician profession. The characters
誣 (to accuse falsely) and *ti* 詆 (to slander), which sometimes are identical
eaning and also make a compound, probably developed from this tradition,
ne aspect of the work of *wu* was to invoke curses.

Furthermore, Wu Keng's 更 name may be interpreted along the same
s, although *keng* usually means "to change." I suspect that this word may
he same as *keng* 梗. The early form of 更 seems to show a hand holding
bones, thus we have such words as *keng* 鯁 or 骾 (fish-bones) and *keng*
to throttle). As for the character *keng* 梗 with "wood" as an element, the
ɔ-wen defines it as a tree with thorns, and the *Fang-yen* says, "as for
e plants which can pierce people, they sometimes are called *keng* 梗 by
people living east of the Pass." The *Kuang-Ya* (*chüan* 2B, "Shih-ku")
ɔly defines this character as *chen* 箴 (bamboo or wooden needle). In the
u li ("T'ien-kuan") the female invoker (*nü-chu*) is described as "having
function of summoning down gods and spirits (*chao* 招), of performing
梗, and of praying for removal of pestilence in order to eliminate diseases
alamities." I would like to suggest that the *keng* 梗 here involves acupunc-
or a ritual in connection with it.

Finally, a word may be said about the two *wu* Lo and Shih. The *Shuo-*
defines *lo* 羅 as "to catch birds with a silk net." This name may be
erstandable in view of the *wu*-physician's association with the yellow
wn) birds in the *Shan hai ching* legend. The similarity of this name to that
he Lo-lo tribe in South China, which has had a culture in which *wu* play
nportant part, may also be noticed. As for *shih* 式, it has a root similar to
of *hsien* 咸, plus a *kung* 工 (craft) which is an attribute of the work of *wu.*

Since so much has been said about the name of *wu,* a word concerning
e major historical and legendary personalities who may have had some
ection with the *wu*-physician may be in order. Earlier I mentioned some
ces which suggest that the ancestor of the ruling family of the Chou
asty, Lady Chiang Yüan's husband, was King K'u of the Kao Hsin clan.
he other hand, with regard to the *chiao-mei* or *kao-mei*, Lady Chien Ti,
being mated to the king of the Kao Hsin clan and swallowing a dark
s egg, gave birth to Hsieh (The Cutter) who was the ancestor of King
g, founder of the Shang dynasty. Therefore, the ancestors of both the
ag and the Chou dynasties were involved in the *kao-mei* tradition and a
of childbirth myth. According to the *Shih-pen*[68] and the *Shih chi,*[69]

8 Quoted in *I-wen lei-chü* 藝文類聚, *chüan* 15, and *T'ai-p'ing yü-lan, chüan* 135; for a
r of *wu* in the Shang dynasty see Ch'en Meng-chia, "Shang-tai ti shen-hua yü wu-shu"
的神話與巫術, *Yen-ching hsüeh-pao*, 20 (1936), 532-76.
9 In the "Yin pen-chi" and "Chou pen-chi" both of which must be based on the "Ti-
ien" of the *Ta-Tai li* 大戴禮.

Chiang Yüan was King K'u's queen and Chien Ti, his concubine. If this is tr
the royal houses of the two dynasties must have originated from the sa
ancestor or clan. Chien Ti's name was sometimes written Chien I 簡易. 1
two characters *ti* 狄 and *i* were homophones in ancient times. One wonder
this name implies any relation to the *wu* tradition in view of the names W
and I-ya, and the moon cult in connection with the *I ching* tradition.

Besides this, it is well known that the rulers of the Shang dynasty w
fond of worshiping gods and spirits and were involved with the *wu* traditi
Even the various names of the founder of the dynasty and his main de
seem quite revealing. His name in the oracle bone inscriptions is often writ
T'ang 唐. According to the small seal form the character may indicate t
hands holding a stem or a shield on the top of a mouth or container. 1
stem also may have been combined with the mouth to depict a musical pi
The *Shuo-wen* defines *t'ang* as a "big flute" and gives its ancient form as
with a mouth element and a main root with the sense of the sun, wh
reminds me of the names King Kao Yang (Chuan Hsü) and Wu Yang.

In the Classics T'ang's name is often written 湯 with a water elemen
the left. The character is sometimes interchangeable with 昜, 崵, or 陽, a
the T'ang Cave (*t'ang ku* 湯谷, 暘谷) was supposed to be the place where
sun rises. The place is also called Hsien T'ang 咸唐 or Hsien Ch'ih 咸池
The *Classic of mountains and seas* mentions a T'ang Stream (*t'ang-shui* 湯
with a note saying that its water can cure diseases most effectively.[71]
character *t'ang* 湯 has the meaning "to eliminate the cruel" or "to rem
pestilence and calamities by prayer and sacrifice."[72] It also means tincture
"medicine in draught," as is often mentioned in the *Huang-ti nei-ching:*
wen (e.g. Chapters 13 and 14). This last meaning may have something to
with King T'ang's name, since several sources relate that the king and his cl
minister, I Yin, were quite familiar with medicine. The *Mo-tzu* ("Kuei
records King T'ang's comparison of I Yin's significance to his governmen
that of an excellent physician and efficacious medicine to a patient. I Yin
also skillful in cooking, as some of the other *wu* were. (I wonder if the w
for natural salt and salty, i.e. *hsien* 鹹, may not have been related to
Hsien's tradition.) According to the *Lü-shih ch'un-ch'iu* ("Hsien chi p'ie
he also gave political advice to the king in terms of medicine. Huang-fu M
his preface to the *Chia-i ching* says, "Tincture was created by I Yin." I

[70] See Yeh Yü-sen, *Yin hsü shu-ch'i ch'ien-pien chi-shih* 殷虛書契前編集釋 (Shang
Ta-tung shu-chü, 1933), 1/56b-57a.

[71] All quoted in *T'ai-p'ing yü-lan, chüan* 45.

[72] "Hsi-fa" quoted in P'ei Yin's *Shih chi chi-chieh* 史記集解; *Feng-su t'ung-i* 風俗注
"Wang pa p'ien"; and *Chou li*, "T'ien-kuan: nü-chu," Cheng Hsüan's commentary
Sun I-jang's *Chou li cheng-i* 周禮正義.

s also traditionally credited with the authorship of the book *T'ang-i lun* n tincture).

If this is regarded as coincidental, I may mention the fact that T'ang's ter name was Li 履 (Treading). This fact appears in the *Analects of Con- ·ius* (20:1) and the *Mo-tzu* ("Chien-ai," *hsia*); the *Shuo-yüan* ("Chun tao en") and Ssu-ma Chen's (8th cent.) *Shih chi so-yin* ("Yin pen-chi") quote imilar passage attributing it to the *Book of history*. Thus the king has a ne in common with one of the twenty-two ancient *wu*. Actually, the 1dbirth myth of treading in sandals became so popular that in later times, ·ording to the *Childbirth prescriptions (T'ai ts'an fang)* quoted in Li Shih- ·n's *Pen-ts'ao kang-mu* (written about 1552-1597), a tincture made by xing the ashes of an old grass sandal in wine may have the effect of ,tening childbirth.

Furthermore, King T'ang's other name was T'ien I 天乙. This is recorded the *Shih chi* ("Yin pen-chi"), the present version of the *Chu-shu chi-nien*, 1 other sources. The *Ti-wang shih-chi* quoted in the *Ch'u hsüeh chi (chüan* says:

> The Yin [i.e. the Shang dynasty] originated from King K'u. Its family name was Tzu (child). Chu Kuei's wife, Fu-tu, caught sight of the moon pierced by white vapor, conceived, and gave birth to T'ang on the day of *i*; so he was named Li, and had the courtesy name T'ien I 天一. [The *Shang-shu cheng-i*, "Yao tien," quotes this more accurately as 天乙. It also reads Ta I.] He later became King Ch'eng T'ang.

e suggestion here that T'ang's courtesy name was derived from the name his birthdate is of course possible in view of the fact that many later kings the dynasty followed that practice. But the fact that his predecessors of : previous dynasty were called Chia, I, Ping, Ting, Jen, and Kuei in such a 1t order according to the ten heavenly stems, must prove that those names re not based on the persons' birthdates. Thus there is room to doubt such interpretation of T'ang's so-called courtesy name. It is known that the 1racters *i* 乙 and *ya* 乙 (the swallow) were the same in ancient times. Since 1ng's ancestor Hsieh was supposed to have been born after his mother 1llowed a swallow's egg according to the *kao-mei* tradition, I feel that 1ng's name may have taken on the meaning of the bird. The family name 1 (child) seems relevant also.

Further evidence of T'ang's relation to the *wu* tradition is his famous .k of praying for rain. The *Mo-tzu* ("Chien-ai," *hsia*), the *Lü-shih ch'un- 'iu* ("Shun-min p'ien"), the *Ti-wang shih-chi*, and other sources all relate in 'ferent ways that after a long (some say five years, others say seven years) ought, King T'ang made a sacrifice and invocation at the *she* of Sang-lin

(Mulberry Forest) and as a result obtained a heavy rain. I have already point
out that to invoke and pray for rain is one of the particular functions of w

While King T'ang definitely followed some of the *wu* traditions,
probably was also aware that the excessive influence of *wu* among his peo₤
could pose a threat to his political authority once he conquered the kingdo₤
The *Mo-tzu* records:

> The Master Mo-tzu said: Making music is wrong! How do we know th
> this is so? The answer is found among the records of the former kin₤
> T'ang's "Governmental code of punishment" says, "If one indulges
> constant dancing (*heng-wu*) in the palace, this is called the 'wir
> (custom) of the *wu* (*wu-feng*). As a punishment, gentlemen shall
> fined two measures of silk; for common men the fine shall be increas₤
> by two hundred silk threads for jade pendants."[73]

The Ancient Text version of the *Book of history* also records that in the fi₤
year of King T'ang's reign (*c.* 1751 B.C.), on the date *i-ch'ou* of the twel₤
month, I Yin advised the king that "those who dare indulge in consta
dancing in the palace and drunken singing in the house are following t
so-called wind (custom) of the *wu*," and should be punished by the blackeni₤
of their faces.[74] Such a code of punishment and the giving of such advice,
factual, may be regarded as evidence of the great popularity of the *wu* t₤
dition at that time. That the fears of T'ang and I Yin were not witho₤
foundation seems plausible in light of the later historical fact of the manip₤
lation of, and later attempts to suppress, the belief in auspicious omens
indications of the Mandate of Heaven by Wang Mang (45 B.C.-A.D. 23).

There is some evidence that King T'ang may have relied on *wu* in ₤
career. One of the prefaces to the *Book of history* attributed to Confucius ₤
Liu Hsiang and Liu Hsin is quoted in the *Shih chi* ("Yin pen-chi"). It sa
that I Yin's son "I Chih praised Wu Hsien for having governed the royal hou
with achievement and so composed 'The protection of Hsien' (*Hsien ai*)." T

---

[73] Sun I-jang (ed.), *Mo-tzu chien-ku* (1907), "Fei-yüeh," *shang*, 8/27a-b. Burt
Watson translates the last sentence as "but for common men the fine shall be two hund₤
pieces of yellow silk," with a note saying, "The meaning of the last sentence is v₤
doubtful." See his *Mo Tzu: basic writings* (New York: Columbia University Press, 196₤
115. I have interpreted the first character of *huang ching* in its early meaning of a ja₤
pendant. See note 76 below. For *heng-wu* we may notice Wu Heng and the moon dan₤
Also *Lun-yü*, 13.22: "人而無恆，不可以作巫醫。"

[74] Chapter 13, "I-hsün." The passage is also followed by denunciations of "le₤
customs" (*yin-feng* 淫風) and "disorderly custom" (*luan-feng* 亂風). Considering ₤
early meanings of *yin* and *luan* and their possible associations with the practices of ₤
as mentioned earlier, this version of the text may not be dismissed lightly, even thou
most scholars believe that the Ancient Text version of the *History* is a forged work.

ok of history ("Chün Shih") also says, "Wu Hsien helped the royal house."
ter scholars have often interpreted these passages as indicating that Wu
ien belonged to the time of King T'ang's great great-grandson, T'ai Wu; but
s seems very doubtful. In the "Enjoinment of wine" (*Chiu kao*) of the
ok of history, the name Hsien is listed right after Ch'eng T'ang. The oracle
ne inscriptions have a piece saying, "Make divination to Hsien and Ta
ia."[75] Here Hsien's name precedes Ta Chia, who was King T'ang's grandson
d, according to the *Shih chi*, succeeded to the throne seven years after T'ang's
ath. Wu Hsien must have been active in King T'ang's time. Later on during
u I's reign (r. c. 1533-1514 B.C.) a Wu Hsien (The Wise) 巫賢 again became
ief minister. The "K'ung commentary" to the *Book of history* suggests
at this Hsien was Wu Hsien's 巫咸 son. This may mean that he was his off-
ring or only that he belonged to the same profession or clan.

Earlier I said that both the Shang and the Chou had King K'u of the
o Hsin clan as their ancestor and that I Yin's birth myth was related to the
Shen clan which might have practiced the *wu* tramping dance. The *Lü-shih
'un-ch'iu* ("Pen-wei p'ien") says:

> A woman from the Yu Shen clan found an infant in a hollow mulberry
> tree when she was gathering mulberry leaves. She presented it to her
> sovereign who let a cook nurse it and investigated the matter. It was
> then told that the infant's mother lived by the River I and was preg-
> nant. In a dream she was told by a god that she should run to the east
> and refrain from looking back when water flows out of the mortar. The
> next day, seeing water flowing out of the mortar, she informed her
> neighbors and ran ten *li* to the east. When she looked back, she saw that
> the whole town was under water, and her body was transformed into a
> hollow mulberry tree. So the infant was named I Yin. And that was how
> I Yin was born in a hollow mulberry tree.

o Yu in commenting on the Yu Shen clan says, "Shen 侁 is read as *hsin*
." In the *Mencius* it is actually mentioned that "I Yin tilled land in the
lds of Yu Hsin 有莘" (Book V, Part I, Section 7). Shen 侁 is sometimes
ritten 侁, 佯 (*Chi-yün*), or 姺 (*Shuo-wen*). I wonder if the Yu Shen (Hsin)
an was related to the Kao Hsin clan. The *hsin* of Kao Hsin means bitter, and
e *hsin* of Yu Hsin with a grass radical on top means a marsh plant, *asarum,* a
me derived from the bitterness of the root, which is used in medicine. A
agmentary passage from the *Ta-Tai li* ("Shih chi") quoted in the *Lu shih
Hou chi*," 9A) says that King K'u (Chün) of the Kao Hsin clan also was born
ter his mother trod in a giant footprint and he was conceived.

[75]Lo Chen-yü, *Yin-hsü shu-ch'i hou-pien* (1916), *hsia*, no. 18.9; see also Li Hsiao-
g, *Chia-ku wen-tzu chi-shih*, *ts'e* 2, pp. 369-71.

Another legendary hero, King Chuan Hsü of the Kao Yang clan, who I have mentioned earlier, is a very significant figure in connection with the *wu* tradition. According to many records, both he and King K'u were offspring of the Yellow Emperor. He was regarded as the ancestor of King Shun and the nobility of the state of Ch'u. The *Ti-wang shih-chi* says that King K'u, when he was fifteen years old, became Chuan Hsü's assistant. The *Kuo-yü* ("Lu yü," *shang*) creates some confusion by saying that the Shang people worshiped Chuan Hsü's offspring, Shun, as their most remote ancestor, and the Chou people worshiped K'u as their most remote ancestor. I am not going to try to unravel this problem here, but I would like to point out that the *Lü-shih ch'un-ch'iu* ("Ku-yüeh p'ien") relates that Chuan Hsü also lived in a hollow mulberry tree and that imitating the sounds of the various winds, created the "music of the eight winds." His name *chuan* 顓, which shows a human figure holding a plant with sprouts and roots, and *hsü* 頊, a figure holding jade, is definitely reminiscent of the *wu* concern with fertility and the invocation of gods.

The name of the Yellow Emperor (Huang-ti) appears in the *Classic mountains and seas*, the *Book of changes* ("Hsi-tz'u," *hsia*), the *Kuo-yü*, the *Tso commentary*, the *Kuan-tzu*, and other sources, but whether the character *huang* in his name was originally intended only to mean "yellow" is very uncertain. I am inclined to interpret it as referring to a type of jade pendant since that was the original meaning of the character and the *Book of changes* particularly mentions the Emperor's care about clothing, though the color may also have been implied.[76] If this is true, the Jade Emperor (Yü-ti) who is worshiped as the supreme god in popular Taoism may not be as late a development as has been thought.

Chinese mythology relates that the Yellow Emperor's ancestors were Fu Hsi and Nü Kua. I have already discussed the myth of Fu Hsi's birth when his mother trod on a footprint and his possible relationship to the *kao-mei* institution. Since he has been studied by Wen I-to and many others in detail, a few remarks about him and his wife or sister, Nü Kua, may be enough. Both of them are depicted as figures having human heads and snake bodies with their tails usually entwined together. This apparently symbolizes sex and fertility. Fu Hsi's family name was said to be Feng (wind). He was supposed to be the first to use sacrificial animals for cookery; thus he was also named Pao Hsi. He was credited with the invention of not only the eight trigrams but also pathogenetic theories, medicine, and acupuncture. In addition he was said to have established the institution of marriage. Moreover, Nü Kua was regarded as a divine matchmaker.

[76]See Kuo Mo-jo, *Chin-wen ts'ung-k'ao* 金文叢考 (Tokyo: Bunkyū-dō, 1932), "Shih huang," 180-92; also Li Hsiao-ting, *Chia-ku wen-tzu chi-shih, ts'e* 13, pp. 4039-46.

The above study indicates that, centering around the major sacrifices d the *wu* tradition, fertility and economic production were two of the basic ncerns of the ancient Chinese. The symbolic meanings of the footsteps, the ants, the snake, and the wind later contributed to the development of inese philosophical ideas of life as well as of human nature and the natures animals and things. A strong desire for life is evident in early literature and also indicated by the growth of medical science. The symbolic significance the footstep and the movements of the sun and moon may also have been strumental in the development of a philosophy with great emphasis on ovement and constant change. In addition, abstractions derived from the aracteristics of jade gradually evolved into the ideas of order, eternal prinple, and reason. All these practices and concepts, significant in the history Chinese thought and institutions, seem to have been related to the *wu* adition in antiquity.

The early use of the tally in China*

Lao Kan

Knotting string is said to have been the earliest form of record keeping in Chinese culture. This method of keeping records is also found in the Ryukyu Islands as well as among the Indian tribes in South America. In the case of the Indians, the knots indicated the dates of festivals or eclipses. The Indians of British Columbia, instead of using knotted string, are found to have used sticks and hairs to show the numbers of different animals.[1] These facts show that strings or sticks have been widely used for record keeping among the primitive peoples of the world. Their ways of using them may offer valuable comparisons with the ancient custom of the Chinese people.

Both strings and sticks were widely used during the development of Chinese culture. The use of sticks is particularly significant. Many aspects of ancient Chinese culture were related to the use of sticks, and traces of such use are still observable in many Chinese cultural phenomena.

Firstly, the Chinese numerals may be traced to the use of notches in sticks. The relics discovered in Pan-p'o at Sian indicate that the numerals may be the earliest form of Chinese characters.[2] This finding casts doubt on the hypothetic assumption that hieroglyphics or pictorial symbols appeared first in the development of Chinese characters and also helps to explain the origin of Chinese numerals and the manner in which they were first written down. These notches in sticks can be compared to the marks on notched tallies. Such a comparison may help to explain why the ancient Chinese numerals were arranged as they were.

Secondly, the mechanical counting tools of the modern world can be

*I am indebted to Dr. Tzay-yüeh Tain for his assistance in the preparation of this article.
[1] Franz Boas, *General anthropology* (Boston: Heath, 1938), 271.
[2] Chung-kuo K'o-hsüeh-yüan: *Hsi-an Pan-p'o* 西安半坡 (Peking: 1963), 197.

traced back to the calculations by means of sticks and the abacus of th
Chinese people. Stick calculating is a method which uses sticks instead
writing. The sticks are arranged in different denominations of singles, ten
hundreds, thousands, and so forth. To represent a desired number, the stic
are placed into position according to their respective denominations. Eac
position is limited to five sticks. If the number exceeds five in any positio
then different forms of arrangement are used. Addition is performed b
adding sticks and subtraction by taking them away in a manner similar to th
way in which the beads on an abacus are manipulated. In principle, stic
calculating is the same as abacus calculating. The only difference is that th
abacus has beads instead of sticks. If the abacus is acknowledged to be relate
in any way to the modern computer, we should recognize the fact that stic
calculating in China was its earliest forerunner.

Thirdly, bamboo was traditionally cut into oblong slips for use a
writing material. Therefore, early Chinese books were in the form of bundl
of slips connected and bound together by cords. This is quite different fro
the Babylonian bricks or Egyptian papyri, and is due to the Chinese speci
system of using sticks. In the post-Han period, when paper became wide
used in China, books were written, and later printed, in vertical columns i
imitation of the old form of collected slips.

Fourthly, chopsticks also fall into the category of the uses to whic
sticks were put. Chopsticks, like other kinds of Chinese sticks, are usual
made of bamboo, occasionally of wood. They were one of the earlie
attempts to use tools instead of hands. This is a further extension of the oth
usages of sticks which have already been alluded to. The use of sticks in div
nation, as in the case of the *Book of changes*, is another form of stick using.

Aside from these examples of the use of sticks, the most important an
the most widely diffused over the world among non-Chinese speaking people
is as tallies. A tally is a combination of two sticks with matched notches fc
use as a certificate of monetary credit, as an order of purchase, as a passpor
or as an identification of the status of an aristocrat. As described in ancien
records and discovered among the artifacts in modern archaeological find
tallies may be made of wood, bamboo, bronze, or even the most expensiv
jade.

Now, I would like to itemize the different forms of Chinese tallies.

The earliest known tallies are notched sticks of wood or bamboo. Thei
use was recorded by ancient scholars in the classics. In the *Hsi-tz'u* 繫辭, o
Commentary on the appended judgements of the Book of changes, it is sai
that in remote antiquity the ancients used knotted strings in the conduct o
government affairs. It is also said that in later times the sages substitute
records in the form of notches on sticks for the purpose of managing th

rious officials and supervising the people.[3] This explanation of the origin of
Chinese record keeping is just a hypothesis, but it is a hypothesis so full of
possibility that we can find no logical ground to reject it.

According to the classics, the first stage in the evolution of Chinese
writing was the formation of *shu-ch'i* 書契. Here *shu* means to write with a
brush and *ch'i* means to carve with a knife.[4] Many scholars are of the opinion
that in ancient times the characters on wooden or bamboo slips were carved.
This opinion is not substantiated by material evidence. Among recent archaeological finds, there are no carved slips except for those with cut marks on
the side intended to be used as tallies. A close examination of the slips will
show that it would be very difficult to inscribe characters on such thin pieces
of wood or bamboo. That is why it was never in fact done. Thus the early use
of *ch'i* or carving is limited to the tally only.

Now, let us examine the construction of the ancient character *ch'i* for a
moment. Its meaning and its application will become clear through such an
examination. The character *ch'i* 契 is composed of three parts. The bottom
part is the character *ta* 大, which is a variation of *mu* 木, which means wood.
The upper part is composed of *chieh* 丰 and *tao* 刀. The latter, *tao*, means a
knife while the former, *chieh*, is a depiction of notched teeth. Therefore it is
clearly a tally. This shows that in ancient times carving was limited to the
tally as we have asserted above. And this is supported by archaeological
evidence.

This kind of tally may be considered to be the original form. There are
many records from the Chou dynasty through the Han concerning the uses
and forms of the wooden or bamboo tally. Moreover, some genuine specimens of tallies have been found in the Tun-huang and Chü-yen sites, which
fact indicates that tallies were widely used in the ancient Chinese world.

Aside from wood or bamboo, the tally could be made of bronze. Both
seals and tallies were used in ancient China and both could be made of bronze.
For identification purposes, they were used in a similar way. In the ruins of
Anyang, a seal was found. Some scholars contend that though seals were
widely used in the ancient Near East, it is still possible that the ancient
Chinese conceived of them independently. They claim that the seal is of
Chinese origin, but they cannot prove it. The finding of many things of Western origin such as the chariot and the spear in the Anyang ruins indicates the
possibility that the Anyang civilization was not as homogeneous as has been
supposed. Thus whether the seal was of Chinese origin is still difficult to say.

---

[3] *Chou-i chien-i* 周易兼義, 8/4 (Taipei: I-wen, 1955 reprint), 166.
[4] Ting Fu-pao, *Shuo-wen chieh-tzu ku-lin* 說文解字詁林 (Taipei: Commercial Press,
1959 reprint), 1865-66.

However, the use of the seal by the Chinese gradually became common durin the Warring States period. During the Ch'in-Han period seals became th standard form of legal identification from the emperor down through the d ferent ranks of officials in all parts of China. The seal thus replaced the tal for the most part. In the "Yü-fu chih" 輿服志 [Treatise on carriage an dress] of the *Hou Han shu*, it is said that a seal was provided for every offici in charge of a management post.[5] Tallies, on the other hand, were only give in special cases. The seal was also used in lieu of signature by private person This use may have started during the Warring States period, and has co tinued through the Ch'in and Han periods down to the present time. It is ve common among the modern Chinese as well as Japanese and Koreans. B study of the evidence indicates that in early times the use of various kinds jade tallies was more important than that of seals.

Excavation has revealed the presence of jade in many Shang and ear Chou sites, but seals have been found in very few of them. This is just the r verse of the findings at sites later than the Warring States and Ch'in-Ha periods. In the *Chou li*, it is recorded that the main varieties of jade are in fi patterns: *kuei* 圭, *pi* 璧, *chang* 璋, *huang* 璜, and *tsung* 琮.[6] These are call the *wu-jui* 五瑞 or five auspicious (jade tablets) in the *Po-hu t'ung* 白虎通. A cording to the terminology used by scholars in the field of Chinese archa ology, *kuei* is identified as a jade knife or jade ax, *pi* as a jade disc with aperture in the center, *huang* as half of a *pi* sometimes used as a main part a jade pendant, and *tsung* as a jade tube. All these patterns are familiar iter in collections of ancient Chinese jade. But it is very significant that no examp of a *chang* has been positively identified.

In the classics, the term *chang* is frequently mentioned. For example, the *Book of poetry*,[7] a *chang* is referred to as a toy for a new born boy. For new born girl, the toy is not a *chang*, but a *wa* 瓦 or piece of pottery. This stat ment is often quoted by the Chinese people in referring to the birth of a ma child. However, nobody knows how to describe a *chang*, except that it was object made of jade. Since it was so common and so important, why have examples of *chang* been found so far? I am of the opinion that the fact th no *chang* has been identified as such does not mean that no *chang* exist What it probably means, instead, is that scholars have failed to recognize it.

The problem of identifying just what a *chang* is stems from the expl nation of the word *chang* in the *Shuo-wen*. It is said there that the *chang* is

---

[5] *Tung-kuan-shu* 東觀書, quoted in the commentary of *Hou Han shu* 後漢書; s *Hou Han shu chi-chieh*, 30/15 (Taipei: I-wen, 1955 reprint), 1386.

[6] Sun I-jang, *Chou-li cheng-i* 周禮正義 (Kuo-hsüeh chi-pen ts'ung-shu ed.), 1-13.

[7] *Mao-shih chu-su* 毛詩注疏, 11-2/10-12 (Taipei: I-wen, 1955 reprint), 387-88.

alf of a *kuei*.[8] Later commentators on this definition have described the *ang* as having a hole and stated that if it is separated into two halves, there ust be half of a hole on the side of each half. This explanation is unclear. ver since the *Shuo-wen* was compiled (c. 100) no actual half ax or half knife as been discovered. If we cling to this definition of *chang*, its identification ill remain impossible. A commentator named Hsü Hao (1810-1879) of the h'ing dynasty stated that the object normally considered as "half of a *kuei*" ould not be considered as such. A *kuei*, in his opinion, is indeed the half of whole. Separately, they are called *kuei*, but when put together, they consti- te one *chang*. In other words, the *chang* is a set of two *kuei* which are used counterparts in one unit. And the unit is called a *chang*. In actual usage, e is to be held in the office while the other is given to the messenger as a eans of identification. This is a new idea and a very valuable one in the fort to identify the *chang* among the thousands of pieces of ancient Chinese de.

Unfortunately, scholars in the Ch'ing dynasty did not pay much atten- on to Hsü Hao's opinion. Everybody still clung to the obscure *Shuo-wen* xplanation. This conflict can best be resolved by re-examining the archae- ogical finds. But Ch'ing dynasty antiquarians did not take the hint from chaeology. Consequently a category of jade which can clearly be identified chang was given many unsuitable names during the time of the Ch'ing ynasty.

This category of jade occupies a very important position among all types f ancient jade. It is a disc with a cavity in the center and with teeth around e circumference. The teeth are irregular in size as well as in arrangement. his type of jade is identified as *hsüan-chi* 璇璣 . It was believed by Wu Ta- 'eng (1835-1902) to be an astronomical instrument. Since there was no tter explanation, many scholars accepted his idea, including Berthold Laufer his outstanding work *Jade, a study in Chinese archaeology and religion*. though Laufer was somewhat doubtful of the explanation, he could not fer a more satisfactory one.

Wu Ta-ch'eng's theory was based on the chapter "Shun-tien" 舜典 in e *Book of history*. It is said there that the ancient king brought into har- ony the seven regulators (prayed for the regularity of the seven luminaries) ith *hsüan-chi* and *yü-heng* 玉衡 . What are *hsüang-chi* and *yü-heng*? If we ompare the explanation given in the *Shuo-wen* (c. 100) with those expressed little later by Ma Jung (76-166), Cheng Hsüan (127-200), and Ts'ai Yung 33-192), we find that a significant change has taken place. The *Shuo-wen* fines both *hsüan-chi* and *yü-heng* simply as jade, but the scholars in the

ing Fu-pao, *Shuo-wen chieh-tzu ku-lin*, 140-41.

later part of the Eastern Han said that they were astronomical instrument
This shows that the theory that *hsüan-chi* and *yü-heng* were astronomic
instruments was strictly a later development. It should not be accepted as t
original meaning of *hsüan-chi* and *yü-heng*. If this explanation is only
product of the late second century, it certainly should not be applied to t
Chou dynasty.

Moreover, jade is fragile and is not very suitable for use as any part
an instrument with moving parts. The theory of Han scholars that jade objec
were used as parts of an instrument or machine was just a fantasy. Such i
terpretations are not reliable. However, since this explanation has formed
tradition of its own, Wu Ta-ch'eng accepted it and used it in order to identi
the jade discs with toothed edges. If the toothed jade was really a part of
machine, it most closely resembles a gear. If it were any kind of gear, ho
ever, the teeth would have to be regular, for no gear has irregular teeth. Fu
thermore, the irregularly arranged teeth on the so-called *hsüan-chi* are ve
narrow. The only comparable object would be, say, the toothed edge of a ke
Taking all these points into consideration, such a disc with irregular tee
should not be considered to be a gear, and the only possibility is that it is
kind of tally.

According to the *Chou li*, the only type of jade object with teeth w
the *chang* and one kind of *chang* which was especially designed to raise troo
was called *ya-chang* 牙璋,[9] or tusked *chang*. After a re-examination of t
extant examples of ancient jade, we would argue that the jade disc with tee
should be identified as *chang*, and the jade disc with three wings and wi
teeth on the wings should be identified as *ya-chang*. Both of these have bee
referred to as *hsüan-chi* and thus wrongly considered to be astronomic
instruments.

Aside from *chang*, there are other varieties of jade. For example, t
tiger-shaped jade (it is called *hu* 琥, a composite character consisting of t
symbols for jade and tiger) was said in the *Shuo-wen* to be an auspicious ja
tally designed for raising troops. No mention of such use of the *hu* can l
found in the *Chou li*. Sun I-jang (1848-1908) has stated that the use of *hu*
raise troops was a practice of the Warring States period, not of the Cho
dynasty, for it is first recorded in the *Lü-shih ch'un-ch'iu*.[10] If we compa
the extant *hu* from the Warring States period with the Shang jade tiger (fro
the George Eumorfopoulos Collection in London), we will find that the
both have irregular teeth on the tiger's head and tail. These articles were use

[9] Sun I-jang, *Chou-li cheng-i*, 13.

[10] The particular passage in which this information is given cannot be found in t
present text of the *Lü-shih ch'un-ch'iu* 呂氏春秋, but survives in a quotation in t
T'ai-p'ing yü-lan 太平御覽, *chüan* 808 (Taipei: Hsin-hsing, 1959 reprint), 3522.

tallies. They could come in different shapes, but had as a common feature
eth of irregular sizes.

During the Warring States period the tally used to raise troops was
hanged from jade to bronze and was called *hu-fu* 虎符. The term *hu-fu* first
ppears in the biography of Lord Hsin-ling in the *Shih chi*, in which a very
xciting story of the stealing of a *hu-fu* in order to relieve the state of Chao is
ven.[11] There are bronze tiger tallies among archaeological finds which are
alled *hu-fu* of Yung-ling and Hsiu-ch'i. Both of them have been shown in a
udy by Wang Kuo-wei (1877-1927) to be relics of the state of Ch'in from
he Warring States period. The use of the tiger tally was continued through-
ut the two Han dynasties as evidenced in the *Han shu* and the *Hou Han shu.*

The *chieh* 節 was also used as a kind of identification. In the "Treatise
n the bureaucracy" in the *Hou Han shu*, the *Fu-chieh ling* 符節令, or the
irector of the Department for Tallies and Tokens, had the duty of keeping
oth *fu* and *chieh*. The *chieh* was a tasselled staff given to an imperial messenger to show his authorization. Because the pole was made of wood, no
ctual examples have survived the ravages of time. But we can still see them in
an paintings. The *chieh* can be considered as an extension of the tally. The
riginal meaning of the word *chieh* is joint or knot of wood or bamboo. In
hat sense, it may be related to the notches on the edges of tallies.

Henri Michel has suggested that this kind of toothed jade might be an
stronomical instrument, because each of the three parts around the disc
hows the same arrangement as the seven points in the Great Dipper.[12] I do
ot find this explanation convincing. To triplicate the points of the Dipper
round the disc does not make sense for purposes of observation. The use of
he seven points seems more likely to be a code in the pattern for a tally. This
ode was used only for certain particular discs because other jade discs could
ot be adapted to this code.

In conclusion, there were various kinds of Chinese tallies as recorded in
he classics. The most common ones were made of wood or of bamboo in
zes like those of wooden slips or bamboo chopsticks. These different kinds
f tallies were used for a long time, even after the invention of paper. Besides
vood and bamboo, other materials were adapted to the making of tallies. A
ronze tally for military use in the Warring States and in the Han dynasty was
n the form of a tiger. It was so important it was controlled by the emperor
imself.

In the Early Chou there were no tiger tallies to raise troops. The Chou
ings used the *chang* or toothed tally made of jade to authenticate messages.

[11] *Shih chi* 史記, 77/4 (Taipei: I-wen, 1955 reprint), 958.
[12] "Sur les jades astronomiques chinois," in *Melanges chinois et bouddiques*
Bruxelles: 1951), 151-60.

However, no extant *chang* was ever identified as such during the Su?
dynasty. This was caused by the misunderstanding of scholars who identifi?
toothed jade discs as jade plates, astronomical instruments, or axes. The on?
satisfactory explanation, in my opinion, is that these irregularly toothed ja?
discs should be regarded as tallies.

Changing conceptions of the hegemon in Pre-Ch'in China*

Sydney Rosen

he term *pa* 霸 generally is translated as "lord protector" or "lord of the ovenants" or "chief of the feudal lords," or by the term which is being sed interchangeably with it in this study—the hegemon.

According to tradition there were five hegemons during the Spring nd Autumn period, but traditions differ when it comes to identifying the ve. In the *Hsün tzu* they are listed as Huan of Ch'i (685-644),[1] Wen of 'hin (635-628), Chuang of Ch'u (613-591), Ho-lü of Wu (514-496), and .ou Chien of Yüeh (496-465).[2] In later texts the last two names usually re replaced by Hsiang of Sung (650-637) and Mu of Ch'in (659-621).[3] ome modern scholars have suggested that there were really only two egemons: Huan of Ch'i and Wen of Chin. So there is no agreement as to he duration of the institution or the identities of the title-holders.

Since the Warring States period the institution has been the topic of a eemingly unending debate. Chinese scholars have worried about whether the egemony, under any circumstances, could be morally defensible. Were the egemons of the Spring and Autumn period justified, even if they were surpers against the king, in holding power as saviors of Chou civilization or s practitioners of "good" government? Could one who usurped power from legitimate monarch govern well? This has been the framework of their dis- ussions.

*An abbreviated version of this article was read at the Asian Studies on the Pacific 'oast Conference in San Diego, California, June 16, 1974.

[1] All dates are B.C. and accord with the chronology of P. M. Tchang's *Synchronismes .hinois* (reprint ed., Taipei: Ch'eng Wen Publishing Co., 1967).

[2] *Hsün tzu* (*SPPY* reprint ed., Taipei: Chung Hua Book Company, 1966). 10/6b/2-4.

[3] See W. Allyn Rickett, *Kuan tzu: a repository of early Chinese thought* (Hong Kong: Iong Kong University Press, 1965), I, 143, n. 101.

The problem with these debates is the failure of the debaters to consider which hegemon they were discussing, or whether all the hegemons wer, usurpers, or what was the nature of each hegemon's exercise of authorit. The concentration on the moral dilemma of the relationship of means an ends has kept people from turning the magnifying glass upon the institutio itself and the significance of early memories of it. The hegemony has bee treated as a static institution, which emerged full blown when Duke Huan (Ch'i was accepted as the first hegemon in 679.

But a close study of the *Tso chuan,* generally considered the mo. reliable source for the period, reveals that the hegemony underwent conside able evolutionary change during the course of the Spring and Autumn perio Futhermore, later conceptions in the literature of the Warring States perio of what the hegemony had been, differ radically from the institution depicte in the *Tso chuan.* An examination of the changes in the hegemony, of th changing expectations from it and of the various memories of it sheds som light on the changing political *milieu* and ideas in the Spring and Autumn an the Warring States periods.

THE HEGEMONY OF CH'I

Duke Huan was the first hegemon, but when he assumed the position (ruler in 685 his state of Ch'i already was well on the road to the position (*pa* or leader of the states. From its infeudation, the state had had close tie with the Chou royal family.

The first Ch'i ruler, Duke T'ai, had performed great military service fo the House of Chou.[4] There was intermarriage between the royal family an the ruling family of Ch'i, the Chiang family. The *Ch'un ch'iu* classic recorc that the king sought to wed one of his daughters to Duke Hsiang, Huan's pr decessor. Political considerations must have been paramount, because Hsian was hardly an ideal choice for a father or a Chou king to make. He was in volved at the time—very publicly—in a passionate love affair with his siste who was the wife of the Duke of Lu. Nevertheless, the marriage betwee Duke Hsiang and the royal princess took place (and the lady is said to hav pined away).[5] Thus there were formal links between Ch'i and the House (

---

[4] *Tso chuan,* Duke Hsiang, Yr. 14. James Legge, *The Chinese classics,* V, *The Ch'u Ts'ew with the Tso Chuen* (reprint ed.; Hong Kong: Hong Kong University Press, 1960 p. 462/15-16. See also Hsi 4, p. 139/2-4; Hsi 26, p. 197/6. All references will be to th Chinese text in the Legge edition, which I have collated with the *SPPY reprint editio) Ch'un ch'iu Tso chuan cheng i.* The texts are identical unless otherwise note References to the *Tso chuan* hereafter will be abbreviated to *Tso.*

[5] *Ch'un ch'iu,* Chuang 1; Legge, *The Chinese classics,* V, p. 72/7; see also *Ch'un ch'it* Chuang 2, p. 74/5-6 and Legge translation, p. 74, par. 3.

ɔu just before Duke Huan became duke and hegemon.

The importance of Ch'i to the Chou king who found it necessary to rry off his daughter so unfortunately and even immorally probably was at st partly the result of that state's policy of steady expansion, starting long 'ore Huan's accession to the dukedom. As early as 715 Duke Hsi, then ruler Ch'i, is believed to have called the first recorded meeting of more than two tes, to mediate difficulties between the states of Sung and Wei on the one d, and Cheng on the other.[6]

Clearly Ch'i had established a special relationship with the state of eng by that year, with Ch'i handling the details of the Earl of Cheng's visit the Chou court.[7] By 706 Ch'i was able to call upon Cheng for troops to in defense against the northern barbarians[8] and in 694 Ch'i punished the irper of the Cheng earldom.[9]

If the state of Lu was not a satellite of Ch'i before Huan's accession to dukedom, it was at least carefully cognizant of the superior power and ight of Ch'i. In 695 Ch'i fought Lu in a border dispute[10] and in 691 Lu l Ch'i together invaded Wei.[11] When the Duke of Lu was murdered in Ch'i, viously by orders of Duke Hsiang during the course of the latter's affair h the Duke of Lu's wife, the state of Lu handled the situation gingerly, liout demanding action against Ch'i or its ruler. The punishment meted t to the immediate perpetrator of the crime was accepted as sufficient.[12] d when the small state of Chi sought aid from Lu against the depredations Ch'i, the Duke of Lu said quite frankly that Lu was not able to help.[13]

Chi began to be a victim of Ch'i ambitions as early as 707, when Duke planned, with Cheng, a surprise attack.[14] The state was divided finally in l and 690.[15] Ch'i also attempted, in 712, the disposal of the small state Hsü, though with less success in this case.[16]

The exercise of naked power was only one way in which Ch'i was ming the leadership of the states even before Duke Huan took the

[6]*Tso,* Yin 8, p. 25/4-5,9-11. The Duke of Sung presided at this meeting, but com-ntators say it was called by Ch'i. Since Ch'i was the mediating state, it is quite prob-e that this tradition is correct.
[7]*Tso,* Yin 8, p. 25/6-7.
[8]*Tso,* Huan 6, p. 47/11.
[9]*Tso,* Huan 18, p. 69/14-17.
[10]*Tso,* Huan 17, p. 67/4-7.
[11]*Tso,* Chuang 3, p. 75/2-4.
[12]*Tso,* Huan 18, p. 69/1-13.
[13]*Tso,* Huan 6, p. 48/16-18.
[14]*Tso,* Huan 5, p. 44/4.
[15]*Tso,* Chuang 3, p. 75/7-10; Chuang 4, p. 76/16-17.
[16]*Tso,* Yin 11, p. 31/2-12.

dukedom. Rulers of Ch'i had already begun to take the initiative in re;
lating the relations between the states and, to some extent, the affairs of t
ruling houses. The mediation between Sung, Wei, and Cheng already has be
cited, as has been the punishment of the usurper to the Cheng earldom. In 7'
Ch'i and Cheng conducted a punitive attack on the city of Ch'eng, which h
violated a decree of the Chou king by failing to join in an interstate acti
against Sung earlier that year.[17] In 691 Ch'i acted to restore the deposed ru
of Wei.[18]

　　Huan became duke in 685 and was acknowledged officially as *pa* or l
gemon in 679. The final steps are easy to trace. In 684 Duke Huan extinguish
the small state of T'an, the ruler of which had offended him.[19] In 683 he m
ried a Chou princess.[20] In 681 there was a meeting of the states to consider c
order in Sung. Commentators assert that it was called by Ch'i, although tha'
not clear in the text of the *Tso chuan*. The little state of Sui did not send a re
resentative and that summer Ch'i extinguished Sui. In the winter of the sa:
year Lu concluded a peace pact with Ch'i.[21] The Ch'i ruler requested troc
from the king and thus, with royal armies, led the feudal lords under the kin
banner, in a disciplinary action, against Sung. The state of Sung submitted.
And in 679, at a meeting of the feudal lords, Ch'i "for the first time was *pa*.'

　　Who thought of giving a title to the role which the rulers of Ch'i seemin;
had begun to play fully thirty years earlier? The sources are silent about th
It might have been the king, for all we know—although there is evidence tl
the royal house was ambivalent in its attitude toward the new hegemoi
seeming sometimes to approve the role Ch'i was playing and sometimes to
nore it.[24] According to tradition, the hegemony was the creation of Du
Huan and his minister, Kuan Chung. But it has been demonstrated that Du
Huan probably was not a creative political thinker and that Kuan Chung ;
parently did not become influential in Ch'i until about seventeen years af
Huan became the official hegemon.[25]

[17] *Tso*, Yin 10, p. 29/18.
[18] *Tso*, Chuang 3, p. 75/1-4; for explanation, see p. 75, par. 1.
[19] *Tso*, Chuang 10, p. 85/18.
[20] *Tso,* Chuang 11, p. 87/14.
[21] *Tso*, Chuang 13, p. 90/3-13.
[22] *Tso*, Chuang 14, pp. 91/1, 92/15-16.
[23] *Tso*, Chuang 15, p. 93/1-7.
[24] See *Tso*, Chuang 20, p. 99/1-4; Chuang 30, p. 117/1-6 for examples of the Ho'
of Chou turning for aid to other states and ignoring "its" hegemon.
[25] See Sydney Rosen, "In search of the historical Kuan Chung" (unpublished Ph
dissertation, Department of Far Eastern Languages and Civilizations, University
Chicago, 1973), Chapters I and IV.

Regardless of who conceived of the formalization of Ch'i policy, it is
ar that the position rested at first on two pillars—the unbridled use of
itary power against the Chou states for the purpose of enhancing the pres-
e of Ch'i and the Chou king's acceptance, however reluctant, of the pre-
inence of Ch'i. At the time the hegemony was acknowledged by the other
tes, it seems clear that the feudal lords and the king were simply accepting
mination by the biggest bully among them.

There does not seem to have been any functional justification for the
titution of *pa* or hegemon in the beginning. The hegemon occasionally acted
behalf of the king in regulating interstate affairs or interfering with suc-
sion problems within states, but this was not a consistent or formally
fined function. Mostly the military might of Ch'i was exercised against the
er Chou vassal states wilfully, for the personal prestige of the ruler of Ch'i.

This situation changed radically after 662, if the *Tso chuan* is to be
lieved. From 662 to the death of Duke Huan, the policy of Ch'i as hegemon
s to serve as defender of the Chou vassal states against the barbarian,
her than as an attacker of Chou states. This sharp shift occurs just at the
e that Kuan Chung becomes prominent in the records of Ch'i as they ap-
ar in the *Tso chuan*.

Kuan Chung became a member of Duke Huan's court in 685, almost im-
diately after the duke's accession.[26] But from 685 to 662 his name does not
pear in the records, although Duke Huan and Ch'i are prominent in them.
d when Kuan Chung does begin to appear as a close adviser to the duke,
changes in policy are notable. It seems to have been Kuan Chung who con-
ved of the hegemon as the protective arm of the king, rather than as preyer
on the states.

In 662 a city was walled for Kuan Chung.[27] Whatever the reason for this
t from the duke, it seems to have resulted in (or accompanied) Kuan Chung's
ofound influence over the duke for the rest of Huan's tenure.

In 661 the small state of Hsing was overrun by barbarians and Kuan
ung advised the duke to move for its relief.[28] The barbarians are in-
iable, Kuan Chung warned, implying that Hsing would not be the last
ou state to fall if they were not stopped. He reminded the duke of the poem
the *Shih ching* in which the troops reveal their longing to return home and
eir fear of "those memorandum tablets."[29] According to Kuan Chung, those
lets were orders to the troops to relieve victims from evil. The tablets, he

[26] *Tso*, Chuang 9, p. 83/1-17.
[27] *Tso*, Chuang 32, p. 119/1.
[28] *Tso*, Min 1, p. 123/2-5.
[29] *Shih ching*, II/I/viii. See Legge, *The Chinese classics*, IV, *The She King or The Book
Poetry* (Hong Kong: Hong Kong University Press, 1965), 264/1-3.

implied, applied now to Duke Huan. The duke took his adivce.

It can be inferred that the duke's role as *pa* or hegemon was, in Ku
Chung's opinion, a position of special responsibility in carrying out the roy
obligations. H. G. Creel has pointed out that during the Western Chou peri
vassal states were dependent upon the help of the king's armies when co
fronted with barbarians. He says it was consistently the troops under roy
command, not the armies under noble command, who stemmed the tide
barbarian incursions.[30] Kuan Chung seems to have seen the hegemon as
suming this royal function.

The new policy continued with support of the Duke of Wei against t
Ti Barbarians, arbitration between the Chou monarch and the Jung B
barians, and with an unsuccessful attempt to relieve the small state of H
from an attack by the non-Chou state of Ch'u.[31] In 656 the duke led t
allied armies of the Chou states in an incursion into Ch'u—a rising pow
menacing the borders of the Chou vassal states. Kuan Chung accompanied t
ruler and, when a Ch'u delegation met the armies to inquire about their pr
ence, it was Kuan Chung who spoke for the northern states—or, more speci
cally, for Ch'i. He claimed that the founder of the state of Ch'i had be
charged, in the early days of the Western Chou, with duties to uphold t
House of Chou in the area, that Ch'u had not sent its proper tribute of rusl
and that a former Chou king had disappeared in the southern region. Ch'i a
its allies wanted to know why. Clearly the *pa* was presented as one who serv
as a policing agent for the king.[32]

Duke Huan died in 644. From 662 to 644 Ch'i did not once exert fo
upon a Chou vassal state. Its military activities were carried out solely as t
protector of the king and his feudal lords.

Kuan Chung seems to have added one other new element to the conce
of *pa*. He asserted that the feudal lords could be attracted to support t
hegemony only by the practice of virtue on the part of the hegemon, i
plying also that hegemony required voluntary acceptance by the feudal lor
Power was not enough.

In 653 Duke Huan met with the other feudal lords at Ning Mu, to co
sider dealing with disorders in the state of Cheng. The minister Kuan Chu
reportedly spoke to the duke, saying: "Your minister has heard it said, 'Beck
the disaffected by means of *li* 禮 , cherish the distant by means of virt
When virtue and *li* do not waver, there are none who will not cherish (you).
The *Tso chuan* reports that the duke then behaved with courtesy to the otl

[30] H. G. Creel, *The origins of statecraft in China* (Chicago: University of Chic
Press, 1970), I, 316.

[31] *Tso*, Min 2, pp. 126/13-127/5; Hsi 12, p. 159/8-18; Hsi 15, p. 164/1-2,8.

[32] *Tso*, Hsi 4, p. 139/1-9.

dal lords.

At this meeting Kuan Chung also stopped the duke from supporting the
el son of the Earl of Cheng, insisting that treachery was not the way to win
feudal lords.[33]

While Kuan Chung seems to have been responsible for redefining the
e of the hegemon, giving him an important function within the Chou
tem, the change also may reflect developments within the empire as well.
e Chou king was continually losing ground during those early years of the
ring and Autumn period. In 674 there was a revolt in the royal court and
ng Hui was forced to seek temporary asylum in the state of Cheng. There
s another revolt at court in 664.[34]

In 650, after the death of King Hui, the new king was the candidate
ored by Duke Huan. In fact, the king owed his throne to the support of the
gemon.[35] It appears that the tie between the Chou king and the hegemon
s strengthened as the king's position weakened, and the legitimacy of the
gemon's position was thus reinforced.

There was a void and the most powerful state stepped into it. Because
king's myth was still strong even though his actual power was dissi-
ting, this lent legitimacy to the aspiration of the powerful vassal. The
ssal lord of Ch'i no longer needed to be aggressive to satisfy his hunger
glory.

This new view of the hegemony was to last after the deaths of Kuan
ung and Duke Huan. It was the rulers of the state of Chin, and the ministers
o stood behind them, who intermittently carried on the institution of the
gemony—substantially as it had been practiced in the later years of Duke
an and Kuan Chung, but with some interesting variations.

THE HEGEMONY OF CHIN

Reading through the *Tso chuan* page by page and column by column, I
ve found no evidence that after Duke Huan any ruler other than those of
in was acknowledged as *pa*, or consistently performed the functions and
joyed the honors of a hegemon for any period of time. Others aspired to the
sition, as, for examples, the Duke of Sung immediately after the death of
ke Huan, the kings of Ch'u over a long period of time and, later, the rulers
Wu and Yüeh. But the *Tso chuan* indicates that they did not achieve their
pirations.

The *Tso chuan* makes it clear that at least four rulers of Chin unques-

[33] *Tso*, Hsi 7, p. 148/8-17.
[34] *Tso*, Chuang 20, p. 99/1-4; Chuang 30, p. 117/1-6.
[35] *Tso*, Hsi 8, p. 150/1-3,13; Hsi 9, p. 152/3-9.

tionably were hegemons. These were Duke Wen (635-628),[36] Duke Hsia (627-621),[37] Duke Ling (620-605),[38] and Duke Tao (573-558).[39] The gemony was questionable and occasionally a matter for contention during years of six other Chin rulers: Dukes Ch'eng (606-600),[40] Ching (599-581) Li (580-573),[42] P'ing (557-532),[43] Chao (531-526),[44] and Ch'ing (525-512) It was during the rule of Duke Ting (511-475) that Chin finally, unequivoca lost the leadership of the states and the institution ceased to be a factor in terstate relations.[46] Later attempts to revive it were not successful.

Even during the periods when Chin's leadership was weak and in fective, no other state won the position from it. The king of Ch'u seemed challenge Chin's position successfully in 579 when the two states signe covenant calling for both to relieve other states in distress, and again at Sung disarmament conference of 546,[47] but in fact the 579 treaty was in fective and the Chou states did not fully accept Ch'u as a hegemon after Sung conference. In 538 the heir to the throne of Ch'u raised the question whether Chin would allow Ch'u the hegemony, and it seemed as though time was ripe for the southern kingdom. But the excesses of the Ch'u lead ship alienated the feudal lords.[48]

When the institution of hegemon fell intermittently into relative (b not total) disrepair—the rulers of Chin, their ministers and many other Ch states continued to see Chin as having the obligations of hegemony even wh its rulers were not fulfilling those obligations. And the rulers continued expect that the perquisites of the position could be theirs—until the to collapse of the hegemony during the tenure of Duke Ting.

Duke Wen of Chin, the famed wanderer Chung-erh, was the first ru after the death of Duke Huan to be declared *pa*. In 632 he was commission

[36] *Tso*, Hsi 28, p. 205/10-16.

[37] *Tso*, Wen 1, p. 228/2-4; Wen 4, pp. 238/1-2, 235/17, 236/12-16, 238/3; Chao p. 585/2.

[38] *Tso*, Wen 13, p. 263/10-12; Wen 14, p. 265/8-14; Wen 18, pp. 276/11-277/14.

[39] *Tso*, Ch'eng 18, p. 407/8-13; Hsiang 3, p; 418/11-13; Hsiang 4, p. 422/2-16; Hsia 8, p. 433/7-8.

[40] *Tso*, Hsuan 7, p. 299/1-17.

[41] *Tso*, Hsuan 12, p. 312/10; Ch'eng 1, p. 336/13-18; Ch'eng 3, p. 351/3-9.

[42] *Tso*, Ch'eng 13, p. 380/17-18; Ch'eng 16, pp. 391/6-10, 393/9-10.

[43] *Tso*, Hsiang 26, p. 520/7-8; Hsiang 27, pp. 528/10-15, 529/2-5, 530/5-7; Hsia 28, p. 537/5.

[44] *Tso*, Chao 13, p. 645/3-4, 9-646/7-8; Chao 16, p. 661/2-3.

[45] *Tso*, Chao 21, pp. 685/16-686/1; Legge's note, p. 688, par. 2; Chao 23, pp. 695 696/1.

[46] *Tso*, Ting 7, p. 764/6; Legge's note, p. 765, par. 3.

[47] *Tso*, Ch'eng 12, p. 377/3-5; Hsiang 27, pp. 529/2-5, 530/5-7.

[48] *Tso*, Chao 4, pp. 593/1,5-594/4.

the king to tranquilize the states in the four quarters, and to punish and
nove those who committed wrongs.[49] From the beginning Duke Wen—and
r his successors—subscribed to Duke Huan's later conception of the hege-
n as a protector of the loyal Chou states and an armed referee of their
utes. And they accepted Kuan Chung's views about the importance of
d faith and courtesy in attracting the feudal lords. The legitimacy of the
emony lay in the hegemon's relationship to the king and in the consent of
feudal lords. The latter had to be won.

For instance, in 620 one of the leading ministers of Chin persuaded the
me minister of the moment, Chao Hsüan Tzu, to return to the state of Wei
ne land that had been seized earlier by the state of Chin. The argument was
t:

> [If a state] rebel and be not punished, by what means [do we] proclaim
> [our] majesty? [If a state] submit and be not overwhelmed with our kind-
> ness, by what means [do we] proclaim [that we] cherish it? [If we] do
> not punish and do not cherish [the states], by what means do we pro-
> claim our virtue? Without virtue, by what means [do we] preside over
> the covenants?[50]

Kuan Chung might have given the same advice to Duke Huan, and dukes
d first ministers of Chin often were to receive and often were to act upon
ilar advice. But the dukes and leading ministers of Chin also had additional
as about the bases for a hegemon's legitimacy and the privileges of a hege-
n that seem not to have occurred to Duke Huan or Kuan Chung.

It has been shown that, contrary to the tradition of Kuan Tzu, Duke
an's rise to hegemony was not based upon internal reforms in Ch'i and that,
eed, he seems not to have been greatly concerned with internal admin-
ation.[51] This was not the case with Duke Wen of Chin.

The *Tso chuan* reports that when Duke Wen first took his place as the
er of Chin, he trained his people for two years (presumably in the arts of
rfare) before planning to use them in battle, and then he also devoted his
ention to making them happy, teaching them the value of good faith and
correct behavior (*li* 禮 and *i* 義). "In one battle [he became] *pa*. It was
cause of Wen's teaching [of his people]," the *Tso chuan* says.[52] While the
ory is at least somewhat apocryphal (since it took more diplomatic and
litary maneuvering than is indicated in this passage), the connection it
kes between competence in domestic affairs and the position of hegemon

[49] *Tso*, Hsi 28, p. 205/10-16.
[50] *Tso*, Wen 7, p. 247/13-18. See also Hsiang 26, p. 520/8-9.
[51] Rosen, "In search of the historical Kuan Chung," *passim.*
[52] *Tso*, Hsi 27, p. 200/14-18.

seems to be valid. The effectiveness of later Chin rulers and ministers wit\[
their own state repeatedly was discussed as a basic element of their position
hegemon.

When Duke Tao recovered the hegemony for Chin in 573, after it \[
been almost completely lost, it is clearly indicated that news of his refor
and domestic appointments led the feudal lords back to his court.[53] When \[
rulers of Chin were not good governors, the hegemony tended to slip te
porarily from their grasp. The title returned to Chin when the rulers were a\[

This connection between internal stability and external prestige was \[
unique to Chin, of course. Increasingly the link between domestic tranq\[
lity and external power was recognized during the course of the sixth centu
But it is significant, I think, that gradually the concept of the hegemony its
became linked, in a limited way, with the concept of effective government.
the same time the hegemony began to assume some imperial aspects.

There is no evidence in the *Tso chuan* that Duke Huan as hegemon \[
particular emphasis upon having other states pay tribute visits to the court
Ch'i. He expected states to attend meetings when he called them,[54] but th\[
is no indication of a regularized regime of court visits. The Chin hegemons,
the other hand, set up a routine of periodic visits. The *Tso chuan* states t\[
under the hegemony of Dukes Wen and Hsiang there was a rule that feu\[
lords should appear at the court of Chin every five years, and that they sho\[
send friendly missions every three years.[55] This was in addition, of course,
attending special meetings for covenants and other affairs.

It is not clear whether these visits were seen purely in terms of c\[
tributing to the honor of the hegemon, or whether they were used for adm\[
istrative purposes. There is no evidence of the latter. That idea apparently \[
to come later. Nevertheless, the demand for visits increased as Chin strugg\[
to retain the hegemony in the sixth century. In 565 the Duke of Lu went \[
the Chin court to learn from the newly installed duke how many court vis\[
and visits of friendly inquiry would be required, and later that year there w
a meeting of the states to give them their instructions about this matter.[56]
551 Tzu Ch'an of Cheng wrote a letter protesting the exactions of the duke
Chin. He cited annual missions of friendly inquiry to Chin and the burden
responses to a continuous and irregular stream of requirements for service.

The development of regularized court visits was accompanied by otl
exactions too. The *Tso chuan* nowhere suggests that Duke Huan collectec

[53] *Tso*, Ch'eng 18, p. 407/8-13; see also Ch'eng 18, p. 408/3-4; Hsiang 9, p. 437/10-\[
[54] *Tso*, Chuang 13, p. 90/3-13.
[55] *Tso*, Chao 3, p. 585/2-3.
[56] *Tso*, Hsiang 8, p. 433/1,7.
[57] *Tso*, Hsiang 22, p. 493/3-11.

ute tax for himself or for Ch'i as part of the rewards of hegemony. He
ected presents on the occasion of his becoming duke, but he does not ap-
r to have collected taxes—except on behalf of the king.[58] The Chin ru-
did collect tribute as hegemons. In 609, for example, a minister of Cheng
t a letter to the prime minister of Chin wearily promising to "[collect] all
poor levies [and] to wait at Yü, just as [your] *chih shih* 執事 [a petty
cial] commands us."[59] The *Tso chuan* entry for 549 notes that Chin's re-
rements for presents were heavy.[60] The following year a new chief minister
tened the burden.[61] The nature of these taxes or presents is not known.

Chin's innovations in the conduct of the hegemony could indicate a
t in the concept of the hegemon—away from that of a servant of the king
towards that of a rival to the king. When emphasis upon administrative
ity and virtue is considered in combination with required court appearences
some form of direct tribute tax, there seems to be a suggestion of the
innings of a new imperial structure, separate from the Chou imperial struc-
e. But that would be an exaggeration. The hegemon continued to be closely
l to the Chou king and the Chou system throughout the period.

The Chin rulers and ministers do not seem to have conceived of the
emony in terms of government. They did not deal with affairs in a state
er than their own) below the level of the feudal lord. And while the re-
onship of the hegemon to the king may have been something other than
t of a totally submissive servant, the Chin rulers continued to see themselves
gents of the king—not as substitutes for him.

It has been suggested that the evolution of the position of Ch'i as hege-
n from an aggressor to an arbiter and royal aide was partly a move to seek
timacy for the new honorific and perhaps partly a deliberate move to
ster a weakened, but still revered, royal house. Both of those factors were
n more apparent in Duke Wen's assumption of the hegemony.

After the death of Duke Huan the House of Chou again found itself in a
of troubles. In 636 the king was at odds first with the state of Cheng and
n with the Ti Barbarians who forced him to flee to Cheng.[62] In 635 the
ly installed Duke Wen of Chin was told, "If you seek [the acceptance of]
feudal lords, you could do nothing better than to aid the king. The feudal
ls will take confidence from that and, moreover, it would be appropriate
)...."[63] Duke Wen took the advice and later that year the king enter-

---

[58]*Tso*, Chuang 10, p. 85/17-18; Hsi 4, p. 139/1-4.
[59]*Tso*, Wen 17, p. 277/11.
[60]*Tso*, Hsiang 24, p. 505/6.
[61]*Tso*, Hsiang 25, p. 511/16.
[62]*Tso*, Hsi 24, pp. 189/6-190/4.
[63]*Tso*, Hsi 25, p. 194/3.

tained his savior in the royal capital.

It was the king who, in 632, appointed Duke Wen as hegemon, c(
missioning him to keep the states tranquil and to correct or remove (
doers.[64] This is the only report in the *Tso chuan* of a clear-cut royal appo(
ment to the hegemony, but the relationship of the hegemon to the k(
throughout the period is fairly, if intermittently, clear in the text. The ru(
and ministers of Chin arbitrated disputes within the royal court protected
court from barbarian incursions, presented the spoils of war to the king, (
occasional use of royal troops and harbored the king when he was tempora(
exiled from his own court.

During the course of the sixth century the influence of the Chou k(
was continually diminished—and at the same time the hegemony became
and less effective in terms of performing real services to the Chou states. (
paralysis of the hegemon was the result of the weakness within Chin as wel(
that of the royal court, of course. But it is difficult to understand why, un(
the circumstances of Chin's relative impotence through much of the centu(
the Chou states continued to recognize its nominal leadership—and even
for it. The most probable explanation is the connection between the hegen(
and the king to whom lip service still was offered.

This tie was recognized by the ministers governing Chin in 533. A fu(
tionary of Chin, involved in a quarrel, had allowed the Jung Barbarian(
attack royal property. In the king's moving remonstrance to Chin he poi(
out that:

> ... I am to you as the cap or crown to the other garments, or the sp(
> to the stream, as their counselor to the people. If you tear the cap (
> break the crown in pieces, tear up the root, stop up the spring and t(
> it on you to cast the counselor away, what can be expected by me,
> One Man, from the Jung and the Ti?

And a minister of Chin, discussing the matter with the chief minis(
carried the king's argument a step further. He said:

> Even Wen, as leader of the states, was not able to change the orde(
> the kingdom. He acted as supporter of the Son of Heaven, show(
> towards him extraordinary respect. Since the time of Wen, our vi(
> has decayed generation after generation, and we have tyrannized (
> and reduced lower and lower the head of Chou, thereby proclaiming(
> extravagance of our course. Is it not right that the states should bec(
> disaffected to us? And moreover, the king's words are right. Do you (
> sider the case well.[65]

[64] *Tso*, Hsi 28, p. 205/12-13.
[65] *Tso*, Chao 9, p. 624/4-11. This is Legge's translation, p. 625-26.

The chief minister, Hsüan Tzu, agreed and the matter was promptly
tified. On the basis of the information in the *Tso chuan*, the minister had
ggerated Chin's misuse of the king, but the point was well made.

Later however, in 510, Chin finally did abandon the king. He had
gested that Chin wall the royal capital in order to save itself the continual
in of defending it, and Fan Hsien-tzu of Chin said: "Rather than guard the
ntiers of Chou, it would be better to wall it. The Son of Heaven [himself]
spoken accurately. [Then] whatever happens later, Chin [need] not be
cerned about it . . . ." He added that it would relieve the feudal lords.[66]
the following year, under the leadership of Chin, the feudal lords walled
Chou capital.[67] By 503 the feudal lords were making their own covenants,
ependently of Chin or any other leading state.[68] There was no longer a
emon.

Chin was no less effective then than it had been during many other ducal
iods. The new element was the decision to cease to be responsible for, or
the king. And the separation of the hegemony from the king seems to have
n ultimately a *coup de grace*—for both.

THE MYTH OF HEGEMONY

For if the feudal lords of the Spring and Autumn period saw the hege-
n essentially as an agent of the king, with limited functions and less limited
ards, this was not the case for some of the influential political thinkers of
Warring States period who were searching their inherited memories of
u's earlier days to find new solutions for new problems. It was they who
le the sharp distinction between the king and the hegemon that has set the
ns for debate about hegemony to this day. And some of them found in the
emony a useful compromise with their ideals as they searched for a more
le government.

Mencius was not, basically, a compromiser and his negative view of the
emon has been perhaps the most influential over the centuries. He said the
emon had won his position by force[69] and had coerced the feudal lords
) punishing their peers. By such coercion the hegemon had committed an
nse against the king.[70]

But although he could not approve of it, Mencius believed the hegemony
l promoted some laudable governmental practices. He said Duke Huan had

[66] *Tso*, Chao 32 p. 739/5; full context, pp. 738/14-739/10.
[57] *Tso*, Ting 1, p. 742/1-2.
[58] See, for example, *Tso*, Ting 7, p. 764/6.
[59] *Meng tzu chu shu*, (*SPPY* ed.), 3b/1a/3.
[70] *Meng tzu chu shu*, 12b/1a/3,8-9.

drawn up a covenant which bound the feudal lords, among other things, abolition of hereditary office, recruitment and promotion of worthy aid and concern for the aged and the young.[71] (There is no record in the *chuan* of Duke Huan's having proposed such a covenant and there are m indications that he would not have thought of it.[72] While these were practi Mencius himself advocated, he still insisted that the hegemon could not h been truly virtuous. His virtue was feigned because it was not inherent.[73] matter how effective the hegemons had been in government, they must considered moral offenders. The hegemony was not a desirable instituti but the policies imputed to it were essential if kingship was to flourish.

If Mencius was the most persuasive thinker for the dynastic peri after the Han, Hsün Tzu was at least as influential in the very late Wari States, the Ch'in, and the Han periods. And he disagreed with Mencius in latter's disdain for the hegemony as an institution of coercion. In fact, he not see it as such. Hsün Tzu drew a third distinction, which Mencius did make, between the hegemon and the conqueror by force. He saw three alte⟩ tive forms of government—that of the true king who ruled by the exan of his innate virtue, that of the hegemon who regulated an alliance or c federation by the example of his administrative skill within his own state, that of the conqueror by force.[74]

In his understanding of the hegemon, Hsün Tzu came close to the C hegemony depicted in the *Tso chuan*, but he enlarged the functions of govе ment within the state of the hegemon and he saw the hegemony as an ir tution separate from the royal house and alternative to it. Like Mencius, he tinguished between the true king, who governed by means of innate virtue, the hegemon who used virtue with virtuosity.[75] And like Mencius, he prefe⟩ and advocated the empire of the true king. But Hsün Tzu apparently was optimistic about the probability of achieving that empire. And so he turneе the hegemon as the less desirable—but nonethless viable—alternative.

The hegemon, within his own state, opened lands, filled granaries, itiated useful production, recruited and promoted men of virtue and abiⅡ used rewards and punishments to protect the weak and restrain the vioⅡ and, in interstate relations, he was not aggressive. So the feudal lords, in absence of a true king, turned to him as their leader in alliance or con eration.[76]

[71]*Meng tzu chu shu*, 12b/1a/11-1b/2.
[72]See Rosen, "In search of the historical Kuan Chung," Chapters I, III, and IV
[73]*Meng tzu chu shu*, 13b/3a/3-4.
[74]*Hsün tzu*, (*SPPY* ed.), 5/4a/11-5a/6.
[75]*Ibid.*
[76]*Ibid.*; see also 5/11b/10-12a/9.

Mencius envisioned the *pa* as functioning wrongly, while establishing irable administrative objectives and procedures, within the Chou system. in Tzu saw the *pa* as the effective administrator who, because of his eftiveness, led an alliance of states without a king (or without a true king).

The unknown author of Chapter six of the *Kuo yü*, the "Ch'i yü" ipter, had still a different conception. This chapter, probably written late the Warring States period,[77] is devoted entirely to the history of Duke an of Ch'i and records in detail a version of his hegemony which differs rkedly from that of the *Tso chuan* and from all other extant references in Warring States period.

The hegemon is seen as one who controlled the disposition of military ces in the other states of the hegemony.[78] He exercised commercial conls over the markets of the other states.[79] As a measure of control, he wed the free use of his state's resources by the other states[80] and he used court visit as an overt technique of administrative supervision.[81] While the stence of the Chou king at the time of Duke Huan is mentioned, he is seen having played a peripheral role in the system. Duke Huan gave him tribute l he honored Duke Huan. But it was admiration for the duke, not revnce for the king, which bound the other feudal lords to the system.

When, in the *Kuo yü's* description of hegemony, the commercial ties are wed in context with the right of the hegemon to assign military duties to er states and with the administrative use of court visits to the hegemon, at emerges is a ruler, governing with the consent of a titular king, rather n a leader or arbitrator among equals. The hegemony "remembered" by : author of the "Ch'i yü" chapter steps beyond the Chou feudal system and gests the outlines of a centralized empire.

A consideration of the history of the institution of *pa* as it is depicted the *Tso chuan* and by these differing writers of the Warring States period ds some light, I think, on the significance of the institution to the Chou tem. The recognition in 510 by the king and the hegemonic state that they l nothing more to offer each other seems in a sense to have been also a renition that neither had anything more to offer the empire as a whole. That ognition led to the end of the hegemony.

[77] See Bernhard Karlgren, "The authenticity and nature of the *Tso chuan*," *Göteborgs gskolas Arsskrift*, XXXII (1926), 3-65.
[78] *Kuo yü*, (*SPPY* ed.), 6/8b/11-9a/6.
[79] *Kuo yü*, 6/8a/7-11.
[80] *Kuo yü*, 6/11b/3-5.
[81] *Kuo yü*, 6/5b/11-6a/10.
[82] *Kuo yü*, 6/9b/1-2; 10a/9-10b/7.

A passive shell of Chou kingship lingered on, but the system fell ap
after the collapse of the hegemony—probably as a result of the causes for
collapse as well as because of the collapse itself. The institution of hegemo
seems to have slowed the pace of disintegration of the Chou system, althou
it was not immune to the forces leading to that disintegration.

In the succeeding two centuries, as political philosophers looked b
upon the kingship and the hegemony as alternative institutions, rather tl
as components of one institution—and as they saw in the hegemony aspe
of empire and imputed to it functions and powers it had not had in fact—
unthinkable possibility of a different system as successor to the Chou syst
became thinkable.

These men were influential in their own times and immediately af
Mencius lectured at great length to the rulers and ministers of several of
Warring States; Hsün Tzu taught Han Fei Tzu and Li Ssu—two men who w
to contribute a great deal to the form of the Ch'in and Han empires. 1
development of the Kuan Tzu tradition strongly indicates that the "Ch'i y
chapter of the *Kuo yü*, or similar works, must have been widely read. A
these three works probably were only three of many roughly contemporane
re-interpretations of the hegemony and its relationship to the Chou syste

The rulers of the Spring and Autumn states vied for hegemony in s
port of a weakened king and an accepted system. The rulers of the Warr
States vied for empire, demonstrably conceiving of it in terms of new c
ceptions of government which were formed, at least in part, by their und
standing of the hegemony.

Emphatic negatives in classical Chinese

Edwin G. Pulleyblank

a well-known article published in 1935 Ting Sheng-shu advanced the
position that the negative particle *fu* 弗 was equivalent to the more
quent and generalized negative particle *pu* 不 + the object pronoun *chih* 之.
texts of the classical Late Chou period the equation does, in fact, work in
rge number of cases. That is, *fu* appears in front of active transitive verbs
ich have no object expressed in the sentence and for which the sense would
uire *chih* if the object were to be expressed, for example 弗知 "does not
 w [it]." Since there is a rule by which a personal pronoun object is nor-
ly placed between the negative particle and the verb—e.g. 不我知 "does
 know me"—one might also expect *不之知, but this is seldom, if ever
nd. Hence it looks as if 弗 stands for *不之.

Ting did not explicitly suggest that *fu* originated as a phonetic contrac-
 of *pu chih* but when one looks at the phonetic history, there is clearly a
sibility of this, as Boodberg (1937) pointed out soon after. In Middle
nese *fu* was a *ju-sheng* word ending in -*t*. This consonant could have
resented the initial consonant of *chih*. Such contractions, or "fusion
rds," are a well-known feature of both ancient and modern Chinese. A
se parallel is provided by 盍 *ho* "why not," which formerly ended in -*p*
 is equivalent in meaning to 何不 *ho pu*. (The problem of the fusion
ation for *fu* from a phonetic point of view will be discussed more fully
ow.)

Unfortunately, in spite of its attractiveness both from a phonetic and
m a semantic point of view, there are serious difficulties about this hy-
hesis which Ting did not fully take into account. Lü Shu-hsiang (1941)
 forced to recognize this when he attempted to extend the theory to the
allel case of the prohibitory negative *wu* 勿 (also a former *ju-sheng* word
ing in -*t*) which looks as if it could be a fusion of *wu* 毋 (*p'ing sheng*) +

chih.[1] Ting had already noted that the equation *fu* = *pu chih* did not worl
the *Shu ching* but dismissed this as the result of textual corruption in
transmission of that notoriously problematical text. Lü showed that for b
fu and *wu* the fusion equations also break down on bronze inscriptions a
on the oracle bones, where there can be no question of textual corrupti
Hence these negative particles could not have originated as fusions but m
have been differentiated from the non-*ju-sheng* forms in some other w
Nevertheless Lü remained impressed by the fact that one can so often und
stand the *ju-sheng* forms as fusions in texts of the classical period. He thou
that what had originally been emphatic forms became secondarily interpre
as fusions.

The matter becomes further complicated when we consider the hist
of these particles from the Han dynasty onward. In texts of that period
fusion interpretation again manifestly breaks down. As Lü shows, there
good reason to think that in the colloquial language the *ju-sheng* forms end
in -*t* replaced the *p'ing-sheng* forms completely. It is true that, as far as
graph is concerned, 不 replaced 弗, but the modern pronunciation of 不
all dialects goes back to an alternative reading in -*t*, e.g. Cantonese *pǝt*. As
Fang-kuei had already suggested to Ting Sheng-shu,[2] this does not mean t
the graph 不 originally had such an alternative reading in -*t*, which wo
conflict with its phonetic series. Rather it means that, because of its ident
of meaning, 不 continued to be used as the most common negative parti
even after the *ju-sheng* form had driven out the non-*ju-sheng* form in spee
The imperative negative has not survived in modern dialects but Lü sho
that in medieval times 勿 or *mo* 没 (also a *ju-sheng* form in -*t*) had simila
replaced 毋.

There is no obvious reason why a contraction should replace *one* of
elements of which it is made up. On the other hand, as Lü himself poin
out, there are good parallels in Chinese as well as in other languages for
replacement of weaker and less emphatic forms by stronger and more e
phatic forms when such forms exist side by side. For example, of the t
classical forms of the first personal pronoun, *wu* 吾 and *wo* 我, only
latter, which was originally the stronger of the two, survived into later tim
Applying this principle to 弗 and 勿, Lü argued that, having begun as e
phatic forms and then acquired a different significance as fusion words, th

[1]See also Graham (1952). Graham notes that von der Gabelentz (1881) had alre
suggested a fusion etymology for 勿. In the case of 弗, however, von der Gabele
(p. 452) merely noted a parallel tendency for the omission of *chih* and did not
Graham states, propose a fusion equation, no doubt because his reading *put* for 不 it
ended in -*t*.
[2]Ting (1935), 996, appended note.

emerged as emphatic forms in Han times. Huang Ching-hsin (1958) argued
at this was complicated and unconvincing. Moreover Huang was able to
ow that there are far too many counterexamples to the fusion hypothesis
en in classical texts. Lü, whose attention was focused mainly on 勿, found
ly a half dozen or so absolutely clear counterexamples and felt that these
re few enough that they could be ignored as possibly resulting from textual
rruption. Huang was able to show that there were far more such exceptions
the case of 弗—and his search was by no means exhaustive.

Huang made another telling argument. He pointed out that *pu,* as well
fu, regularly appears in front of transitive verbs where the sense requires
h as object.[3] That is, 不知, as well as 弗知, means "does not know [it]."
is means that there was a general rule allowing the deletion of *chih* when
was the object of a verb negated by *pu.* If there were no other obstacle to
 fusion equation, one could save the hypothesis by assuming that the
letion rule was optional, but the existence of such a rule at all obviously
eatly weakens the force of the argument that 弗 *must* contain 之 because
the non-occurrence of *不之. One would wish to find some further principle
account for the failure to delete in some cases and the deletion in others.
oreover there are, in fact, many cases in which it is quite impossible to
ply *chih.* One is therefore driven to the conclusion that the real difference
all periods between the negative particles ending in -*t* and the related forms
thout this ending had nothing to do with the presence or absence of *chih.*

The earliest explanation of the difference between 弗 and 不 is that of
 Hsiu (129-182) who, in his commentary to the *Kung-yang chuan,* stated
at *fu* was a "deeper" (深) form of *pu.*[4] What "deep" means in this connec-
n is, of course, open to conjecture but it has usually been interpreted as
mething like stronger or more emphatic. Coming from a time so much
ser than we are today to when our texts were written, this comment is
viously deserving of attention. Though it is difficult to demonstrate con-
sively by objective means that emphasis was intended when the *ju-sheng*
rms were used, emphasis is a well recognized linguistic concept and it is not
fficult to find parallels in other languages for the existence of emphatic
rms of negation.

All languages have devices for giving special prominence to one element
 a sentence rather than another. Often this is achieved by means of supra-
gmental features, for example, the sentence stress in English. Whether this
 s so in Old Chinese is impossible to say but we do know that there were
ecial syntactical devices of word order and also special particles and, in

---

[3] Dobson (1959), 42, rejects the fusion equation for *fu* on similar grounds.
[4] 弗者不之深也, commentary on Duke Huang 10/3. Nearly the same words occur
 in under Duke Hsi 26/2. See *Kung-yang chuan chu-shu,* 5/4a and 12/3b.

some cases, word forms used for this purpose. For example, the two forms
the first person pronoun already alluded to are partly distinguished by
positions in which they can occur, but where either one is permitted, as
the subject position before a verb or as possessive in front of a noun, *wo*
more emphatic (Kennedy, 1956). This comes out even more clearly in
case of the *ju-sheng* forms of the demonstrative *shih* 實 , EMC *ʑit* (for *dʑi*
and *shih* 寔 EMC *dʑik*, which are used in the *Shih ching, Tso chuan*, and *K*
yü to recapitulate the subject and give it contrastive emphasis (Pulleybla
1958).[5] The primary function of the *ju-sheng* negatives in -*t* seems to
similar, that is, to give relative prominence to the fact of negation rather th
to what is negated. It is obviously impossible to test this hypothesis on
classical texts. In many cases, even though the meaning in context wou
support such an interpretation, objective criteria are hard to find. In wh
follows I shall concentrate my attention on cases in which such criteria see
to reveal themselves, and especially on cases where the fusion hypothesis
impossible.

One situation in which we might expect emphasis on the negati
particle is where we find the same verb repeated, first in the affirmative a
then in the negative. In such a case the verb, being predictable, gives l
information than the particle. (Compare the contrastive stress on the nou
in "a red chair and a red table" with the contrastive stress on the adjecti
in "a red chair and a blue chair.")

Examples of this kind are:

(1)   公子呂曰：國不堪貳，君將若之何? 欲與大叔，臣請事之; 若弗與
則請除之，無生民心。 (*Tso* 3/Yin 1/3)
"Kung-tzu Lü said, 'The country cannot stand two allegianc
What are you going to do about it? If you wish to give [Chen
to T'ai-shu, I beg to be allowed to serve him. If you do *not* gi
it, then I beg to be allowed to get rid of him, so as not to distu
the people's minds'."

(2)   夫禮樂慈愛，戰所畜 ···· 虢弗畜也。 (*Tso* 73/Chuang 27/fu)
"Rites, music, kindness, and love are what one must cultivate f
the sake of going to war . . . Kuo has *not* cultivated them."

(3)   始，吾敬子。今子魯囚也，吾弗敬子矣。 (*Tso* 59/Chuang 11/4
"Formerly I respected you. Now you are a prisoner in Lu an
respect you no more."

---

[5] In reconstructed forms of Chinese EMC stands for Early Middle Chinese, i.e. my n
reconstruction of the phonology of the *Ch'ieh-yün*. This has not yet been published
detail. A preliminary outline was given in Pulleyblank (1973b).

Note that *fu* could not be understood as *pu chih* in this example, since the object *tzu* is repeated as well as the verb.

(4)   故其好之也一，其弗好之也一。 (*Chuang-tzu* 16/6/19).
"Therefore his liking was one and his not liking was one." (Watson, 79)

It is true that immediately after this we get two parallel cases where *pu* is used instead of *fu*:

其一也一，其不一也一；其一與天爲徒，其不一與人爲徒。
(*Chuang-tzu* 16/6/19-20)
"His being one was one and his not being one was one. In being one, he was acting as a companion of Heaven. In not being one, he was acting as a companion of man." (Watson, 79-80)

This vacillation is difficult to explain on any interpretation of the distinction between *pu* and *fu*. Perhaps all that one can say is that in classical Chinese grammar marked forms are generally optional rather than obligatory.

(5)   泰清以之言也，問乎无始曰：若是則无窮之弗知，與无爲之知，孰
      是而孰非乎？无始曰：不知深矣，知之淺矣；弗知內矣，知之外矣。
      於是泰清卬而歎曰：弗知乃知乎？知乃不知乎？孰知不知之知？
(*Chuang-tzu* 60/22/59)
"Great Purity asked No Beginning about these words, 'In this case which is right and which is wrong—No End's not knowing or No Action's knowing?' No Beginning said, 'Not knowing is deep. Knowing is shallow. Not knowing is inner. Knowing is outer.' Thereupon Great Purity looked up and sighed, saying, 'Is not knowing knowing? Is knowing not knowing? Who knows the knowing of not knowing?' "

Here again one finds *fu* where it is explicitly contrastive, though not to the exclusion of *pu* in apparently identical situations.

Though the verb may not be explicitly repeated, it may be already implicit from the context, so that the negative particle is still the main new element.

(6)   冬十月庚申，改葬惠公，公弗臨，故不書。 (*Tso* 4/Yin 1/*fu* 5)
"In winter, tenth month, on the day *keng-shen* they changed the place of burial of Duke Hui. The duke did *not* look on. Therefore [the historian] did not record it."

The duke ought to have participated in such a ceremony. Note that *c.* could be supplied as object of both the verb *lin* "look on," which is nega* by *fu,* and the verb *shu* "record," which is negated by *pu.*

(7)   遂滅息。以息嬀歸，生堵敖及成王焉。未言，楚子問之，對曰
       一婦人而事二夫，縱弗能死，其又奚言？ (*Tso* 62/Chuang 14/:
       "[The Viscount of Ch'u] went on to overthrow Hsi. He returr
       with the consort of the ruler of Hsi whose surname was Kuei a
       had as children by her Tu Ao and [the future] King Ch'eng. ;
       never spoke. The Viscount of Ch'u asked her why. She said,
       being one woman, have served two husbands. Though I was *
       able to die, how should I venture to speak again?' "

One could supply *chih* as object of *ssu* "die" in the sense of "die someone" but the real explanation for *fu,* rather than *pu,* is probably th though duty called for her death, she did not do so. In the following exam the verb is definitely intransitive and *chih* would not be possible.

(8)   大子曰：吾其廢乎？對曰：⋯且子懼不孝，無懼弗得立。脩己ī
       責人，則免於難。 (*Tso* 84/Min 2/*fu* 2)
       "The Crown Prince said, 'Shall I be set aside?' [Li K'o] repli
       '... Moreover you should be afraid of being unfilial. Do not
       afraid of not coming to the throne. If you cultivate your o
       virtue and do not blame others, you will avoid danger.' "

(9)   今也不然，師行而量食，飢者弗食，勞者弗息。 (*Mencius* 6/1B
       "Now it is not like that. As the royal host moves, provisions ;
       consumed. The hungry do *not* eat and the weary do *not* rest."

The contrast here is with the idealized ancient times when a royal t of inspection allegedly did bring relief to the hungry and weary. One could necessary supply *chih* as object of *shih* "eat," referring to "provisions," this would be somewhat forced. It is more natural to take *shih* as neuter, th is, as having an indefinite object. The second verb, *hsi* "rest," clearly has to intransitive.

It has been noted that *fu* is frequently found with verbs like 許 * "consent," 聽 *t'ing* "listen, agree to," etc. This frequent type of collocati can readily be accommodated in the interpretation of *fu* as an empha negative used when the negation rather than the verb is stressed. The us situation is that a subordinate has made a proposal to a superior. The expec response is either acceptance or refusal and, when it is the latter, it is negative particle which conveys the essential new information.

It is, of course, impossible here to discuss exhaustively all cases of

classical Chinese. One set of examples which deserves special attention is
made up of those which have the final particles *i* 矣, *i* 已, or the combination
已 *yeh i* after a verb negated by *fu*. Of the twenty-two examples which I
find in the *Tso chuan* all, without exception, have intransitive verbs or trans-
tive verbs with an explicit object, so that it is impossible to regard *fu* as
incorporating the pronoun object *chih*. One of these examples has already
been given above—example (3). The rest are given below.

(10) 多行無禮，弗能在矣。 (171/Wen 15/12)
    "Doing many things contrary to ritual requirements, he cannot
    survive."

(11) 弗過之矣。 (187/ Hsüan 6/*fu* 5)
    "He will not live beyond that point."

(12) 自今鄭國不四五年弗得寧矣。 (264/Hsiang 8/3)
    "Within four or five years from now the country of Cheng will
    have no peace."

(13) 必死於此，弗得出矣。 (267/Hsiang 9/3)
    "I will certainly die here. I shall not be able to get out."

(14) 弗能久矣。 (287/Hsiang 18/4)
    "He cannot long hold out."

The same expression occurs in (15) 296/Hsiang 22/*fu* 3, (16) 333/
Hsiang 31/*fu* 1, (17) 344/Chao 1/*fu* 7, (18) 374/Chao 11/4, and (19) 419/
Chao 25/*fu* 4. *Chiu* 久 can be either transitive or intransitive. That is, it can
be followed by *chih*, meaning "to continue it for a long time," or made passive
by *k'o* 可 "is possible," as in example (20). On the other hand there are
thirteen affirmative examples of 能久 "can hold out" in the *Tso chuan* and
no cases of *能久之. There are also three examples of 不能久, none of which
have final 矣.

(20) 不義而克，必以爲道。道以淫虐，弗可久已矣。
    (340/Chao 1/*fu* 1)
    "When he conquers unrighteously, he will certainly make that his
    way. A way that makes use of licentiousness and cruelty cannot
    be long maintained."

In most texts of the classical period, including the *Tso chuan*, it is a
firm rule that *k'o* 可 can only be followed by a passive transitive verb with
the subject of *k'o* as its underlying object. Before intransitive verbs and active
transitive verbs one finds *k'o i* 可以 instead (see Chou Fa-kao, 1950). If *fu*
were equivalent to *pu chih*, one should therefore never find *fu k'o* in examples

(21), (24), (25), (26), (27), (28), (29), and (30). *Fu k'o*, without a followi
已 or 矣, occurs in 417/Chao 25/8 and 423/Chao 27/3.

(21)   弗可爲矣。(360/Chao 6/*fu* 1)
       "It can no longer be done."

(22)   蔡侯般弒其君之歲也，歲在豕韋，弗過此矣。(374/Chao 11/4)
       "It is [the return of] the year in which Pan, Marquis of Ts'a
       murdered his ruler. The year star is in the constellation Shih-we
       He will not survive past this."

(23)   歸，弗來矣。(377/Chao 12/4)
       "When he returns, he will not come again."

(24)   雖賤，必書地以名其人，終爲不義，弗可滅已。(433/Chao 31/6
       "Though he was of low rank, it was necessary to record th
       territory and therewith to name the man, so that in the end h
       unrighteous act could not be obliterated."

(25)   弗可改也已。(98/Hsi 7/3)
       "[His nature] cannot be changed."

(26)   天之棄商久矣，君將興之，弗可赦也已。(119/Hsi 22/4)
       "Heaven has long abandoned Shang. You intend to raise it u
       again but its offense cannot be pardoned."

(27)   政亡，則國家從之，弗可止也已。(211/Ch'eng 2/2)
       "When the government perishes, the state will follow it. It cannc
       be stopped."

(28)   若由是二者，弗可爲也已。(344/Chao 1/*fu* 7)
       "If [his illness] has arisen from these two causes, nothing can b
       done about it."

(29)   以楊楯賈禍，弗可爲也已。(499/Ting 6/5)
       "You have purchased misfortune with those poplar shields
       Nothing can be done about it."

(30)   寡君以爲苟有盟焉，弗可改也已。(484/Ai 12/3)
       "Our ruler considers that if a treaty has been made with them, i
       cannot be changed."

The final particle *i* 矣, like modern *le* 了, is primarily aspectual i
meaning. That is, it is used when an action is looked upon as already ac
complished or when a new state or situation has arisen or will have arisen. I
can at the same time convey emphasis by vividly presenting a situatior

ecially a future situation, as already accomplished rather than merely tential. It is not surprising, therefore, to find other emphatic words, such the emphatic negative particles, associated with it.

The form *i* 已, which occurs both as a full verb "to stop, finish" and as inal particle, is cognate, though not identical, with *i* 矣. It occurs, especially comparatively early texts like the *Tso chuan* and the *Lun-yü*, after *yeh* 也 here *i* 矣 is excluded) and sometimes alone, as if replacing *yeh i* 也已, in ces where *yeh* 也 would be possible.

Examples of *fu* followed by these particles, similar to those in the *o chuan,* are found in other texts as well. It is remarkable how many of em have intransitive verbs or verbs with explicit objects.

(31) 壺子曰：追之。列子追之不及，反以報壺子，曰：已滅矣，已失矣，吾弗及已。 (*Chuang-tzu* 20/7/27)

"Hu-tzu said, 'Pursue him.' Lieh-tzu pursued him but did not catch up to him. He returned and told Hu-tzu, 'He's vanished! He's lost! I could not catch up with him!' "

Note that in the narrative we have simply *pu chi* 不及 but in the words of Lieh-tzu, where the matter is reported vividly and with emphasis, we have *fu chi i* 弗及已.

(32) 出而謂列子曰：嘻！子之先生死矣，弗活矣。
(*Chuang-tzu* 20/7/20)

"He came out and said to Lieh-tzu, 'Ah! Your master is dead! He is no longer alive!' "

(33) 故曰：正者正也，其心以爲不然者，天門弗開矣。
(*Chuang-tzu* 38/14/55)

"Therefore it is said, 'The corrector must be correct. If the mind cannot accept this fact, then the doors of Heaven will never open.' " (Watson, 162)

(34) 惡乎至？有以爲未始有物者，至矣，盡矣，弗可以加矣。
(*Chuang-tzu* 63/23/58)

"How far did it go? To the point where some of them believed that things have never existed—so far, to the end where nothing can be added." (Watson, 257)

(35) 其得罪於君也，將弗久矣。 (*Chuang-tzu* 26/24/54)

"It would be no time at all before he did something you considered unpardonable." (Watson, 269)

(36) 子曰：君子博學於文，約之以禮，亦可以弗畔矣夫。
(*Lun-yü* 11/6/27. See also 23/12/15)

"The Master said, 'A gentleman who is widely versed in lett(
and at the same time knows how to submit his learning to t(
restraints of ritual is not likely, I think, to go far wrong.' " (Wal(
121)

(37) 獲於上有道，不信於友弗獲於上矣；信於友有道，事親弗說，弗
於友矣。 (*Mencius* 28/4A/13)

"There is a way to be accepted by one's superiors. If one is n(
trusted by one's friends, one will not be accepted by one's s(
periors. There is a way to be trusted by one's friends. If, in servi(
one's parents, one does not give them pleasure, one will not
trusted by one's friends."

It must be noted that in the continuation of this passage (
twice find *pu . . . i* in phrases that are apparently quite parallel
the above examples with *fu . . . i.* In the latter cases the verbs a(
active, while in the former they are passive, but I have no theo(
to offer as to why this should lead to the use of different negati(
particles. What is very clear is that the use of *fu* in front of passi(
verbs is quite inconsistent with the fusion hypothesis.

(38) 雖與之俱學，弗若之矣。 (*Mencius* 44/6A/9)

"Though he studies along with him, he does not come up to him(

(39) 得一善，則拳拳服膺，而弗失之矣。 (*Chung-yung* 8)

"When he got hold of one good thing, he clasped it firmly to h(
bosom and did not lose it."

(40) 子曰：素隱行怪，後世有述焉，吾弗爲之矣。君子遵道而行，半
而廢，吾弗能已矣。 (*Chung-yung* 11)

"The Master said, 'To live in obscurity, and practice wonders,
order to be talked about in future ages—I will not do that.
gentleman, proceeding along the right path, may abandon it ha(
way—but I cannot stop.' "

In not more than one or two of these examples would it be possible (
interpret *fu* as incorporating an object pronoun. Instead we find the obje(
pronoun *chih* explicitly present between the verb and the final particle
three cases where it is required, as in example (11) above from the *Tso chua(*
In the *Lun-yü* we also find a number of examples in which *chih* appears befo(
the final particle *i* after verbs negated by *pu.* 吾不欲觀之矣 (4/3/10), 聖人(
不得而見之矣…善人吾不得而見之矣(13/7/26), 吾不知之矣 (15/8/16), 出三(
不食之矣(18/10/6). I have not found similar examples of *pu . . . chih i* (
other texts but there are also very few examples of *pu . . . i* in which *ch(*

uld be supplied as the understood object. It would appear, therefore, that
ıe must posit a general rule inhibiting the deletion of *chih* after a negated
:rb when followed by the particle *i.*

Such a rule will also account for some of the cases that have been noted
ɪ Lü Shu-hsiang and others in which we find *chih* between *fu* and the verb
negates, in many of which we find final *i.* Though there are also a few
:amples of *fu* + *chih* + verb without final *i,* it seems clear that we should
ɛk to explain all such cases in terms of the failure to delete *chih* rather than
 showing the incomplete fusion of *pu* with *chih,* as Lü Shu-hsiang has
ıggested—something like 不之 **p∂* **t∂* → 弗之 **p∂t-***t∂* → 弗 **p∂t.* Lü's
ıggestion is phonetically quite plausible but could not be applied to cases in
hich *chih* appears *after* a verb negated by *fu.*

The case of *wu* 勿 is largely parallel to that of *fu* and will not be
lustrated in detail here. The most important difference appears to be that,
hile both *pu* and *fu* are common in situations where *chih* has been deleted,
u 毋 (or 無) is comparatively rare in such situations. Nevertheless *wu* 勿,
ke *fu* 弗, does occur in front of intransitive verbs or transitive verbs with the
bject expressed, so that unless óne arbitrarily explains away all such examples
s the result of textual corruption the fusion hypothesis will not work. The
orrespondence between *fu* and *wu* emerges very clearly in the pattern with
nal *i.* The rule against the deletion of *chih* applies here also and in such cases
ᴴih mostly appears after the verb, in spite of which we find 勿 rather than
丰 or 無 .

(41) 人皆謂我毀明堂，毀諸已乎？…王欲行王政，則勿毀之矣。
    (*Mencius* 6/1B/5)
    "People all tell me to destroy my Hall of Light. Shall I destroy it,
    or let it be? . . . 'If your Majesty intends to put into practice
    Kingly government, then don't destroy it.' "

    Note that the use of the emphatic negative is appropriate
    here because the verb *hui* "destroy" is repeated and the question
    is one of affirmation or negation.

(42) 請勿敢復見矣。 (*Mencius* 17/2B/11)
    "Please let me not again venture to see you."

    One could perhaps understand *chih* as omitted object here,
    referring to second person, but it is not certain that the passage
    must be construed in that way. Another possible interpretation
    would be to construe the verb as passive, ". . . venture to be seen."

(43) 勿言之矣。 (*Chuang-tzu* 11/4/67)
    "Don't say it."

(44) 君若勿已矣。 (*Chuang-tzu* 65/24/24)
"If you are not going to stop . . "

In discussing this passage, Graham pointed out that the ve~
i "stop" can be either transitive or intransitive, but here it is mo~
natural to take it as intransitive.

(45) 勿問之矣。 (*I ching* 26/42)
"Do not ask about it."

Compare also 勿聽之也 (without final 矣) in the *Chan-kuo ts'e* 8 and 勿
之有悔焉耳矣 (with *chih* between the negative and the verb) in the *Li ch*
T'an-kung 檀弓, cited by Lü Shu-hsiang (1941, p. 20).

Even if we decide that *fu* and *wu* 勿 were primarily emphatic forms ~
pu and *wu* 毋 respectively, it remains true, as many scholars from von d~
Gabelentz onward have observed, that there is a high (though imperfec~
correlation between their use and situations in which an underlying *chi*
which has been deleted can be inferred. How are we to account for this?
have no fully adequate explanation to offer but it seems evident that it is
question that must be studied in a larger context than simply that of th~
negative particles. We need to know much more about the rules for th~
deletion of *chih*. How can we, for example, account in terms of a gener~
theory of Chinese sentence structure for the previously unsuspected rule tha~
we have revealed about the non-deletion of *chih* before the final particle ~
Perhaps it has something to do with prosodic features—the rhythms o~
speech. But these are matters that are very difficult to investigate in a dea~
language.

Perhaps one can account for the tendency to use the emphatic negative
when a deleted *chih* can be understood, at least in part, by the fact that, if
transitive verb is already given in the context or is predictable from th~
context, situations in which, we have suggested, emphasis is likely to be shifte~
to the negative particle, the object of the verb will also very likely be alread~
given in the context. Conversely, if the object is not predictable and henc~
replaceable by a pronoun, the verb and object together are more likely to b~
more important in terms of information content than the negative particle
This would not account for an absence of the emphatic negatives in front o~
intransitive verbs, but, as we have seen, there is really no such absence in a~
absolute sense and it has not even been demonstrated that there is a signifi~
cant relative rarity.

Lü Shu-hsiang's theory that, though not originally fusion words, th~
emphatic negatives came to be interpreted as such at a certain period, has ~
certain plausibility but it is difficult to test, and even he assumes that th~

lder emphatic meaning must have survived at the same time.

Two other negatives ending in *-t* have been largely ignored by modern
nguists. They are comparatively rare and each is confined to certain texts.
ieh 蔑, EMC *met,* occurs principally in the *Tso chuan* and *Kuo-yü.* The
ollowing examples include all those in the *Tso chuan* and those that have
een noted in the *Kuo-yü,* excluding cases where it is an active verb meaning
destroy" or "despise" (懱).

(46) 君納重耳，蔑不濟矣。(*Tso* 104/Hsi 10/*fu*)
   "If you then restore Ch'ung-erh, everything will be successful."
      A more literal rendering of the last phrase would be "there
   will be no not succeeding."

(47) 雖我小國，則蔑以過之矣。(*Tso* 174/Wen 17/5)
   "Though ours is a small state, [others] have no means to surpass
   it."

(48) 夫狄焉思啓封疆以利社稷者，何國蔑有？(*Tso* 227/Ch'eng 8/*fu*)
   "What country does *not* have those who craftily think to enlarge
   its boundaries in order to benefit the altars of land and grain?"

(49) 封疆之肖，何國蔑有？(*Tso* 340/Chao 1/3)
   "What country does *not* have [concerns about] encroachments
   on its borders?"

(50) 寧事齊楚，有亡而已，蔑從晉矣。(*Tso* 245/Ch'eng 16/12)
   "We had better serve Ch'i or Ch'u. [If we go on] there is only
   destruction. We should no longer follow Chin."

(51) 我斃蔑也，而事晉，蔑有貳矣。(*Tso* 245/Ch'eng 16/12)
   "I will kill Mieh, and serve Chin with no wavering."

(52) 有死而已，吾蔑從之矣。(*Tso* 293/Hsiang 21/4)
   "There is only death [by which I can respond]. I will *not* follow
   him."

(53) 雖甚盛德，其蔑以加於此矣。(*Tso* 327/Hsiang 29/8)
   "Even the most ample virtue would surely have nothing to add
   to this."

(54) 其蔑以復矣。(*Tso* 338/Chao 5/*fu* 1)
   "He will surely have no way to return."

(55) 其蔑不濟矣。(*Tso* 358/Chao 5/*fu* 1)

"Surely they will be completely successful."

(56) 若使先濟者知免，後者慕之，蔑有鬬心矣。 (*Tso* 445/Ting 4/16)
"If you let the first ones who cross know that they can escape
the rest will be anxious to follow in their footsteps, and will have
no will to fight."

(57) 吾有死而已，蔑從之矣。 (*Kuo-yü* 8.8b, p. 71a)
"Death would be my only recourse. I will not follow them."
(Compare examples 50 and 52 above.)

(58) 然後用之，蔑不欲矣。 (*Kuo-yü* 10.20a, p. 89a)
"If afterwards you try to employ them, they will no longer be
unwilling."

(59) 始與善，善進善，不善蔑由至矣；始與不善，不善進不善，善亦
由至矣。 (*Kuo-yü* 12.1b, p. 96a)
"If you begin with good men, the good will advance the good and
the bad will have no way to get there. If you begin with bad, the
bad will advance the bad and the good likewise will have no way
to get there."

(60) 君苟輔我，蔑天命矣。 (*Kuo-yü* 8.13b, p. 73b)
"If only you will assist me, we shall no longer lay claim to the
mandate of Heaven."

(61) 自此其父之死，吾蔑與比而事君矣。 (*Kuo-yü* 14.8a, p. 108a)
"Since the death of this one's father, I have no one with whom
to stand side by side and serve my lord."

(62) 天占既兆，人事又見，我蔑卜筮矣。 (*Kuo-yü* 19.13a, p. 142b)
"Heaven's omens are revealed and the human situation is also
apparent. Let us take no more oracles from the yarrow stalks."

(63) 包胥曰：善哉。蔑以加焉。 (*Kuo-yü* 19.14b, p. 143a)
"Pao Hsü said, 'Good! There is nothing to add to it.' "

There is also a single occurrence in the genuine chapters of the *Shu ching*.

(64) 文王蔑德，降于國人。 (*Shu ching, Chün shih* 13)
"Wen Wang would have had no virtue to send down on the state's
people." (Karlgren, 61)

According to some interpretations *mieh* is the negative particle also in
the phrase 蔑資 which occurs in *Shih ching* 254.5 and 257.3, meaning "here
are no resources." Others, however interpret it here as "destroy" or "despise."
In all these examples *mieh* could be replaced by *wu* 無, either in the

se of the negative verb "not have" or as a preverbal negative particle. In
o cases, (60) and (64), it has a noun object, to which may be added the
o *Shih ching* examples if they are accepted. It must also be construed as a
rb in those examples where it is followed by *i* 以, meaning "not have
ereby to . . . ." Compare the common constructions *yu i* "have whereby
. . . ," *wu i* "not have whereby to . . . ." Examples (59) and (61) are quite
nilar to this except that the preposition verbs *yü* 與 "accompany; with"
d *yu* 由 "follow along; from" replace *i* 以 "use; by means of." *Mieh* is no
ubt also to be construed as a verb in examples (46), (55), and (58), where
is followed by a verb negated by *pu.* Compare 事無不濟 (*Tso* 388/Chao
/5). In the remaining cases, where it is directly in front of a full verb, it is
s obvious that one should interpret *mieh* as "not have" rather than simply
a particle of negation but it shares this ambiguity with *wu.* Note especially
e cases of 蔑有 in (48), (49), (51), and (56) and compare 無有, which occurs
ne nine times in the *Tso chuan.*

Apart from its denotative equivalence to *wu* 無, the association of
ieh with emphatic statements should be obvious from these examples. Note
pecially the frequent association with the final particle *i* 矣, which is similar
what has been noted in the case of 弗 and 勿 .

The examples of *mo* that resemble *mieh* are found in the *Lun-yü* and
-tzu.

(65) 雖欲從之，末由也已。 (*Lun-yü* 16/9/11. Quoted in *Shih chi* 47
      [Takigawa edition, p. 79] with 蔑 instead of 末.) "Yet though I
      long to pursue it, I can find no way of getting it at all." (Waley,
      140. Literally: "I have no along which.")

(66) 說而不繹，從而不改，吾末如之何也已矣。 (*Lun-yü* 17/9/24)
      "For those who approve but do not carry out, who are stirred,
      but do not change, I can do nothing at all." (Waley, 143)

(67) 子曰：不曰如之何，如之何者，吾末如之何也已矣。
      (*Lun-yü* 31/15/16)
      "If a man does not continually ask himself, 'What am I to do
      about this, what am I to do about this,' there is no possibility of
      my doing anything about him." (Waley, 196)

(68) 果哉！末之難矣。 (*Lun-yü* 30/14/39)
      "How bold! He makes no difficulty in it."
          I take *nan* as transitive 'to regard as difficult with *chih* as
      its object. I believe this is a better interpretation than Waley's
      "That is indeed an easy way out," or Legge's, "How determined
      is he in his purpose! But this is not difficult!"

(69) 子路不說曰：末之也已，何必公山氏之之也。(*Lun-yü* 35/17/4)
"Tzu-lu was displeased and said, 'When there was no one y·
would go to, why must you go to Kung-shan?"
   Compare Waley, p. 210 "After having refused in so ma
cases, why go to Kung-shan of all people?"

(70) 吾末予子酒矣。(*Mo-tzu* 87/48/65)
"We will *not* [as we promised] give you wine!"

The similarity to *mieh* is obvious. In examples (65), (66), and (67) *m*
could be replaced by *wu* "not have" as far as the denotative meaning
concerned. In (68), (69), and (70) it comes directly in front of a verb as
negative particle, with the kind of absolute, existential negation that
associated with the *m*- series, as opposed to the *p*- series. This is like the cor·
sponding examples of *mieh*. Compare (57) "I will no longer (*mieh*) follc
him" and (70) "we will not [as we promised] give you wine." Note also th·
in all these examples *mo* is followed by 矣 or 也已(矣). The close similari·
in meaning and construction between *mieh* and *mo* and the fact that th·
never occur in the same texts suggests that they are dialectal forms of the sam·
word. This suggestion is strengthened by the fact that we actually find *mi·*
substituted for *mo* in example (65) from the *Lun-yü* as quoted in *Shih chi* 4

A few additional examples of *mo* as a negative particle allegedly occ·
in the *Li chi*, the *Kung-yang chuan*, and the *Lü-shih ch'un-ch'iu* but these a·
all rather different from the ones we have been discussing.[6] In most of t·
cases *mo* 末 appears to be equivalent in meaning to *wei* 未 and could easi·
be merely a graphic error for the latter. In one passage in the *Wen Wang shi·*
tzu 文王世子 section of the *Li chi* it seems to be equivalent to 勿 "do not.·
This is of interest for the present study but can hardly be relied upon since
is an isolated example. Similarly isolated is *mo pu i* . . . 末不亦 "Is it not th·
. . ." as a rhetorical question formula in *Kung-yang chuan* 487/Ai 14/1.

MORPHOLOGY

Though *fu* 弗 was never semantically equivalent to a fusion of *pu ch·*
不之, the hypothesis that it was formed from *pu* by the addition of a suffix·
element -*t* works very well phonetically. This is somewhat obscured in Ka·
gren's Archaic reconstruction, since he has *piŭg* for 不 and *piwət* for 弗 Th·
final -*g* is, however, quite problematical. If there was a final consonant in th·
rhyme group in question, it was probably a weak fricative - ð or a semivocal·
glide -*i*, Moreover, as far as the head vowel is concerned, words in -*iŭg* belon·

[6]See Yang (1928), 27; and Ōno (1968), 305.

the *əg* rhyme group and the hypothetical *-ŭ-* is posited to account for later ∙und changes. My own reconstruction departs from Karlgren's in other ∙spects also, since I eliminate his medial *yod -i-* already at the Middle Chinese ∙ge giving *puw* instead of *pi̯ə̆u*. In Old Chinese I reconstruct this as **pə̀*, the ∙al glide being left unwritten since it was an automatic feature found when ∙ere was no other consonant or glide in this position. The grave accent ∙presents one of two possible prosodic features that are assumed to have ∙aracterized all syllables in Old Chinese. It is the feature which gave rise to ∙ade III type syllables in the Chinese rhyme table phonology, which Karl- ∙en reconstructed with medial *-i-* and for which I reconstruct high tense ∙wels *-i-*, *-i-*, *-u-*, in Early Middle Chinese, *-i-*, *-y-* in Late Middle Chinese.[7] ∙ccording to the same principles 弗 would be Old Chinese **pə̀t*.

The phonological analysis of the relation between 勿 and 毋 is a little ∙ore complicated. In Middle Chinese 毋 was identical in pronunciation with ∙. Karlgren has *mi̯u*, which I would revise to EMC *mua* (phonetically [*muo*] [*muə*] because of the effect on the nuclear vowel *-a-* of the preceding ∙nse medial *-u-*), Karlgren also gives the same Archaic reconstruction for ∙th forms, namely *mi̯wo*. As other scholars have pointed out, however, ∙arlgren's *-o* rhyme group is not to be separated from his *-ag̑* group. As far as ∙e final consonant is concerned, the same remarks apply as in the case of the ∙g group and my Old Chinese reconstruction corresponding to Karlgren's ∙i̯wo is **mà*. On the other hand 勿, which rhymes with 弗 in both Middle ∙d Old Chinese, implies Old Chinese **mə̀t*. If one, wishes to account for **mə̀t* ∙ a parallel formation to **pə̀t*, one requires a form **mə̀* as the primitive to ∙hich the suffix *-t* was added. This would yield EMC *muw*, corresponding to ∙i̯ə̆u in Karlgren's system, instead of the attested *mua* (Karlgren *mi̯u*).

What is no doubt the solution to this dilemma has been pointed out by ∙.F. Mulder (1959). Though 毋 and 無 were regarded as homophonous in ∙iddle Chinese and had, indeed, become interchangeable already in Late ∙ou texts, there is good reason to believe that they were originally distinct. ∙raphically 毋 is merely a variant of 母 EMC *mow'* (Karlgren *mə̯u*), which ∙rlier rhymed in Karlgren's *-əg* group. It seems likely, therefore, that it was ∙iginally read **mə̀*, being an ablaut alternant of 無 **mà*. Later **mə̀* became ∙solete as a spoken form, being replaced by **mà*, and the pronunciation ∙à was transferred to the graph 毋 in reading tradition also. (Karlgren notes

---

[7]Arguments to show that Karlgren's *yod* was of secondary origin and should be ∙minated from the phonology of Old Chinese were given in Pulleyblank (1961). At that ∙ne I postulated vowel length as the distinguishing feature which later gave rise to it. Pulleyblank (1970-71) reasons are given for eliminating it at the Middle Chinese stage. ∙e theory that the distinction in question originated from an accentual opposition is ∙umbrated in Pulleyblank (1973).

in *Grammata serica recensa,* no. 107, that a reading *mi̯ŭu,* i.e. EMC *muw,* w
preserved for the character in a special usage as part of the name of a type
ritual cap.)

We can thus posit precisely the same morphological relationship betwee
*mə̀t and **mə̀* as between **pə̀t* and **pə̀* and this allows us to posit a suff
*-t which could be added to negative particles. The semantic effect of th
suffix was evidently to give prominence to the negation as such, rather tha
to what was negated. Can this same morpheme be recognized in *mieh,* EM
met and *mo,* EMC *mat?*

The form to which the suffix was presumably added in this case w
*mà 無. As we have seen, *mieh* and *mo* can be looked on as strong forms
wu < **ma,* so the proposed derivation works very well semantically. Phonet
cally there are still problems, however. In the case of *mo,* which we m
reconstruct as Old Chinese *mát,* the only obstacle is the "acute" prosod
which was responsible for the Grade I vowel in Middle Chinese. While I hav
no explanation to offer for the shift from "grave" to "acute" in the deriv
form, one can at least say that alternations of the same kind are found qui
commonly in word formation in Old Chinese, both in grammatical particl
and in full words. Compare, for example, 安 EMC *ʔan* < **ʔán* "how, where
and 焉 EMC *ʔɨan* < **ʔàn* (Karlgren *ˈɨän* < *ˈɨän*), which are clearly variants
one another, or 莫 EMC *mak* < **mâk,* "no one, nothing," which is anoth
derivative of *wu* "not have."

The front vowel in 蔑 EMC *met* presents more of a difficulty. Karlgre
reconstructs Archaic *miat.* I suspect that the fronting of the vowel is actuall
to be attributed to a prefix, though there is insufficient evidence to reco
struct its exact form. One could provisionally posit a form **C^j mát,* whe
C^j represents a palatal or palatalized consonant. The question then aris
whether this reconstruction applies to all meanings associated with the chara
ter or, perhaps, only to the meaning "destroy," as with the cognate word 滅
EMC *mjiat* "destroy" < **C^j mat.* Since the negative particle written with th
character was probably already obsolete in speech in Late Chou times, it
quite possible that, as with 毋, the true reading has been lost. The expecte
form to be derived from **mà* + **-t* would be **màt,* giving EMC *muat,* Moder
Mandarin *wa.* It is worth noting that the character now read *mieh* is in fa
phonetic in 韈 *wa,* EMC *muat* < **màt* (Karlgren *mi̯uɐt* < *mi̯wăt*). Thoug
corroborative evidence is lacking, I suspect that, as a negative particle 蔑
should also be read **wa* rather than *mieh.*

Ōno Tōru, one of the few grammarians to discuss *mieh* and *mo,* als
recognizes them to be variants of one another and to be emphatic equivalen
of *wu.* Etymologically, he derives them from the verb *mieh* "destroy."
seems to me, however, that all the **m-* negatives must be derivatives of th

ne root and that the meaning of existential negation is primary rather than
:ondary. *Mieh* "annihilate, destroy" (i.e. "cause to be nothing") in both its
d Chinese forms, *C^jmát* and *C^jmàt*, is to be recognized as a derivative of
s same root rather than the other way around. The other full meaning of
e character "despise" represents a closely related semantic extension of the
ne root, i.e. "regard as nothing." Other full words derived from this root
:lude: 亡 *wang*, EMC *muaŋ* < *màŋ*, "disappear, die, lose," which is cer-
nly very closely related to *wu* "not have," the graph 亡 being the earliest
ıy of writing this latter meaning; *wang* 忘 EMC *muaŋ* < *màŋ* "forget";
ɔ 沒 EMC *mot* < *mət* "disappear, die, drown." More remote connections
ıy be suspected with the extensive word families with initial *m- and the
neral meaning "small" and "dark." I shall not explore these here however.

Other important questions that are left for further study are the exact
ations on the one hand, between the forms *mə̀* and *mà* as negative
rticles and, on the other hand, between *mà* as a negative particle and *mà*
the verb "not have."

SUMMARY

A morpheme *-t is posited for the earliest stages of Old Chinese which
uld be added to negative particles, as follows:

$$*pə̀ \; 不 \; + -t \longrightarrow \; *pə̀t \; 弗$$

$$*mə̀ \; 毋 \; + -t \longrightarrow \; *mə̀t \; 勿$$

$$*mà \; 無 \; + -t \; {\longrightarrow \; *màt \; 蔑 \atop \longrightarrow \; *mát \; 末}$$

ıe forms in -t differed from corresponding forms without -t in the degree of
ıphasis that was placed on the negation as such. The coincidence that this
ffix *-t was phonetically the same as the initial consonant of *chih* 之, EMC
: < *tə̀ may possibly have led in the Late Chou period to a greater tendency
r the use of *pə̀t and *mə̀t in cases where *tə̀ could have been inserted but
ey were never confined to such situations. The forms *màt and *mát,
ıich seem to have been dialectal variants of one another, both died out well
fore the end of the Chou period. *mə̀ also died out, being replaced by *mà,
ıt the corresponding strong form remained *mə̀t. *pə̀t and *mə̀t persisted
d from Han times onward drove out the corresponding less emphatic forms
the spoken language.

REFERENCES

References for examples from the *Chuang-tzu*, *I ching*, *Lun-yü*, *Kur yang chuan*, *Mencius*, *Mo-tzu*, *Shih ching* and *Tso* [*chuan*] are to the Harva Yenching Indexes. For the *Kuo-yü* reference is made to the *Ssu-pu ts'ung-k* edition in the Taiwan photographic reprint in Western binding. For the *Sr ching* reference is made to Karlgren (1950). For the *Chung-yung* reference made to J. Legge, *The Chinese classics*, Vol. I, reprinted by Hong Kong U versity Press. Translations are the author's except where otherwise indicatec

Boodberg, Peter A. (1937). "Some proleptical remarks on the evolution Archaic Chinese," *HJAS*, 2, 329-72.

Chou Fa-kao 周法高 (1950). "Shang-ku yü-fa cha-chi" 上古語法札記 , *CYY* 22, 171-207.

Dobson, W.A.C.H. (1959). *Late Archaic Chinese.* Toronto.

Gabelentz, Georg von der (1881). *Chinesische grammatik.* Leipzig. Reprir Berlin; Deutsche Verlag der Wissenschaften, 1953.

Graham, A. C. (1952). "A probable fusion word: 勿 *wuh* = 毋 *wu* + 之 *jy* *BSOAS*, 14, 139-48.

Huang Ching-hsin 黃景欣 (1958). "Ch'in Han i-ch'ien ku Han-yü chung ti fo ting tz'u 'fu' 'pu' yen-chiu" 秦漢以前古漢語中的否定詞弗不研究, *Yuy yanjiu*, 3, 1-24.

Karlgren, Bernhard (1950). "The book of documents," *BMFEA*, 22, 1-81.

_____ (1957). "Grammata serica recensa," *BMFEA*, 29, 1-332.

Kennedy, George A. (1956). "Tsai lun wu wo" 再論吾我, *CYYY*, 28, 273-8 Reprinted in *Selected works of George A. Kennedy* (New Haven: Ya University, 1964), 434-42.

Lü Shu-hsiang 呂叔湘 (1941). "Lun wu yü wu" 論毋與勿 , *Studia Serica*, 4 Reprinted in *Han-yü yü-fa lun-wen chi* 漢語語法論文集 (Shanghai, 195. 12-35.

Mulder, J.W.F. (1959). "On the morphology of the negatives in Archa Chinese," *T'oung Pao*, 47, 251-80.

Ōno Tōru 大野透 (1968). *Kambumpō no sogenteki kenkyū* 漢文法の溯源的 究 , I. Tokyo: Sōundō shoten.

Pulleyblank, E. G. (1960). "Studies in Early Chinese grammar," *Asia Maje* 8, 36-67.

_____ (1962). "The consonantal system of Old Chinese," *Asia Major*, 58-114 and 206-65.

_____ (1970-71). "Late Middle Chinese," *Asia Major*, 15, 197-239; 1 121-68.

_____ (1973a). "Some new hypotheses concerning word families Chinese," *Journal of Chinese Linguistics*, 1, 111-25.

_____ (1973b). "Linguistic evidence for the date of Han-shan," paper presented to the International Congress of Orientalists, Paris.

ng Sheng-shu 丁聲樹 (1935). "Shih fou-ting tz'u fu pu"釋否定詞弗不, in *Ch'ing-chu Ts'ai Yüan-p'ei hsien-sheng liu-shih-wu sui lun-wen chi* 慶祝蔡元培先生六十五歲論文集, II (1935), 967-96.

ıley, Arthur (1938). *The analects of Confucius.* London: Allen and Unwin.

ıtson, Burton (1968). *The complete works of Chuang-tzu.* New York and London: Columbia University Press.

ıng Shu-ta 楊樹達 (1928). *Tz'u ch'üan*詞詮. Shanghai: Commercial Press.

What *did* the master say?

Göran Malmqvist

INTRODUCTION

Kung-yang commentary contains six statements which have been attri
ed to Confucius. One of these is found in the first entry under the 12th
 of Duke Chao, where the *Ch'un-ch'iu* states as follows: "In the 12th
, in Spring, Kao Yen of Ch'i led an army and introduced the earl of
thern Yen into Yang." *Kung-yang*: "What is meant by [the three words]
ü yang 伯于陽 ? It was Kung-tzu Yang Sheng. The master said: 'I was already
re of that.' Someone present said: 'Since you were aware of this, why did
 not correct it?' [The Master] said: 'What about that which you do not
w? The *Ch'un-ch'iu* is so faithful to historical facts that the [relative]
r [of the feudal lords] is [that established by Duke] Huan of Ch'i and
ke] Wen of Chin and that [the order in which the princes are listed at]
tings is that determined by the president of the meeting. As for the
ressions [of praise and blame?], I, Ch'iu, am the guilty one.'" (376/12/1)[1]

Four statements attributed to Confucius are found in the very last
y of the *Kung-yang* which relates the capture of a *lin* 麟 : " ... The *lin* is a
evolent beast. When there is a true king it appears. When there is no true
 it does not appear. Someone informed [Master K'ung] of this, saying:
re is a fallow-deer and it is horned!' Master K'ung said: 'For whose sake
 it come? For whose sake has it come?' He turned his sleeves and wiped
face. Tears wet his robe. When Yen Yüan died the Master said: 'Alas!
ven has caused me this loss!' When Tzu Lu died the Master said: 'Alas!
ven is cutting me off!' When a *lin* was captured in a hunt in the west
ter K'ung said: 'My way has come to an end!' " (487/14/1)

The remaining statement attributed to the Master serves as a comment on

All references to the *Kung-yang* are to the text of the *Harvard-Yenching sinological*
x series.

a vivid account of the meeting at Yeh-ching, when the marquis of Ch'i c
doled with Duke Chao of Lu, who in the 25th year of his reign (517 B
was forced to leave his state after an abortive attempt at ousting the *de fa*
ruler of Lu, the head of the powerful Chi clan. The account of the ri
which was observed at the meeting and which moved both the particip:
and the spectators to tears concludes as follows: "When they had finis
crying they placed men to serve as a fence, used a chariot-cover as a mat
a saddle as a table. Thus they met in accordance with the rites proper
chance meeting. Master K'ung said: (1) '*Ch'i li yü ch'i tz'u tsu kuan i* 其
其辭足觀矣.' " (416/25/7)

The comment attributed to Confucius has been variously interpre
K'ung Kuang-sen (1752-1786), a descendant of Confucius in the sevent
generation and one of the greatest *Kung-yang* scholars of the Ch'ing peri
paraphrases as follows: (2) 是禮也與？乃若其辭則有足觀矣。譏昭公不知
之本而威儀文辭是亟，故不能以禮爲國致有此辱也。 "Were these the [prop
rites? As regards the speeches they were quite impressive. [The *Ch'un-ch*
criticizes Duke Chao for excelling in decorum and elegant speech while h
the same time was ignorant of the basic tenets of ritual. His inability
govern his state in accordance with *li* therefore brought about this hur
ation." (*Ch'un-ch'iu Kung-yang t'ung-i,* sub Chao 25). This interpretatio
followed by Ch'en Li (1809-1869) in his monumental work *Kung-yang i-sl*

A present-day student of the *Kung-yang* may disagree with this
terpretation. But considering the awe-inspiring authority of the two grea
Kung-yang scholars of the Ch'ing period he had better examine his data be
rejecting their interpretation. Even the slightest acquaintance with the *Ki*
yang would make him aware of the presence in the text of certain grammat
and stylistic idiosyncrasies which markedly deviate from the dictates of
mative grammars of classical Chinese.

The correct interpretation of the passage obviously hinges on
function of the form *yü* 與 . K'ung Kuang-sen and Ch'en Li treat it as an
ponent of the interrogative sentence suffix. William Hung and his assoc:
editors of the Harvard-Yenching Index text indicate, by their punctuati
that the graph here serves as a marker of coordination.

Since Master Kung-yang is no longer available we shall have to use
text—and the entire text—as our informant. By observing all occurrer
of the graph the investigator may—and again may not—uncover data wh
will help him to determine the function of the graph in the relevant pass:
If he does—so much the better. If he does not, he will at least, in the pro
of his investigation, have observed certain grammatical usages and sema
distinctions which otherwise might have eluded him.

An exhaustive investigation of this kind which requires a full account

and a description of each occurrence of a particular graph is bound to
~~d~~ much information the presentation of which may seem extrinsic to the
~~ler~~. At the same time it is bound to raise questions the answers to which
~~v~~hile falling outside the immediate frame of reference—may prove useful
determining the grammatical and semantic idiosyncrasies of the text. The
~~1~~ity of such observations may eventually prove useful for the dating of
text and for determining its relation to other texts.

~~'~~HE FUNCTIONS AND MEANING OF THE GRAPH *YÜ* IN THE *KUNG-YANG*

~~T~~he interrogative sentence suffix *yü*[2]

~~1~~. *Yü* in the pattern "*Ch'i chu* x *yü*?" "Could this perhaps be x?"

(3) *Tzu Kung-yang tzu yüeh*: "*Ch'i chu i ping Huan yü*?"　子公羊子
曰：其諸以病桓與？"Our Master Kung-yang says: 'Could this
[entry] perhaps be meant as an embarrassment to [Duke]
Huan?'" (33/6/5)

(4) *Tzu Ju tzu yüeh*: "*I Ch'un-ch'iu wei Ch'un-ch'iu. Ch'i wu Chung-
sun. Ch'i chu wu Chung-sun yü*?" 子女子曰：以春秋爲春秋。齊
無仲孫。其諸吾仲孫與？"Our Master Ju says: 'We must accept
the *Ch'un-ch'iu* such as it is. There was no Chung-sun [family] in
Ch'i. Could this perhaps refer to [a member of] the Chung-sun
family of Lu?'" (81/1/6)

(5) *Ch'i chu shih yü yu pu tsai ts'e che yü*? 其諸侍御有不在側者與？
"Could it perhaps be that one of your favorite attendants was
not at your side?" (88/2/3)

(6) *Lu tzu yüeh*: "*Shih wang yeh. Pu neng hu mu che, ch'i chu tz'u
chih wei yü*? 魯子曰：是王也。不能乎母者，其諸此之謂與？
"Master Lu says: 'This was the king. Could the statement that he
was unable to get along with his mother perhaps refer to this
instance?'" (125/24/4)

(7) *Tzu Kung-yang tzu yüeh*: "*Ch'i chu wei ch'i shuang shuang erh
chü chih che yü*?" 子公羊子曰：其諸爲其雙雙而俱至者與？"Our
Master Kung-yang says: 'Could it perhaps be that the two of them
arrived together?'" (185/5/5)

(8) *Ch'i chu chün tzu lo tao Yao Shun chih tao yü*? 其諸君子樂道堯
舜之道與？"Or could it perhaps be that the superior man took
pleasure in narrating the way of Yao and Shun?" (187/14/1)

The pattern "*Ch'i chu* x *i*" is found once in the *Kung-yang*:

(9) *Ch'i chu tse i yü tz'u yen pien i*? 其諸則宜於此焉變矣？"Was it
perhaps proper to indicate the vicissitudes on this occasion?"
(205/15/9)

Apart from these instances I have found only one other occurrence
this construction in the entire pre-Han literature:

(10) *Ch'i chu i hu jen chih ch'iu chih yü*? 其諸異乎人之求之!
"Would this perhaps be different from the way in which oth
seek it?" (*Lun-yü*, Harvard-Yenching Index edition 1/10/1)

This construction is obviously related to constructions such as (11) (
huo che ... hu? 其或者……乎？, *huo che ... hu*? 或者……乎？, *)
chu ... hu? 或諸……乎？, and *ch'i che ... yü*? 其者……與？, wh
are all found in Han texts.[2]

2. The interrogative suffix *yü* in disjunctive questions.

Twelve instances of *yü* are found in disjunctive questions of
pattern "*Tse wei chih ch'i wei* x *yü* y *yü*." "But it is not known whet
it is a case of x or of y."

(12) *Tse wei chih ch'i tsai Ch'i yü Ts'ao yü*. 則未知其在齊與曹與 "
it is not known whether this [criticism] applies to Ch'i or
Ts'ao." (35/9/4)

(13) *Tse wei chih ch'i wei Hsüan fu-jen yü Ch'eng fu-jen yü*. 則未知
爲宣夫人與成夫人與。 "But it is not known whether she was
spouse of [Duke] Hsüan or of [Duke] Ch'eng." (254/2/7)

(14) *Tse wei chih Kung-tzu Hsi Shih ts'ung yü Kung-tzu Fu C
ts'ung yü*. 則未知公子喜時從與公子負芻從與。 "But it was
known whether prince Hsi Shih or prince Fu Ch'u had follo
[him]." (399/20/2)

(15) *Tse wei chih ch'i wei Wu kung yü I kung yü*. 則未知其爲武公
公與 "But it is not known whether she was [the spouse of] D
Wu or Duke I." (433/31/6)

(16) *Tse wei chih ch'i wei Lu kung-tzu yü Chu-lü kung-tzu yü* 則未
其爲魯公子與邾婁公子與。 "But it is not known whether it w
prince of Lu or a prince of Chu-lü." (433/31/6)

(17) *Tse wei chih ch'i wei shih yü, ch'i chu chün-tzu lo tao Yao SI
chih tao yü*. 則未知其爲是與，其諸君子樂道堯舜之道與。 "I
not known, however, whether it was for this purpose [that
Ch'un-ch'iu was written] or whether it perhaps could be that
superior man took pleasure in narrating the ways of Yao
Shun." (487/14/1)[3]

3. Other instances of the interrogative sentence suffix *yü*.

(18) *Tz'u fei nu yü*? 此非怒與？ "Was this not an excessive display

<hr />

[2]For this see Chou Fa-kao, *A historical grammar of Ancient Chinese, Part III: S
stitution* (Taipei, 1959), 234, 411.

[3]The second part of this passage has already been discussed above (sentence [8]).

anger?" (50/4/4)

(19) *Chün pu t'u yü*? 君不圖與? "Does not [your] lord have plans [for an invasion of Lu] ?" (61/13/4)

(20) *Jan tse shan chih yü*? 然則善之與? "If so, does [the *Ch'un-ch'iu*] then approve of him?" (79/32/3)

(21) *Ch'in pu an yü*? 寢不安與? "Did you not sleep restfully?" (88/2/3)

(22) *Yü Kuo hsien yü*? 虞郭見與? "Did [the states of] Yü and Kuo appear before you?" (88/2/3)

(23) *Jan tse shih wang che yü*? 然則是王者與? "If so, was this one of the king's men?" (159/9/1)

Yü[2] as a suffix in subordinated clauses

In two instances *yü* serves as a suffix in subordinated clauses. This function of *yü* is similar to that of the "dilemma *ba*" of modern *P'u-t'ung-hua*.[4]

(24) *Chiang ts'ung hsien chün chih ming yü, tse kuo i chih Chi Tzu che yeh. Ju pu ts'ung hsien chün chih ming yü, tse wo i li che yeh.* 將從先君之命與，則國宜之季子者也。如不從先君之命與，則我宜立者也。 "If we are to follow the command of our late lord, then the state should properly go to Chi Tzu. And should we fail to follow the command of our late lord, then I am the one who should be set up as ruler." (326/29/8)

Yü[3] as a marker of coordination

(25) *Wu yü Cheng jen mo yu ch'eng yeh. Wu yü Cheng jen tse ho wei mo yu ch'eng*? 吾與鄭人末有成也。吾與鄭人則曷爲末有成? "Between us and the men of Cheng there was not yet peace. Why was there not yet peace between us and the men of Cheng." (14/6/1)

(26) *Ch'ing i Ch'ü ch'an chih sheng yü Ch'ui-chi chih pai pi wang.* 請以屈產之乘與垂棘之白璧往。 "I request leave to go forward [to Yü] with your team of horses from Ch'ü and your disc of white jade from Ch'ui-chi." (88/2/3)

(27) *Nan I yü pei Ti chiao, Chung kuo pu chüeh jo hsien.* 南夷與北狄交，中國不絕若綫。 "If the southern I and the northern Ti were to join forces [the fate of] the Central States would be as precarious as if they were suspended by a [thin] thread." (91/4/4)

(28) *Sung kung yü Ch'u tzu ch'i i sheng chü chih hui.* 宋公與楚子期以乘車之會。 "The duke of Sung and the viscount of Ch'u had agreed on an unarmed meeting." (117/21/6)

(29) *Sung kung yü Ch'u jen ch'i chan yü Hung chih yang.* 宋公與楚人

For "dilemma *ba*" see Chao Yuen-ren, *A grammar of spoken Chinese* (Berkeley, 5), 1094.

期戰于泓之陽。 "The duke of Sung and men from Ch'u agreed to battle on the northern bank of the river Hur (119/22/4)

(30) *Po Li Tzu yü Chien Shu Tzu chien yüeh.* 百里子與蹇叔子諫 "Po Li Tzu and Chien Shu Tzu remonstrated, saying:" (141/3:

(31) *Po Li Tzu yü Chien Shu Tzu sung ch'i tzu erh chieh chih yi* 百里子與蹇叔子送其子而戒之曰。 "Po Li Tzu and Chien Shu saw their sons off and warned them, saying:" (141/33/3)

(32) *Po Li Tzu yü Chien Shu Tzu ts'ung ch'i tzu erh k'u chih.* 百 與蹇叔子從其子而哭之 "Po Li Tzu and Chien Shu Tzu follow their sons and cried over them." (142/33/3)

(33) *Jan erh Chin jen yü Chiang Jung yao chih Hsiao erh chi c* 然而晉人與姜戎要之殽而擊之。 "However, the men from C and the Chiang Jung invited them to battle at Hsiao and defe. them there." (142/33/3)

(34) *Fu-jen yü kung i t'i yeh.* 夫人與公一體也。 "The spouse and duke are one body." (177/1/3)

(35) *Chin Hsi K'o yü Ts'ang-sun Hsü t'ung shih erh p'in yü Ch'i.* 克與藏孫許同時而聘于齊。 "Hsi K'o of Chin and Ts'ang-sun at the same time paid a courtesy visit to Ch'i." (212/2/4)

(36) *Wei Ning Chih yü Sun Lin-fu chu Wei hou erh li Kung-sun P* 衞窜殖與孫林父逐衞侯而立公孫剽。 "Ning Chih of Wei and Lin-fu expelled the marquis of Wei and appointed in his s Kung-sun P'iao." (315/27/4)

(37) *Meng shih yü Shu-sun shih tieh erh ssu chih.* 孟氏與叔孫氏迭 之。 "The Meng clan and the Shu-sun clan took turns to pro him with food." (452/8/16)

(38) *Ch'i Chiang yü Miu Chiang.* 齊姜與繆姜。 "Ch'i Chiang and Chiang." (254/2/7)

(39) *Hsün Yin yü Shih Chi Yeh che ho wei che yeh?* 荀寅與士吉射 爲者也? "Hsün Yin and Shih Chi Yeh, what kind of men v they?" (460/13/7)

(40) *Yeh yeh, Yü Chai yeh, I Mo yeh yü Chi Tzu t'ung mu che* 謁也、餘祭也、夷昧也與季子同母者四 "This Yeh, this Yü C this I Mo and Chi Tzu were the four sons of the same moth (326/29/8)

(41) *Erh shih wu chün, wu shou erh kuo, shih wu yü erh wei ts' yeh.* 爾弒吾君，吾受爾國，是吾與爾爲篡也。 "You assassin. my lord. If I were to receive the state as a gift from you, then and I would become accomplices in the rebellion." (326/29/8

(42) *Miu kung chu ch'i erh tzu Chuang kung P'ing yü tso-shih Po.*

逐其二子莊公馮與左師勃。 "Duke Miu expelled his two sons P'ing [who later became] Duke Chuang and Po who held the office of *tso-shih*." (9/3/7)

(43) *Ch'en yu Pao Kuang-fu yü Liang Mai Tzu che*. 臣有鮑廣父與梁買子者。 "Among the ministers there were a certain Pao Kuang-fu and a certain Liang Mai Tzu." (433/31/6)

(44) *Kao Tzu chih tan ssu yü ssu t'ing fu*. 高子執單食與四脡脯。 "Kao Tzu carried a basket of cooked rice and four slices of dried meat." (416/25/7)

(45) *Chin Chao Yang ch'ü Chin-yang chih chia, i chu Hsün Yin yü Shih Chi Yeh*. 晉趙鞅取晉陽之甲，以逐荀寅與士吉射。 "Chao Yang of Chin took the guards from Chin-yang and expelled with their help Hsün Yin and Shih Chi Yeh." (460/13/7)

(46) *Ch'u wo che fei Ning shih yü Sun shih, fan tsai erh*. 黜我者非甯氏與孫氏，凡在爾。 "The one who expelled me was neither the Ning clan nor the Sun clan. It all rested in you!" (315/27/4)

In 18 instances (sentences [25] – [41]) the resultant coordinative ⸥ression is found in preverbal position or as the topic of a nominal sentence. ⸤ive instances the resultant expression is found in postverbal position or as predicate of a nominal sentence (sentences [42] – [46]).

*⸥ü*³ as a preposition

(47) *Wei ch'i yü kung meng yeh*. 爲其與公盟也。 "It was on account of the fact that he made a covenant with the duke." (2/1/2)

(48) *Yü kung meng che chung i*. 與公盟者衆矣。 "Those who had made covenants with the duke were already quite many." (2/1/2)

(49) *Kung ho wei yü wei che meng*? 公曷爲與微者盟？ "Why did the duke make a covenant with a man of low rank?" (17/8/8)

(50) *Kung ho wei yü ta-fu meng*? 公曷爲與大夫盟？ "Why did the duke make a covenant with a great officer?" (55/9/2)

(51) *Wei ch'i hui yü ta-fu meng yeh*. 爲其諱與大夫盟也。 "This was in order to conceal the fact that the duke made a covenant with a great officer." (55/9/2)

(52) *Huan kung hsia yü chih meng*. 桓公下與之盟。 "Duke Huan got down [from the platform] and made a covenant with him." (61/13/4)

(53) *Hui yü ta-fu meng yeh*. 諱與大夫盟也。 "It was in order to conceal the fact that [the duke] made a covenant with a great officer." (68/22/5; 147/2/3)

(54) *Chu-hou pu k'o shih yü kung meng*. 諸侯不可使與公盟。 "The feudal lords could not be induced to make a covenant with the

duke." (156/7/8)

(55) *Tieh Chin ta-fu shih yü kung meng yeh.* 眜晉大夫使與公盟
"[They] winked at a great officer of Chin and made him ma
covenant with the duke." (156/7/8)

(56) *Chih te yü Chin hou meng.* 至得與晉侯盟。"When he arrive
was given an opportunity to make a covenant with the mar
of Chin." (166/13/10)

(57) *Tai yü Yüan-lou erh yü chih meng.* 逮于袁婁而與之盟。
caught up [with Kuo Tso] at Yüan-lou and made a covenant v
him there." (212/2/4)

(58) *Wei ch'i yü Yüan Ch'iao meng yeh.* 爲其與袁僑盟也。"It wa
account of the fact that he had made a covenant with Y
Ch'iao." (256/3/7)

(59) *Wu ch'ing yü tzu meng.* 吾請與子盟。"I request to mak
covenant with you." (315/27/4)

(60) *Wu yü yü chih meng.* 吾欲與之盟。"I wished to make a cove
with him." (315/27/4)

(61) *Hsi ch'i ch'i tzu erh yü chih meng.* 攜其妻子而與之盟。"He t
the hands of his wife and his children and made a pact v
them." (315/27/4)

(62) *Yü kung yu so yüeh, jan hou ju.* 與公有所約，然後入。"She
not enter until she had made a certain agreement with the du
(70/24/5)

(63) *Wu yü chih yüeh i sheng chü chih hui.* 吾與之約以乘車之會
have agreed with him on an unarmed meeting." (117/21/6)

(64) *Tzu ku wei wo yü chih yüeh i.* 子固爲我與之約矣。"You r
confirm this agreement with him for my sake." (315/27/4)

(65) *Kung-tzu Chuan pu te i erh yü chih yüeh.* 公子鱄不得已而與之
"Prince Chuan had no choice but to confirm the agreement v
him." (315/27/4)

(66) *Hsien yü Cheng jen chan yeh.* 嫌與鄭人戰也。"It may be wro
assumed that he fought with men of Cheng." (39/12/9)

(67) *Wan ch'ang yü Chuang kung chan.* 萬嘗與莊公戰。"Wan (
fought with Duke Chuang." (59/12/4)

(68) *Yü Min kung po.* 與閔公博。"He played chess with Duke M
(59/12/4)

(69) *Kung ho wei yü wei che shou?* 公曷爲與微者狩？"Why did
duke hunt with a man of low rank?" (50/4/7)

(70) *Hui yü ch'ou shou yeh.* 諱與讎狩也。"[The *Ch'un-ch'iu*] conc
the fact that [the duke] hunted together with a feud enem
(50/4/7)

(71) *Mo chung hu ch'i yü ch'ou shou yeh.* 莫重乎其與讎狩也。 "Nothing could warrant a more severe criticism than the fact that [the duke] hunted with his feud enemy." (50/4/7)

(72) *Yü chih yin chiu.* 與之飲酒。 "[The marquis of Ch'i] drank wine with him." (46/1/2)

(73) *Sui yü chih ju erh mou yüeh.* 遂與之入而謀曰。 "He then withdrew and deliberated with him, saying:" (88/2/3)

(74) *Yüan yü tzu lü chih.* 願與子慮之。 "I wish to consider this with you." (88/2/3; 237/15/2)

(75) *Yü ch'i tzu chü lai ch'ao yeh.* 與其子俱來朝也。 "He came and paid court together with his son." (94/5/2)

(76) *Yü chu ta-fu li yü ch'ao.* 與諸大夫立於朝。 "[Chao Tun] was standing in the court together with the other great officers." (186/6/1)

(77) *Yü chih li yü ch'ao.* 與之立于朝。 "Together with him [Chao Ch'uan] established himself at the court." (187/6/1)

(78) *Sung Hua Yüan ho wei yü chu-hou wei Sung P'eng ch'eng?* 宋華元曷爲與諸侯圍宋彭城？ "Why did Hua Yüan of Sung together with the feudal lords lay a siege on the Sung city of P'eng?" (252/1/2)

(79) *Ch'i Kuo Hsia ho wei yü Wei Shih Man Ku shuai shih wei Ch'i?* 齊國夏曷爲與衞石曼姑帥師圍戚？ "Why did Kuo Hsia of Ch'i together with Shih Man Ku of Wei lead an army to lay a siege on Ch'i?" (469/3/1)

(80) *Wei Shu-sun Pao shuai erh yü chih chü yeh.* 爲叔孫豹率而與之俱也。 "It was on account of the fact that Shu-sun Pao led [the mission] and took him on as a partner." (259/5/3)

(81) *Shu-sun Pao tse ho wei shuai erh yü chih chü?* 叔孫豹則曷爲率而與之俱？ "Why did Shu-sun Pao lead [the mission] and take him on as a partner?" (259/5/3)

(82) *Tz'u ho wei yü ch'in shih che t'ung?* 辭曷爲與親弑者同？ "Why are the expressions the same as those used of someone who has been personally involved in an assassination?" (79/32/3)

(83) *Tz'u ho wei yü ch'in shih che t'ung?* 詞曷爲與親弑者同？ "Why is the wording the same as that used of someone who has been personally involved in an assassination?" (338/1/2)

(84) *Mien mu yü Ch'ing kung hsiang ssu.* 面目與頃公相似。 "His features resembled those of Duke Ch'ing." (211/2/4)

(85) *I fu yü Ch'ing kung hsiang ssu.* 衣服與頃公相似。 "His clothes resembled those of Duke Ch'ing." (211/2/4)

(86) *Yü Chü wei ching yeh.* 與莒爲竟也。 "They created a boundary

against Chü." (343/1/8)

(87) *Yü Chü wei ching, tse ho wei shuai shih erh wang*? 與莒爲竟，
莒爲帥師而往？ "If they created a boundary against Chü, w
did they go forward leading an army?" (343/1/8)

(88) *Hsiang yü chi lü erh yü.* 相與跨闔而語。 "They talked togeth
leaning on the gate." (212/2/4)

(89) *Hsiang yü shuai shih wei An chih chan.* 相與率師爲鞌之戰
"Together they led their armies and fought a battle at A
(212/2/4)

(90) *Ku hsiang yü wang tai hu Chin yeh.* 故相與往殆乎晉也。 "The
fore they went forward together to lay their suspicions (?) bef
[the ruler of] Chin." (259/5/12)

(91) *Chü chiang mieh chih, tse ho wei hsiang yü wang tai hu Ch*
莒將滅之，則莒爲相與往殆乎晉？ "If Chü was about to
tinguish them, why did they go forward together to lay th
suspicions before [the ruler of] Chin?" (259/5/3)

(92) *Tzu ch'ü wo erh kuei, wu shu yü ch'u yü tz'u*? 子去我而歸，吾孰
處乎此？ "If you leave me and return, with whom shall I rem
here?" (203/15/2)

(93) *Ch'ou che wu shih yen k'o yü t'ung.* 讎者無時焉可與通。 "At
time is it permissible to communicate with one's feud enem
(50/4/7)

In 43 out of a total of 49 occurrences the preposition *yü* is followed
a nominal expression. The combination *hsiang yü*, "together," occurs f
times (sentences [88] – [91]). The expression *shu yü*, "with whom," is fou
once (sentence [92]). There is one occurrence of pregnant *yü* (sentence [93

E. *Yü*[3] in the pattern " A *chih yü* B"

The pattern "A *chih yü* B" is found four times within the corpus:

(94) *Ch'i chih yü jen* 器之與人。 (25/2/5)

(95) *Chih hu ti chih yü jen* 至乎地之與人。 (25/2/5)

(96) *Huan kung chih yü Jung Ti* 桓公之與戎狄。 (77/30/7)

(97) *Nan-ying chih yü Cheng hsiang ch'ü shu ch'ien li* 南郢之與鄭相
數千里 (195/12/3)

The full context must be given for the first three instances of th
construction. The first instance is contained in the comment on the followi
Ch'un-ch'iu passage: "In Summer, in the fourth month, [the duke] took t
great tripod of Kao from Sung." *Kung-yang*: "Here [it is stated that] he to
it from Sung. Why, then, is it referred to as 'the tripod of Kao'? [In referri
to] vessels [one] follows the name [of the original owner]. (Ho Hsiu [1]
182]: "One names it after the original owner.") [In referring to] land, [on

ows the [name of the present] owner. (Ho Hsiu: "One follows the name
the later owner.") Why is this so? (98) *Ch'i chih yü jen, fei yu chi erh.*
之與人，非有即爾。(On this passage Ho Hsiu comments as follows: "*Chi*
ans 'to approach'. . . . Whenever a man takes possession of an object from
>ther state, the ownership is not [immediately] established by [merely]
»roaching [the object]. Those who take possession of an object all consider
t the ownership is fully established first when they have brought the object
:k with them. In order to safeguard the identification of the object for the
ure, they correctly adhere to the original name of the object." It has been
gested (Wang Yin-chih [1766-1834], *Ching i shu wen*) that Ho Hsiu's
nment is based on the reading *fei chi yu erh*. I suggest the following
nslation of the passage: "*As to the correlation between objects and man,
nership may not be [immediately] established by [mere] approach.*"

The second instance is found in the continuation of the same *Kung-
ıg* passage: "Sung first took possession of this tripod of Kao through an
ighteous deed. Therefore it is referred to as 'the tripod of Kao.' *When it
nes to the correlation between land and man, it is not so.* Ownership of
d may be established in a single instant [by the act of taking the land in
ssession]. If so, may then the act of taking possession [of land] be regarded
[equivalent to the establishment of full] ownership [of the land]? The
wer is no. And why? This is like the king of Ch'u marrying his younger
er: at no time can such an act be allowed."

The third instance of the pattern "A *chih yü* B" is found in the
lowing context: the *Ch'un-ch'iu* states that "men from Ch'i attacked the
ın Jung." (77/30/7) The *Kung-yang* comments as follows: "This was the
rquis of *Ch'i*. Why does the Text refer to him as 'men'? In order to degrade
ı. Why degrade him? Master Ssu-ma says: '[The *Ch'un-ch'iu*] obviously
ısiders that he pressed them (i.e. the Shan Jung) in a too harassing manner.
s was obviously a battle. Why does the Text not refer to a battle? In the
'un-ch'iu the term *chan* ("battle") is used only of matched opponents. *The
relation of [the strength of] Duke Huan [on the one hand] and of the
ıg and the Ti [on the other] was such that he could simply drive them out.*"

The fourth instance is found in the following sentence:

(97) *Nan-ying chih yü Cheng hsiang ch'ü shu ch'ien li.* 南郢之與鄭相
ɪ千里。"As to the [spatial] correlation between Nan-ying and Cheng,
y are separated by a distance of several thousand *li*." (195/12/3)

Yü[4] as a verb = "to participate in"

(99) *Kai Teng yü hui erh.* 蓋鄧與會爾。"It was obviously so that [the
ruler of] Teng took part in the meeting." (26/2/8)

(100) *Ch'i yü fa erh pu yü chan.* 齊與伐而不與戰。"Ch'i participated
in the [initial] attack, but not in the ensuing battle." (57/10/5)

(101) *Li K'o chih ch'i pu k'o yü mou.* 里克知其不可與謀。 "Li
knew that [Hsün Hsi] would have no part in his plot." (102/10

(102) *Sung kung yü fa erh pu yü chan.* 宋公與伐而不與戰。 "The d
of Sung participated in the [initial] attack, but not in
[ensuing] battle." (113/18/3)

(103) *Kung yü wei erh yeh. Kung yü wei nai ho? Kung yü i erh y*
公與爲爾也。公與爲奈何？公與議爾也。 "The duke participa
in the undertaking. Under what circumstances did he do so?
participated in the deliberations." (118/21/8)

(104) *Pu chien yü meng yeh.* 不見與盟也。 "[The duke] was not invi
to take part in the covenant." (171/16/1)

(105) *Kung-tzu Sui chih ch'i pu k'o yü mou.* 公子遂知其不可與謀
"Prince Sui knew that [Shu-chung Hui-po] would have no par
his plot." (237/15/2)

(106) *Kai Cheng yü hui erh.* 蓋鄭與會爾。 "It was obviously so that [
ruler of] Cheng took part in the meeting." (274/11/8)

(107) *Kung pu yü meng che ho? Kung pu chien yü meng yeh. Kung
chien yü meng, ta-fu chih, ho i chih hui?* 公不與盟者何？公不
與盟也。公不見與盟，大夫執，何以致會？ "What is meant
the phrase *kung pu yü meng*? The duke was not invited
participate. Since the duke was not invited to participate in
covenant and since a great officer was arrested, why is the meet
referred to in the report of the return [of the duke]?" (383/13

(108) *Yü shih kung yeh.* 與弒公也。 "He participated in the assass
ation of the duke." (10/4/5; 46/1/2; 87/1/10)

(109) *Ch'i yü shih kung nai ho?* 其與弒公奈何？ "Under what circ
stances did he participate in the assassination of the duk
(10/4/5; 46/1/2)

(110) *Chün-tzu ch'ih pu yü yen.* 君子恥不與焉。 "The superior n
considered it a disgrace that he did not participate in
(383/13/5)

(111) *Ch'u ch'i so erh ch'ing yü yeh.* 處其所而請與也。 "He remai
at his place and requested leave to participate [in the covenant
(99/8/2)

(112) *Ch'i ch'u ch'i so erh ch'ing yü nai ho?* 其處其所而請與奈
"Under what circumstances did he remain at his place and requ
leave to participate [in the covenant]." (99/8/2)

(113) *Jo fu yüeh yen wei hsin, tse fei ch'en p'u shu nieh chih so kan
yeh.* 若夫約言爲信，則非臣僕庶孽之所敢與也。 "But to confi
agreements and act as guarantor, those are duties in which sim
servants and sons of concubines do not presume to participa

(315/27/4)

(114) *Chi Tzu ch'i erh chih chih, tse pu te yü yü kuo cheng. Tso erh shih chih, tse ch'in ch'in. Yin pu jen chien yeh.* 季子起而治之，則不得與于國政。坐而視之，則親親。因不忍見也。"[It may be argued that] Chi Tzu could have risen and controlled them, but [this was impossible on account of the fact that] he was not in a position to participate in state administration. [Again, it may be argued that] he could have let things take their course, but [this was impossible since] he loved his relatives and consequently was unable to bear to witness [what was going on]." (73/27/3)

In a majority of instances the verb *yü* is followed either by a single gatable term (15 instances in sentences [99] – [107]) or by a verb-object pression (5 instances, sentences [108] and [109]). In the first sentence of e passage (114) in which a non-negatable expression (*kuo cheng*, "state ministration") serves as object, the verb *yü* is replaced by *yü yü*.

Yü[3] as a verb = "to give"

(115) *Ju wu yü erh i i.* 如勿與而已矣。"It would have been better had he not given [him the city of Ching]." (2/1/3)[5]

(116) *Lu jen pu yü.* 魯人不與。"The people of Lu refused to give it." (87/1/9)

(117) *Ch'ien tz'u che Chin jen lai ch'i shih erh pu yü.* 前此者晉人來乞師而不與。"Prior to this men from Chin had come to request troops, but no troops had been given." (244/16/11)

(118) *Chao kung pu yü.* 昭公不與。"Duke Chao did not give [it to him]." (443/4/14)

(119) *Hsien chün chih so wei pu yü ch'en kuo erh na kuo hu chün che, i chün k'o i wei she chi tsung miao chu yeh.* 先君之所爲不與臣國而納國乎君者，以君可以爲社稷宗廟主也。"The reason why the late lord did not give the state to me, but handed it to you, Sir, was that he considered you more suited to act as head of the state and of the ancestral temple." (9/3/7)

(120) *Tzu pu yü wo kuo, wu chiang sha tzu chün i.* 子不與我國，吾將殺子君矣。"If you do not surrender your state to me I shall kill your lord." (117/21/6)

(121) *Yü wo Chi hou chih hsien!* 與我紀侯之甗！"Give us the *hsien* vessel which formerly belonged to the marquis of Chi!" (212/2/4, 2 instances)

(122) *Chin jo shih tso erh yü Chi Tzu kuo, Chi Tzu yu pu shou yeh.* 今若是迮而與季子國，季子猶不受也。"If we were to act in a

[5] For the considerations underlying the translation see G. Malmqvist, "Studies on the ngyang and Guuliang commentaries I," *BMFEA*, 43 (1971), 70.

great hurry and hand over the state to Chi Tzu he would ref
to accept it." (326/29/8)

(123) *Hsien chün chih so i pu yü tzu kuo erh yü ti che, fan wei Chi 1
ku yeh.* 先君之所以不與子國而與弟者，凡爲季子故也。"That
late lord did not hand the state to his son, but instead hande
to his younger brother, was entirely on account of you, Chi Tz
(326/29/8)

(124) *Yü chih yü chieh erh tsou chih.* 與之玉節而走之。"He gave h
a jade token and hustled him off." (475/6/8)

(125) *Ch'ing wu yü tzu erh yü ti.* 請無與子而與弟。"I suggest that [
ruler] hand over the state, not to his son, but to his youn
brother." (326/29/8)

H. *Yü*[3] as a verb = "to grant [someone] the right to"

  1. *Yü* in the pattern "*yü* [N] V"

(126) *Pu yü nien mu yeh.* 不與念母也。"[The *Ch'un-ch'iu*] does r
grant [Duke Chuang] the right to think of his mother." (46/1/

(127) *Pu yü kung fu ch'ou yeh.* 不與公復讎也。"[The *Ch'un-ch'i*
does not grant the duke the right to take revenge." (56/9/6)[6]

(128) *Ho wei pu yü kung fu ch'ou?* 曷爲不與公復讎？"Why does [
Ch'un-ch'iu] not grant the duke the right to take revenge
(56/9/6)

(129) *Pu yü chu-hou chuan feng yeh.* 不與諸侯專封也。"[The *Ch'
ch'iu*] does not grant a feudal lord the right to enfeoff vassals
his own accord." (85/1/2; 87/2/1; 106/14/1; 252/1/2; 353/4
385/13/6)

(130) *Ho wei pu yü?* 曷爲不與？"Why does [the *Ch'un-ch'iu*] r
grant this right?" (85/1/2; 87/2/1; 106/14/1; 167/14/8; 193/11
436/1/2)

(131) *Shih yü erh wen pu yü.* 實與而文不與。"[The *Ch'un-ch'iu*] d
in fact grant this right, without, however, expressing it explici
in the text." (85/1/2; 87/2/1; 106/14/1; 167/14/8; 193/11
436/1/2)

(132) *Chu-hou chih i pu te chuan feng, tse ch'i yüeh shih yü chih h
諸侯之義不得專封，則其曰實與之何？"Since the duties of
feudal lord did not comprise enfeoffing vassals on his own acco
why does the Text state that [the *Ch'un-ch'iu*] in fact grants t
right?" (85/1/2; 87/2/1; 106/14/1)

(133) *Pu yü Ch'i hou chuan feng yeh.* 不與齊侯專封也。"[The *Ch'i

---

[6]By extension of meaning the sentence may also be interpreted as follows: "[T
Ch'un-ch'iu] does not give the duke credit for the revenge."

ch'iu] does not grant the marquis of Ch'i the right to enfeoff vassals on his own accord." (88/2/1)

(134) *Yü Huan wei chu yeh.* 與桓爲主也。 "[The *Ch'un-ch'iu*] grants [Duke] Huan the role of leader." (91/4/4)

(135) *Ch'ien tz'u che yu shih i, hou tz'u che yu shih i, tse ho wei tu yü tz'u yen yü Huan kung wei chu*? 前此者有事矣，後此者有事矣，則曷爲獨於此焉與桓公爲主？ "Before this there were events [reflecting duke Huan's leadership] ; after this there were [similar] events. Why, then, does [the *Ch'un-ch'iu*] single out this instance for granting [Duke] Huan the role of leader?" (91/4/4)

(136) *Pu yü mieh yeh.* 不與滅也。 "[The *Ch'un-ch'iu*] does not grant [Chin] the right to extinguish [Yü]." (96/5/9)

(137) *Ho wei pu yü mieh?* 曷爲不與滅？ "Why does [the *Ch'un-ch'iu*] not grant [Chin] the right to extinguish [Yü]?" (96/5/9)

(138) *Yü shih t'ing chih yeh.* 與使聽之也。 "[The *Ch'un-ch'iu*] grants an envoy the right to settle the case." (131/28/4)

(139) *Pu yü chih T'ien Tzu yeh.* 不與致天子也。 "[The *Ch'un-ch'iu*] does not grant [the duke] the right to summon the Son of Heaven." (134/28/10)

(140) *Pu yü tsai chih T'ien Tzu yeh.* 不與再致天子也。 "[The *Ch'un-ch'iu*] does not grant [the duke] the right to summon the Son of Heaven a second time." (135/28/17)

(141) *Pu yü ta-fu chuan fei chih chün yeh.* 不與大夫專廢置君也。 "[The *Ch'un-ch'iu*] does not grant a great officer the right to discard and establish rulers on his own accord." (167/14/8)

(142) *Pu yü fa T'ien Tzu yeh.* 不與伐天子也。 "[The *Ch'un-ch'iu*] does not grant [Chao Ch'uan] the right to attack the Son of Heaven." (179/1/13; 410/23/4)

(143) *Pu yü wai t'ao yeh.* 不與外討也。 "[The *Ch'un-ch'iu*] does not grant [Ch'u] the right to punish [someone] abroad." (193/11/5)

(144) *Pu yü wai t'ao che, yin ch'i t'ao hu wai erh pu yü yeh.* 不與外討者，因其討乎外而不與也。 "The phrase *pu yü wai t'ao* indicates that the right to punish was not granted as the punishment was executed abroad." (193/11/5)

(145) *Sui nei t'ao i pu yü yeh.* 雖內討亦不與也。 "[The *Ch'un-ch'iu*] does not grant [a feudal lord] the right of punishment, even though the punishment be executed in his own state." (193/11/5)

(146) *Chu-hou chih i pu te chuan t'ao, tse ch'i yüeh shih yü chih ho?* 諸侯之義不得專討，則其曰實與之何？ "Since the duties of a feudal lord do not comprise punishing on his own accord, why does the Text state that [the *Ch'un-ch'iu*] in fact grants this

right?" (193/11/5)

(147) *Pu yü Chin erh yü Ch'u tzu wei li yeh* 不與晉而與楚子爲禮也
"[The *Ch'un-ch'iu*] grants the right of [the correct use of] t
ritual, not to Chin, but to the viscount of Ch'u." (195/12/3)

(148) *Ho wei pu yü Chin erh yü Ch'u tzu wei li yeh*? 曷爲不與晉而
楚子爲禮也？ "Why does [the *Ch'un-ch'iu*] grant the right of [t
correct use of] the ritual, not to Chin, but to the viscount
Ch'u?" (195/12/3)

(149) *Pu yü tang yeh.* 不與當也。 "[The *Ch'un-ch'iu*] does not gra
him the right to govern the state." (408/22/10)

(150) *Pu yü tang che, pu yü tang, fu ssu tzu chi, hsiung ssu ti chi ch*
tz'u yeh. 不與當者，不與當，父死子繼，兄死弟及之辭也。"
to the expression *pu yü tang*, it is an expression used when
father dies and his son succeeds him, or when an elder broth
dies and his younger brother gains the throne." (408/22/10)

(151) *Pu yü ta-fu chuan chih yeh.* 不與大夫專執也。 "[The *Ch'un-ch'i*
does not grant a great officer the right to seize [someone] on I
own accord." (436/1/2)

In all these examples *yü* functions as a link verb.

2. *Yü* in the pattern "*yü* N *chih* V"

(152) *Yü Hsiang kung chih cheng Ch'i yeh.* 與襄公之征齊也。 "[T
Ch'un-ch'iu] grants Duke Hsiang the right to punish Ch'i
(113/18/3)

(153) *Ho wei yü Hsiang kung chih cheng Ch'i*? 曷爲與襄公之征齊
"Why does [The *Ch'un-ch'iu*] grant Duke Hsiang the right t
punish Ch'i?" (113/18/3)

(154) *Pu yü I Ti chih chu Chung kuo yeh.* 不與夷狄之主中國也。 "[T
Ch'un-ch'iu] does not grant the I and the Ti the right to lord
over the Central States." (410/23/8; 485/13/3)

(155) *Pu yü I Ti chih chu Chung kuo, tse ch'i yen huo Ch'en Hsia Nie*
ho? 不與夷狄之主中國，則其言獲陳夏齧何？ "If [the *Ch'un
chiu*] does not grant the I and the Ti the right to lord it over tl
Central States, why does the Text here speak of the capture t
Hsia Nieh of Ch'en?" (410/23/8)

(156) *Pu yü I Ti chih chu Chung kuo, tse ho wei i hui liang po chih tz*
yen chih? 不與夷狄之主中國，則曷爲以會兩伯之辭言之？ "
[the *Ch'un-ch'iu*] does not grant the I and the Ti the right t
lord it over the Central States, why are they here spoken of in tl
context of having a meeting with two leaders [among the feud.
lords]?" (485/13/3)

$Yü^3$ as a verb = "to associate with"

(157) *Chung kuo pu tsu kuei yeh, tse pu jo yü Ch'u.* 中國不足歸也，則不若與楚。 "Since the Central States are not to be depended on, it would be better to side with Ch'u." (263/7/9)

SUMMARY

Functions and meanings	Occurrences	Sentences
A. $Yü^2$ as a sentence suffix		
1. in the pattern *"Ch'i chu* x *yü"*	6	(3)–(8)
2. in disjunctive questions	12	(12)–(17)
3. other occurrences	6	(18)–(23)
B. $Yü^2$ as a suffix in subordinated clauses	2	(24)
C. $Yü^3$ as a marker of coordination	23	(25)–(46)
D. $Yü^3$ as a preposition	49	(47)–(93)
E. $Yü^3$ in the pattern "A *chih yü* B"	4	(94)–(97)
F. $Yü^4$ as a verb = "to participate in"	25	(99)–(114)
G. $Yü^3$ as a verb = "to give"	13	(115)–(125)
H. $Yü^3$ as a verb = "to grant the right to"		
1. in the pattern *"yü* [N] V"	54	(126)–(151)
2. in the pattern *"yü* N *chih* V"	6	(152)–(156)
I. $Yü^3$ as a verb = "to associate with"	1	(157)

The wide functional and semantic range of the graph sometimes results potential ambiguity. Removed from its context, sentence (116) *"Lu jen pu i"* could be interpreted as meaning either "The men from Lu did not give" or "The men from Lu did not participate in it."

The following two sentences are apparently structurally identical: (142) *Pu yü fa T'ien Tzu yeh."* and (108) *"Yü shih kung yeh."* The contexts of these two sentences make it perfectly clear that the first sentence must be interpreted as "[The *Ch'un-ch'iu*] does not grant [Chao Ch'uan] the right to attack the Son of Heaven.", while the second sentence means "He participated in the assassination of the duke."

In one instance the context fails to solve the ambiguity: (115) *"Ju wu yü erh i i."* Accepting Ho Hsiu's amendment of *ju* into *pu ju* ("it would be better") the sentence may be interpreted as "It would have been better if [the earl of Cheng] had not given [his younger brother Tuan the city of Ching].", or as "It would have been better if [the earl of Cheng] had not taken part [in the undertaking]."

In a number of instances we find two occurrences of the graph *yü* in the same sentences. The two forms invariably have the same function and meaning, as may be exemplified by the following sentences:

(13)   *Tse wei chih ch'i wei Hsüan fu-jen yü Ch'eng fu-jen yü.* "But it not known whether she was the spouse of [Duke] Hsüan or [Duke] Ch'eng."

(100) *Ch'i yü fa erh pu yü chan.* "Ch'i participated in the [initia attack, but not in the [ensuing] battle."

(125) *Ch'ing wu yü tzu erh yü ti.* "I suggest that [the ruler] hand ov the state, not to his son, but to his younger brother."

(131) *Shih yü erh wen pu yü.* "[The *Ch'un-ch'iu*] does in fact gra this right, without, however, expressing it explicitly in the text."

In texts other than the *Kung-yang* two occurrences of the graph *yü* the same sentence do not necessarily have the same function and meaning

CONCLUSION

We now return to the statement by Confucius which triggered th study. The results of the investigation do not lend support to K'ung Kuan sen's interpretation, as it finds expression in his somewhat tortuous paraphras (It is possible that K'ung Kuang-sen erroneously regarded the first three wor of the statement as an elliptic form of "*Ch'i chu li yü*?" 其諸禮與? "Cou this perhaps be the [correct] ritual?") We may safely conclude that *yü* he functions as a marker of coordination and that the passage must be i terpreted as follows: "Their rites and their speeches were indeed wor

[7] Although this investigation is strictly confined to the *Kung-yang* text perhaps I m; be allowed to digress further and discuss the following passage in the *Lun-yü*: (158) *T: han yen li yü ming yü jen.* 子罕言利與命與仁。(Harvard-Yenching index edition, 15/9/1 Wing-tsit Chan gives a short survey of the various attempts at interpreting this passa; (*A source book in Chinese philosophy* [Princeton University Press, 1963], 34-35). It interesting to note that all these attempts are based on the assumption that the tv occurrence of *yü* have the same function, serving either as a marker of coordinatic ("and"), as a verb ("to give forth"), or as a preposition ("compared with; than"). If v base our interpretation of the passage on the hypothesis that the two forms hav *different* functions, we arrive at the following translation which well tallies with what known of the topics of the Master's teaching: "The Master spoke more rarely of prot and human destiny than of humanity." This statement tallies well with the statisti provided by Wing-tsit Chan: "It is true that the topic of profit is mentioned in tl *Analects* only six times and destiny or fate only ten times, but fifty-eight of the 4! chapters of the *Analects* are devoted to humanity and the word *jen* occurs 105 times Reference may also be made to the partially identical structure in (159) *Fu-tzu chih y(hsing yü t'ien tao pu k'o te erh wen yeh.* 夫子之言性與天道不可得而聞也。 "The Maste discourses on human nature and on the way of Heaven cannot be heard." (*Lun-y* 8/5/13). It should finally be added that *yü* in the sense of "to compare with; than" attested in the *Lun-yü*, e.g. in 4/3/4.

bserving!"

We have no means of knowing whether Confucius, who was 34 years of ge at the time, personally witnessed the show at Yeh-ching. But had he done o, the wretched spectacle of the spineless Duke Chao crying in self-pity after is expulsion from the state which he had failed to govern for 25 years, would ardly have impressed the Master.

Professor Herrlee G. Creel has aptly defined *li* as "good taste." The tter lack of good taste in Duke Chao's performance at Yeh-ching no doubt rovoked the Master to his sarcastic remark.

Marshes in *Mencius* and elsewhere

A lexicographical note

Derk Bodde

veryone who reads Professor Creel (hereafter Herrlee in these pages) knows
1at he can never be dull. To his writings he always brings a disciplined
nagination, a limpid style, an unerring ability to focus on vital issues, and a
oncommitant ability to stimulate the mind of the reader—sometimes quite
ontroversially so. Such is the stuff of great scholarship.

It is not Herrlee the scholar but Herrlee the pedagogue, however, who
as quite unwittingly stimulated the writing of the present article. This he
id long ago by preparing, with his collaborators Chang Tsung-ch'ien and
lichard C. Rudolph, the three volumes of *Literary Chinese by the inductive
method* (Chicago, 1938-39, 1952) on which generations of students of classical
Chinese have been raised. Despite competition in recent years from other
exts, as well as certain recognized weaknesses of its own, I have remained
aithful to *Literary Chinese* for one all-compelling reason: the fact that it,
nore than any other textbook in its field I know, provides a genuinely cul-
ural, as well as linguistic, introduction to Chinese civilization. Indeed, a very
itting subtitle for it might be *Chinese culture by the inductive method.*

In the third volume, that of *The Mencius,* I have nonetheless always
egretted the decision to stop with the first three books, thereby depriving the
tudent of some of the most famous chapters, notably the debates between
Mencius and Kao Tzu on human nature. However, though there are some arid
tretches in these first books which might have been deleted, they are of
course balanced by other chapters of outstanding importance. One of the best
s IIIa, 4, with its lengthy debate between Mencius and the follower of the
griculturalist Hsü Hsing. This provides one of the most vivid statements of
Confucian social and economic theory, but besides this, the chapter is pep-
pered with other cultural tidbits. At the very beginning the mention of the
urious agricultural implements *lei* 耒 and *ssu* 耜 (wrongly rendered by Legge

and others as "plow handles and shares" or the like) allows the teacher to sa
something about early Chinese agricultural technology. A little later, the iro
implement used by Hsü Hsing gives opportunity to mention the beginning o
the iron age in China. The "shrike-tongued barbarian of the south" wh
appears near the end vividly illustrates how intolerant Confucian culturalisr
could sometimes be. And somewhat earlier comes the unexpected excursio.
into Chinese mythology, with its description of the primeval flood, th
conquest of which enabled the world to become fit for sedentary (and there
fore, for the Chinese, civilized) human habitation.

In this same paragraph (the seventh in James Legge's arrangement) ther
is a sentence that has always puzzled me. It reads, in Legge's translation:[1]

> Shun committed to Yih the direction of the fire to be employed, an
> Yih set fire to, and consumed, *the forests and vegetation on* the moun
> tains and *in* the marshes, so that the birds and beasts fled away to hid
> themselves. [Legge's italics]

How, one wonders, could marshes be set on fire? The commentator
give no help—after all, there is nothing ethically or philosophically significan
in a marsh—and the translators, for the most part, do no better. Thus, from
the latter, we have the following renditions of the key second part of th
sentence: "I mit le feu dans les montagnes et les marais et les purifia pa
l'incendie" (Couvreur).[2] "Yi fired the hills and bogs, and burnt them" (Lyall).
"Yih then burned away the undergrowth of mountain and marsh" (Giles).
"He then set fire to the mountains and marshes so that they were reduce
to ruins" (Ware).[5] "Shun sent Yi with a burning torch to set fires in the hill
and fens, and to burn them off" (Dobson).[6] The only translators who seen
to be tacitly aware of the problem are Richard Wilhelm and D. C. Lau. Th
former translates: "I legte Feuer an die Berge und Dschungeln und verbrannt
die Urwälder."[7] And Dr. Lau writes: "Yi set the mountains and valleys aligh
and burnt them."[8] Neither scholar, however, warns the reader that there i
anything peculiar about the word paraphrased as "jungles" or "valleys."

[1] James Legge, *The Chinese classics,* II (Hong Kong & London, 1861), 126.

[2] Séraphin Couvreur, *Les Quatre livres* (Ho Kien Fou, 1895), 423. I am indebted t
Professor Hans Bielenstein of Columbia University for sending me the wording o
Couvreur's rendition.

[3] Leonard A. Lyall, *Mencius* (London & New York, 1932), 78.

[4] Lionel Giles, *The book of Mencius* (London, 1942), 60.

[5] James R. Ware, *The sayings of Mencius* (Mentor Books, 1960), 85.

[6] W.A.C.H. Dobson, *Mencius* (Toronto, 1963), 117.

[7] Richard Wilhelm, *Mong dsi (Mong ko)* (Jena, 1916; 2nd printing, 1921), 56. I am
indebted to Professor Emeritus Hellmut Wilhelm of the University of Washington fo
sending me the wording of his father's rendition.

[8] D. C. Lau, *Mencius* (Penguin Books, 1970), 102.

The word in question is *tse* 澤, which during most of its history has ormally signified "marsh" but today is undoubtedly best known as the first llable in the personal name of Mao Tse-tung. In Herrlee's *Mencius,* vocabu- ry entry no. 712 defines *tse* as: "A marsh, a pool, moisture. Favor, kindness, neficial influence. To moisten, to enrich, to benefit, to anoint. Smooth, ossy, slippery." These definitions are in general agreement with the standard ctionaries. In what follows, we will confine our discussion to the two imary concrete meanings of "marsh" and "pool" (broadening the latter, owever, to include "pond/lake"), together with any further concrete mean- gs that may develop from these.

In Chou dynasty texts it is evident that *tse* was a general designation for most any stationary, and probably usually shallow, expanse of water. Some- mes the *tse* was so shallow and covered with reeds and grasses as to be a real arsh, but at other times it was deep enough to permit the movement of oats or erection of fish-weirs; in such instances it seems better to term it lepending on size) a pool, pond, or lake. The former situation is illustrated y a speech in the *Tso chuan* under the year 522 B.C., in which the statesman en Tzu tells the duke of Ch'i: "The trees of the mountain forests are main- ined [for your use] by the Heng-lu [an official title], the reeds and rushes f the marshes (*tse*) by the Chou-chiao [another title], and the fuel for fire f the thickets by the Yü-hou [still another title]."[9] The situation in which *tse* corresponds to a lake is illustrated by a sentence in the *Chuang-tzu* escribing the age of pristine perfection: "In that age the mountains had no aths or trails, the lakes (*tse*) no boats or fish-weirs."[10]

The distinction between *tse* as "marsh" and as "pool/pond/lake" is ometimes so vague that any precise translation becomes arbitrary.[11] The mbiguity of the word emerges clearly in another statement in the *Tso chuan* here we read: "When a stream is blocked up, it becomes a *tse*."[12] Generally

[9] Chao 20: Legge, *Chinese classics,* V (London, 1872), 683b; Couvreur, *Tch'ouen s'iou et Tso Tchouan* (Ho Kien Fou, 1914), III, 323.

[10] Chap. 9: *Ssu-pu pei-yao* ed. (hereafter *SPPY*), 4/7a; Burton Watson, *The Complete orks of Chuang Tzu* (New York & London, 1968), 105. The word liang 梁, translated fish-weirs," is rendered by Watson as "bridges," but there are many passages in which occurs in conjunction with *tse* and refers to a dam or other barrier built into the water trap fish. See the decisive statement in the *Mo-tzu*, chap. 9: *SPPY* 2/3b; Y. P. Mei, he ethical and political works of Motse (London, 1929), 37, which tells how the irtuous administrator collects taxes on "the profits (*li* 利) of the mountain forests and f the lake weirs (*tse liang* 澤梁)," "Profits" can only signify fish profits here. See milarly *Mencius*, Ib, 5 (Legge, 38), as well as passages in other works.

[11] See, for example, the *Tso chuan* passage cited at note 16 below, where Legge anslates *tse* as "marshes" and Couvreur as "bords des lacs." Actually, as we shall see, oth renditions are probably inaccurate.

[12] Hsüan 12 (597 B.C.): Legge, 317b; Couvreur, I, 618.

speaking, however, it would seem, on the basis of many occurrences not cite
here, that in early Chou times *tse*, in the meaning of "marsh," was somewh.
less common than in later times, but in the meaning of "pool/pond/lake" w.
considerably more common. A possible reason, suggested here only ve:
tentatively because much more research would be needed, is that *tse* meani.
"marsh" was rivaled in early Chou times by another and possibly more popul.
word, *hsi* 隰, "swamp," which later declined in importance.[13] *Tse* as "poo.
pond/lake," on the other hand, started by having the field pretty much .
itself; from late Chou times onward, however, it was more and more replace.
by *hu* 湖, a word that eventually became the standard designation for "lak.
but, because of its southern origin, is not found in the early Chou literature.

The basically aquatic significance of the word *tse* is of course indicate.
by the occurrence in the written character of the graphic element meani.
"water." It is natural enough, therefore, that *tse* should usually be thought .
in conjunction with low-lying terrain. The classical expression of this idea—
formulated in a deliberately reversed manner for paradoxical effect—occu.
in one of the famous riddles enunciated by Hui Shih: "Heaven is as low as t.
earth; mountains and *tse* are on the same level."[15] Other texts can be foun.
however, in which *tse* seems to have very little connection with water, an.
there are even rare instances in which the word's associations seem to be wit.
heights rather than depths. Illustrative of the second point is a *Tso chua.
passage stating (in Legge's translation) that certain officers of the Chin arm.
were sent to "examine all the difficult places in the hills and marshes (*tse*).
As translated by Couvreur, the officers are said to have explored "les passag.
escarpés dans les montagnes et sur les bords des lacs (*tse*)."[16] The key wor.
here, *hsien* 險, can, in a secondary sense, signify "dangerous" or "difficult.
(hence Legge's "difficult places"). Its primary meaning, however, is "steep .
rugged terrain" and the like, and this is surely what the word means when, .

[13] According to the Harvard-Yenching *Concordance to Shih Ching*, *hsi* appears in n.
less than fifteen poems (nos. 38, 58, 84, 115, 126, 132, 148, 163, 164, 204, 210, 22.
228, 250, 290), whereas *tse*, in its concrete primary meanings, occurs in only three (no.
145, 181, 261). However, there is some ambiguity about the word *hsi* itself, becau.
although it does mean "swamp" in many contexts, in some others it apparently simp.
means "lowland."

[14] *Hu* does not occur in the *Shih ching, Shu ching, Lun yü* or *Tso chuan*. Howeve.
it occurs once in the *Mo-tzu*, chap. 15: *SPPY* 4/5a, Mei, 85; once in the *Kuan-tzu*, cha.
84: *SPPY* 24/16b; Lewis Maverick (ed.), *Economic dialogues in ancient China, selectior.
from the Kuan-tzu* (Carbondale, Illinois, 1954), 202; and seven times in the *Chuang-tz.
(see the Harvard-Yenching *Concordance to Chuang Tzu*). In the *Kuan-tzu* and *Chuan.
tzu, hu* is invariably linked with another well-known word of southern origin, *chiang* 江
"river."

[15] *Chuang-tzu*, chap. 33: *SPPY* 10/20b, Watson, 274.
[16] Hsiang 18 (555 B.C.): Legge, 478b; Couvreur, II, 335-36.

re, it occurs in conjunction with *shan* 山 , "mountains." Hence Couvreur's
passages escarpés" is much better than Legge's "difficult places"; by the
me token, however, his "bords des lacs" for *tse* is fully as incongruous as
gge's "marshes." The decisive factor is that the word *tse* is conjoined here
oth with *shan* and with *hsien* (the phrase in question, *shan tse chih hsien*
澤之險, literally means "the *hsien* of mountains and of *tse*"). The only
asonable conclusion, it seems to me, is that these *tse* were located *among*
e mountains, rather than below and away from them.

Even more conclusive, though many centuries later, is a passage wherein
an Yeh (398-446), in his *Hou Han shu* [Later Han history], describes the
rly habits of the Southern Barbarians (in modern Hunan).[17] Here, having
rrated the origin of these "barbarians" from the union between a dog and
e daughter of the mythological Chinese sage ruler Ti K'u, Fan Yeh says of
em: "They loved to enter mountain gorges but did not enjoy flat expanses.
he Sovereign [i.e. Ti K'u], in accordance with their notions, bestowed on
em famous mountains and broad *tse*." The stated preference here for
mountain gorges" (*shan ho* 山壑 , translated by Streffer as "tiefe Gebirgs-
ler") as against "flat expanses" (*p'ing k'uang* 平曠,translated by Streffer as
ffenem Flachland"), followed by the linking of "famous mountains"
ning shan 名山) and "broad *tse*" (*kuang tse* 廣澤) with one another, makes
impossible, in my opinion, for the latter to be thought of as either low-lying
narshes" or "lakes" that are below the mountains. Surely they must be
ateau-like expanses among the mountains themselves. Streffer, I think, is on
e right track when he translates (though without comment): ". . . weitem
uchtbaren Boden bei berühmten Bergen."

As to the usually aquatic associations of *tse*, passages can nevertheless
e found wherein flora and fauna seemingly quite out of place in a damp
vironment are associated with *tse*. The *Kuan-tzu*, for example, says in a
assage in which the very term just cited, *kuang tse*, appears: "The tiger and
e leopard are the most ferocious of beasts. So long as they dwell in deep
rests and broad *tse* (*kuang tse*), men will be fearful of their awesomeness
d respect them."[18] The *Chuang-tzu*, likewise, speaks about "the *tse*
heasant" (*chih* 雉 , the ring-necked pheasant), which Burton Watson translates
congruously as "swamp pheasant."[19] It would seem that in both passages,

[17] *SPPY* 116/1b. Translated in Johanne Michael Streffer, *Das Kapitel 86 (76) des
ou Han Shu* (Göppingen, West Germany: Verlag Alfred Künmerle, 1971), 80. The
ading of this passage with students several years ago first suggested to me that *tse*
ight have meanings other than those found in the dictionaries.

[18] Chap. 64: *SPPY* 20/3a. See W. Allyn Rickett, *Kuan-tzu, a repertory of early
hinese thought*, I (Hong Kong, 1965), 125, where he conventionally translates *kuang
e* as "broad marshes."

[19] *Chuang-tzu*, chap. 3: *SPPY* 2/3a, Watson, 52.

grasslands would fit the situation better than would swamps or marshes.

Other references seem to indicate, however, that these grasslands—they were indeed such—could on occasion grow shrubs, bushes, and ev*
trees in addition to grass. Thus the *Chuang-tzu*, in a passage to be quoted lat*
(see note 25), associates the Chinese oak (*shu* 杼) and Chinese chestnut (*li* 栗*
with what it calls the "great *tse*" (*ta tse* 大澤)—apparently a *tse* of co*
siderable extent. And the *Kuan-tzu*, in a passage likewise cited below (s*
note 32), describes what it calls "the northern *tse*" in the state of Ch'i (mode*
Shantung) as an important source of cooking fuel. The term rendered "fue*
is actually a binom, *hsin jao* 薪蕘, which Yin Chih-chang (d. A.D. 718*
commentator on the *Kuan-tzu*, explains by saying: "What is large is *hsin*, wh*
is small is *jao*." It is evident that *hsin* (the standard word for "firewood"*
here refers to pieces of wood of larger size, while *jao* is the term coveri*
smaller branches, twigs, shrubs, and grasses.

The word *tse* occurs a number of times in the *Tso chuan* as a suffix*
place names; Legge usually translates by the formula, "at the marsh of X*
while Couvreur, more cautiously, usually leaves *tse* untranslated as part of t*
place name ("at X-*tse*"). It happens more than once that these *tse* are t*
locales for military or political events such as would ordinarily never *
imagined as occurring either in a "marsh" or a "lake." In 638 B.C., f*
example, when the viscount of Ch'u had gained an important victory ov*
Sung, the two wives of the earl of Cheng offered him a congratulatory fea*
at a place in Cheng called "the *tse* of K'o."[20] In 580 the son of a decease*
ruler of Cheng signed a treaty with the state of Chin at the *tse* of Hsiu.*
Other treaties, between other states, were likewise signed in 579 and 570*
the *tse* of So and *tse* of Chi respectively.[22] In 549 the viscount of Ch'*
besieged the capital of Cheng at its eastern gate, for which purpose he campe*
his army at the *tse* of Tz'u.[23] And in 505, somewhat similarly, the Lu arm*
marched through the capital of Wei and then halted at the *tse* of T'un.[24] *
each instance, the actions make excellent sense if we visualize them as occu*
ring at a meadow, heath, or other expanse of non-wet open land.

Not only could *tse* be the locales for treaty-signings and military e*
campments, however. Sometimes recluses or primitives lived in them as we*
The *Chuang-tzu*, with characteristic humor, tells how Confucius, after learnir*
Taoist wisdom, "said goodbye to his friends and associates, dismissed h*
disciples, and retired to the great *tse*, wearing furs and felted clothing an*

[20] Hsi 22: Legge, 183b; Couvreur, I, 336.
[21] Ch'eng 11: Legge, 373b; Couvreur, II, 83.
[22] Ch'eng 12 and Hsiang 3: Legge, 378a and 420a; Couvreur, II, 94 and 193.
[23] Hsiang 24: Legge, 508b; Couvreur, II, 414.
[24] Ting 5: Legge, 762b; Couvreur, III, 527.

ing on acorns and chestnuts."[25] And the *Huai-nan-tzu*, in a description of imitive man, states that "the people of old lived in *tse* in covered-over pits." cause, however, they suffered from cold and damp in winter and heat and ects in summer, the sages proceeded to build houses of clay and wood for em.[26] These "covered-over pits" (*fu hsüeh* 復穴) are mentioned already in e *Shih ching*, where it is said that Tan-fu, ancient ancestor of the Chou ople, formed coverings (*fu*) and pits (*hsüeh*) for his people at a time when uses as such did not yet exist.[27] The terms at once suggest the pit dwellings hose foundations have been uncovered at various Chinese Neolithic sites. irther, their mention in the poem in conjunction with Tan-fu (in Northwest iina) suggests that the *tse* where the *Huai-nan-tzu* says the ancients had their overed-over pits" may also have been located in the northwest loess high-ids.

By now so much has been said about various kinds of *tse* that the reader ay almost have forgotten the original context. The key words in *Mencius*, Ia, 4 read (in my rendition): "Yi ignited the mountains and *tse* and burned em off." This theme of a sage who anciently clears the land by fire is by no eans unique. The *Kuan-tzu*, in two successive chapters, attributes the same it to Huang Ti, the Yellow Sovereign, and then to Yü, founder of the Hsia nasty. In both cases the sentences run: "He set fire to the mountain forests, stroyed the dense thickets, and burned off the luxuriant *tse*."[28] Regardless which sage is involved, it is evident that the theme is that of clearing the nd from primeval growth and thus making the world suitable for settled iman habitation. In other words, it is a culture myth symbolizing the rmation of sedentary agrarian civilization.

The same act of burning off the land, devoid of any mythological sociations, is also mentioned quite casually in a number of other passages. us the *Kuan-tzu*, in the course of enumerating several matters about which e ruler should be particularly careful, mentions among them that of "the ountains and the *tse* not being saved from fire; plants and trees not being anted."[29] The *Huai-nan-tzu* warns similarly that "when fire is released in a e, the [neighboring] forest becomes anxious [lest it catch fire] ."[30] And the 'uang-tzu* remarks poetically of the Taoist adept: "The Perfect Man is dlike. Though the great *tse* burns, it cannot roast him; though the Ho and

[25] Chap. 20: *SPPY* 7/12a, Watson, 214. This is the passage, mentioned earlier, which iplies that oaks and chestnuts grew in the *tse*.
[26] *Huai-nan-tzu*, *SPPY* 13/1a.
[27] *Shih ching*, no. 237.
[28] *Kuan-tzu*, chap. 78: *SPPY* 23/4b, Maverick, 151; chap. 79: *SPPY* 23/4b, Maverick, 50-61. The sentence is repeated no less than three times in the second reference.
[29] Chap. 4: *SPPY* 1/13b, Maverick, 42.
[30] *SPPY* 16/7a.

Han rivers freeze, they cannot chill him."[31]

Of particular interest is yet another passage from the *Kuan-tzu*, one of the many in which the model minister, Kuan Chung, advises his ruler, Duke Huan of Ch'i (r. 685-643 B.C.).[32] It begins with the statement: "The northern *tse* in Ch'i was set on fire." The text then goes on to say that when this happened, Kuan Chung congratulated his ruler, saying: "Our cultivated land (*t'ien yeh* 田野) will now be extended, and the peasants will be sure to have a hundred-fold profit." His prediction proved accurate, for by the ninth month of that year all the grain taxes had been collected and the quality of the grain was excellent. On being asked the reason, Kuan Chung explained: "Whether it be a state of a myriad or a thousand chariots, no one can cook without fuel. Now with the burning of the northern *tse*, there has been no continuation [of the former supply of fuel from that area], so that the peasants have been able . . . to sell their fuel at ten times more per bundle [than formerly]." This, he concludes, has given them the means effectively to carry out their agricultural work (by hiring additional labor?), which is why they have been able to bring in their tax grain so early. Not only, as mentioned earlier, do this passage indicate that some trees, at least, grew in the *tse* besides shrubs and grasses. It also implies that the burning of the *tse* led to its conversion into agricultural land ("Our cultivated lands will now be enlarged"). Unless the burning were in fact followed by drainage operations—and there is no mention of these in the text—it is hard to see how the *tse* from which the new lands were converted could possibly have been either a marsh or a lake.

Two technical terms occur in the texts to describe the act of burning. The primary one is *fen* 焚, the graph of which appropriately consists of the elements signifying "fire" and "forest." *Fen* appears in the *Mencius* passage, the first of the *Kuan-tzu* passages, and the *Chuang-tzu* quotation; in each instance I have rendered it as "burn" or "burn off." The other, more general term is *shao* 燒, found in the first and third *Kuan-tzu* passages, where I have translated it as "set fire to" or "set on fire." Yin Chih-chang, commenting on the third *Kuan-tzu* passage, explains: "To circulate fire for hunting is called *shao*." That *shao* and *fen*, used technically, are practically synonymous is indicated by the *Shuo-wen* dictionary, which says under *fen*: "*Fen* is to set on fire (*shao*) for hunting."[33] Though there is ample evidence that fire was

---

[31]Chap. 2: *SPPY* 1/21b, Watson, 46, who translates: "Though the great swamp blaze." We have already encountered the term *ta tse*, "great *tse*," in an earlier quotation from *Chuang-tzu* (see at note 25).

[32]Chap. 80: *SPPY* 23/14b, Maverick, 169-70. This is the passage referred to earlier because of its mention of the firewood and other fuel derived from the *tze*.

[33]*Shuo-wen chieh-tzu, Ssu-pu ts'ung-k'an* ed., 10A/8b.

d in early China to drive out the game in mass hunts,[34] our texts clearly
gest that it was also used—probably not only prehistorically but much
r as well—to clear the land for agriculture. Perhaps the process was similar
the "slash and burn" agriculture still practiced in parts of Southeast Asia
ay.

The foregoing evidence, I hope, supports the conclusion that the word
anciently covered a considerable range of meanings. Starting as a desig-
ion for a low-lying area of either marsh or outright water, the word—no
bt because of the concept of openness ever present in it—was extended
cover other kinds of open terrain as well. Some of these had probably
le or nothing to do with water, and some seem to have been located quite
h in the mountains. For the most part, no doubt, these non-aquatic *tse*
sisted of open meadow or grassland, but in some instances such land was
arently interspersed to some extent by bush and even trees. While many
were presumably small, certain ones were probably large enough to be
asured in miles. English words that come to mind as possible synonyms
lude grassland, meadow, heath, moor, bush, plateau, alpine meadow.

Before concluding, it is worth pointing out that our own word "marsh"
vides an interesting semantic parallel when used as a dialect word in south-
stern England. In Somersetshire, for example, the word carries with it "no
plication of bog or swamp. 'The marshes' are some of the richest grazing
d in Somerset." And in southern Devonshire the word is "applied loosely
meadows by the riverside, whether dry or marshy."[35] From this part of
gland these dialect usages apparently passed to Australia, and more specifi-
ly to Tasmania, where a resident informs us: "A 'marsh' here is what in
gland would be called a meadow."[36]

What this article has discussed is admittedly of no great consequence.
ough the excuse for writing it has been the desire to explain a puzzling
ssage in a textbook prepared by Herrlee Creel, the result in no way pretends
match the intellectual interests of the man to whom it is affectionately
dicated. If there is any general moral to be drawn, it is simply that no easy
rtcuts are possible for the serious study of classical Chinese civilization and
guage. Resort to the dictionaries and similar aids is not enough. They must

---

[34] See, *inter alia*, the account of the hunt in *Shih ching* no. 78, which (in Bernhard
lgren's rendition, *The Book of odes* [Stockholm, 1950], 53) speaks of "rows of fires"
t "surge everywhere."

[35] See Joseph Wright (ed.), *The English dialect dictionary* (6 vols.; London, Oxford
ew York, 1898-1905), IV, 44, *sub* "marsh (4)."

[36] Mrs. Louisa Anne Meredith, *My home in Tasmania during a residence of nine years*
vols.; London, 1852), I, 163. Quoted in Edward E. Morris, *Austral English, a dictionary
Australasian phrases and usages* (London, 1898), 287, s.v.

be supplemented at every turn by eternal readiness to do one's own explori —usually laboriously, often unproductively, and not infrequently leadi into obscure byways as well as along the better-known highways. Herrle every writing testifies to his full awareness of this principle and his lifelo commitment to the task of exploring.

The organization of the Mohist *Canons*

A. C. Graham

ɇ six dialectical chapters of *Mo-tzu* are the principal surviving documents
ancient Chinese disputation.[1] They consist of four chapters of *Ching* 經
ɩnóns] and *Ching shuo* 經說 [Explanations of the Canons] (on topics in
ɩc, ethics, and science), followed by the *Ta ch'ü* 大取 [Bigger pick] and
ɩao ch'ü* 小取 [Smaller pick], which appear to be selections from the
ʿecta membra* of two documents,[2] the *Yü ching* 語經 [Expounding the
ɩons] (a sequence of canons and explanations on ethics) and the *Ming shih*
ɩ [Names and objects] (a consecutive treatise on a discipline which for the
ɩment we shall call "logic"). All belong to the last century of the Mohist
ɩool, which died out after the suppression of the schools by the Ch'in in
ɩ B.C.

Modern editors have succeeded in fitting most of the *Explanations* to
ɩr proper *Canons*, and in solving many of the formidable textual difficulties,
ɩ they have been content to examine the consecutive sections piecemeal,

[1] The present paper builds on the results of my two most recent articles on later
ɩhism: (G 1) "Later Mohist treatises on ethics and logic reconstructed from the *Ta-ch'ü*
ɩpter of *Mo-tzu*," *Asia Major*, NS, 17/2 (1972), 137-89; (G 2) "The concepts of
ɩessity and the 'a priori' in later Mohist disputation," *Asia Major*, NS, 19/2 (1975),
ɩ-90. References to *Mo-tzu* and *Hsün-tzu* are to the *Ssu-pu ts'ung-k'an* editions. The
ɩnbering of the Canons follows the edition of T'an Chieh-fu, *Mo-pien fa-wei* 墨辯發微
ɩking, 1958), which rearranges some of the relevant sections, but reproduces the plain
ɩt of the *SPTK* on pp. 24-23; the sections of *Expounding the canons* (EC) and *Names
ɩ objects* (NO) are numbered as in (G 1), 152-64, 173-78.

In the Chinese texts the following editorial conventions are used:

*X X is an emended character.	(X) X is parenthetic and a suspected gloss.
⟨X⟩ insert X.	(Y)*X Read X for Y.
(X) X is head character of the *Explanation*.	[X] Delete X.

[2] (G 1), 139-47.

without looking for an overall structure. However in 1972 I pointed ou
curious symmetry in the successive groupings of definitions and propositi●
in the Canons:

Definitions		Propositions	
A 1-6	'Reason,' 'knowing,' 'thinking'	A 88-B 12	Logic
A 7-38	Ethics	. . . .	
A 39-51	Space, time, and change	B 13-15	Space, time, and chan
A 52-69	Geometry	B 16-31	Optics, mechanics,
			economics
A 70-75	Disputation	B 32-82	Problems in disputati
(A 76-87:	Appendix to definitions,		
	analysing ambiguous words)		

There are no propositions on ethics, but this gap would be filled
Expounding the canons, judged on linguistic and other grounds to be ●
oldest of the documents.[3] We seem to discern the outlines of an organi●
summa dividing disputation into five branches, the most important of whi●
ethics, was the first to be written down. *Names and objects*, the latest of ●
documents, and the only one not composed in canon/explanation form, wo●
be outside this summa. In a more recent paper I have considered the sign●
cance of the third of the five pairs of sequences ("Space, time, and change●
and argued that the driving-force of later Mohist thought is a conviction t●
times have changed, the authority of the sages is discredited, and only lo●
can discover truths invulnerable to time.[4] The propositions of B 13-15, whi●
analyze the relation between space and duration, lead up to the conclusi●
in B 15 that "in 'Yao is good at ruling,' we locate him in the past fron●
standpoint in the present; if someone located him in the present from
standpoint in the past, it would be 'Yao is unable to rule.' " (10/13A/4-6) 堯
治，自今在諸古也。自古在之今，則堯不能治也。 The corresponding series
definitions begins with space and duration (A 39 " 'Duration' is pervasi●
of different times"; A 40 " 'Space' is pervasion of different places." (10/2B
久，彌異時也。（守）＊宇，彌異所也。) and concludes with the two ba
concepts in Mohist logic, the "staying" (*chih* 止) of name with object as lo
as a description of a changing situation remains true, and the logical or cau
"necessity" (*pi* 必) which is eternal (A 50 "To 'stay' is to endure as it wa●
A 51 "The 'necessary' is the unending." (10/1A/3) 止，以久也。 (10/1A/3,
必，不已也。). The placing of the "Space, time, and change" sequen●
suggests that the first two disciplines are conceived as having only the te●
porary validity of *chih*, the last two as having the unchanging validity of *p●*

[3](G 1), 150-152.
[4](G 2).

gestion which we shall shortly try to substantiate.

Two of the Mohist's four disciplines fit neatly into Western categories, ~ics" and "science," but the first and last both seem to come under the ~ding of "logic." That he should treat them separately is a very interesting ~ which suggests that we may have missed some distinction basic to later ~ist thinking. I believe we can find a clue to it in a Canon analyzing the ~ces and objects of knowledge:

A 80. "*Knowing*. By report, by explanation, by experience. The name, the object, how to relate them, how to act.

(Explanation). Having received it at second hand is knowing by report. That something square will not rotate[5] is known by explanation. Having been a witness oneself is knowing by experience.

What something is called by is its name. What is so called is the object. The mating of name and object is relating. To intend and to perform are to act."

(10/2A/5) 知。（間）*聞，說，親，名，實，合，爲。(10/10A/4)（知）。傳受之，聞也。方不（厈）*運，說也。身觀焉，親也。所以謂，名也。所謂，實也。名實耦，合也。志行，爲也。

Of the three sources of knowledge, the *Canons* are concerned only with ~lanation; but they deal with all the four fields of knowledge, and the ~sibility at once arises that this is the basis of the fourfold arrangement of ~ *Canons* before and after the "Space, time, and change" sequences. ~owing how to act" would be the ethics of A 7-38 and *Expounding the* ~*ons*, "knowing about objects" the geometry and physics of A 39-51 and ~6-31, and "knowing about names" and "knowing how to relate (names to ~cts)" the two disciplines which we have confused under the heading of ~ic." The reason why the four disciplines are presented in a different order ~n that of A 80 would then be that the two concerned with *chih* belong ~ore the bridging sequence and the two concerned with *pi* belong after it. ~re is no space to work out the consequences in detail within the limits of ~ present paper, but the following is a broad summary:

(1) A 1-6, A 88-B 12, "knowing how to relate (names to objects)": the ~ of consistent description of changing objects, calling the similar by the ~e name and the different by different names. The key concepts are *t'ung*

The corrupt graph 厈 looks like the 庫 in A 48 which Wu Yü-chiang convincingly ~tified as *yün* 厙 (= 軍) "rotate" written without its radical in a form attested for the ~netic on bronze inscriptions. *Cf.* A. C. Graham and Nathan Sivin, "A systematic ~roach to the Mohist optics," in *Chinese science*, edited by Nakayama and Sivin, ~nbridge: MIT Press, 1973), 121, 141.

i 同異 "the same and the different," (A 89, 94, 95 : B 1, 3, 6, 9), and purpose of the art is to "fix," cause names to stay in objects throughout t duration (*chih* used transitively as well as intransitively, A 89, 95 : B 1).

(2) A 7-38, *Expounding the canons*, "knowing how to act": the ar weighing the relative importance of desires and dislikes in changing situati Here the key concepts are *li hai* 利害 "benefit and harm" (A 26, 27 : EC 2 6-8, 10, 11). We do not find the word *chih* in these sequences, but elsewI we do find it in the phrase *chih so yü* 止所欲 "fix which you desire" (A 7S

(3) A 39-51, B 13-15. The bridging sequences on space, time, change, the definitions of which end with *chih* and *pi*.

(4) A 52-69, B 16-31, "knowing about objects": the art of fin necessary relations between objects. The Mohist physics of B 16-31 is st lingly different from the traditional proto-sciences of China in that through explanations are purely causal and causal relations are conceived as necess (Cf. A 1 *"Minor cause* [necessary condition]. Having this, it will not nec arily be so; lacking this, necessarily it will not be so. . . . *Major cause* [neces and sufficient condition] : having this, it will necessarily be so; lacking necessarily it will not be so." A 77 "Dampness is the cause: it is necessa required that what it does come about." (10/6A/7) 小故。有之不必然 之必不然。(10/6A/8) 大故。有之必〈然〉無〈之必不〉然。 (10/9B/8) 濕 也。必待所爲之成也。) The word *pi* "necessarily" recurs throughout physics sections (B 21-23, 25, 29).

(5) A 70-75, B 32-82, "knowing about names," the art of fin necessary relations between names. The key concepts are *shih fei* 是非 "b X or not-X"; one judges whether something is or is not by deductions star from the definitions of names. "In 'disputation,' one says that it is, the ot that it is not, and the one who fits the fact is the winner" (B 35). "One s it is an ox, the other that it is not. . . . Such being the case they do not b fit the fact; and if they do not both fit, necessarily one of them does not (A 74). Under the definition of *pi* in A 51 we find "Being X or not-. necessary." (10/16A/1, 2) 「辯」也者 ，或謂之是 ，或謂之非，當者勝 (10/9A/6-8) 或謂之牛 ，或謂之非牛…是不俱當。不俱當，必或不當。(10/8 是非，必也。 In these sequences we find *pi* in the logical sense of "necessari in A 74 : B 35, 49, 51, 60, 64, 69-71, 73.

It can now be seen that the same fourfold classification underlies account of disputation from *Names and objects* which stands at the hea the *Hsiao ch'ü* chapter:[6]

[6]NO 9. In (G 1), 189 I treated the last sentence as a separate fragment and plac in NO 11, but the relation to the organization of the *Canons* confirms the unity o passage. I now follow T'an Chieh-fu in taking the particle *yen* 焉 , both here and in N (*cf.* (G 1), 150) as the conjunction *yen* "only then."

"The purpose of disputation is

(1) by clarifying the portions of X and not-X, to inquire into the principles behind order and misrule ('Knowing about names'):

(2) by clarifying points of sameness and difference, to discern the patterns of names and objects ('Knowing how to relate names to objects'):

(3) by settling the beneficial and the harmful, to resolve confusions and doubts ('Knowing how to act'):

only after that may one by describing summarize what is so of the myriad things ('Knowing about objects'), by assorting seek out comparables in the multitude of sayings."

(11/7B/5-7) 夫辯者，將以明是非之分，審治亂之紀：明同異之處，察名實之理：處利害，決嫌疑：焉摹略萬物之然，論求群言之比。

Since disputation is concerned primarily with "Knowing about names" an be seen from our quotations from A 74 and B 35), this discipline is first; otherwise the order is that of the groupings of the *Canons*. We can discern the fivefold arrangement of the *Canons* behind the classification ur kinds of doubt in B 10, which at first sight seems quite unsystematic:

"Doubt. Explained by accidental, easy, coinciding, or transient circumstances.

(Explanation) . . . 'accidental circumstances.'

To lift things when they are light and put them down when they are heavy is not a test of strength (for example, stone and feathers), to shave wood along the grain is not a test of skill: 'easy circumstances.'

Whether the fighter's breakdown is due to drinking wine or to the midday sun cannot be known: 'coinciding circumstances.'

'Is it knowing? Or is it supposing the already ended to be so?': 'transient circumstances.'"

(10/3B/7) 疑。說在逢，循，遇，過。(10/12B/5)（疑）。蓬爲務則士爲牛，廬者夏寒，蓬也。舉之則輕，廢之則重，非有力也：沛（＝柿）從削，非巧也（若石羽），楯（＝循）也。鬭者之敝（＝弊）也，以飲酒若以（日）＊日中，是不可智（＝知）也：愚（＝遇）也。智（＝知）與，以已爲然也與：（愚）＊過也。

Now we have argued that the fundamental doubt which the Mohist utation is designed to clarify is the one which underlies the bridging ences on "Space, time and change": how do we establish fixed standards a changing world? This is the doubt due to transient circumstances ("Is it wing? Or is it supposing the already ended to be so?"). To counter it, the

Mohist has developed the logic of necessary relations between names (A
"The 'necessary' is the unending"; A 84 "The 'necessary,' accept and do
doubt." (10/1A/3, 4) 必，不已也。　(10/10B/1)「必」也者，可〈而〉勿疑
"Knowing about names" therefore has no place in his categories of doubt
first sight one might expect the same of "knowing about objects," whic
knowledge through the sciences of necessary relations between objects.
although he conceives causal relations as necessary, it is only in such scie.
as optics and mechanics (the ones treated in the *Canons*), not for examp
medicine, that causes are easily isolated. The stock example in the *Can*
and elsewhere in *Mo-tzu*, of an event with several possible causes is sickn
"Knowing about objects" therefore allows the doubt which arises f
coinciding circumstances (whether a spell of weakness is due to drunken
or to the heat). In the realm of "knowing how to act," the judgment th
man is righteous or strong or skillful is doubtful if he demonstrates these
in easy circumstances. The corrupt passage on accidental circumsta
presumably belongs to the realm of "knowing how to relate." It ma
noticed that except in the case of transient circumstances (which are put
the order is again that of the groupings of the *Canons*.

In Confucian literature there is one essay which resembles the
Mohist writings so closely that one is tempted to regard it as a digest of
Mohist techniques adapted to Confucian purposes, Hsün-tzu's *Cheng n*
正名 [The right use of names]. This begins like the *Canons* with a serie
definitions, and proceeds with three sections on:

(1) "The purpose of having names," which is to communicate
    similarities and differences between objects. "If noble and base
    not clarified, if the similar and the different are not distinguis
    we are inevitably in trouble with the intention not being conve
    and action being hampered and made ineffective."

(2) "What we depend on to recognize similarity and difference," w
    is observation of objects by the five senses in conjunction with
    mind.

(3) "The pivotal requirements for instituting names": the compoun
    of names when a single one is insufficient, classification of na
    at different levels of generality, agreed conventions for the us
    each name.

[7]In the opening sentences of the first *Universal love* chapter (*Mo-tzu*, chapter 1
is said that the sage must be able to identify the source of disorder as a phys
diagnoses the source of an illness. *Cf*. A 77 quoted above ("Dampness is the cause"),
the example of illness in B 9, where "the reason why it is so" is that "someone wou
him."

(*Hsün-tzu* 16/3B/3,4A/6) 所爲有名。(10/4A/1, 2) 貴賤不明，同異不別，如是則志必有不喻之患而事必有困廢之禍。(16/5B/5) 所緣而以同異。(16/7B/1, 2) 制名之樞要。

If we ask what kinds of knowledge result from the three lines of inquiry, :an answer with three of the four disciplines of the later Mohists, and in order in which they treat them in the *Canons* (although it must be itted that Hsün-tzu seems uninterested in the Mohist concept of logical causal necessity):

> Knowing how to relate names to objects.
> Knowing about objects.
> Knowing about names.

After general reflections on the uses and limitations of the study of es and objects Hsün-tzu concludes with a discussion of the weighing of :es similar to that in *Expounding the canons* (EC 7-9). At first sight this is to have no connection with the rest of the essay; it is only after referring he Mohist scheme that we see that Hsün-tzu is winding up the essay with one remaining discipline,

> Knowing how to act.

Hsün-tzu lists, unfortunately without explanations, examples of faulty ment in his first three disciplines (two of which however he refutes in il at the end of his *Cheng lun* 正論 [Essay on corrections]. A point which kens one's interest in them is that as in the *Canons* there are two varieties :h a Westerner is tempted to class together as logical; by scrutinizing them nay hope to get closer to the elusive distinction between "Knowing how :late" and "Knowing about names":

> " 'To be insulted is not disgraceful,' 'The sage does not love himself,' 'Killing robbers is not killing people,' these are cases of disordering names by confusion in the use of names. If you test them by the purpose of having names, and observe which alternative applies, you can forbid them."

(*Hsün-tzu* 16/7B/4-8) 見侮不辱，聖人不愛己，殺盜非殺人也，此惑於用名以亂名者也。驗之所「以」爲有名而觀其孰行，則能禁之矣。

Why does Hsün-tzu think that to refute these claims it is sufficient to :al to the *purpose* of having names? Because the objection is not that they factually or logically wrong but that they are semantically misleading; ' "disorder names by confusion in the use of names." By referring back to n-tzu's account of the "*purpose* of having names" we see that the weak- of such language is simply "the intention not being conveyed and action

being hampered and made ineffective." The trouble with "To be insult«
not disgraceful," as we learn from the *Cheng lun*,[8] is that it exploits
ambiguity of the word "disgrace"; to be insulted is not morally disgra«
but it is socially disgraceful. "Killing robbers is not killing people" is a M«
thesis; we shall see shortly that for the Mohists too it belongs to the real
"Knowing how to relate names to objects," and that they defend i
grounds not of logic but of semantic consistency.

" 'Mountains are level with abysses,' 'The essential desires are '
'Fine dishes do not improve the taste, the great bell does not imp
the music,' these are cases of disordering names by the use of obj
If you test them by what one depends on to recognize similarity
difference, and observe which alternative accords, you can forbid th«

(*Hsün-tzu* 16/8A/1-7)　山淵平，情欲寡，芻豢不加甘，大鐘不加樂，此惑
實以亂名者也。驗之所緣（無）* 而以同異而觀其孰調，則能禁之矣

In these cases (from the Mohist's realm of "knowing about obje«
the description is wrong because the facts are wrong; they "disorder n«
by confusion in the use of objects." We test them by "what one depen«
to recognize similarity and difference" (that is, as Hsün-tzu has already
us, by the five senses and the mind). The *Cheng lun* criticizes "The esse
desires are few" on factual grounds, that the desires essential to man ca
seen to be many.[9]

" 'You introduce yourself by what is not your name (?),' 'The
has the ox (?),' 'A horse is not a horse,' these are cases of disord«
objects by confusion in the use of names. If you test them by
convention for the name, and use what one accepts to show
fallaciousness of what one rejects, you can forbid them."

(*Hsün-tzu* 16/8A/8-8B/4)　非而謁，楹有牛，馬非馬也，此惑於用名以亂
也。驗之名約，以其所受悖其所辭，則能禁之矣。

This type of proposition, unlike the first, is mistaken in fact; unlik«
second it derives not from neglect of observation but from bad logic
analogy with the other two, we should expect this type to be tested b‹
"pivotal requirements for instituting names." But only one of these rec
ments is relevant, the "convention for the name" (its definition). You r
Kung-sun Lung's "A white horse is not a horse" (the only intelligible exar
by appealing to the logical relations between names, starting from
definitions. This, we have suggested, is precisely what the Mohist mea«
"knowing about names."

[8]*Hsün-tzu*, 12/20A/6-22B/1.
[9]*Hsün-tzu*, 12/22B/1-23B/6.

The fourfold classification of knowledge in A 80 is based on the dis-
tion between *ming* "names" (a term which for the Mohist embraces the
le of language), and *shih*, literally "solids," concrete, particular transient
cts. This dichotomy leads the Mohist to distinguish between three kinds
xplanation, of the logical relations between names, the causal relations
veen objects, and the semantic relations between name and object, and
es room for a fourth realm, that of not describing but prescribing actions.
are now ready to come to grips with the two branches of disputation
ch seemed to concern logic, one of which we can already see is more like
ad of practical semantics.

The sequences which deal with the logical relations between names are
0-75, B 32-82. Even here the Mohist is not exploring logical forms like
totle in his syllogistics, but defining logical terms and giving examples of
ori reasoning. I have pointed out elsewhere[10] that many of the definitions
1-75 compose chains, in which all the major ethical definitions derive
the terms "desire" and "dislike" (undefined, but analyzed in A 84), and
definition of the circle follows from the undefined *jo* "be like" and *jan*
" This explains why it is said in EC 2 that "Whatever the sage desired or
ked *beforehand* on behalf of men, men necessarily get from him by means
s *ch'ing* (what it is in itself, as laid down in its definition)," and in a
age arbitrarily rearranged in T'an Chieh-fu's edition under A 89, 92, that
en we go over the wall the circle 'stays' (is fixed on objects throughout
duration). By the things that follow from each other or exclude each
r, it is admissible that we know *beforehand* what it is." (11/4B/6) 諸聖人
爲人欲。(5B/3, 4) 惡者,人 (右)＊必以其請(＝情) 得焉。(10/11A/4) 超
(＝圓)止也。相從相去 ,先知是可。 (There is evidence both that
"beforehand" has the logical sense of *a priori* and that the Mohist's
edure is to imagine an object behind a wall and ask how much one knows
t it from the implications of its name without going over the wall to
rve it.)[11] The practical examples of *a priori* reasoning in B 32-82 are
fully developed towards the end of the series; we give a few of the later
ples:

B 71. "To suppose that all statements are fallacious is fallacious.
Explained by: his own statement.

(Explanation) To be fallacious is to be inadmissible. If this man's
statement is admissible (and so not fallacious), it follows that he
recognizes something as admissible. If this man's statement is inadmissible, to suppose that it fits the fact is necessarily ill-considered."

(G 2). That the ethical definitions form a chain was already noticed in (G 1), 165-67.
(G 2). *Cf.* (G 1), 154, n. 8.

(10/5A/8)以言爲盡誖，誖。說在其言。 **(10/20B/3-5)** （以）。誖。不可
（出入）＊之＊人之言可，是不誖，則是有可也。之人之言不可，以當必不

B 73. "Being limitless is not incompatible with doing something
every one. Explained by: whether it is filled or not.

(Explanation) (Objection:) The south if limited is exhaustibl
limitless is inexhaustible. If whether it is limited or limitless is not
knowable, then whether it is exhaustible or not, whether men fill it
not, and whether men are exhaustible or not, are likewise not
knowable, and it is fallacious to treat it as necessary that men ca
exhaustively loved.
(Answer:) If men do not fill the limitless, men are limited, and the
no difficulty about exhausting the limited. If they do fill the limit
the limitless has been exhausted, and there is no difficulty at
exhausting the limitless."

(10/5B/2) 無窮不害兼，說在盈否。 **(10/20B/8-21A/5)** （無）。南者有窮
盡，無窮則不可盡。有窮無窮未可智，則可盡不可盡〔不可盡〕未可智
之盈之否未可智，〔而必〕人之可盡不可盡亦未可智，而必人之可盡愛也
人若不盈（先）＊無窮。則人有窮也：盡有窮無難。盈無窮則無窮盡
盡（有）＊無窮無難。

B 76. "It is a fallacy to suppose that benevolence is within
righteousness outside. Explained by: matching with the face.

(Explanation) To be benevolent is to love (as defined A 7: "T
'benevolent' is to love individually"), to be righteous is to benefit
defined A 8: "To be 'righteous' is to benefit"). Loving and benefi
are on this side, the loved and the benefited are on that side. Nei
loving and benefiting nor the loved and the benefited are within
outside each other. To suppose that benevolence is within but righte
ness outside is to refer to loving and the benefited, which is refer
arbitrarily, like the left eye being excluded from the head but the r
eye included."

(10/5B/6) 仁義之爲外內也（內）＊誖。說在仵顏。**(10/22A/7-22B/3)**（仁
仁愛也，義利也。愛利此也，所愛所利彼也。愛利不相爲內外，所愛
不相爲外內。其爲仁內也義外也，舉愛與所利也，是狂舉也，若左目
右目入。 **(10/1A/6)** 仁，體愛也。…義，利也。

B 79. "To reject denial is fallacious. Explained by: he does not reje
(Explanation) If he does not reject his own denial he does not re

denial. Whether his rejection is to be rejected or not, it amounts to not rejecting denial."

(10/6A/2)非誹者（諱）＊誹。說在弗非。(10/21B/7-22A/1) 不（誹）非己之誹也，不非誹。（非）＊誹可非也，不可非也，是不非誹也。

Turning now to the semantic relations between names and objects, se belong to the discipline of "Knowing how to relate names and objects," ch is expounded in A 1-6, A 88-B 12, and also in the independent essay *nes and objects* (as is clear from its very first sentence, "Names and objects not necessarily related" (11/4B/6) 名實。名實不必（名）＊合。). There is space here to consider the very problematic Canons of A 88-B 12, but it ns to me that they begin to be intelligible only when we appreciate that y lay down procedures, not for logical proof, but for consistent description objects. That the argumentation in this discipline has nothing in common the strict demonstrations we have just quoted is obvious from the long ment of *Names and objects* which makes up the main body of the *Hsiao* i. This contrasts three series of parallel propositions, of which represen-ve examples are:

(1) "White horses are horses; to ride white horses is to ride horses."
(2) "Her younger brother is a handsome man; loving her younger brother is *not* loving a handsome man."
(3) "To be about to fall into a well is not to fall into a well; to stop someone being about to fall into a well is to stop him falling into a well.

(11/8B/8) 白馬馬也，乘白馬乘馬也。(11/9A/3, 4) 其弟美人也，愛弟非愛美人也。(11/9B/6, 7) 且入井非入井也，止且入井止入井也。

The second series includes the most famous or notorious of later Mohist ments. I have myself changed my mind about it in public once already,[12] shall now do so again:

"Huo's parents are *jen* (people), but Huo's serving her parents is not serving *jen* (serving a husband). Her younger brother is a handsome man, but loving her younger brother is not loving a handsome man. A carriage is wood, but riding a carriage is not 'riding wood' (an unidentified idiom). A boat is wood, but entering a boat is not entering wood (piercing or soaking into wood). Robbers are people, but abounding in robbers is not abounding in people, being without robbers is not being without people.

How shall we make this clear? Disliking the abundance of robbers is

[2](G 1), 179, n. 3.

not disliking the abundance of people, desiring to be without robbe
not desiring to be without people. The whole world agrees that th
are right; but if such is the case, there is no longer any difficult
allowing that

> loving robbers is not loving people,
> not loving robbers is not not loving people,
> killing robbers is not killing people.

The latter claims are the same in kind as the former; the world d
not think itself wrong to hold the former, yet thinks the Mohists wr
to hold the latter...."

(11/9A/3-9B/3) 獲之（視）＊視人也，獲事其親非事人也。其弟美人也，
弟非愛美人也。車木也，乘車非乘木也。船木也，（人）＊入船非＊人木
盜人人也，多盜非多人也，無盜非無人也。奚以明之。惡多盜非惡多人
欲無盜非欲無人也。世相與共是之。若若是，則雖盜人人也，愛盜非
也，不愛盜非不愛人也，殺盜人非殺人也〔無難盜〕無難矣。此與彼同
世有彼而不自非也，墨者有此而非之。…

It is commonly assumed that since the *Hsiao ch'ü* is free of the tex
difficulties of the other dialectical chapters it is safe to read it without ta
account of the *Canons*. But if we do so we condemn ourselves to miss
fundamental Mohist distinction between semantic and logical questions;
mistake the comparisons of parallel propositions for a fumbled attemp
establish logical forms, in which the Mohist fails to advance beyond argun
from analogy or to perceive that his examples are vitiated by the chan
meanings of words in different combinations. It is quite impossible to ad
that the Mohist, who has a whole sequence of *Canons* analyzing ambigu
words (A 76-87), and in the logical demonstrations we have quoted disp
a peculiar, almost scholastic rigor, could be thinking in such a primitive v
On the contrary, it is precisely because of the semantic confusions in th
examples that he puts them in the province of "Knowing how to relate na
to objects." *Sha tao* "killing robbers" suggests the execution of robbers
legitimate authority (*cf.* EC 6: "Killing robbers on your own authority is
killing robbers." (11/4A/1) 專殺盜非殺盜也。); *sha jen* "killing peo
suggests murder or wanton slaughter, as can be seen from the many exam
of the phrase in *Mencius*. In "Robbers are people, therefore killing robbe
killing people," the logical form is unchallengeable yet the conclusio
unjustified, because it would commonly be understood as "Executing rob
is murder." The Mohist's method of clearing up this confusion is to off
series of parallel sentences in which a semantic change (whether idiomati
simply a shift in the meaning of *jen* from the men who are robbers to me

eral) similarly reverses the conclusion. This is not a matter of crude
ment from analogy; what a sentence is taken to mean depends very much
explicit or implicit parallelism with other sentences, a fact which is
cially obvious in the Chinese language, which in some styles uses paral-
m almost as much as syntax to limit the potential meanings of a sentence.

The form "X is Y, but doing something to X is not doing it to Y"
ears also in B 54, in the second of the logical sequences. There the example
A dog is a hound, but killing a dog is not killing a hound"; I have failed to
e the idiomatic sense of the second clause (killing a domestic dog for
ag is not committing the offence of killing someone's hunting hound?).
parison with the *Names and objects* passage on killing robbers shows that
problem presented both a semantic and a logical aspect, each considered
in the discipline appropriate to it:

(1) When words in combination change semantically, one establishes
arallelism whether doing something to X is or is not doing it to Y.

(2) Logically, if X is Y, to do something to X *is* to do it to Y; it must
efore still be possible to say, in the neutral sense of the words, that one
do it to Y. If there were no sense in which the executioner of robbers
d be said to kill people, we should have to admit that robbers are not
le. This is the point made in B 54:

> "A dog is a hound, yet it is admissible that killing a dog is not killing a
> hound. Explained by: their identity.
>
> (Explanation) A dog is a hound; it is admissible to call it 'killing a
> hound.' "

(10/4A/4, 5) 狗犬也，而殺狗非殺犬也可。說在重。(10/18A/7)（狗）。狗犬
也，謂之殺犬可。

To take an example from English idiom, suppose that someone is
zled by my claim that although a man's legs are his lower limbs, pulling
eg (teasing him) is not tugging at a lower limb. I might answer, like the
or of *Names and objects*, by other examples (a goose is a bird, but
king one's goose is not cooking a bird . . .); I might also, like the author of
4, add that there is no logical contradiction because tugging at his lower
can also be called "pulling his leg."

The nature of the Ch'in "Reform of the Script" as reflected in archaeological documents excavated under conditions of control

Noel Barnard

my recently published *The Ch'u silk manuscript—translation and com-
ntary* some consideration has been given to the appreciably large number
"descendantless graphs" which are present in this famous brush-written
: document. The possible significance of this aspect of pre-Ch'in Chinese
ipt has not been particularly well investigated by earlier scholars. Accord-
ly, I put forward several observations firmly supported by the script evi-
ice in the Ch'u Silk Manuscript itself:

> That an important change occurred in respect of a substantial proportion
> of the multi-element graphs that were in common use in late Chan-kuo
> times is well attested amongst the CSM characters. That the change was
> strongly influenced by phonetic considerations is likewise most sugges-
> tive. The significance of these data [see Figs. 19 and 20, *op. cit.*] in
> regard to the reconstruction of archaic Chinese sounds—and the dating
> of such reconstructions—would appear to be obvious.[1]

wever, there being some possibility of argument to the effect that the Ch'u
k Manuscript descendantless graphs may reflect something of the Ch'u
ritten) "dialect" rather than more general characteristics of pre-Han charac-
structures employed throughout the "Middle States," it is useful to explore
situation more extensively. The sources consulted comprise inscriptions in
ne, bronze, lacquer, bamboo, jade, etc. and all examples cited are derived
m archaeological documents which have been excavated under conditions
control or are otherwise acceptably attested. Before embarking upon the
•ject proper, a very brief note on earlier (and still currently held) views on
nature of the pre-Ch'in script is presented. This note is intended mainly to

[1] Noel Barnard, *The Ch'u silk manuscript—translation and commentary* (Canberra:
stralian National University, 1973), 51.

refresh the reader's mind on several fundamental points which I believe n
require reconsideration in the light of the rapidly growing corpus of archae
logical documents.

EARLIER VIEWS ON THE NATURE OF THE ARCHAIC SCRIPT

Unfortunately we do not know as much as we might wish in regard
everyday literature in Shang and Western Chou times, and it is general
conceded that the oracle bone texts and bronze texts are surely but limit
facets of all that was written. Notwithstanding this restricted variety of doc
ment-type it has often been asserted that certain "primitive" elements p
meated the archaic script of the earlier periods and that it was essentially
somewhat crude medium of expression when compared with that of Han:

(a) The pre-Ch'in script comprised, for the greater part, characte
lacking "radicals":

> In our current Chinese writing, which goes back, in principle, direct
> to Ch'in and Han times, the phonetic compounds (*hsieh-sheng*), chara
> ters consisting of one signific ("radical") and one "phonetic", form t
> great majority; so-called *chia-chieh* phonetic loans, where a charact
> without the addition of any signific, stands for another word becau
> of sound similarity, e.g. *wan* "scorpion" used for *wan* "ten thousand
> are comparatively rare. In Chou time, on the contrary, the *chia-chi*
> were extremely common, and the phonetic compounds much rarer th
> in later times. In fact the majority of the latter seem to have be
> created out of *chia-chieh* characters by a later (late Chou, Ch'in a
> Han) addition of elucidating, specifying significs ("radicals"). What
> now the "phonetic half" of the character, was in middle Chou time, t
> entire character used as a *chia-chieh*, phonetic loan . . . .[2]

(b) Generally, as has just been noted, the phonetic alone existed. Th
form of graph was freely employed as a "loan character" (*chia-chieh*) f
others words of identical or similar sound:

> It was the great phonetic similarity, sometimes homophony, of lar
> groups of monosyllabic words that gave rise to the principle of phone
> loans (*chia-chieh*), the character for one word being applied, as a loa
> to a totally different word that was identical or similar in sound, a pr
> ciple which in its turn, by the elucidating addition of determinativ
> ("radicals"), led to the creation of the great, even dominating catego
> of characters known as *hsieh-sheng*, phonetic compounds, consisting

[2] B. Karlgren, "Some fecundity symbols in ancient China," *BMFEA*, 2 (1930), 4.

one "Radical" and one "Phonetic".[3]

ıus the character 求 : 求 g'i̯ôg/ch'iu "pray" was used both in the sense of ▸ray" and of "fur"—the latter, according to some authorities, being the ımary meaning of the graph. Similarly 萬 : 萬 mi̯wân/wan cited above was ed for "scorpion" and for "ten thousand." In this way a graph was "loaned" denote other words (presumably lacking a character) when required in iting. However, in an earlier study, Karlgren came to the conclusion that ₃ employment of radicals forming hsieh-sheng phonetic compounds "may vertheless have been in practical use in everyday life and in profane writing eady in Chou time";[4] the records we know in bronze ritual vessels and, in ang times, in the oracle bones being thus representative of a special and ¿red form of writing:

> It is possible to write without distinguishing radical as long as the subject is limited to a few well-known religious formulae (as on oracle bones or ritual bronzes). It is practically impossible when it comes to writing extensive lay texts with thousands of different words. The ambiguity in using one and the same chia-chieh for a dozen different words would be unendurable ... the great majority of chia-chieh loan characters must have been supplied with elucidating radicals (i.e. changed into hsieh-sheng) in the moment there arose a real literature, i.e. already in Chou time. The hsieh-sheng characters which we find in the Shuo-wen are therefore, in principle and composition, those that were in regular use when the Chou culture flourished; only their technical execution was abbreviated and simplified and normalized through the hsiao-chuan reform of Li Ssu's.[5]

ıe concept of chia-chieh "loan characters" is thus closely associated with ⪡t-types and in ordinary writing it is supposed that "radicalized" charac-ɾs were in common use at an early period (i.e. from about 600 B.C.). It is ;o considered that the hsiao-chuan script of the Shuo-wen dictionary which ṣulted from Li Ssu's reforms during the reign of Shih-huang-ti (221-209 B.C.) ıs necessarily a "normalization" of the earlier graphs—the reforms involving ▸ major structural alterations of the characters. H. G. Creel, too, wrote to ɹch the same effect: "Such abbreviation of characters and alterations in eir form were already being made during the time of the [Shang] bone ṣcriptions, and are in constant evidence in inscriptions on bronzes .... This, ₃n, was merely to follow in the long established line of the natural evolution

---

[3] B. Karlgren, "Grammata serica," BMFEA, 12 (1940), 1.
[4] B. Karlgren, "On the script of the Chou dynasty," BMFEA, 8 (1936), 178.
[5] Ibid., 177.

of the Chinese script."[6]

In opposition to the approach of the "radical + phonetic" propone
Creel made a strong case for the ideographic nature of Chinese script a
sought to view the phonetic aspect of the script as being a highly overra
feature. Although his arguments are stimulating and manifest most inter
ingly the impact of archaeological data upon Western scholarship in terms
down-to-earth studies—and these conducted by one who was almost al
among Westerners at the time in really understanding the significance
archaeological evidence and capable of bringing the full fruits of West
historical methodology into the field of pre-Han studies—his conclusions
this particular problem are now, nevertheless, somewhat open to questi
This is due simply to the accumulation of a great deal of new evidence a
the tremendous increase in details of provenance which has resulted fr
controlled archaeological excavations. Many new archaic graphs have beco
available and indicate, I believe, not only the important rôle of radica
phonetic combinations in pre-Ch'in characters but also the fact that there w
indeed a "reformation" of the script.

There are other features, no doubt, which may be observed am
various studies of the archaic script but the preceding passages seem to co
the most important views that will receive specific attention in the pres
paper and they are certainly of a fundamental nature in regard to the cou
of recent research applied to the reconstruction of archaic Chinese pronu
ation. Investigations in this sphere have a considerable bearing upon translat
techniques especially those concerned with pre-Ch'in inscriptions. Chin
scholars have long observed the fact that many archaic characters in th
archaic context do not possess the meaning normally associated with
same characters (when transcribed into modern form) as they appear in la
texts. For example, characters such as 白 : 白 b'ăk/*po* "white," 女 : 女 n
nü "woman," 畏 : 畏 ·įwər / *wei* "fear," etc. are to be found employ
respectively in the sense of 伯 băk/*po* "official title," 汝n'įo/*ju* "you" (o
如n'įo/*ju* "like"), 威 ·įwər/*wei* "majesty." Although the original context n
show the meanings in many instances, consultation of ancient rhyme tab
"dictionaries," the *Shih ching* rhyme system, and other such sources is of
undertaken to prove an identity of sound between two sometimes qu
dissimilar graphs. In commentaries on the inscriptions, Chinese scholars h
applied this method of interpretation assiduously and, it is to be fear
frequently in a rather too fanciful way.

The reconstruction of early Chinese pronunciation was first put ont
systematic basis through the application of Western linguistic principles

[6] H. G. Creel, "On the nature of Chinese ideography," *T'oung Pao*, 32 (1936), 143

Karlgren. The data employed ranged from the study of dialects in China, early alien records of Chinese pronunciation (e.g. Japanese *on* sounds, Tibetan, etc.), the rhyming sources mentioned above and, in particular, the rhymes of the *Shih ching*. Although this is quite an inadequate resume of the tremendous work involved, the important thing to observe is that almost the entire body of data comprises textual material, originating, in the form we now know it, no earlier than the Han period, and the earliest extant "original" texts seldom date before T'ang times. Pre-Ch'in inscriptions were, of course, consulted and individual graphs are employed profusely in illustration, however, Karlgren's aim was to draw only upon "ancestral" characters whose "descendant" graphs demonstrated an essentially unbroken line. Hundreds of characters which had become obsolete prior to the Han period were accordingly placed aside, or simply disregarded. Consequently, an unbalanced assessment of the general nature of Chinese script, its development, the role of Li Su's "reforms," etc. results, while the significance of certain limitations attending the evidence has unfortunately not been generally realized.[7] It is, of course, immediately obvious that the *Shih ching*—supposed to have been compiled between 900 and 600 B.C.—must, indeed, be proved to be a faithful version of the phonological form it originally possessed to allow its use in linguistic research. In other words, it is essential that the *hsieh-sheng* phonetic compounds in the various Han and later versions of the *Shih ching* should comprise the same radical + phonetic structures as those employed in Chou times. If, however, it should be discovered that any considerable number of characters in pre-Ch'in archaeological "documents" contain phonetic elements (or that these elements existed as characters without additional radicals) which have no relationship to the phonetic elements employed since Ch'in and Han times for the same written words, then linguistic research conducted on the written language in general should take into account more fully the obvious implications of such visually unrelated phenomena.

To put the problem in another way: we cannot assume that Han period versions of ancient texts supposed to have been transmitted from the earlier periods reflect reliably, in the characters used, the radical + phonetic combinations in which the originals were written. For instance, we cannot take a verse of the *Shih-ching* and simply archaize the characters and state that this

[7]Note, in this connection, the useful appraisal in Paul L.-M. Serruys' "Note on Archaic Chinese dialectology" (*Orbis* Tome IX, No. 1, 1960) which describes in more detail and with greater authority the many deficiencies and uncertainties attending Karlgren's system (pp. 42-49). This short summary of his major work: *The Chinese Dialects of Han time according to Fang Yen* is directed towards linguists not acquainted with the particular problems of the Chinese language, but for those of us who are not trained in linguistics it is to be found most valuable in its general explanation of technicalities of the discipline as applied in the main work.

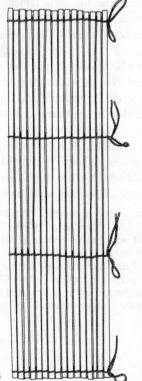

Figure 1A

Figure 1B

a reconstruction of the original form. Although quite a few *Shih-ching*
aracters are known in their archaic forms there is absolutely no certainty
at simple element-by-element substitutions—the phonetic portions in
rticular—will invariably result in the original graphs that were employed
r the same meanings and sounds. Many characters in the "classics" are
known among archaeological documents—because of limited contexts and
ucity of materials this is not surprising. However, among the bone, bronze,
mboo, pottery, and other such texts there are, on the other hand, many
aracters of which there is no traditional record. The possible significance of
is situation will be our main concern throughout this survey.

Before an acceptable reconstruction of pre-Ch'in character sounds is
tempted, it may be granted that extensive study of the structural nature of
e characters is absolutely essential. The student should concern himself first
ainly with visual aspects and only when these are thoroughly explored and
derstood should he then be in a position to attempt reconstructions of the
unds with a reasonable degree of confidence in the validity of his work.

AN ANALYSIS OF THE ARCHAIC GRAPHS

The archaic characters may be divided into four general groups for the
rpose of this investigation. The examples cited and illustrated, it should be
served, are derived not only from the script of oracle bone and bronze
xts but also from inscriptions in pottery (seal-impressions and incised
aracters), lacquer (incised characters), silk and bamboo-tablets (brush-
itten in ink), etc. With this variety of materials and of associated writing
struments, as well as the use of brush and ink, we must keep in mind the
ssible physical and structural effects of these variables upon the "normal"

gure 1 A: Portion of a Han-period inventory of various items of military equipment
ployed in actions against barbarian incursions in the vicinity of Chü-yen, Inner
ongolia. The complete inventory comprises 75 or so wooden tablets with brush writing
riting omitted in the sketch above) all of which was executed on the tablets before
ey were strung together—no allowance being made for the binding. B: Drawing
sed upon a reconstruction of a set of brush-written tablets containing a section of
e *I li* (士相見之禮). In this case the tablets were in bound form prior to the writing—
, spaces were left open during the process of writing so as to allow for binding after-
ards (after *Wu-wei Han-chien*, Pl. 24). Each tablet, with the exception of the first and
st, is numbered at the bottom. The last tablet lists the total number of characters
,020 altogether) immediately following the conclusion of the text. In its rolled state
e last line of text is inside and naturally is last to emerge as the text is unrolled and
ad. On the outside and on the backs of two tablets the section title and its number are
itten.

Figure 2 Examples of simple single element graphs all of which are directly ancestral to their modern character forms (and parallels). Their transition through the Ch'in "reform of the script" was purely a matter of slight technical change.

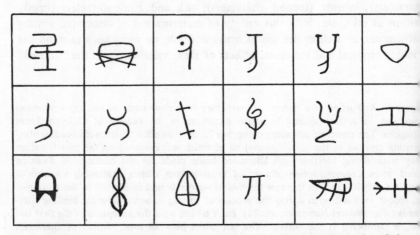

Figure 3 Simple single-element graphs which lack descendants, i.e. their *modern character equivalents* (or *replacements*) are unknown. As several of the examples derive from pottery seal texts some may not be true characters but symbols.

orm of the character. It will be appreciated that characters incised in metal
urfaces by means of a stylus-like implement will vary somewhat from the
ncised graphs in bone or tortoise shell; graphs incised in clay during the
reparation of molds for casting will exhibit nuances different from the
receding while brush-and-ink writing will manifest further differences. More
etailed observations have been offered in respect of brush-written characters
n the Ch'u Silk Manuscript.[8]

. Simple Single-element Graphs

The majority of these, in respect of their basic structures, are directly
ncestral to their *modern character parallels* and have suffered only slight
echnical changes through the transition periods of Ch'in and Han. In the
election below it will be observed that characters such as 王 giwang/*wang*
"King"; 弓 kịŭng/*kung* "bow"; 子 tsiəg/*tzu* "son"; 于 giwo/*yü* "in"; etc. are
learly direct parallels of the modern characters 王；弓；子；于. Examples
uch as 矢 śiər/*shih* "arrow"; 氏 ḓiĕg/*shih* "Mr."; 土 t'o/*t'u* "earth"; etc.
nanifest a quite close structural connection with 矢；氏；土. The nature of
he technical evolution involved is a matter of some interest. The pronounced
hickening in the centers of vertical strokes as in 矢 and 土 has given way to a
imple horizontal cross-stroke in the post-Ch'in forms 矢 and 土；the head of
he "arrow" graph is written now as ⼇ instead of 亼. In the archaic graph 夨
'ien/*t'ien* "heaven," the round head of this anthropomorphic drawing has
imilarly evolved into a simple cross-stroke; so, too, the 夨 -shaped arms: 天.
ngularity of execution becomes the rule in later calligraphy; circles, crescents,
urves, etc. so characteristic of Chou and Chan-kuo writing lose their graceful
inuosity: 子 is rendered with a triangular head and a straight body 子, the
uxom graph 母 məg/*mu* "mother" now possesses distinctly square breasts
母, while the egg-shaped symbol 白 b'ak/*po*, "white" has preserved a sugges-
ion of its former oval shape in the small slanting-stroke surmounting the
nodern character parallel 白.

Many scores of such simple single-element characters of antiquity are
hus easily recognized purely upon comparison with their modern descendants;
n their archaic context, too, we find them employed in much the same way
s in later times—their meanings are practically identical. It has often been
issumed that the technical changes described above were largely the result of
he invention of the brush attributed to the Ch'in general, Meng T'ien;
itherto, writing was done with some sort of stylus on wooden tablets and
he characters either engraved or applied in lacquer. However, recent archaeological discoveries of both writing brushes and brush-written characters in

[8] See Barnard, *The Ch'u silk manuscript*, 19-53.

Figure 4 A selection of complex single-element graphs whose *modern character parallels* are directly descendant from the archaic forms.

k on silk and on wood and bamboo tablets datable several centuries anterior
to the close of the Chan-kuo period illustrate the need for quite a different
approach to this problem. Evidence of the use of brush and ink alone is, of
course, amply verified as early as Shang in the oracular records. Variations of
 technical kind in the mode of writing the characters seem now to be but
one aspect of a major revolution in the structural form of the characters—
this reform of the script reached its climax after the unification of the feudal
states under Ch'in. By Han times the brush had been radically improved in
design to cope with the requirements of the "new" script—again a fact
amply attested upon comparison of pre-Ch'in brush-writing with recently
excavated examples of early Han characters.

Numbers of simple single-element archaic graphs lack descendants and
present no indication at all of possible later equivalents. Practically none of
the characters in Figure 3 have yet been defined in terms of meaning or sound;
they represent a small but steadily growing group of characters occurring in
inscription texts which are often too brief in content to permit the context to
indicate possible meanings—as to their archaic pronunciations we may never
be able to find means of reconstruction. Some of these graphs will sooner or
later turn up as radical, or as phonetic, elements in more complex characters,
while within many of the multi-element archaic groups which follow will be
noted further similar enigmatic elements which presumably were individually
employed as characters in their own right and which now have no counterparts. The element 屮 in 艸 : 茻 , for example, may later be discovered as
 character but at present neither this element nor the character is fully
understood.[9]

Among simple single-element graphs, however, the majority shows a
direct ancestor-descendant line through the Ch'in script reform and only a
small number of descendantless examples may be allocated to the present
group.

. Complex Single-element Graphs

In apportioning single-element characters into groups of "simple" and
complex" graphs, the aim is primarily one of general convenience yet the
division does serve to indicate a feature that might otherwise escape notice:
simple single-element characters which succeeded in surviving the Ch'in script
reform have suffered only minor shape and structural adjustments; complex
single-element characters, however, presented greater opportunity for technical change and consequently the feature is more easily and extensively
found. Indeed, the more complex the element, the more severe the degree of

[9]*Ibid.*, passage: 070.

modifications effected. Characters such as 里: 里 li̯əg/*li* "village"; 平: 平 b'iĕng/*p'ing* "level"; 戈: 戈 kwa/*ko* "ko-dagger-axe"; 止: 止 ti̯əg/*chih* "possessive article"; etc. exhibit only slight technical change. Graphs such as 金 ki̯əm/*chin* "bronze"; 冊: 冊 ts'ĕk/*ts'e* "bundle of bamboo tablets"; 非 piwər /*fei* "negative particle"; 正: 正 tieng/*cheng* "first (month)"; etc. evince more striking modification. Others such as 萬: 萬 mi̯wan/*wa* "10,000"; 長: 長 d'i̯ang/*ch'ang* "long"; 民: 民 mi̯ən/*min* "the people"; 年 nien/*nien* "year"; etc. manifest an increasing degree of alteration in shape and structural change. When placed alongside their later counterparts the may, nevertheless, be easily recognized even by the inexperienced eye bu somewhat more difficult are such parallels as: 庚: 庚 kǎng/*keng* "cyclic character"; 享: 享 xi̯ang/*hsiang* "sacrifice"; 鬯: 鬯 t'i̯ang/*ch'ang* "aromati wine"; 齊: 齊 dz'i̯ər/*ch'i* "Ch'i (State)"; 京: 京 kli̯ǎng/*ching* "capital"; 昌 t'i̯ang/*ch'ang* "abundance"; 馬: 馬 mǎ/*ma* "horse"; 車: 車 t'i̯ǎ/*ch* "chariot"; etc.

It will be appreciated, of course, that in using the term "reform of th script" and generally dating in Ch'in times the transformations described an illustrated in these pages I am, nevertheless, leaving open to question mor general aspects of character evolution prior to Ch'in times. This is a large fiel of study and only one or two examples of the research undertaken to dat can be conveniently illustrated here. The complex graph above for "chariot, for example, was so written in Shang and Western Chou times but becam obsolete long before the unification under Ch'in, in fact, the simpler archai form 車: 車 also frequently occurs in Western Chou inscriptions; the comple graph does not appear in Ch'un-ch'iu or Chan-kuo inscriptions. However, th evolution of the graph 金 "bronze" to the later form 金, on the other hanc did not result in the disappearance of the more complex earlier structure. O

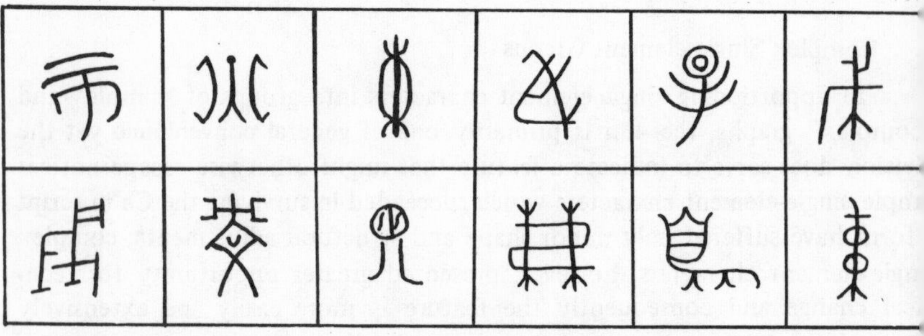

Figure 5 Complex single-element graphs lacking descendants, i.e. their *modern character equivalents* (or *replacements*) are unknown. Examples presented here are mainly personal names.

contrary, it seems to have maintained its popularity at least to within a
ntury of the Ch'in unification.

Anterior to 655 B.C. this character may be observed in recently exca-
ed bronze texts from the state of Kuo and is written therein as 𝕩 , a
aree-stroke" form. In combination, the three short strokes are omitted and
 graph (functioning as a radical) is abbreviated to 𝕩 in the character 𦇧 :
𝕩 which is part of a compound term for a type of Ting-cauldron. Earlier
t unattested inscriptions of Western Chou style often employ a "two-stroke"
aph written variously as 𝕩 and 𝕩 ; the "three-stroke" form is thus prob-
ly characteristic only of late Western and early Eastern Chou. By middle
stern Chou times the "three-stroke" graph had developed into the "four-
oke" graph 𝕩 which appears as the radical of the character 銘 : 銘 mieng/
ng "inscription" in the famous Piao Bells' text. In inscriptions from the
tes of Ts'ai and Wu (the series recently unearthed at Shou-hsien and
table within a decade or so of 500 B.C.) the same mid-Eastern Chou struc-
re is preserved 𝕩 , 𝕩 , 𝕩 , 𝕩 , 𝕩 , etc. From the same general area,
ceptably-attested Ch'u bronzes of Chan-kuo date, the Ch'u Silk Manuscript,
e cache of brush-written bamboo tablets recovered at Hsin-yang and the
cently excavated Chiang-ling tablets—all datable roughly between 500 and
0 B.C.—similarly employ the "four-stroke" form. Most of our reliably
tested examples illustrate thus a very strong continuity of the "four-stroke"
 element (or character) over a period of more than two centuries. Mean-
ne, however, the simplification of the graph towards a new "two-stroke"
rsion 𝕩 was in process. The position occupied by the two strokes was
ctated by the "four-stroke" graph and in no way does it seem to have been
fluenced by the much earlier "two-stroke" forms: 𝕩 or 𝕩 . Among some
 the Ch'u documents already referred to, comprising incised bronze texts

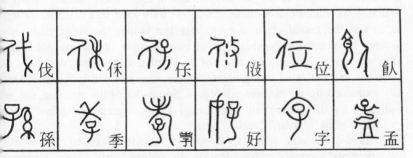

Figure 6 Simple multi-element graphs and their modern character forms. The
selection here is representative of a fairly large number which passed through
the Ch'in "reform of the script" practically unscathed.

and brush-written characters on bamboo strips, the nature of the process
abbreviation which actually involved a coalescing of the vertical pairs
strokes in the "four-stroke" graph is well demonstrated: 龟 , 鞶 , etc.

It may be assumed, therefore, that one aspect of the Ch'in script refor
involved standardization of such natural developments in the script at tl
expense of any long-cherished archaisms which still persisted—these we
firmly proscribed but not altogether forgotten because of their close affini
with the ancestral structures of antiquity. Ch'in's reformation of the scrip
however, proceeded further than this and made itself especially evide
among complex single-element characters such as those incorporated
Figure 5, which like the examples of simple single-element graphs list
earlier presumably came to be replaced by unrelated forms. Exactly wh
graphs were selected as substitutes by the Ch'in reformers seems to have be
forgotten even in early Han times; the Ch'in—so Confucian tradition tells
—not only applied a firm policy of standardization of characters, litera
style, weights and measures, etc. but also strictly enforced their regulatio
by a harsh system of punishments and effectively combated reactiona:
opposition by a well-calculated program directed towards the destruction
the foundations of the ancient Chou culture.

3.   Simple Multi-element Graphs

There probably exists a practical limit governing the extent to whic
single-element graphs—whether simple or complex—can be created an
effectively employed for writing. No doubt, an ingenious scribe might see
to invent thousands of graphs and if the principle of character creation ha
been restricted only to single-element graphs and a phonetic system of writir
never conceived, a hieroglyphic—and to some extent, ideographic—vocab
lary of cumbersome size and complexity might have eventuated in ancier
China. This, however, did not happen and in the earliest samples of writir
available we find single-element characters were kept to a manageable min
mum and the manufacture of new characters tended increasingly towards
process involving the combination of two or more of the available singl
element graphs. In many cases one of the combined elements functioned as
phonetic and indicated in a general way the sound of the spoken word vis
ally expressed by the element concerned. Some idea of the meaning, too, w
indicated by the appropriate addition of a simple graph or radical such
"water," "grass," "man," "metal," etc.

It is often very difficult, however, to decide in various cases wheth
two or more elements in combination do, indeed, form radical + phonet
graphs; "man" + "grain" 𥝋 : 休 (corrupted in Ch'in and Han times to "man
+ "tree" 休—a rendering unknown among the numerous examples in a

sted inscriptions) may well express the ideas of "ease," "grace," etc. with-
ut recourse to the phonetic value of either element. The reconstructed pro-
unciation of modern 休 is xi̯ôg/*hsiu*, thus neither 禾 g'wa/*huo, ho* nor 人
ẹn/*jen* in the archaic structure, nor 木 muk/*mu* in the later form have any
ggestion of phonetic affinity. This is not, of course, an original observation
—the *Shuo-wen* dictionary first records the opinion that the graph is simply
representation of a man reclining against a tree. However, when we consider
e following points, even so apparently obvious an explanation as that in the
huo-wen may be discovered to state the case far too simply. First, in Shang
racle bone texts there is, indeed, a character 休 "man" + "tree" which
ccurs in both attested and unattested documents; always, however, it
ppears as a place-name and never as a meaning. Secondly, among unattested
estern Chou texts, there are about a dozen cases of 休 used in the meaning
f 休 "grace" in the formula "to respond and extol the King's grace"—
efore Ch'in and Han times these are the only instances of the "man" + "tree"
raph used as a meaning. This group of inscriptions, however, comprises
veral items that are obvious fakes and several of the others are strongly
uspect. Thirdly, in the majority of unattested inscriptions using this same
rmula the character is written "man" + "grain" (over 40 examples). Lastly,
 all attested inscriptions (over 30 examples) the character is "man" +
grain." The evidence is thus highly suggestive that two different characters
re involved: a place-name 休 (sound and meaning unknown), and 休 "grace".
he "man" + "tree" graph is attested in Shang times but does not appear
gain in reliable documents until Ch'in and Han times. As there are several
h'un-ch'iu and Chan-kuo period examples of 休, we may assume that this
rm was dispensed with in Ch'in times and in place of it a character 休
man" + "tree" established. From the time of this substitution all record of
e "man" + "grain" graph disappeared. Exactly what prompted this change
 difficult to determine at present.

Returning now to the representative group of simple multi-element
raphs in Figure 6, we may observe that characters such as 伐 : 伐 bi̯wăt/*fa*
attack"; 位 : 位 gi̯wεd/*wei* "position"; 孫 : 孫 swən/*sun* "grandson"; 好 :
子 xôg/*hao* "good"; etc. manifest practically no structural changes. On the
ther hand, the graphs 保 : 保 pôg/*pao* "cherish" and 攸 : 鋚 d'i̯ôg/
iao "metal ornaments on reins," show in the former case a marked struc-
ural variation which is, nevertheless, highly suggestive of the general shape of
e archaic 保 ; in the second case an entire new element is added. Examples
f this additional element, however, also appear in a few unattested pre-Ch'in
scriptions. Simple multi-element graphs which maintain such direct, or
early direct, associations with their post-Ch'in descendants occur in appreci-
ble numbers.

Although these archaic forms may be easily aligned with *mode character parallels*, or as in the case of 㑶: 保 with *modern character equ alents*, we are still confronted by many others in this group which lack eith parallel or equivalent modern forms (*cf.* Figure 7).

4. Complex Multi-element Graphs

The arbitrary division of multi-element characters into groups "simple" and "complex" forms again serves the convenient purpose of ill trating the greater degree of technical modifications attending the more co plex forms. Figure 8 shows the feature quite clearly in respect of the a companying *modern character parallels* and the *modern character equivalen*. Among the former may be observed examples of practically unmodifi structures, 㝉 : 寶 pôg/*pao* "valuable" is transmitted as 寶 involving mere an alteration in the location of the constituent elements, 叀 : 惠 g'iwɛd/*hu* "gracious" is close to the modern character 惠, etc. But the character 彝 "*I*-vessel"—a generic term for bronze vessels—exhibits a drastic chang particularly, in the sudden appearance from Ch'in and Han times of t elements 米 "grain" and 糸 "silk." An evolution towards this complex stru ture is evident, however, in the Chan-kuo period graph 彌 : 㣙 but ev here there is no "silk" or "grain" element—simply the element 丝 "small In a number of unattested bronze inscriptions of Western Chou style t archaic form is written as 彝 suggesting thus a quite early corruption of t

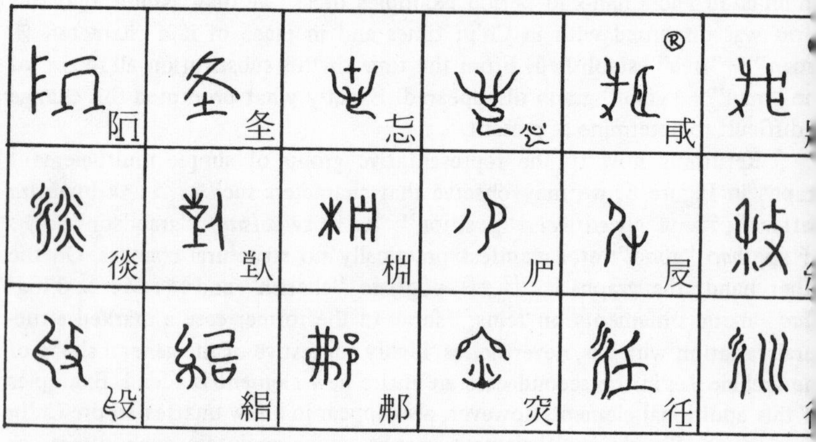

Figure 7 Simple multi-element graphs lacking descendants, i.e. their *modern character equivalents* (or *replacements*) are unknown, or are still to be satisfactorily demonstrated.

ht-hand section ⸺ into ⸺ which in Chan-kuo times came to be written
ȣ : 幺. It is perfectly evident that originally there was no element ȣ : 幺
this character (*cf.* Figure 9).

A similar instance of character evolution involving corrupt changes
ich exhibit a complete disregard for the basic structure is that of the
aracter 敢 kâm/*kan* "to presume." The *modern character equivalent* 敢
s only a loose affinity with the archaic graph 設 ; the transition of the
t-hand section from 設 to 敢 , and the right-hand section from 設 to
can be traced in some detail from Western Chou to Han times as illus-
ted in Figure 10. It may be observed that Ch'un-ch'iu and Chan-kuo period
amples often have the major "hand" element rising from the "mouth"
ment but maintain the cross-stroke through the "wrist" of the "hand"; the
ht-hand element of all pre-Ch'in examples in attested materials is distinctly
⸺ "hand" and not a "hand-holding-object" ⸺ or ⸺ element (modern 攵,
or 夂). In the Small Seal form of the *Shuo-wen* a certain degree of affinity
maintained in so far as the fundamental elements can be recognized and
gned with those of the attested pre-Ch'in examples—closer than the *ku-*
n and Large Seal structures, let it be observed—but the significance of the
aracter structure was apparently misunderstood by Hsü Shen. He came to
e conclusion that the character comprised the "radical" 受 and the "pho-
tic" 古 ko/*ku* "ancient"—our examples from pre-Ch'in sources, however,
ustrate quite clearly that there was no 古 element which would, of course,
ve been quite unsuitable as a phonetic and, moreover, they exhibit a con-
derable lack of correspondence with the *Shuo-wen*'s *ku-wen* form as well as
e Large Seal form.

Similarly the modern character 揚 diang/*yang* "to extol" appears in the
nall Seal as 揚 and the *Shuo-wen* records also the *ku-wen* form of 揚 , i.e.
:; both vary thus from Western Chou character structures which appear
her as 揚 or as 揚 in all attested examples. The element 丮 is the equiv-
nt of modern 丮 and pictures a man clutching an object with both hands.
her such cases of disparity between the structures of attested pre-Ch'in
aphs and those of the *ku-wen* and Large Seal forms recorded in the *Shuo-*
n may be cited. This is an avenue of research which requires a great deal
ore investigation than would be possible here but there is now more than
fficient evidence available to prove invalid Wang Kuo-wei's theory of (a)
'in's "preservation" and "re-establishment" of the Large Seal script of
pposed Western Chou origin, and (b) the co-existence of the Li script with
e Large Seal from an early period.[10]

---

[10] See Derk Bodde, *China's first unifier* (Leiden, 1938) for a convenient exposition of
ing's theory.

Figure 8 Complex multi-element graphs and their *modern character parallels* where directly ancestral, and their *modern character equivalents* where appreciable variations among the constituent elements are to be noted, e.g. f-4, e-5, f-5, e-6, etc.

RADICALS IN PRE-HAN CHARACTERS AND
DESCENDANTLESS MULTI-ELEMENT GRAPHS

The classification of archaic characters into single-element and multi-
ment groups has illustrated in the case of the former an essentially un-
thed passage of the greater majority of single-element characters through
Ch'in script reform—the more complex the character, however, the
ater the tendency towards technical modification, but complex single-
ment characters so affected are, on the whole, easily paralleled with their
estral structures. Thus a comparatively small proportion of single-element
phs lacks descendants. Multi-element characters, however, illustrate in the
complex structures studied in the preceding section that an appreciable
nber became obsolete in Ch'in times. It remains now to investigate the
ation of multi-element characters more exhaustively and with particular
erence to the more complex archaic examples. Quite a considerable num-
(Figure 8 is merely representative) came through the Ch'in period with
ying degrees of technical adjustments. The modifications so effected, in an
preciable proportion of the graphs, resulted in structural changes of little
sequence—these often classifiable simply as changes in shape. Those with
jor modifications, such as the several individual cases studied earlier,
vide interesting side-light on evolutionary tendencies before the Ch'in
iod as well as on aspects of the script reform. However, by far the most
portant body of multi-element characters is that considerable corpus com-
sing graphs which became obsolete no later than the Ch'in period (Figure
). Here are provided the materials requiring really urgent study for the very
d reason that it is precisely these characters which have been discarded
m linguistic consideration.[11] Not only this, the fact that we are dealing
h multi-element structures brings to our notice the problem of the
dical."

One of the immediate features manifested by our materials is the
stence of large numbers of "radicalized" characters appearing in the
nze inscriptions—Karlgren's "sacred" texts as opposed to "profane" or
ryday writing. It is, of course, well enough known that the inscriptions
er only a limited range of vocabulary and their contexts tend to be re-
icted to set formulae concerned generally with records of feudal investi-
es. This aspect of the "sacred" texts is clearly noted by Karlgren in his
per "On the script of the Chou dynasty" but we are now in a far better
sition in possessing not only a somewhat larger stock of "sacred" texts
an was available when he wrote, but also we are able to divide the materials
o groups of "attestation-types." As a result we may the better test the

---

[11] Karlgren, "Grammata serica," 2.

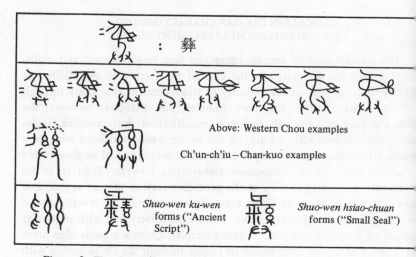

Above: Western Chou examples

Ch'un-ch'iu – Chan-kuo examples

Shuo-wen ku-wen forms ("Ancient Script")

Shuo-wen hsiao-chuan forms ("Small Seal")

Figure 9 The character *i*, a generic term for bronze vessels, and its development from early Western Chou to Han times.

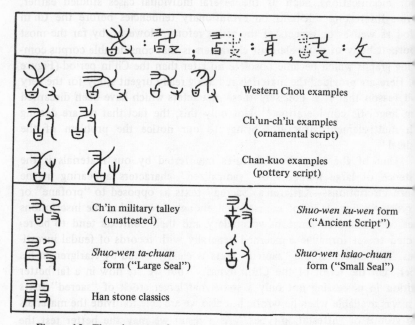

Western Chou examples

Ch'un-ch'iu examples (ornamental script)

Chan-kuo examples (pottery script)

Ch'in military talley (unattested)

Shuo-wen ku-wen form ("Ancient Script")

Shuo-wen ta-chuan form ("Large Seal")

Shuo-wen hsiao-chuan form ("Small Seal")

Han stone classics

Figure 10 The character *kan* "to dare" and its development from early Western Chou to Han times.

ications of his admission that there existed a number of real *hsieh-sheng*,
hia-chieh furnished with extra radicals[12] but which he maintained were
e whole extremely scarce in Shang and Chou archaeological documents.

Karlgren was concerned with two major questions (a) were the same
etic loans made in early Chou as in the Small Seal (or Ch'in and Han
d script) i.e. was the choice of phonograms made already in *Shih ching*
s (900-600 B.C.), and (b) were the additional radicals added already at
early period, or did their addition to the characters constitute an inno-
n attributable to the Ch'in reforms of about 221 B.C.? We are concerned
the second of the two queries at the moment. To illustrate the situation
gren conveniently lists the two ways characters in the *Shih ching* might
been written in Chou times:

麟,舜,鄰,顛,塡,聞,etc.,

　　　or

舜,舜,舜,眞,眞,眞,etc.

oncludes quite justifiably that the radicalized characters must have been
oyed but this immediately raised the problem, as he saw it, of explaining
apparently so few radicalized characters appear in the inscriptions:

One of the largest "radicals" in our present dictionaries is no. 140 艸
"grass". In the *Shuo-wen* it has a very large section. In the Ch'in and
Han inscriptions it is quite frequent. In the ritual bronze inscriptions of
the Chou, on the contrary, there is hardly a single reliable example of
this radical. How could this be explained if it were true that the regular
hsieh-hsing, with radicals, were fully current in the great literature of
early and middle Chou, of which we have no contemporaneous manu-
scripts? Why should the only documentary evidence from that epoch,
the bronze inscription, directly discredit our conclusions? Must we not
judge the lost script after the pattern of the survivals?

　　Not necessarily. There is here the difference between sacred script
and profane script. The former is always much more conservative than
the latter. An archaic simplicity and austerity is considered desirable
and dignified. In the conventional and well-known formulae of the
ritual bronzes there was little inconvenience in writing simple *chia-chieh*,
without radicals, such as 屯右 "pure happiness" for 純佑; it could entail
no misunderstanding, and it looked infinitely more ancient and dignified. When it came to the needs of everyday life, its struggles and
business intercourse, its manifold duties and functions, and when the
scribe had to take down administrative data, Royal orders, and to keep

Karlgren, "On the script of the Chou dynasty," 177.

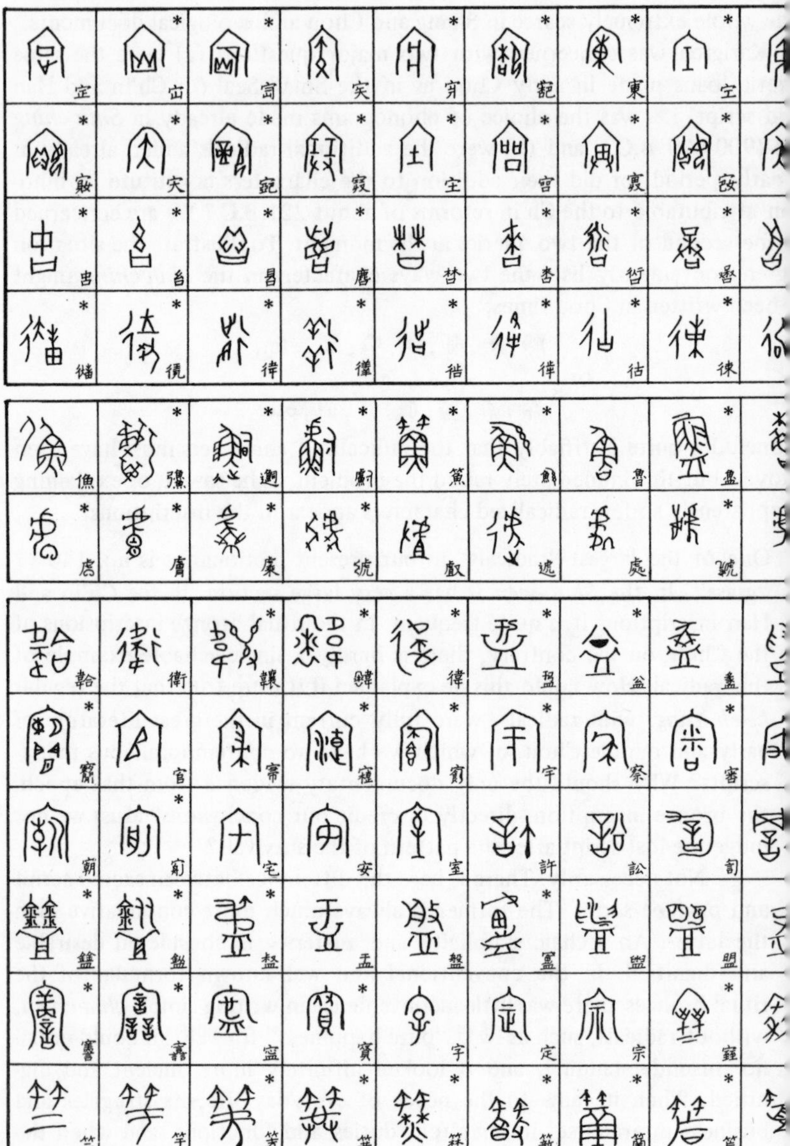
東
魚
衛
益
官
察
宅
安
室
許
盤
盟
宇
定
宗
竿

accounts and so on, he was glad to be able to add to his *chia-chieh* some elucidating radicals, which made all the crazy homophones or semi-homophones distinguishable. . . .[13]

ough I am in full agreement with the general argument advanced towards existence of radicalized characters, I feel it necessary to correct the ortunate impression created in respect of their stated rarity in "sacred" :s. Obviously the context of these documents is such that very, very few racters that now possess "grass" radicals were needed in the compilations! s was a rather ill-chosen and certainly misleading example to illustrate the it. If, for instance, the element "water" had been employed in illustration te the contrary conclusion would have resulted for it will be appreciated t combinations of "water" plus other elements will for the most part prise "radical" + "phonetic" combinations—particularly as the bulk of ription examples are geographical names (Figure 12).

Karlgren is, nevertheless, correct in his observation to the extent that ain archaic characters in the inscriptions were written without radicals— *modern character parallels* being radicalized. His examples above of 屯: 右: 佑 are representative of this feature, and there are, of course, others. m my own knowledge of the archaeological documents, however, I am from convinced that both radicalized and unradicalized pairs of characters e employed—one for everyday purposes and the other for special texts. s true, of course, that the one character may appear in one document with radical and in another without it. Although this feature is not remarkably racteristic of the inscriptions, there are to be observed a very small nber of instances of radicalized and unradicalized forms in bronze texts of same vintage and provenience—and in a few cases, in the same inscrip- i—thus we know definitely that radicals were occasionally added or itted within the bounds of some of the "sacred" texts themselves, and on basis of the contexts concerned we learn also that the variation lacks any n of regulation—it is simply a matter of the whim of the writer.

If, on the other hand, we take a character such as 純 d̂iwən/*ch'un* ire" and find it written invariably as 屯 in the inscriptions, what basis is re to the opinion that in ordinary everyday writing the radical "silk" uld have been added and the resulting graph used for the same meaning? In

[3]*Ibid.*, 178.

re 11 Multi-element graphs of Shang, Western Chou, and Eastern Chou—an mbly compiled expressly to illustrate the advanced nature of the *hsieh-sheng* form haracter from the earliest times of which we have examples. Among these, characters :h lack descendants or *modern character equivalents* (or, *replacements*) are indicated isterisks.

Chan-kuo period documents we do, indeed, find a character 絉 : 純 am
the Yang-t'ien-hu cache of brush-written bamboo tablets (e.g. items 2:8,
11:11, etc.) and in an unattested inscription several times published since
late 19th century it is written as 𦀃 . In the latter case it is part of a pers
name and thus no indication of its meaning is given. In the bamboo tab
however, this character is found in several character-compounds forr
terms related to various kinds of wearing apparel which were obvio
manufactured entirely or partly of silk. Its meaning cannot be determ
with precision but it seems unlikely in context to possess the abstract ide
"pure" although it may mean in one case "pure-silk." In the Talley ins
tion the simple graph 屯 d'wən/*t'un* appears several times but with
meaning of "assemble together." Thus in Western Chou times we find it v
out radical in unattested inscriptions in the phrase "pure happiness" bu
Chan-kuo times used as a verb "to assemble." With the addition of the "s
radical in Chan-kuo times it possesses some meaning connected with art
made of silk. With such limited evidence at our disposal this is about as fa
we can proceed in matters of interpretation until more textual exam
come to light.

    The "silk" radical is found in many characters among the Yang-t'ien

Figure 12   Characters with the "water" radical copied from Shang, Western
Chou, and Eastern Chou sources. Those lacking descendants, i.e. *modern
character equivalents* or *parallels* are denoted by asterisks.

boo tablets, the Ch'u Silk Manuscript, and other contemporaneous
ces; a variety of 40 or more different characters is listed in my files (see
re 13). The majority of these occur in bamboo tablets which comprise
rds of the artifacts buried with the occupants of the tombs. In Western
u times a similar range of vocabulary would have been required for the
articles of clothing, or other apparel of similar style, but we cannot
tantiate this contention with reference to the lists of benefices incor-
ted in recently excavated Western Chou inscriptions because silk clothing
ldom mentioned. Characters in Figure 13 which lack descendants are
ted by asterisks; the high proportion under this one radical provides an
esting view of this situation as it existed about the fourth century B.C.

Among Ch'un-ch'iu and Chan-kuo documents we find a number of
acters with the "grass" radical (Figure 14). Again, if we search through
general corpus of Western Chou inscriptions we find there are, indeed,
al with "grass" radicals, e.g. 𝕏 , 𝕏 , 𝕏 , 𝕏 , 𝕏 , etc. but only two
nples among the attested inscriptions published to date— 𝕏 and 𝕏 .

A more comprehensive view of the extent of radicalized characters
ars in Figure 11 wherein examples from Shang, Western Chou, and
ern Chou documents are assembled. Those from Shang exhibit the situ-
n of multi-element graphs classifiable under three radicals only. Many
her examples are available, and the reader may seek these conveniently in
Hsiang-heng's *Hsü chia-ku-wen pien*, Shima Kunio's *Inkyo bokuji sōrui*,
other such compendia. As a matter of interest attention might be drawn
he character index to the *Hsü chia-ku-wen pien*: oracle bone characters
ch have modern equivalents determined amount to 1,048 items, those
ch do not appear in the *Shuo-wen* dictionary amount to a further 1,585
s. A total of some 2,600 graphs is thus recorded in this work and about
of these became obsolete some time between the fall of Shang and 221
Of course it would be highly incautious to assert that these descendant-
multi-element graphs all continued to be employed throughout the Chou
od. There is not yet enough documentary material from the later era to
w reliable conclusions. The chances are, nevertheless, rather in favor of
view that the majority of these graphs continued to be used.

Western Chou multi-element graphs in the next section of this figure
drawn from properly provenanced inscriptions. The arrangement is on
lar lines and this is followed, too, for the graphs culled from attested
ern Chou texts; the latter form a larger body of materials than is at
ent available from Western Chou sources. Although the data from unat-
d inscriptions have been omitted, it should be appreciated that their
usion would add fuel to the arguments resulting from the present materials.
ful study of the characters assembled here will result in a clear impression

紡	結	紅	絡	縞*	絕
絅	糾*	紀*	緋*	純*	綏
繪	紗*	緒*	純	絹	絅
綷	絆*	繆*	緺*	絆*	綷
戀*	綺*	繡*	縞*	繩*	綺
縑*	繢*	縱*	繰*	纏*	紱
絹*	縷*	纏*	纏*	經	絰
紕	縈*	絼*	給*	繼*	絘
紺*	紛*	綠*	絲*	綫*	絽

ɔ the quantity of multi-element graphs which became obsolete sometime
ɾ to 221 B.C. That many of these are, moreover, definitely radical +
netic combinations is evident where a series such as the following can be
mbled: 豐 : 鑑 , 瑿 : 盤 , 登 : 盉 , 盂 : 盤 , 𡨄 : 𧰨 ,   etc.   The
ɛr element 皿 mi̯ăng/*min* "vessel" certainly functions as a radical in the
three cases at least. As these are vessel-names we may be sure that they
ʌld not all have been pronounced mi̯ăng. Several other series of similar
ʌficance may be noted, but where there is at present only one character
ɛr what might appear to be a radical—and no other combination avail-
with that same "radical"—we cannot, of course, arbitrarily regard it as
sieh-sheng graph until further relevant examples come to light. However,
ɔes not seem necessary to worry excessively about phonetic consider-
ns in the first stage of the argument. The important point is that so many
ɾacters, especially in the Eastern Chou group, and many datable within
or three centuries of the Ch'in script reform, vanished from record in the
ɹity of 221 B.C. It is obvious that entirely new characters, or new combi-
ɔns of elements, replaced them. The basis of substitution then becomes
crucial subject of study and here, indeed, we must become deeply con-
ɪed with the pronunciation of the obsolete graphs.

The new characters we know well enough because the majority are in
today, or if some fell out of use at various times over the last two mil-
ʌia, they still remain recorded for the most part. What we do not know,
ɾever, are their ancestors. Many of such ancestral forms, nevertheless, are
ɾrded in these pages, but the genealogical line has been sundered beyond
ɔgnition. There are thus two general groups of archaic characters upon the
s of which we may summarize our attempts to reconstruct the nature of
ʃcript reform: (a) characters which survived Li Ssu's measures in whole or
ɾart, and (b) characters which were discarded and replaced by entirely
ɛrent structural combinations. In the first group the following features in
ɛct of phonological considerations may be noted:

(1) A considerable number of single-element graphs including numerals,
ɪcal characters, and characters such as: 月, 王, 于, 大, 立, 中, 用, 白, 天,
女, 止, 曰, 不, 其, 夫, 年, 戈, 玄, 市, 人, 永, 川, 工, 乃, 乍, etc. main-
ɛd their basic structures with generally minimum modification from their
ɪest Shang appearance. Meanings for the greater part are identical with
ɹe associated with the same graphs today. As to pronunciation, however,
characters present no indication within their construction—sound

ɾe 13 Characters with the "silk" radical copied mainly from Chan-kuo period
ɪments. The majority appears in bamboo tablets with brush-written tomb lists of
ɾal artifacts.

changes that occurred over a period of time would be simply custo
associations. The sound dįwər was just as adequately indicated by 隹
500-200 B.C. as was įwi a thousand years later and as *wei* in modern Pe
or *wai* in modern Cantonese. For this reason the majority of pre-Ch'in si
element graphs has persisted without alteration for phonological purp
Some, however, were provided with radicals by the Ch'in reformers, e.g
which occurs in pre-Han texts in the meaning of "you" appears after 221
as 汝; 白, a title, has the "man" element added 伯; 不 "great" is writte
丕, etc. These "unradicalized" graphs and a few other examples serve
represent instances of two or more different meanings with practi
identical sounds, but at the time of the script reform it was felt necessa
differentiate the meanings by providing additional elements. To this exte
may be suggested phonological considerations came into play.

    (2) Among multi-element characters many have maintained
original components. In terms of their being radical + phonetic combina
we may assume that in Ch'in times the phonetic portions still functi
reasonably well to represent the sounds associated with each. Others w
suffered severe modifications usually have the phonetic portion prese
e.g. 繸 : 㡭 became 率 slįwət/*shuai* "lead troops" (the original form, it
be noted, is recorded in the *Shuo-wen*); 㝵 : 障 tswən/*tsun* "honor"
the radical 阝; 㥁 : 德 tək/*teh* "virtue" had the radical changed from 彳
彳, etc. Instances of this kind seem to suggest that the Ch'in reformers
definitely interested in preserving as much as possible complete charac
or particular elements of characters, that presented at the time—I belie
correct to assume—a clear indication of the current pronunciations.

    (3) Corrupt changes involving a sheer disregard for the original na
of the elements of various characters occurred and may be taken to illus
the Ch'in reformers' concern with the problem of making the script an u
date vehicle of writing. They were not interested in the background c
development nor were they prepared to maintain all its natural paths of
ution. Thus the radical 丂: 丂 was arbitrarily transformed into 丂. The
absolutely no structural foundation for this change. In the particle 於:
於 įo/*yü* "in," "at" the left-hand element has also been transformed int
while the upper right-hand element 入 has become 丿. There is again no
for such a transformation.

    When we turn our attention to the numerous multi-element gr
recorded from Shang to Chan-kuo times which disappeared from the s
no later than 221 B.C. it becomes increasingly evident that phonolo
considerations had much to do with the discarding of these graphs. The
fact that so many of them are clearly radical + phonetic combinations do
itself seem proof of the matter. However, let us consider the follo

racteristics of the obsolete graphs; so far as possible we shall limit obser-
on to examples datable close to the Ch'in era:

(1) Many obsolete multi-element graphs contain the same radicals as
se employed among the characters which were left unmodified by the
rmers. Of the 214 radicals according to the *K'ang-hsi Dictionary* the
ler may easily recognize such elements as: 人 9, 匚 23, 厂 27, 又 29, 宀 40,
0, 心 61, 戈 62, 日 73, 月 74, 皿 108, 辵 [辶] 162, 阝 163, 門 169, etc., all
which appear in series of several characters each. In fact, there are only a
tively few elements among those which seem to function as radicals that
not be transcribed into modern parallels.

(2) Individual elements in pre-Ch'in characters—well known in Han
later graphs—appear with the function of phonetics in conjunction with
icals but form combinations unknown except in pre-Ch'in archaeological
uments. Examples such as 徚,江,任,盛,闉, etc. when transcribed thus
ctly into *modern character form* appear to be normal characters but upon
ching for them one soon discovers that they are unrecorded. Although we
suggest the probable pronunciation on the basis of what appears to be
phonetic element we cannot assert that a modern character with a similar
nd is, in fact, the *modern character equivalent*. Any attempt to find such

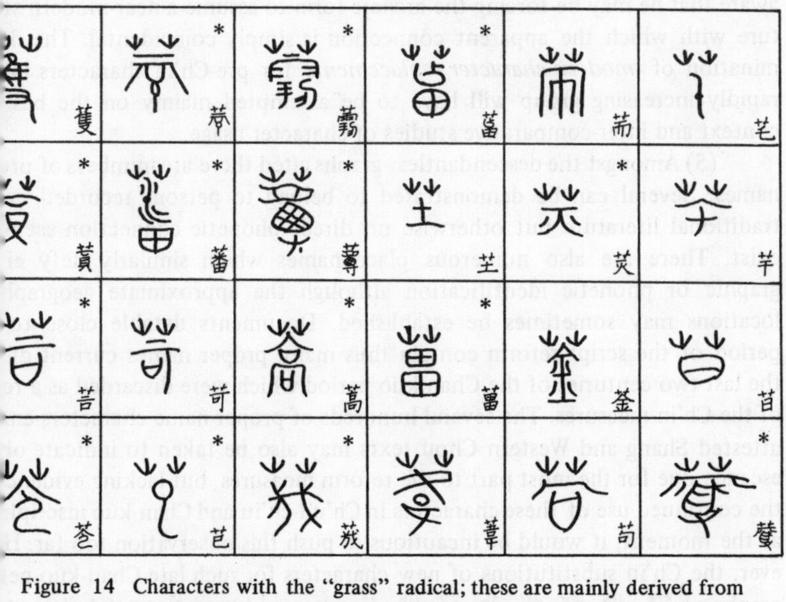

Figure 14 Characters with the "grass" radical; these are mainly derived from
archaeological documents of Eastern Chou date. Those lacking descendants or
modern character equivalents are indicated by asterisks.

phonetic equivalents must be made with careful attention to the orig
context, and should a series of different archaic sentences show the s.
graph employed consistently in the meaning of the proposed *modern cha*
ter equivalent, we may then accept that a case of phonetic substitution
been proved. The modern character, in such a case, might perhaps be ter
a *modern character replacement*—this would indicate that the connec
lost around 221 B.C. has been reconstructed upon the basis of character u
and phonetic similarity.

(3) In the phonetic portions of many obsolete characters may be no
a more complex situation than that just described—the phonetic consist
two or more definable post-Ch'in elements forming combinations of a n
unusual kind. Some may be found among rarely used modern character fo
but with different radicals. However, the majority of these complex phon
elements are quite unknown, e.g. 譎, 霻, 唇, 敊, 簸, etc. Ch'in period sut
tutions will be exceedingly difficult to determine although, in some instan
an individual component element may be found to indicate the sound of
phonetic as a whole.

(4) Phonetic portions of many of the graphs contain elements wl
defy definite transcription, e.g. 徬, 紴, 綏, 杒, 鼜, 鑀, etc. Although sc
degree of "modernization" can be attempted, the transcriber is only too sa
aware that he may be forcing the archaic form to assume a near-modern st
ture with which the apparent connection is simply coincidental. The de
mination of *modern character replacements* for pre-Ch'in characters in
rapidly increasing group will have to be attempted mainly on the basis
context and inter-comparative studies of character usage.

(5) Amongst the descendantless graphs cited there are numbers of pro
names. Several can be demonstrated to belong to persons recorded in
traditional literature but otherwise no direct phonetic connection seem:
exist. There are also numerous place names which similarly defy eit
graphic or phonetic identification although the approximate geograph
locations may sometimes be established. Documents datable close to
period of the script reform contain thus many proper names current du
the last two centuries of the Chan-kuo period which were discarded as a re:
of the Ch'in measures. The several hundreds of proper name characters am
attested Shang and Western Chou texts may also be taken to indicate ob
escence due for the most part to the reform measures, but lacking evidence
the continued use of these characters in Ch'un-ch'iu and Chan-kuo inscripti
at the moment, it would be incautious to push this observation too far. H
ever, the Ch'in substitutions of new characters for such late Chan-kuo per
graphs as 譖, 罶, 邞, 濡, 菽, 肛, 屑, 芭, etc. would most certainly have b
effected with full regard to the third century B.C. pronunciation of th

er names—the new characters would have had identical sounds. As each
h of newly excavated inscriptions appears the general stock of proper
e characters increases. That a very high proportion of those uncovered
ι Chan-kuo period sites over the last decade or so comprise descendantless
i-element graphs is a feature that must be accepted as a highly significant
mentary on the phonological aspect of the script reform. *Unless the
unciation of proper names was maintained and effectively indicated by
ιew phonetic elements in the modern character replacements sheer con-
ιn would have resulted.* Possibly future research directed towards the
tion of *modern character replacements* with pre-Ch'in geographical and
ιnal names may be found, in cases of reliably demonstrated connections,
eful means of determining the pronunciations of the phonetic elements
erned.

(6) Among the graphs listed in our figures are several which are names
essel-types current about 500 B.C. and later, e.g. 盨, 鎡, 鬲, and 鬴. In
of these it is perfectly evident that the elements 銓, 从, 于, and 升
tion as phonetics; the Chan-kuo period sounds of three of these can be
ssed with some degree of certainty: 从 dz'i̯ung/*ts'ung* "to follow"; 于
ι/*yü* "to," "in"; and 升 śi̯əng/*sheng* "rise." The graph 鎡 *ts'ung*(?)
rs in a vessel which until recently has usually been called a P'ing 餅, or a
ι豆. The graph 鬲 *yü*(?) is descriptive of a form of Ting, while another
ι of Ting is represented in the graph 鬴 *sheng*(?). The first character
e (盨) appears in a long inscription in a vessel normally termed a Tsun
Other vessels from the same site, however, employ other vessel-name
s which coincide with those already known. It would appear, therefore,
some of the descendantless characters may well comprise words (or
s) which became obsolete altogether. In the case of some vessel-names
ι obsolescence could have occurred but so far as the entire group of these
matic graphs is concerned it would be unusual to find more than a very
ι number of instances of both "word" and "graph" having become
ιct before Ch'in times.

Characters from inscribed artifacts excavated under controlled con-
ιns over the last four decades studied in this way illustrate conclusively
ιgh that the script reform briefly recorded in the *Shih chi* by the four
acters 同書文字 did, indeed, involve a major change effected upon an
eciably large number of characters. It was not sufficient, however, to
e a complete cleavage between pre-Ch'in and Han period scripts. Fortu-
ly, many characters of antiquity survived the measures which, in any
, were not directed to the total destruction of the ancient script. Li Ssu
ιly sought to rationalize the written language along lines which have yet

to be assessed more fully than it is possible to attempt here. His substitut
of Small Seal characters for the descendantless multi-element pre-Ch'in gra
such as those listed in the appended figures was, apparently, effected v
careful consideration of the contemporaneous pronunciation of the arcl
originals. We know these pre-Ch'in characters from the inscriptions; in se
cases the context indicates the meanings but we do not know how they v
pronounced either when they were in current use, or when Li Ssu rejec
them and replaced them by Small Seal graphs. Exactly what Small
characters were substituted is thus the essential problem.

Furthermore, we must realize that the available inscription vocabu
of Ch'un-ch'iu and Chan-kuo times is obviously only a fraction of the t
number of characters then in use. It is my considered opinion that there
a total of at least 6,000-7,000 characters. From attested pre-Ch'in docum
a variety of approximately 3,000 graphs may be culled from the oracle bo
inscribed bronzes, bamboo texts, etc. This total may be justifiably asserte
indicate firstly, the minimum number of characters that would have accu
lated by late Chan-kuo times, and secondly, the general nature of that fun
characters. Now, of the 3,000 available characters several scores of sir
element graphs have *modern character equivalents*, while very few post-C
single-element graphs remain without known ancestral forms. The remair
of the character vocabulary of both general chronological eras is, for the n
part, multi-element in form. Of assessable *hsieh-sheng* structure less than
the total of archaic examples passed through the Ch'in period and contir
unchanged—the greater proportion of these *hsieh-sheng* graphs comp
those that were either severely modified or were replaced by quite diffe
multi-element combinations. What proportion of the remaining, but as
unknown, vocabulary of Ch'un-ch'iu and Chan-kuo times still buried ben
the soil will comprise the same descendantless characters as well as
examples? We can be reasonably certain, upon reviewing the vocabul
content of the relevant documents excavated over the last few decades
we may expect an average of not much less than 25% to eventuate; this
fairly conservative estimate. Careful study of the examples in our figure
relation to the documents from which they have been selected results
distinct impression that there will be considerable additions to our alre
extensive vocabulary of archaic graphs and constituent elements which
modern character parallels or *equivalents*.

Although the substitution of *modern character replacements* for arc
multi-element graphs has been demonstrated to have been largely effec
upon a phonetic basis—the old phonetic element being no longer repre
tative of the current character pronunciation—we must not lose sight of
possibility that the replacement of complete graphs (or of their phon

ments) may at times reflect something over and above mere phonological
ιnipulations. The choice of elements substituted may have been dictated,
 some extent, by "political" policy—the Ch'in as the conquering and
ifying power would naturally seek to leave its particular imprint in the
wly established characters. Wang Kuo-wei's theory referred to earlier
mediately comes to mind—did the Ch'in come to adopt the Western Chou
ipt, preserve it for several centuries in the west, then when ultimately
ιning ascendancy over the Contending States, re-establish the old Western
ιou script in the form of the Seal characters—our *modern character*
lacements? This hypothesis, feasible as it may sound, has practically no
ιndation. First, we know a fair amount about the Western Chou script and
ve record of many of its multi-element graphs. Numbers of these were
viously proscribed by the script reforms—those accepted by Li Ssu, how-
ιr, were already widely employed throughout the various States in Chan-
ι times. Unfortunately, examples of Ch'in inscriptions prior to the unifi-
tion period are rare and the two best known texts—if genuine—would be
ιtable only about 150 years before the Empire. Comparison of character
ιuctures in these texts (the Ch'in Kung Chung and the Ch'in Kung Kuei—
ιther acceptably attested) with those of the "weight and measure" inscrip-
ιns of the Imperial period (of which there are properly provenanced
ιamples) and the "Imprecations against Ch'u" text suggests that the latter
ιo may have provided the stimulus for the former.

    Just to what extent character structures that might later be discovered
 be peculiarly Ch'in in origin supplanted structures current among the
ιnquered States is accordingly difficult to assess at present. One thing only
ιms certain in the present state of our knowledge—Ch'in substituted
ιphs comprising combinations of elements that for one reason or another
ιre favored by the reformers. Interesting parallels with the current "refor-
ιtion of the script" might be proposed, but this would necessarily become
ι subject of another paper.

Han Confucianism and Confucius in Han

Benjamin E. Wallacker

Han Confucianism I mean the school of thought called *Ju* 儒; by Con-
ius in Han I mean the tradition of the great teacher as it was manifest in
Former Han dynasty. Which of these, if they are usefully distinguishable,
s "victorious" in "The victory of Han Confucianism"? What "Confu-
nism" was the subject of "The establishment of Confucianism as a state
gion during the Han dynasty"?[1] Was there a victory of Confucianism in
n? If so, was it a victory of the *Ju* or of the tradition of Confucius? Was an
hodoxy of thought established? Then what schools were declared hetero-
<?

It is a commonplace, almost a proverbial truism, that what allegedly
oyed ideological triumph in Han was Confucianism heavily admixed, and
burden of much study has been analysis, qualitative and quantitative, of
amalgam. Strong doses of Legalism have been discerned as well as drafts
the magic of *Yin-yang* 陰陽 and Five Elements. Recently the influence of
hism has been explored in detail. Can there have been officially adopted
oherent system of thought containing so many disparate elements?

What after all is the evidence for the official prescription during Han of
ingle system of thought and the proscription of other systems? There is the
posal of the tenth month of 140 B.C., the first month of the first full year
the reign of Wu-ti.[2] Prime minister Wei Wan, a holdover from the reign of
ing-ti, proposed to the new emperor that certain exclusions be made in the
ft of government officials then being broadcast. The prime minister asked
t those among the responding candidates who adhered to the words of

---

[1] H. H. Dubs, "The victory of Han Confucianism," *JAOS*, LVIII (1938), 435-49. Hu
h, "The establishment of Confucianism as a state religion during the Han dynasty,"
CBRAS, LX (1929), 20-41.

[2] Wang Hsien-ch'ien, *Han-shu pu-chu* 漢書補注 (*HS*). I-wen edition. 6.1b-2a, p. 84.

"Shen and Shang and Han-fei, of Su Ch'in and Chang I," be removed fr
consideration because of their espousal of doctrines that would bring disor
to the country. The five proscribed thinkers were Shen Pu-hai, Shang Ya
and Han-fei Tzu, generally classed as Legalists, and Su Ch'in and Chang
specialists in diplomacy and foreign policy during the Warring States period

The emperor accepted the prime minister's suggestion, in so do
officially condemning certain thinkers at least so far as concerned the hir
of government employees. Of course Wei Wan's proposal merely denies
does not affirm any schools except by implication. A statement at on
stronger and more affirmative is attributed to Tung Chung-shu in his *Han s*
biography.

"At the present time," says Tung Chung-shu in a presentation of
certain date,[3] "teachers differ in their ways and men differ in their discours
The hundred schools are of varying method and their purport and mean
are not the same. Your servant, although stupid, believes that whatever d
not lie within the curriculum of the Six Refinements, within the meth
ology of Confucius, tends to rupture the Way. Let them not then tra
abreast [with us]; let all preaching of perversion and speciousness be
tinguished and put to rest."

Tung Chung-shu's pronouncement, by its very existence, suggests t
Wei Wan's proposed exclusion of certain schools had not been enforced.
Wan's brief tenure under Wu-ti had been followed by the premature atten
of the emperor's uncle, T'ien Fen, to dislodge the aged empress dowag
waving the banner of Confucianism before her passionate adherence to
teachings of the Yellow Emperor and Lao-tzu. The empress dowager h
soon put down the court insurrection and left T'ien Fen to bide his time
she should die.

Nor is it likely that Tung Chung-shu's strong statement brought gr
changes during his own lifetime, whatever importance was attached to
writings after his death. He held no high position in the government, nor v
he an intimate of the emperor. His statement is part of the famous th
questions and answers which supposedly passed between the emperor a
Tung Chung-shu and which evoke expansive praise from Liu Hsin in
closing panegyric to Tung Chung-shu's biography.

Tung Chung-shu's views must be given their due weight irrespective
the date of his rise to prominence. He explicitly elevates the *Liu-i* 六藝,

---

[3] *HS* 56.19a, p. 1172. On dating problems see Fukui Shigemasa, "Some problems
the establishment of Confucianism," *Shigaku zasshi*, LXXVI (1967), 1-34, and
valuable earlier work of Hirai Masashi to which Fukui refers. Fukui's conclusion is t
the question and answer sessions took place not in 140, as the standard texts would h
it, but in 135.

Refinements, and the methods of Confucius as his criteria of excellence.
 of the multitude of contemporary philosophical schools which do not
ve therefrom, he seems clearly to say, should be banned. Yet Tung Chung-
himself achieved an admixing of large dollops of non-Confucian mechan-
 magic in developing the theory of resonance which is attributed to him.
Tung Chung-shu obviously the question of whether a given system of
ught was or was not traceable to Confucius and the *Liu-i* was a matter of
rpretation.

The most substantial evidence of the imposition of orthodoxy of
ught during the reign of Wu-ti is found in the *Ju-lin* accounts in *Shih chi*
 Han shu.[4] We read there of the momentous events which followed the
th in 135 of Wu-ti's powerful grandmother, the empress dowager. T'ien
, whose earlier offensive the old lady had scotched, was now moved into
post of prime minister. "He banished the words of the Yellow [Emperor]
 Lao[-tzu], the *Hsing-ming* 刑名, the Hundred Schools; and he extended
self toward literary scholars and *Ju* numbering in the hundreds."

Here the *Ju* are promoted and all other schools are condemned, with
cial attention reserved for the Taoism beloved of the late empress dowager
 the *Hsing-ming* favored by her late husband, Wen-ti. It is worth noting
t this text, unlike the two cited earlier, occurs also in *Shih chi*, an indi-
ion of surer authenticity. But was the policy of T'ien Fen carried out?
re *Ju* taken into government service in droves and Taoists and *Hsing-ming*
alists refused entry? Were the *Ju*, in short, given the stamp of official
hodoxy?

We are fortunate in having two semi-official sources, the one pre-dating
 other post-dating the reign of Wu-ti, which afford us assessments of the
ef philosophies extant in Han China. The earlier view is that of Ssu-ma
n, father of Ssu-ma Ch'ien, recorded in the great history which he en-
ged and his son accomplished.[5] The later view is contained in the biblio-
phical chapter of the *Han shu*,[6] a chapter based upon the labors of Liu
ang and his son Hsin.

Ssu-ma T'an's famous critical assessment considers six schools of
ught: *Yin-yang* 陰陽, *Ju* 儒, *Mo* 墨, *Ming* 名, *Fa* 法, and *Tao-te* 道德. All
se schools have as their concern, says Ssu-ma T'an, the creation of orderly
ernment. In his remarks on the various schools the author gives both the
d points and the shortcomings. *Yin-yang*, for example, he values highly

---

[4]*Shih chi* 史記 (*SC*), see Takigawa Kametarō, *Shiki kaichū kōshō* 史記會注考證 (I-
n reprint of Tokyo, 1932-34 edition), 121.8-9; *HS* 88.3b, p. 1544. See also the Annals
the year 124, *HS* 6.11b, p. 89, and the biography of Liu Hsin, *HS* 36.33a, p. 978.

[5]*SC* 130.7-9 and *HS* 62.4b-5b, pp. 1247-48.

[6]*HS* 30.32a, pp. 890ff.

for its accuracy in calendrical computation. He says however that the atte
ant magical fascination with auspicious and inauspicious dates and ti
makes of a man's life a forest of fearful situations, tabus and prohibition
be obeyed.

The *Ju*, according to the account, take as their ancestor Confuc
They are to be valued for their ordering of the forms which properly ob
between lord and vassal and between father and son, for their clear per
tion of the relationship between husband and wife and between elder
younger brothers. But the *Ju* are so weighed down with ritual observan
says Ssu-ma T'an, that it is practically impossible for a man to follow them

Ssu-ma T'an approves strongly of the Mohists' stress on the fundan
tal things in life and their measured and moderate expenditures, but he ta
them to task for the extreme frugality which makes their teachings diffi
to live by.

The Legalists, valued for their lucid recognition of the distinct
between ruler and ruled, superior and inferior, are criticized for their exces
strictness, their total neglect of the importance of kindness.

The Nominalists are praised for their knowledge of the differe
between name and thing, but Ssu-ma T'an believes their sophistry has
them to lose sight of the practical world.

Ssu-ma T'an closes with the Taoists. They turn out to have perforr
in their philosophy precisely what Ssu-ma T'an has achieved in his revi
Taoism has adopted what is worthy from each of the other schools and
acquired the skill to shift with changes in circumstances and to adapt to
times. In its inclusive flexibility, its lack of prejudice, Taoism has bece
ideologically transcendant. Ssu-ma T'an's Taoism is not one of the hund
schools, each competing for favor against its fellows. Rather it has rai
itself above the host of philosophies by seeing each school in the contex
the whole. Embracing all schools in its understanding, Ssu-ma T'an's Tao
is supreme.

The schools taken up by Ssu-ma T'an are the first six discussed in
bibliographical chapter or *I-wen-chih* 藝文志 of *Han shu*, in the follow
order, *Ju, Tao, Yin-yang, Fa, Ming, Mo*. Four schools are added, the Di
matists, the *Tsa-chia* 雜家, the Agriculturalists, and the *Hsiao-shuo* 小訪
petty narratives. The treatment of the schools, like that of Ssu-ma T'an, s
out the good and the bad points. Unlike Ssu-ma T'an however, no sir
school is exempt from criticism. There is no counterpart among the
schools for the Taoism of Ssu-ma T'an.

But the *Ju* are slightly favored, perhaps by their appearance at the h
of the list and surely by the line or so of additional space given them in
account. The *Ju* association with the Six Classics and their stress on

cepts of *Jen* 仁 and *I* 義 are stated. The *Ju* desire "to lend weight to their
ds" is given as the reason for tracing their pedigree back to the demigods
) and Shun and to the Chou kings Wen and Wu as well as to Confucius.
Ju of later days, the account states, have on occasion lost the true way,
arted from the basic truths of the tradition. Thus the account appears to
rove the Confucian tradition and must therefore disapprove departure
m it.

The Taoists are praised in the *I-wen-chih* for their humility and their
ity, qualities the text deems valuable in a ruler, but they are condemned
their rejection of the traditionally Confucian *Jen* and *I* as well as ritual
dies. The Taoists are accused of relying upon their inner purity and empti-
s as their sole tools of government.

Yin-yang, in the view of the *I-wen-chih* as in that of Ssu-ma T'an, is
ch to be valued for its skill in calendrical computations, but it is weighed
wn with superstitious tabus. Legalism's sureness and certainty in applying
ard and punishment are accepted with approval by the *I-wen-chih* as
pporting the system of rites." But the school's total reliance on penal law,
want of positive educative indoctrination, are deemed faults.

The Nominalists seem to be valued chiefly for their contribution to the
es, from whose ancient office they are supposedly derived. Their work is
ociated with the famous "rectification of names" of Confucius, but they
condemned for their latter-day nitpicking.

The Mohists, the last of the six schools treated in common by Ssu-ma
n and the *I-wen-chih*, are criticized only for excessive zeal in observing
ir worthwhile beliefs. Thus their excessive frugality is seen as destructive
Rites, and their universal love is condemned for its disregard of the degrees
distance which must obtain between people. Other Mohist virtues are
mired without serious qualification, their prizing of excellence in officials,
ir honoring of ghosts, their anti-fatalism, and their insistence upon tight
te order and discipline.

Of the four remaining schools discussed in the *I-wen-chih* only the *Tsa-
ia*, the school of overt eclecticism, need detain us. The school is praised for
receptivity to bits of truth no matter where they are found, in the *Ju* and
e *Mo,* the *Ming* and the *Fa*, but comes under criticism for its loose flexi-
lity which provides nothing to which one can "send home his heart," as the
xt nicely puts it.

It is apparent that neither Ssu-ma T'an nor the *I-wen-chih* is pro-
uncedly doctrinaire. Neither sets up a single school of thought to the
clusion of all others. Both reviews are inclusive rather than exclusive. The
incipal differences between them lie in the base of their inclusiveness and in
e degree of explicitness in stating the identity of the base. We have seen

that Taoism is the chosen doctrine of Ssu-ma T'an, but its chief attract
seems to be its openness, its hospitality to all philosophies. The *I-wen-chi*
not so explicit as Ssu-ma T'an in indicating its preference, but there is
doubt that the *Ju*, or at least the Confucian tradition as preserved by the
is favored. The school comes first, gets more space, and again insofar as
school carries the Confucian tradition, it serves as the model against wh
several of the other schools are measured.

But it is not the *Ju* who are the counterpart of Ssu-ma T'an's Taoi
rather it is an eclectic summary to the *I-wen-chih* section on the philosoph
The various schools, says the summary, arose in that time in history when
kingly way had fragmented and the feudal lords were pursuing politics
force. The diverse tastes and propensities of the competing political lead
brought forth in response a wide range of ideologues, a swarm of philosoph
Each of the schools concentrated upon a single aspect of the great truth a
has, therefore, a governmental use. All the schools derive at least in so
sense from the Six Classics or Six Refinements.

The assertion of filiation with the *Liu-ching* 六經 or *Liu-i* is crucial
the question we are pursuing. If Tung Chung-shu's criterion of ideologi
respectability is derivation from the Six Refinements and if all schools are
derived by the *I-wen-chih*, then what is heterodox? We have seen that neitl
Ssu-ma T'an nor the *I-wen-chih* seeks to expunge any of the philosophies a
whole but rather selects from each those parts worth preserving. And althou
the *I-wen-chih* does show a preference for the *Ju* in the section we ha
discussed above, it is a preference for the tradition of Confucius as faithfu
carried by the *Ju*. The *Ju* receive criticism from *I-wen-chih*; they are not giv
unqualified approval.

The preference of *I-wen-chih* for the tradition of Confucius is evident
the implicit base from which several of the schools are evaluated. The Taoi
are criticized for their rejection of Rites, *Jen,* and *I*; Legalism is praised for
effective support of Rites; the Nominalists are valued for their rectification
names and their understanding of the Rites; and the Mohists are condemn
for their neglect of Rites and their ignorance of *Jen.*

The introduction to the *I-wen-chih* itself, a preamble to its presentati
of the entire written corpus of culture, provides a transcendent view of Co
fucius. In the very first sentence we read, "When, long ago, Chung-ni died a
his fine words were cut off," there occurred a dispersion of the grand t
dition which he had codified. *Spring and autumn* scholarship split into fi
schools; and that of the *Odes* broke up into four. During the Warring Stat
period the various philosophers, the *chu-tzu* 諸子, emerged in contentio
rivalry. The Ch'in state forbade the currency of much classic literature,
policy tardily reversed by Han.

The time of Wu-ti, the introduction continues, brought encouragement
classical scholarship. The emperor lamented the decline of Rites and Music
he realm and established facilities for the gathering and copying of scat-
d texts. The great work thus begun included the collecting of the *chu-tzu*
well as the Confucian texts. Under Ch'eng-ti was begun the cataloguing
ject of the father and son Liu. When Liu Hsiang died, his son Hsin took
r the labor which produced the catalogue and the classic bibliographic
gories. The first place in the catalogue, and in the library on which it was
d, was given to the Six Classics. The second great category was the *chu-*
, the philosophers.

The pre-eminence of the classics over all other books is parallel to the
eminence of Confucius over all other thinkers. Some Chinese of Han
es, it would appear, viewed the past as a lost paradise to which one could
onably aspire to return. The sole link with the lost paradise was Confucius,
h a symbol of the past and a key to its treasures. At his death, as we have
1, the truth he embraced became dispersed and ever since that time man
tried to reconstitute the whole.

Liu Hsin's catalogue, on which the *I-wen-chih* drew so heavily, was
ed the *Ch'i-lüeh* 七略 "Seven outlines," and we make the transition from
rary to political evidence in a passage from that work which is preserved
commentary to the *Wen-hsüan*:[7]

> Hsiao-wu Huang-ti ordered Prime Minister Kung-sun Hung broadly to
> open the pathways for presentation of books. In the space of a hundred
> years the books piled up like a mountain.

Kung-sun Hung was the first man who carried the label of scholar, not
say Confucian, to reach the office of prime minister. In his own person
refore he bridges the chasm between the world of the bookman and that
the practical government administrator. It is in the words of Kung-sun
ng that Professor Creel uncovered one of the more compelling pieces of
lence on the influence of Legalism upon Han thinking. The words were
ered by Kung-sun Hung in a review of four cardinal virtues of Confu-
ism, *Jen* 仁, *I* 義, *Li* 禮, and *Chih* 智,[8] often rendered Benevolence, Pro-
ty, Rites, and Wisdom.

Kung-sun Hung states that *Chih* is the origin of *Shu* 術 or "method," a
hnical term of the school of Shen Pu-hai. *Shu* is the means by which the
er is able to make tough decisions and to carry them out. It is the ideo-
ical underpinning of that pragmatic governmental administration which

---

[7] *Wen-hsüan* 文選 (Commercial Press edition), 38.847.
[8] *HS* 58.3b, p. 1215. The material is not included in the version of Kung-sun Hung's
graphy in *SC* 112.

Legalism provided to the unification of China. Kung-sun Hung has tr
muted the antique Confucian notion of Wisdom into the knowledge of I
efficiently and practically to administer a state.

The glosses Kung-sun Hung gives for *I* and *Li* are standard word-pl.
i "to be appropriate, fit," and *li* "to tread upon." But the word *Jen*, perh
the most fundamental Confucian concept, is defined by Kung-sun Hung v
the word *ai* 愛 "love." An expanded definition follows: "To bring forth j
and to put off loss; to love universally and to lack private concerns: we ca
Jen." Here Kung-sun Hung has defined *Jen*, the discriminating and gra
compassion of Confucius and Mencius with *Chien-ai* 兼愛, Mo-tzu's in
criminate love for mankind, to Mencius the abhorrent opposite of *Jen*.

This intrusion of one of the chief articles of Mohist belief into Kı
sun Hung's testament of Confucianism figures weightily in the thesis
Fukui Shigemasa[9] that Mohism was to a great degree absorbed by C
fucianism before and during Han. The absorption theory would explain
apparent disappearance of adherants to Mohism, a surprising phenomeno
view of the fact that Mohism was the chief rival of Confucianism a cent
or so earlier. We need not accept wholly the Fukui thesis, recalling the
that Mohism holds an important position in the *I-wen-chih*, in order to vi
his having brought together evidence of Mohism's influence upon thinkin
high official places during Former Han.

The signs of Mohist influence in the life and character of Kung
Hung are few but fairly clear. The man was notorious for his personal
gality, indeed the object of some derision. He once proposed the disarmin;
the populace of their crossbows, an idea not inconsistent, it would seem, v
Mohist antipathy to offensive warfare.[10] Finally, Kung-sun Hung express
view of Heaven more consonant with the theism of Mo-tzu than with
agnosticism of Confucius. He says that Chieh and Chou suffered beca
Heaven was punishing them for their evil deeds; Yü and T'ang, having amas
virtue, were given to rule the empire. Heaven seems less mechanical and m
volitional in Kung-sun Hung's view.[11] Kung-sun Hung's purported Co
cianism, it is obvious, was hospitable to ideas from other schools.

If such leading Confucians of the time of Wu-ti as Kung-sun Hung
Tung Chung-shu were eclectic, so also was the government as a whole.
though there were present in the administration of Wu-ti men of literary
scholarly bent, students of Confucian texts, there were also men in
government who stood against Confucian thought or simply ignored it.

[9] Fukui Shigemasa, "The resuscitation of Mo-chia in the former Han dynasty," *Tö
gaku*, XXIX (1970), 1-18.
[10] *HS* 64A.14b, p. 1277.
[11] *HS* 58.4a, p. 1215.

ivalence of the Wu-ti court is well illustrated in the retrospective debate
ch was held shortly after the emperor's death in 87 B.C. and which has
e down to us in the *Yen-t'ieh-lun, Dialogues on salt and iron*. Senior
ernment officials who were economic interventionists and supporters of
ansive foreign policy, were pitted against conservative and passive scholars.
contrast between the activist officials, proponents of the new statism,
the old-fashioned literati, harking back to a fantasy feudalism, is con-
ially enunciated in the dialogues. Ideologically the contest was between
practical arts of statecraft as codified by the Legalists and the older values
simpler society as sanctified by the Confucians.

Han Confucianism, as we have seen, did not assert a clear command of
cial thinking in Former Han. Let us now turn our attention to the looser
cept of Confucius in Han. How did the tradition and teachings of Con-
ius manifest themselves? In what ways did the tradition make its presence
? What skills or knowledge in the Confucian tradition were valued by the
wielding political power?

The tradition of Confucius and the bearers of that heritage had three
able skills to offer the Han state: (1) They had a greater command of
al and protocol than other groups; (2) They placed a higher value upon
racy than did competing schools; (3) Their devotion to historical texts
them the ability to quote classical precedent with facility.

The initial entry of the tradition of Confucius into the Han state was
to Shu-sun T'ung,[12] an expert in Rites who had previously been employed
Ch'in. At the downfall of Ch'in, Shu-sun T'ung offered his services to one
r another of the front-running rebels and ultimately was engaged by Liu
g, the founder of Han known as Kao-tsu. Kao-tsu was no Confucian nor
he an admirer of Confucians. His employment of Shu-sun T'ung was for
practical purpose of acquiring the aid of his knowledge of ritual protocol.
victorious emperor could no longer endure the spectacle of his generals at
rt drinking themselves into a brawling tangle in their ease of military
mph. The emperor required of Shu-sun T'ung that he devise a program of
als, ceremonies, and procedures which he, the emperor, could easily learn
which would assure an atmosphere of civilized calm at court.

Shu-sun T'ung drew his program of rituals not only from older sources
also from the Ch'in ceremonials. There is no reason to believe that he
d to insinuate any of the ideological values of Confucius into the product;
was not a man whom principle unduly hampered in his struggle for survival.
great and lasting contribution to the Confucian tradition was to make

[12]Shu-sun T'ung's biography is in *SC* 99 and *HS* 43. Kao-tsu remarked eloquently
going through the ceremonials Shu-sun T'ung had arranged, "Now, today, I have
e to know the nobility of being emperor." *SC* 99.18, *HS* 43.16b, p. 1032.

himself useful to Han by providing his own specialty. A measure of
importance of Shu-sun T'ung's contribution is the role played by the *Li,*
Rites, in the *I-wen-chih* assessment of schools. We have seen above t
attention to the Rites is a criterion in several of the evaluations. Rites beca
one of the most valuable items in the portfolio of the bearers of the C
fucian tradition.

Literacy was as closely associated with the traditions of Confuciu:
were rituals, and it was by reason of their avowed primacy in letters that
Confucians made their second grand contribution to Han. The bureaucr:
immensity of the centralized Chinese state required great numbers of lite:
people to man offices in the provinces as well as in the capital, there to k
records, make reports, draft orders and memorials.

Lu Chia, a contemporary of Shu-sun T'ung, warned Kao-tsu that
could not hold on horseback that which he had won on horseback.[13] He
an effective proponent of literary as distinct from martial skills in governm
office. Formal nationwide drafts of men for office came into being in
B.C. when a call was issued for the "worthy and excellent," qualities wh
seem to have been measured at least in part by literary attainment and sl
The government came gradually to develop techniques of testing candida
qualifications, moral and ethical as well as literary and intellectual, by
quiring that they answer questions propounded in the name of the empero

A natural development perhaps was the government's decision no lor
merely to examine the education and character of candidates but to un
take to train them further after selection. The chief agent of the cen
government in the construction of the new educational and training faci
was Kung-sun Hung.[14] The system he founded assigned select students dra
from the entire country to the study of specific classic works. The stude
were required to apply themselves effectively to their studies or face dismis
Successful graduates were placed in a pool from which official appointme
were made.

The educational process had within its very choice of texts an elem
of indoctrination, but the best means of imposing a stringent ideolog
orthodoxy would lie in adhering to constrained interpretations placed on
texts. Had Tung Chung-shu been demonstratively active in determining
work of the facility, his apparently strict constructions might be presumec
have been put in force. But under the design of Kung-sun Hung the col
could hardly have been much more strict in ideological purity than was
man himself. The texts chosen for study very likely comprised the work:
the Confucian tradition, those which appear in the first section of

[13]*SC* 97.15-16 and *HS* 43.7a, p. 1028.
[14]*HS* 6.11b, p. 89 and 88.3b-4a, p. 1544; *SC* 121.8-9.

wen-chih a century later, the corpus known as the Confucian classics.

The Confucian classics made one emphatic ideological statement quite ɔart from differing interpretations placed upon the texts: The past must be udied and cherished. Not that every deed and utterance recorded in the ₂xts was a lucid and unambiguous guide for the modern reader, but the total ɔrpus served as a sort of epic by which the Chinese could project themselves ır into the past and could celebrate their lengthy pedigree. The student of a onfucian classic very likely committed the entire text to memory and ɔquired a set of general assumptions about good and evil in government and ɔciety. From the *Ch'un-ch'iu* the student gained a mass of day-to-day events ₁ brief narration, causes and effects for one who would find them, tabus roken and ensuing disaster for those who would seek such links. There was a ʾealth of human experience from which to learn, mistakes to be avoided, ιccesses to be emulated.

To use the past as a model against which to measure the present was learly subversive of contemporary efforts to govern, as Li Ssu, advisor to h'in, realized when he sought to prohibit popular contemplation of historical ₂xts. And Hsüan-ti, a successor to Wu-ti, realized that the *Ju* of his day were otentially subversive in their continual downgrading of their own times as iewed against the Confucian past.[15] But a corpus of records of the past can e used without blanket value judgment. The past can be used not as a model ut as a source of governmental and legal precedent. Classical solutions to roblems analogous to contemporary problems can be sought out and exam-ɪed for possible applicability.

To enlist the past as a storehouse of suggestive guidelines for present ecisions is rational behavior. To use the past in this way is also to cater in a ɪoderate manner to the common desire for a higher sanction for political and ₂gal constraints than resides in mortal rulers. The third great contribution of he Confucian tradition to Han was to offer its historical texts to the state for ɪse as a source of legal precedent and lofty sanction. The bearers of the Con-ucian tradition seem to have consented to assist in the practical adminis-ration of the state provided classical precedent, no matter how distended the ɪt, be sought for acts and policies. This partnership guaranteed the Confucians ₁ important role in government in return for their aid in locating precedents n the literature they so thoroughly controlled. The non-Confucians gained ɔrecisely the kind of traditional sanction for their strong central government ʋhich had been wanting in the Ch'in state.

The architect of this collaborative structure was none other than Kung-ιn Hung, the first avowed adherent of the Confucian tradition to attain high

[15] *HS* 9.1b, p. 122.

and weighty office, the first man to be forced to temper his values and ideology to the practicalities of governmental administration. Kung-sun Hung was the crucible in which began the amalgamation between Confucian tradition and Legalist pragmatism. He was well practiced in "literalizing the law and bureaucratizing affairs," *wen-fa li-shih* 文法吏事,[16] that is, placing the law on a basis of textual authority as opposed to spontaneous fiat, and subjecting all problems to official solution, as opposed perhaps to informal and unofficial compromise. Kung-sun Hung gave a *Ju* methodological lining to the workings of the law, but we have much more detail on how the process worked from the career of Chang T'ang.

Kung-sun Hung was an avowed Confucian; Chang T'ang was an adherent of "the short and the long," apparently an allusion to the politics of the Warring States period. His background was in penal law and he came to occupy the office of minister of justice during Kung-sun Hung's ascendancy. He went on to become grand secretary and then prime minister. Even before he became minister of justice Chang T'ang was co-compiler of a massive corpus of what appears to have been case and judicial law. The corpus was so large as to evoke the criticism that it brought confusion and uncertainty to the task of local magistracy. The very ambiguity and multitude of options meant that more and more clerical assistance was required to seek out precedents from which the magistrate might select the one which best fitted his notion of justice in the case.

At this time the emperor, as the text says,[17] "had turned his gaze increasingly towards literary scholarship." Chang T'ang accordingly began to search out legal precedents from the ancient literature on which to base his judicial decisions. As clerks to make the actual searches he selected students from the training program inaugurated by Kung-sun Hung, students who specialized in the *Shang-shu* and the *Ch'un-ch'iu*. These young scholars were set to the task of "settling doubtful law." Of course the process of legal research is often one of seeking precedent for the decision one has already made, and so it was that Chang T'ang would frequently divine the intent of the emperor and then put his scholars to work finding classical precedent to support the imperial wisdom.

Chang T'ang brought to fulfillment the melding of the Confucian tradition with case-governed Legalism. We have pointed out the importance of Kung-sun Hung in the process; it is possible that Tung Chung-shu played a role also. Chang T'ang is said to have gone at times to seek counsel from the

---

[16] *SC* 112.4, *HS* 58.4b, p. 1215. See also *HS* 89.1a-b, p. 1556, where Tung Chung-shu and Erh K'uan are linked with Kung-sun Hung as *Ju* who were practiced in *wen-fa* and the glossing and adorning of bureaucratic workings with classical sources.

[17] See Chang T'ang's biography: *SC* 122.15 and *HS* 59.2b, p. 1222.

:tired Confucian. If we accept the story as true, the question arises what the
reat minister would have to discuss with Tung Chung-shu. It is perhaps
'orth suggesting that the two men had enjoyed a long association, for which
owever there is no evidence, and that the subject they had in common was
ie legal precedents in the classics. Tung Chung-shu's own labors had led him
） examine and presumably to date, classify, and order hundreds of historical
pisodes from the *Ch'un-ch'iu* in his search for the ties and links of resonance.
ut in the process he surely became well-equipped to help in the finding of
:gal precedents, so familiar must he have been with the material.[18]

It would be ironic indeed were it to develop that Tung Chung-shu's
reat gift to Chinese institutions was not so much in the system of education
r civil service selection but in the wedding of Legalistic methods and Con-
ucian historicism.

To the three great contributions made by the traditions of Confucius to
Ian government, to rituals, to civil service selection and training, and to law
nd administration, must be added the uniquely supreme respect which came
o be awarded to Confucius as sole transmitter of the wealth of antiquity.
lacing Confucius in so elevated a position may appear to constitute a true
ictory of Confucianism. But there was a difference between common respect
or the past and the recognition of the value of Confucius as its repository
nd transmitter, on the one hand, and acceptance of the specific values and
deas of the *Ju*, on the other hand. The *Ju* were a partisan group who believed,
re must assume, in such articles as the superiority of rites over law, kin
elationships over those imposed by the state, man's innate sense of good and
vil over externally dictated norms. Moreover, the *Ju* were very likely not
ilent about their antipathy to Legalism, Mohism, and Taoism. The *Ju*, the
Ian Confucians, indeed sectarian Confucians, thus remained merely one of
everal contesting schools to the end of Former Han.

In a very real sense, however, content-free Confucianism, the tradition
)f Confucius, which was free to accept beliefs and practices from all schools
nd whose own creed consisted almost entirely of simple reverance for tra-
lition, did emerge pre-eminent in Han. Confucius became identified with the
Chinese tradition and thereby became the rightful recipient of universal
espect. But he gained that position at the cost of his supporters' giving up
he attempt to impose his ideas upon the Chinese people to the exclusion of
ompeting ideologies.

[18] Tung Chung-shu is in fact credited with the compilation of a sizable book of
:ases and rules of law, of which we preserve perhaps half a dozen. They are conveniently
:athered in Shen Chia-pen 沈家本, *Han lü chih-i* 漢律摭遺 22.3b, ff. In *Shen Chi-i hsien-*
heng i-shu 沈寄簃先生遺書 (Taipei: Wen-hai Press, 1964).

The resulting Confucianism, which I have called "Confucius in Han," is well outlined by Kung-sun Hung in the presentation of the four Confucian virtues to which we have had occasion to refer. *Jen* has been broadened to coalesce with the universal love of Mo-tzu, the love which was suited to an all-powerful government demanding equal obeisance from all its citizens whatever their kin obligations. *I* was the valuable Confucian notion of intuitive, or at least internalized, knowledge of right and wrong. *Li* was Rites, all customary behavior, culture formed, from mourning ceremonies to state sacrifices. Finally *Chih* was the knowledge of Legalistic methodology in statecraft, basically the art of marshalling the entire populace to do the will of the ruler.

Uncovering the sauce jar:
a literary interpretation of Yang Hsiung's "Chü Ch'in mei Hsin"*

David R. Knechtges

Fifth year of T'ien-feng ... THE WANG MANG GRANDEE YANG HSIUNG DIED. ... The last section of the *Exemplary sayings* written by Yang Hsiung lavishly praises Wang Mang's achievement and virtue as comparable to that of I Yin and the Duke of Chou. Later, he also wrote "Denigrating Ch'in and praising Hsin" in order to eulogize Wang Mang. A gentleman finds this distressing!

Chu Hsi, *T'ung-chien kang-mu*.[1]

*I wish to acknowledge the helpful advice of my former teachers, Hsiao Kung-ch'üan, h Yu-chung, and Hellmut Wilhelm, all professors emeriti at the University of Washing-. I also wish to thank my good friend and colleague, Wang Ching-hsien, for his con-ctive criticism.

Abbreviations used in this paper are as follows:

GSR: Bernhard Karlgren, "Grammata serica recensa," *BMFEA*, 29 (1957), 1-332.

HFHD: Homer H. Dubs, trans. *The history of the Former Han dynasty*. 3 vols. (Baltimore: Waverly Press, 1938-55).

HS: *Han shu* (Peking: Chung-hua shu-chü, 1962 ed.).

MH: Édouard Chavannes, trans. *Les Mémoires historiques de Se-ma Ts'ien*. 6 vols. (1895-1905; Paris: Adrien Maisonneuve, 1969 reprinted with an additional volume).

Records: Burton Watson, trans. *Records of the grand historian of China*. 2 vols. (New York: Columbia University Press, 1961).

SC: *Shih chi* (Peking: Chung-hua shu-chü, 1959).

SPPY: *Ssu-pu pei-yao*.

SPTK: *Ssu-pu ts'ung-k'an*.

WH: *Wen hsüan (SPTK)*.

[1] *T'ung-chien kang-mu* 通鑑綱目 (1701 Wang Kung-hsing ed.), 8.63a-b. Although the g-*mu* was not written entirely by Chu Hsi, this statement is probably from his brush, it is consistent with other similar remarks Chu made about Yang Hsiung (*cf.* his 'u-tz'u hou-yü"楚辭後語, 2.13a-b, *Ch'ung-ting ch'i-shih-erh chia Ch'u tz'u p'ing-lin* 丁七十二家楚辭評林 [1475 Chin-chien lin-jui t'ang ed.]).

Over the ages Confucian scholars have sometimes criticized Yang Hsiung
for his "Denigrating Ch'in and praising Hsin." This is not right. Yang
Hsiung had no choice but to write this piece. In his recitation of the
virtue of the Hsin-Mang, he only is able to praise it over the oppressive
Ch'in. A deeper meaning certainly can be ascertained. When he says in
his preface that Wang Mang "Matches the Five Sovereigns/ Towers over
the Three Kings" and "Since the Creation I have never heard of anyone
greater," this truly is designed to mock Wang Mang. If Hsiung had been
good at flattery, had written portents for the mandate, and had praised
Wang Mang's achievement and virtue in order to seek rank and position,
he ought to have been ranked with the highest ministers of state. How
could he have been as unsuccessful as he was?

Hung Mai, *Jung-chai sui-pi*.[2]

Occasionally in the history of literature one finds an example of a poet who
work has been adjudicated as bad, not on the basis of any objective liter
criteria, but on factors completely unrelated to the work such as "bad char
ter" or "improper behavior." In Chinese literature, the great Han poet Y
Hsiung (53 B.C.-A.D. 18) is perhaps the most famous example of a wr
whose literary reputation has been sullied by such extra-literary consi
ations. One of his works in fact has been condemned, not because it is po
written, but because it was written at all. This piece is Yang Hsiung's mem
"Denigrating Ch'in and praising Hsin" ("Chü Ch'in mei Hsin" 劇秦美新; he
after referred to as CCMH).[3]

The piece, which was considered of sufficient literary quality to
included in the sixth century anthology *Wen hsüan*, has been one of the m
controversial writings in Chinese literature. The controversy has not b
exclusively a literary controversy, however, and the evaluation of the work
been largely related to the question of Yang Hsiung's character and behav

---

[2] *Jung-chai sui-pi* 容齋隨筆 (*SPTK*), 13.5a-6a.

[3] The word *chü* "bothersome," "terrible," "to aggravate," is especially difficu
translate accurately into English. Von Zach (see the reference below) makes nouns
of *chü* and *mei* ("Tadel der Ch'in und Lob der Hsin-Dynastie"), but I prefer to l
their verbal force ("to consider terrible" and "to consider good"). Albert E. Dien's t
lation of the title is ingenious ("The virulent Ch'in and the admirable Hsin"), but a
fails to express the verbal quality of the words; see "Yen Chih-t'ui (531-591+): a Bud
Confucian," in *Confucian personalities*, edited by Arthur F. Wright and Denis Twitc
(Stanford: Stanford University Press, 1962), 50. Another interesting suggestion is m
by the Sung scholar Wang Yu-hsüeh, who glosses *chü* as *hsi-chü* "to play," "to fun,"
mock"; see *T'ung-chien kang-mu*, 8.63b, "Chi-lan." It would be tempting to translat
title "Mocking the Ch'in and praising the Hsin," but unfortunately *chü* in the sen
hsi-chü 戲劇 is a much later usage. The text is contained in *WH* 48.9a-20a.

ely has it been studied as I propose it should be, as a work of literary art.
basic assumption is that a work of literary art is an independent, self-
tained entity, which one should be able to read for its intrinsic quality,
it should not be necessary to consider extrinsic elements such as the
ior's personality, social and political background, or even "intention."

Indeed, one should beware of equating the meaning of a work with its
ntion, for works of literature are continuously being interpreted over time,
as Wellek and Warren rightly assert: "The total meaning of a work of art
not be defined in terms of its meaning for the author and his contem-
aries. It is rather the result of a process of accretion, i.e. the history of its
icism by its many readers in many ages."[4] Thus, although a work may
inally have been written for a non-literary purpose, such as Milton's
opagitica, Edmund Burke's *The impeachment of Warren Hastings, Esq.* or
·ma Ch'ien's "Letter to Jen An," over time it can be appreciated for its
insic literary quality.

CCMH is a good example of a work that has been variously treated over
ages. Much of the opinion has been influenced by the Sung philosopher,
ı Hsi (1130-1200), whose remarks on the piece are quoted at the beginning
this paper. According to this view, CCMH deserves condemnation, not
ause it is a poor literary specimen, but because it praises the "usurper"
ıg Mang (45 B.C.-A.D. 23), who assumed the throne as first emperor of
Hsin dynasty in January A.D. 9.[5] Wang previously had been regent and
ting emperor" for the infant Han rulers at the close of the Former Han
asty. During the short-lived Hsin dynasty, which ended with his assassin-
n iñ A.D. 23, Wang Mang instituted an extensive reform program ostensibly
:d on ancient, classical models. Although his reform has been labelled
:ialistic,"[6] it was actually a utopian scheme that purported to revive the
itutions and practices of the Chou dynasty. It was not his reform, but the
of seizing the throne, that gained for Wang Mang everlasting opprobrium,

[*] René Wellek and Austin Warren, *Theory of literature* (2nd ed. New York: Harcourt,
·e & World, 1956), 31.

There is a controversy whether the name Hsin means "new" or refers to Wang Mang's
of Hsin-tu. It is possible the term refers to both. See *HFHD*, III, 257, n. 36.2 and
exchange between Yang Lien-sheng and Dubs in *HJAS*, 19 (1956), 435-42; 20, (1957),
·32. It has also been discussed by J.J.L. Duyvendak, *TP*, 40 (1950), 216-17 and
uncey S. Goodrich, "The reign of Wang Mang: Hsin or New?" *Oriens*, 10 (1957),
·18.

[*] See Hu Shih, "Wang Mang, the socialist emperor of nineteen centuries ago,"
BRAS, 59 (1928), 218-30; Otto Franke, "Staatssozialistische Versuche im alten und
·elalterlichen China," *Sitzungsberichte der preuss. Akad. d. Wiss. Phil-Hist Kl.* (1931),
·42 and "Staatssozialismus in China im Altertum und Mittelalter," *Scientia*, 52 (1932),
·5; James H. Jacques, "Wang Mang, an early Chinese socialist?" *Eastern World*
idon), 19 (August-September 1965), 15-17.

for his deed was viewed in later times as a usurpation, which was one of most heinous crimes a Chinese statesman could commit. According to m Confucian scholars, it was the duty of an upright and loyal official to ref to serve a usurper, and if necessary, to take one's life rather than continu office.

Yang Hsiung was an official of the Han, albeit a rather low ranking and he did not resign nor did he commit suicide when Wang Mang decla himself emperor. Because of his prominence as a Confucian scholar philosopher, Yang Hsiung seems to have been singled out for special critici Not refusing to serve the usurper, and writing a panegyric for the Hsin, tantamount to what would be called "treason" in the West.

Not all Chinese scholars maintain this view, however, and anot interpretation attempts to exonerate Yang from the charges of being a W Mang partisan. Particularly in the late Ming and throughout the Ch'ing, wl there was increased interest in Yang Hsiung's philosophical works, a num of scholars, in what amounts to an *apologia*, try to demonstrate that Y Hsiung actually was opposed to Wang Mang and that his works contain m veiled criticisms of his policies and his usurpation.[7] There was even an ef by several scholars in the seventeenth century to prove that Yang Hsiung not live into the Hsin period, or even that he did not write the CCMH.[8]

These interpretations are clearly not literary but political, and in they are based on rather limited and highly ambiguous information. primary source for information on Yang Hsiung's role in the Wang M "usurpation" is the "Appraisal" (*tsan* 贊) appended to Yang's Han biography.[9] According to the "appraisal," one of the methods Wang M used to gain support for his claim to the throne was the presentation to court of what were called *fu-ming* 符名, "portents for the mandate." *Fu-m* were auspicious omens, presumably naturally occurring or falsely invent which were interpreted as signs from Heaven confirming Wang Ma legitimacy. A great number of *fu-ming* were presented in the early month his reign, and they were eventually collected in a huge forty-two sect

---

[7] Most representative of this view are Ch'en Pen-li (*fl.* 1878) in his *T'ai-hsüan ch'a* 太玄闡秘 (*Chü-hsüeh hsüan ts'ung-shu*); Yü Yüeh (1821-1906) in "Yang-tzu Fa p'ing-i" 揚子法言評議, *Chu-tzu p'ing-i* 諸子評議, ch. 34-35; Wang Jung-pao (1878-19 *Fa-yen i-shu* 法言義疏 (1933; Taipei: I-wen yin-shu kuan reprint n.d.). Even non-Chi scholars have written defenses of Yang Hsiung. See Kanō Naoki, "Yō Yū to Hōgen" 雄と法言, *Shinagaku* 支那學, 3.6 (August 1923), 399-420 and Fritz Jäger, "Yang H und Wang Mang," *Sinica-Sonderausgabe* (1937), 14-34. A recent review of the ques has been done by Li Hsien, "Yang Hsiung jen-ke p'ing-i" 揚雄人格評議, *Kuo-wen hs pao* 國文學報, No. 2 (April 1972), 185-93.

[8] For details, see the discussion below.

[9] *HS* 87B.3584.

*'ien 篇) book.[10] One of Wang Mang's early supporters was a man named
hen Feng. As Wang assumed more and more power for himself, Chen
:came increasingly uneasy and feared a reaction possibly from the Han house
self. This led to Chen's demotion to a low position. His son, Chen Hsün, was
utraged by the treatment his father had received, and attempted to retaliate
y the use of *fu-ming*. He first presented a *fu-ming* stating the house of Hsin
ιould divide its territory at Shan between Chen Feng and one P'ing Yen,
ho was then serving as Grand Tutor. Wang Mang could not have been pleased,
ut in spite of the fact he had previously issued a prohibition against the
resentation of *fu-ming*, he granted the request. Chen Hsün followed this *fu-
ing* with a second even bolder than the first. This "portent" demanded that
'ang Mang's daughter be married to Chen Hsün. Wang was angered by Chen's
ιdacity and ordered his arrest. Chen Hsün escaped while his father was
»rced to commit suicide. Implicated in Chen Hsün's plot were a number of
αportant officials, including Liu Fen, the son of the great bibliographer, Liu
sin (?-A.D. 23).[11]

To what extent this was an actual conspiracy against Wang Mang is not
nown. At any rate, it did result in the arrest and execution of hundreds of
fficials who were suspected of anti-Wang Mang activities. Liu Fen purportedly
»nfessed his involvement, and in his confession, he mentioned Yang Hsiung's
ame, which meant Yang could be arrested and questioned. At this time,
ang was engaged in the collation of books in the T'ien-lu Gallery, one of the
ιperial archives. Hearing that the prison officers were on their way to arrest
im, Yang jumped from the Gallery in an apparent attempt to commit suicide.
liraculously, he survived the fall.[12]

Word of Yang's attempted suicide reached Wang Mang, who is reported
) have said, "Hsiung never participates in affairs; what guilt could he have in
ιis?" He immediately ordered an investigation, and the authorities discovered
ιat the only reason for Yang's implication was that once Liu Fen had studied
strange script" under Yang Hsiung, who was an expert in the study of
ifficult and rare characters. Wang did not consider this sufficient grounds to
etain him, and he issued a decree not to interrogate him.[13] Yang then

[10]See *HS* 99B.4112-14; *HFHD*, III, 288-94.

[11]See *HS* 99B.4123; *HFHD*, III, 307-11.

[12]See *HS* 87A.3584. The two Ch'eng brothers, Ch'eng Hao (1032-1085) and Ch'eng
(1033-1107), among others, have doubted the credibility of this story of Yang's fall
om the T'ien-lu Gallery; see *Erh Ch'eng ch'üan shu* 二程全書 (*SPPY*) 4.4a. For a
ιmmary of the arguments in English, see Alfred Forke, "The philosopher Yang Hsiung,"
ΙCBRAS, 61 (1930), 108-10.

[13]*HS* 87A.3584. "Strange script" (*ch'i-tzu* 奇字) was a form of writing that was said
) differ from the *ku-wen* 古文 style.

temporarily left the court to recover from the injuries sustained in his fall, b
was summoned back later to what seems to have been a sinecure.[14]

The story of the "*fu-ming* affair" and Yang Hsiung's leap from th
imperial library reads more like romance than history, and it is certainl
possible to interpret the account in different ways. For example, it is possibl
to construe Yang Hsiung's arrest as an indication that certain members of th
Wang Mang regime (if not Wang Mang himself) suspected Yang of associatio
with the anti-Wang Mang group. On the other hand, one could claim that th
fact Wang Mang ordered his release and even promoted him proves that Yan
Hsiung and Wang Mang were on rather good terms, and that his arrest wa
simply a blunder by the authorities. Finally, it is conceivable that Yang Hsiun
was neither a supporter nor an opponent of Wang Mang, but an innocer
scholar in the imperial library who happened to suffer the misfortune of onc
having taught a confessed participant in this political intrigue.

The case of "Yang Hsiung and Wang Mang" is a good illustration of th
hazards involved in using "historical" events to interpret works of literatur
What is assumed to be fact (Yang Hsiung was an enthusiastic devotee of Wan
Mang or alternatively Yang Hsiung was an opponent of Wang Mang) turns ou
to be an unproved assumption, which, if used to support an interpretatio
leads only to questionable and extremely tenuous conclusions. Thus, if on
cannot be certain about Yang Hsiung's role in the Wang Mang regime, when
comes to evaluating a work like CCMH, which is attributed to the period afte
Yang returned to court,[15] the questions of Yang's "sincerity" and "intention
become impossible to answer.

"Intention" and "sincerity" in fact are not proper literary conside
ations, and one should ignore them unless he is prepared to risk the interpre
ative error known as the "intentional fallacy." The fundamental literar
question is not what the message is, but how the author expresses it. The be
method of determining the mode of expression is by a "close reading" of th
piece, paying special attention to the tension, ambiguity, and paradox of th
language. I propose, therefore, to attempt to examine CCMH in this fashio
and I begin with the most basic kind of interpretative reading, a translatio
of the text.

[14] His position was that of *chung-san ta-fu* 中散大夫 or Palace Grandee withou
Specified Appointment. He also held simultaneously the post of *chu-li* 諸吏, for which
know of no good English equivalent.

[15] Ch'en Pen-li assigns the piece to A.D. 10; see the *nien-p'u* in *T'ai-hsüan ch'an-m*
10a. Tung Tso-pin dates it somewhat later in A.D. 14; see "Fang-yen hsüeh-chia Yan
Hsiung nien-p'u" 方言學家揚雄年譜, *Chung-shan ta-hsüeh yü-yen li-shih yen-chiu-s
chou-k'an* 中山大學語言歷史研究所週刊, 8 (June 1929), 88.

Denigrating Ch'in and Praising Hsin[16]

Yang Hsiung, *chu-li* and Palace Grandee without Specified Appointment ocking my head on the ground and bowing repeatedly present a memorial "sealed matters." Your Majesty the emperor: I, Yang Hsiung, whose classi-l learning is shallow and meager and whose deeds and abilities are nothing usual frequently have received your great favor and have been selected)m my equals and ranked with the most noble. I am ashamed that I lack y basis for being worthy of my position. It is my humble opinion that Your jesty, with the virtue of a veritable sage, has risen as a dragon and ascended the throne. You are reverent, enlightened, and esteem antiquity; you act as ther and mother to the people; you serve as lord of the empire. Holding e way of purity and clarity, you shine like a mirror over the world and form yourself of its manners and customs. Your learning is broad and all-compassing:

> You are a partner with heaven, a twin with earth;
> You join with the divine luminaries.
> You match the Five Sovereigns,
> And tower over the Three Kings.

nce the Creation, I have never heard of anyone greater. I am truly delighted make manifest the Hsin virtue and let it shine without limit.

In the past Ssu-ma Hsiang-ju wrote a work on the *Feng* 封 and *Shan* 禪

[16] I use two texts of this piece. One is the *Liu-ch'en chu Wen-hsüan* 六臣註文選 *PTK)* which is a reprint of a Sung edition. The other version, and the preferred one, is e Hu K'e-chia (1757-1816) edition prepared by Ku Kuang-ch'i (1776-1835) and P'eng ao-sun (1769-1821) in 1809. I use the Commercial Press reprint with punctuation blished in Hong Kong, 1960. In addition to the commentary of Li Shan and the Wu-'en paraphrases, I have consulted the following Ch'ing dynasty commentaries on *Wen ian*: Chang Yün-ao (1747-1829), *Hsüan-hsüeh chiao-yen* 選學膠言 , Preface dated 22, Taipei: Kuang-wen, 1966 reprint; Sun Chih-tsu (1737-1801), *Wen-hsüan Li chu -cheng* 文選李注補正, 1798, Taipei: Kuang-wen, 1966 reprint; Wang Shih-han (1707-?), *n-hsüan li-hsüeh ch'üan-yü* 文選理學權輿 , Preface dated 1768, Taipei: Kuang-wen, 66 reprint; Chu Chien (1769-1850), *Wen-hsüan chi-shih* 文選集釋 , Preface dated 1836, ipei: Kuang-wen, 1966 reprint; Liang Chang-chü (1775-1849), *Wen-hsüan p'ang-cheng* 選旁證 , 1834, Taipei: Kuang-wen, 1966 reprint; Hu Shao-ying (1791-1860), *Wen-hsüan en-cheng* 文選箋正, Preface dated 1858, Taipei: Kuang-wen, 1966 reprint; Hsu Sun-ing (n.d.), *Wen-hsüan pi-chi* 文選筆記, Preface dated 1884, Taipei: Kuang-wen, 1966 rint. I have consulted the following translations: *Monzen* 文選, in *Kokuyaku Kambun sei* 國譯漢文大成 (3 vols.; Tokyo: Kokumin bunko kankō kai, 1922), II, 430-39; Erwin n Zach, *Die chinesische Anthologie: Ubersetzungen aus dem Wen hsüan*, edited by e Martin Fang (2 vols.; Cambridge, Mass.: Harvard University Press, 1958), II, 898-905; anklin Melvin Doeringer, "Yang Hsiung and his formulation of a classicism," Unpub-hed dissertation, Columbia University, 1971, pp. 202-10.

sacrifices in order to display the excellence of the Han house.[17] I am co
stantly suffering from dizzy spells and I am afraid one morning my corp
will fill a moat or ditch before I can serve you as a dog or horse.[18] If n
feelings are not expressed I will eternally regret it in the Yellow Springs
dare to fully express my liver and gall and pour forth my belly and heart
have composed a work denigrating Ch'in and praising Hsin. Although I ha
not investigated one part in ten thousand, these are the utmost of my though
Knocking my head on the ground, bowing repeatedly, I inform you as follow

In the beginning, Heaven and Earth had yet to open and all was blurr
and indistinct. Some of it burgeoned as black and some of it sprouted
yellow.[19] When the black and yellow split apart, above and below they beg
to warm each other.[20] It was then that man was first engendered and er
perors and kings initially came into existence. In this time of chaos and da
ness their vigor and reputation were unknown.[21] For generations no o
could speak about them. Of those about whom one could speak:

> In high antiquity no one was more illustrious than Fu Hsi;
> In middle antiquity no one was more splendid than Yao
>   and Shun;

[17]The "Essay on the *Feng* and *Shan* Sacrifices" (*Feng Shan wen*) immediately p
cedes Yang Hsiung's piece in the *WH* (48.1a-10a). It is also found in *SC* 117.3063-71 a
HS 57B.2600-8. It has been translated by von Zach, II, 893-98; Watson, *Records*,
336-41; and recently by Yves Hervouet, *Le Chapitre 117 du Che-ki (Biographie de Ss*
ma Siang-jou) (Paris: Presses Universitaires de France, 1972), 205-26. Hervouet has a
discussed the work in his *Un Poète de cour sous les Han: Sseu-ma Siang-jou* (Par
Presses Universitaires de France, 1964), 198-209.

[18]*Cf.* Chao Ch'ung-kuo's memorial in *HS* 69.2982: "I have received great favor fr
the Son of Heaven. Both my father and sons have been given illustrious rank. My positi
has reached as high as the ministership and my rank is that of marquis. The age of t
dog and horse is seventy-six, and even if you issue a decree for my corpse to fill a mc
or ditch, as long as my reputation does not perish, I will have no cares or concerns." T
term "dog and horse" (*ch'üan ma* 犬馬) is thus a self-humbling expression of an officia
desire to be of service to his lord.

[19]The "black" (*hsüan* 玄) is Heaven, and the "yellow" (*huang* 黄) is Earth. T
locus classicus for the association of these colors with Heaven and Earth is in the *Bo*
of changes, "Wen-yen" commentary; see *Chou i yin-te* 周易引得 (1935; Taipei: Ch'e
Wen Publishing Co., 1966 reprint), 4/2.

[20]I follow Li Shan who equates *ou* 嘔 "to vomit" (GSR 122i, **u*) with *hsü* 吁 "
warm" (GSR 108c′, *xiu*). *Cf. Li chi* (*SPTK*), 11.14b, in which one finds the com
nation *hsü ou* (GSR 122o, **iu*): "The *yin* and *yang* find each other, *warm* and nurt
the myriad things."

[21]I am following Chu Chien who claims the character *hsin* 鼗 of the *Wen hsüan* te
is an abbreviated form of *wei* 亹 (GSR 585a, *miwər*) "vigorous." Chu then points ou
relevant passage from the *Book of songs*: "*Vigorous, vigorous* King Wen/ His go
reputation is unending" (*Mao shih* 235). For Chu's argument, see *Wen-hsüan chi-sh*
23.6b.

Closer to us in time, no one was more notable than Ch'eng
and Chou.[22]

ien Confucius could not find employment, he used the opportunity to
oduce the *Spring and autumn annals*. He said that those blessed by the
ine luminaries and those trusted by the people are none other than those
o speak of the Way and Virtue, Humaneness, Propriety, the Rites, and
sdom.

All alone, Ch'in rose to prominence from the borderlands of the Western
ng, on the Pin wilds, Ch'i and Yung.[23] Following the presumptuous traces
Hsiang, Wen, Hsüan, and Ling, Ch'in established its foundation under Duke
iao, prospered under Hui-wen, and flourished under Chao and Chuang.
en Cheng broke the Vertical Alliance, dominated the Horizontal Alliance,
d swallowed up the Six States, he then called himself First Emperor. He
artily adopted the iniquitous policies of Shang Yang, Chang I, Lü Pu-wei,
d Li Ssu. He avidly promoted the military tactics of Po Ch'i, Wang Chien,
ng T'ien, and Wang Pen.[24] He destroyed the old texts, abolished the sayings
the philosophers, burned books, relaxed the Rites, let the music crumble,
d stopped up the people's ears and eyes. Then, he wished to

Cast off Yao,
Set Shun afloat,
Wash away the Yin,
Sweep aside the Chou.

burned and eradicated the writings of Confucius and had engraved his own
rits and feats. He changed the regulations, measures, axle size, and weights
all were made to conform with the Ch'in standard.[25] Thus, elderly Con-
ian scholars and prominent old men picked up their books and retreated

[22] Ch'eng Chou is ambiguous. It could refer to the ancient city situated near Loyang
one could render it the "Accomplished Chou." Yang uses the same expression in his
rricade hunt rhapsody," which the T'ang *Wen hsüan* commentator, Liu Liang,
lains as King Ch'eng and the Duke of Chou (see *WH* 8.32a).
[23] These areas are near the old Chou ancestral home.
[24] Shang Yang (*ob.* 338 B.C.) was the legalist adviser to Duke Hsiao (361-338 B.C.).
ng I (*ob. c.* 310 B.C.) was the organizer of the Horizontal Alliance. Lü Pu-wei (*ob.*
B.C.) and Li Ssu (280?-208 B.C.) were powerful ministers under the first Ch'in
peror. Po Ch'i (*ob.* 258 B.C.) was a Ch'in general who led the campaigns against Han,
, and Chao. Wang Chien (*fl.* 236 B.C.) led the campaign that resulted in the final
in victory in 221. Meng T'ien (*ob.* 209 B.C.) was the First Emperor's commander-in-
ef and is famous for building the Great Wall. Wang Pen (*fl.* 226 B.C.) was another
in general, who defeated Ch'i in 221 B.C.
[25] I am following the interpretation of Hu Shao-ying and Wang Nien-sun; see *Wen-
an chien-cheng*, 30.21b.

into the distance. Ritual officers and erudites rolled their tongues and wou[l]
not speak. The bird that "comes with fine demeanor" and the beast of "fle[sh]
and horn"[26] considered Ch'in a maneater and would not approach it. Porte[nts]
of sweet dew, good wine springs, luminaries, soaking moisture disappeare[d.]
Evil bewitchments such as great comets, passing meteors, a giant barbaria[n,]
and a "ghost token" appeared.[27] The spirits cut off their divine moisture, a[nd]
the rivers and seas rose *en masse*. In its second generation, Ch'in was destroye[d.]
How terribly suddenly this happened![28]

The Way of emperors and kings requires caution—one must not devia[te]
from it. Those who are able to correctly understand it, will have an exhausti[ve]
supply of good portents; those who deviate from it and are blind to it, w[ill]
suffer the extreme in evil calamities. If one looks into antiquity, there we[re]
cases of rulers who, though they depended on propitious omens, still perishe[d.]
How, then, could one who followed an evil path maintain himself inta[ct?]
Therefore, those who follow antiquity are praised as a Yao or Shun wh[ile]
those who pompously disdain it will fall like Chieh or Chou. It is even m[ore]
impossible for one who completely sweeps aside the thousand-year feats a[nd]
deeds of former sages and concentrates solely on his selfish interest to enj[oy]
divine blessings.

It happened that the Han ancestor ascended as a dragon from Feng a[nd]
P'ei, dashed forth from Yüan and She. At Wu Pass he joined forces w[ith]
Hsiang Yü against Hsien-yang. He created his dynastic enterprise in Shu a[nd]
Han; he began his rise to power in the Three Ch'in.[29] He conquered Hsia[ng]
Yü east of the T'ai-hang mountains and was declared emperor of the wor[ld.]
In response to the times, he removed the most cruel and bothersome aspe[cts]
of the Ch'in government. The use of Confucian scholarship, punishmen[ts,]
calendars and annals,[30] maps and canons little by little increased. Thou[gh]
in conflict with antiquity, the Han continued to follow the remaining Ch['in]
institutions and measures as well as the Hsiang clan titles and ranks. Thus, t[he]
Imperial Canon had gaps and was not repaired; the kingly principles we[re]

[26]These are terms for the so-called Chinese phoenix (*feng-huang* 鳳凰) and unic[orn]
(*ch'i-lin* 麒麟).

[27]The ghost token refers to the appearance in 211 B.C. of a spirit bearing a jade t[ablet]
foretold the impending death of the First Emperor; see *SC* 6.259 and *MH*, II, 183-84.

[28]The word I have translated as "terribly suddenly" is *chü* 劇, the same word t[hat]
occurs in the title of the piece. I suspect that it is used here in a double sense:
"sudden," referring to the short span of the Ch'in dynasty; (2) "terrible," "extrem[e,"]
referring to the oppressiveness of the Ch'in regime.

[29]The Three Ch'in is the area where Hsiang Yü set up three former Ch'in general[s as]
kings. Liu Pang's adviser, Han Hsin, provided him with the strategy to conquer this a[rea]
in 206 B.C.

[30]*Kokuyaku Kambun taisei*, 433, suggests this means "historical records."

axed and not tightened. The Way of Han reached its limit and the fate of
e dynasty came to an end. It was dark, confusing, and they could not turn
ck.

Then, when the great Hsin received the mandate, the Lord on High
urned his aid, and the Sovereign Earth was concerned and comforting.
rk tokens, sacred covenants, yellow omens bubbled forth.[31]

> Swelling, spouting, roaring, and raging,
> Like the flow of a river, welling of the sea,
> Movement of clouds, bending of the wind,
> Gathering of mist, scattering of rain,
> They extend to the eight limits of earth,
> And array themselves above in the court of Heaven.

ke the sound of thunder, rays from the sun, blazing light and soaring echoes
ed the space between Heaven and the Abyss. These were certainly things
t to be declined!

Thereupon, Your Majesty acceded to Heaven's mandate, gained the
most favor and the highest honor. You divided divine tallies with Heaven
d joined in sacred covenants with Earth. You established yourself over the
llions of people and created a model for a myriad ages. Such strange, extra-
linary, fantastic phenomena appeared because of your sacrifices to Heaven
d service to Earth. These unusual things and distinctive anomalies were
served by the Generals of the Five Majesties and were spread into the
pire in forty-eight sections.[32] They mounted up to the celestial vault and
ead out over the earth below. If not the Hsin house, who was worthy of
eiving them? Splendid and magnificent, they were true emblems of a Son
Heaven!

Such things as the white pigeon, vermilion crow, white fish, and severed
pent are worthless compared with these.[33] To receive the mandate is
tremely easy, but to attract such portents is extremely laborious. In the

[31] Wang Mang claimed descent from the Yellow Emperor and ruled under the power
the color yellow.

[32] This was a collection of *fu-ming* published in the year A.D. 9 in forty-two sections,
forty-eight as mentioned here; see *HS* 99B.4112 and *HFHD*, III, 288.

[33] The "white pigeon" is mentioned in a late source (the *Wu lu* 吳錄 cited in Li Shan's
n hsüan commentary to this passage, *WH* 48.15b) as an auspicious omen that appeared
ore T'ang, founder of the Yin dynasty. The vermilion crow, or vermilion bird, was a
orable sign that appeared before King Wu, founder of the Chou; see *SC* 28.1366;
ng-shu ta-chuan 尚書大傳 (*SPTK*), 3.1b. The white fish was a fish that jumped into
g Wen's boat; he took it as a good sign and immediately performed a sacrifice; see
4.120. Before he became emperor, Han Kao-tsu cut a snake in two. This was inter-
ted as a sign that he was destined to overthrow the Ch'in; see *HS* 1.7 (*HFHD*, I, 34-6).

past, the emperors succeeded the sovereigns, the kings succeeded the e
perors, and each followed the former and trod in the footsteps of antiqui
Some maintained order by non-action; others perished by adding and su
tracting things.[34] How could one have known the Hsin house would comr
its attention, collect its ideas, concentrate its thoughts, and extend its devoti
to this extent?

Your Majesty everywhere acts augustly, at dawn is awake, and is dilige
and earnest—these are not things done by Ch'in! If you had not been dilige:
you would be unworthy of your predecessors. If you had not been earne
you would not be in harmony with "upright virtue."[35] Thus, you open t
secret archives and peruse the forest of writings.

> From afar, scholars collect in your park of literature
>   and elegance;
> They soar into your garden of rites and music.
> You continue the lost heritage of Yin and Chou;
> You carry on the vanished customs of Yao and Shun.
> Sublime pitchpipes and excellent measures,
> Golden decrees and jade articles,
> Divine milfoil divination and sacred scapulimancy,
> Old texts on all of these have been discovered.[36]
> Your blazing splendor, shining and luminous—
> There is nowhere it does not spread!
> You use chariots, banners, and pennants to signify
>   distinction;
> You display carriage bells and march music to maintain
>   moderation;
> You apply robes, uniforms, and caps to clarify rank.
> You regulate marriages and funerals to show reverence.
> You make affectionate the nine clansmen and fine
>   worthies to effect harmony.

To change the stipulations for the spirits and earth gods is the high
standard. To reverently cultivate the hundred sacrifices is to put everyth

[34]That is to say, they changed the inalterable principles of government. The lin
derived from the famous *Lun yü* 論語 2.23 passage in which the Master maintains t
the Rites of ten generations in the future can be known, for they are based on preced

[35]*Cf. Shih* 256/2: "Upright is his virtuous conduct."

[36]This passage can be interpreted in two ways: (1) "old texts" (*ku-wen*) on pi
pipes, measures, divination, etc. were discovered; (2) "old texts" *and* pitchpi
measures, divination, etc. were discovered. I prefer the former because of the importa
of the old text "discoveries" during the Wang Mang reign. I discuss the ambiguities of
passage below.

ıe proper sequence. The Bright Hall, Pi-yung, and Ling-t'ai are magnificent
ts. The Nine Temples and Long Life Palace are the ultimate in filial
y.[37] To establish the Six Classics is a great achievement. To obtain the
ζiance of the khan in the north shows the broadest virtue.[38]

As for   Reviving the five ranks,
          Grading the three types of land,
          Administering the well-field system,
          Eliminating human servitude,
          Collating the *Code of Fu*,
          Rectifying the methods of Ssu-ma;[39]

          Grandly exhalting the airs of reverent service,
             resplendent virtue, and sublime harmony,[40]
          And widening the road for scholars to lecture,
             speak admonitions, and recite exhortations:

          As the sound of flocking egrets fills the court,
          And groups of geese and phoenixes approach the stairs.[41]

[7] In A.D. 4 Wang Mang built a Ming-t'ang (Bright Hall), Pi-yung, and Ling-t'ai in
ection with his expansion of the Imperial University; see *HS* 99A.4069 (*HFHD*, III,
. The Nine Temples, which were Wang Mang's ancestral temples, were not built until
20 (see *HS* 99C.4161-2 and *HFHD*, III, 191). Yang Hsiung could not have known
ıeir existence, because he had died two years earlier. See the discussion below. The
; Life Palace was built from the Han emperor Yüan's temple to house the Empress
ager Wang, Wang Mang's aunt. It must have been built *c.* A.D. 8 (see *HS* 98.4034).
[8] Exactly what Yang can be referring to here I do not know. In reality, Wang Mang's
ngs with the Hsiung-nu were disastrous. The Hsiung-nu not only were reluctant to
allegiance to Wang Mang, they even gave protection to anti-Wang Mang rebels. See
4B.3820 ff. and *HFHD*, III, 119-21.
[9] Here Yang is describing some of the institutional changes adopted by Wang Mang.
all of them accord exactly with what Wang Mang actually instituted. For example,
.D. 8 Wang Mang memorialized that *four*, not three classes of land be established
HS 99A.4089; *HFHD*, III, 240-41). It would appear that Yang may be basing himself
ıe "Wu ch'eng" chapter of the *Shang shu* 尚書 (*SPTK*, 6.10b), in which King Wu of
ı is credited with establishing five ranks of nobility and three classes of land to be
ıed to the nobles. I do not know of any specific interest that Wang Mang had in the
· *of Fu*, which is now a chapter in the *Shang shu*, and the treatise on military tactics
ıuted to Ssu-ma Jang-chü. I suspect that nothing specific is meant by these two
s, and that they are merely a metaphorical way of saying Wang Mang was interested
ı and the art of warfare.
[0] I believe the word *feng* 風 here refers to musical airs, for there is a similar passage
·*ou li* 周禮 (*SPTK*) 6.1b: "They teach the sons of the state musical virtues: central
ony, reverent servitude, filial piety, and friendship."
[1] These are metaphors for the scholars who are "flocking" to Wang Mang's court.
cking egrets" is used in *Shih* 278, where it probably refers to distinguished dignitaries
urt.

All of these allow the legacy of the former sages to spread and circulate
no longer remain concealed. How grand and glorious you are! The affai
Heaven and man are flourishing and the expectations of the ghosts and sp
are truly fulfilled. Of the many ministers and former officers[42] not a one
not delight in your standards. Of the robbers, bandits, villains, and trait
not a one did not quake with awe.

> You follow the scions of Shao-tien;
> Make notable the descendants of the Yellow
>   Emperor and Shun.[43]
> Where the Imperial Canon had gaps it was repaired;
> Where the kingly principles were relaxed they
>   are tightened.
> Bright, shining—are you not sublime?

Of those affected by your influence and saturated by your transformation

> The capital was completely inundated;
> The imperial demesne was drenched;
> The vassal states were wetted or had to lift
>   their skirts;[44]
> And the border areas were bathed and washed.

> Following the former canons,
> Inspecting the people in the four directions,[45]
> Reaching the Four Peaks,[46]
> Performing the *Feng* sacrifices on Mt. T'ai,[47]
> And the *Shan* sacrifices at Liang-fu:

These are the standard duty of one who receives the mandate.

[42] Part of this line is derived from *Shih* 258/4: "The many ministers and fo
officers/ They do not help us." The Ch'ing scholar, Wang Nien-sun (1744-1832), n
the interesting claim that the term *hsien cheng* 先正 "former officers" refers to the s
mentioned above, which makes good sense in this context; see *Tu-shu tsa-chih* 讀書
chih-yü, B.64a-b (Taipei: Shih-chieh shu-chü, 1963 ed.).

[43] Shao-tien was the father of the Yellow Emperor; Wang Mang claimed descent
both the Yellow Emperor and Shun; see *HS* 99B.4105 and *HFHD*, III, 274-77.

[44] *Cf. Shih* 34/1: "Where the ford is deep they wet their gowns,/ Where it is sh
they lift their skirts." The image of course is of someone fording a stream. See belo
an explanation of these metaphors.

[45] Or alternatively, the four classes of people.

[46] This refers to the seasonal visit of the emperor to the four sacred mounta
practice that purportedly existed in remote antiquity.

[47] Literally, "to add a mound." The word *feng* originally meant "mound," w
probably designates as a sacrificial term the "sacrificial mound."

One ruler received the mandate but had no time to carry out the sacri-
s, while another did not receive the mandate yet still performed them.[48]
1 greater and more magnificent is the Hsin! It is precisely at this time that
spirits of the lofty peaks, deep seas, and far-reaching rivers all have set up
rs and are anticipating the arrival of the holder of the mandate. Even
ple across the sea and in distant lands stretch their necks, stand on tiptoe,
 their heads, and face the interior, gasping.[49] How can an emperor, as
,ent as he may be, refrain from performing this duty? It would be appro-
te for you to command the most noble and wise to compose an "Imperial
on" and make it an addition to the three old canons,[50] which can be
vn to people of the future and transmitted without limit. This will allow
yriad generations to constantly

> Wear "lofty greatness"
> Walk in "awesome respect."
> They will breathe your fragrant aroma,
> Taste your sweet fruit.
> They will mirror the perfect essence of
>   absolute purity,
> And hear the rectifying sounds of clear harmony.

n, all officers will fulfill their duties and their achievements will all be
lendent.

> You will uphold the course of Heaven,
> Maintain the order of Earth.

se sacrifices are the highest principles in the world. I hope they can be
mpted!

[8] Referring to Han Kao-tsu and the Ch'in First Emperor respectively.

[9] *Cf.* Ssu-ma Hsiang-ju, "Yü Pa Shu hsi," *SC* 117.3044: "They stretch their necks,
heir heels, and gasp."

[0] Li Shan identifies only two "Old Canons": the "Canon of Yao" and the "Canon of
,," both in the *Shang shu* (the "Canon of Shun" is considered spurious). The usual
pretation of this passage is that the "Imperial Canon" of Wang Mang will be a third
n, which will be added to the two *Shang shu* canons, but based on a parallel with
na Hsiang-ju's "Feng Shan wen," which has an analogous line "He will add to the
six classics and make a seventh" (*SC* 117.3068), this interpretation seems less likely.
 reluctant to insist on my interpretation, however, for the notion of the "*Erh tien*"
Two Canons" of the *Shang shu* is a rather common formulation, although interestingly
pseudo-K'ung An-kuo "*Shang shu* preface" names "Five Canons" (*Wu tien*); see *WH*
1b. It is possible the author of CCMH was following a tradition concerning the
g shu canons that is now lost.

AUTHORSHIP

Although it is not necessary to know who wrote this piece in orde achieve a satisfactory literary understanding of it, because the authorship CCMH has been questioned, a brief survey of the arguments in an attemp clarify the issue might be useful. As early as the Sung scholars have b debating whether Yang wrote this work. Wang An-shih (1021-1068), who a great admirer of Yang Hsiung, claimed that it was a late forgery.[51] Dui the Ming and Ch'ing, a number of scholars put forth various amusing, erroneous claims about the authorship. Absolutely absurd is the sugges that the piece was written by Ku Yung (?-9 B.C.) because he has the same (Tzu-yün) as Yang Hsiung. Unless Ku Yung could have written from his gr it would have been impossible for him to write such a glorification of Hsin, for he died almost twenty years before Wang Mang ascended throne.[52] Another suggestion that appears now and again in the literatur that the piece was actually authored by Liu Fen, who had implicated Y Hsiung in the *fu-ming* affair. Again, there is no evidence to support supposition.[53]

A more serious argument, and one that seems to have been in vogu the seventeenth century, is that the customary dates (53 B.C.-A.D. 18) Yang Hsiung are wrong, and that Yang died before the Wang Mang era. claim is based on a corrupt passage from the *Hsin lun* by Yang's friend H T'an (*c.* 43 B.C.-A.D. 28).[54] The date of Yang Hsiung's death is well attes

[51] I have searched in vain throughout Wang An-shih's collection for his spe remarks on CCMH authorship. The only place I have seen him quoted is in *Hsüan-hs chiao-yen* 19.17a. Virtually all of the remarks I did find are laudatory, including tl poems; see Li Pi (ed.), *Wang Ching-kung shih chien-chu* 王荆公詩箋注 , (Peking: Ch hua shu-chü, 1958), 132-34.

[52] This argument has been demolished by Liang Chang-chü, *Wen-hsüan P'ang-ch* 40.8b.

[53] The first to posit this idea seems to be Feng Shih-k'o (*fl. c.* 1567); see *T'ai-hs ch'an-mi, nien-p'u,* 10a. Ch'en Pen-li rightly remarks that "we do not know on what argument is based."

[54] *WH* 7.1a quotes the *Hsin lun* 新論 as saying that Yang Hsiung died the day afte finished his "Sweet springs rhapsody" (*Kan-ch'üan fu* 甘泉賦 , which would put the of his death around 13 B.C. and still in the reign of Emperor Ch'eng (32-7 B.C.). Sch who have been misled by this passage include Hu Chih (1517-1585), Chiao Hung (1 1620), and Wang Wan (1624-1691); see *Chiao-shih pi-ch'eng* 焦氏筆乘 (*Yüeh-ya t ts'ung-shu* 粤雅堂叢書 ed.), 11.31b-33b and *Wen-hsüan p'ang-cheng*, 40.8b-9a. Their e is understandable, for they did not have access to the careful collation of this passag Yen K'o-chün (1762-1843), which did not appear until 1836. See *Ch'üan Hou Han* 全後漢文, 15.3a, in *Ch'üan shang-ku San-tai Ch'in Han San-kuo Liu-ch'ao wen* 全上 代秦漢三國六朝文 (Taipei: Shih-chieh shu-chü, 1963). The passage has been transl. by Timoteus Pokora, "Huan T'an's *fu* on looking for the immortals," *AO*, 28 (19

vever, and there is no doubt that he lived well into the Hsin era.[55]

Some scholars have attached significance to the fact that the CCMH is mentioned in the *Han shu*, where the texts of most of Yang's writings are served. This fact could mean that Pan Ku did not know of the existence of s piece, or if he knew it, he deliberately suppressed it as too embarrassing Yang Hsiung. It could also mean that CCMH did not exist at all during the e of Pan Ku, and that it is a later forgery, as some have claimed. None of se theories can be supported by the evidence, however. Actually, Pan Ku es mention CCMH, not in the *Han shu*, but in his "Elaboration of the on" (*Tien yin* 典引), a piece written in imitation of CCMH.[56] Why Pan did not include CCMH in Yang's *Han shu* biography is puzzling, but I do t think one can conclude he deliberately remained silent about it.[57]

There is, however, one piece of internal evidence that does cast doubt the authenticity. In one passage the author enumerates some of Wang ng's accomplishments. One of these is the building of the nine ancestral nples for the founders of the Hsin house. Construction of the temples began September A.D. 20,[58] and since Yang died in A.D. 18, it seems improbable could have known of their existence. The least one can say is that this ticular line is spurious, and that someone after Yang Hsiung must have npered with the piece.

The existence of one anachronism, however, is not sufficient evidence concluding that the entire piece is a forgery. It is possible that a Wang ng partisan, wishing to bolster support for the Hsin emperor in the waning irs of the dynasty, added an embellishment to Yang's original text. These nples apparently were "more magnificent than anything previously cted"[59] in Han China, and a eulogy for Wang Mang would not be complete

---

. One of the first scholars to refute the theory of Yang's early death is Ch'üan Tsu-ng (1705-1755); see *Chi-ch'i t'ing chi* 鮚埼亭集 (Shanghai: Commercial Press, 1936), 46-47.

[55]The sources for Yang's death date are the "Appraisal" (*HS* 87B.3585) and the ang Hsiung family genealogy" (see *Ch'üan Han wen*, Yen K'o-chün, 54.11b), both of ich give T'ien-feng 5 (A.D. 18).

[56]*WH* 48.21b.

[57]I cannot agree with Dr. Doeringer's claim that "Since Pan Ku admired Hsiung, he y have deliberately remained silent about this work [i.e. his records of the period m Emperor Hsüan to Emperors Ai and P'ing] in order to avoid portraying Hsiung as active supporter of Wang Mang. And certainly Pan Ku was not above ignoring embar-sing works, for he made no reference to Hsiung's essay entitled 'Castigating Ch'in and tolling Hsin' (*Chü Ch'in Mei Hsin*)," "Yang Hsiung and his formulation of a classicism," 201.

[58]See *HS* 99C.4161-2 and *HFHD*, III, 395-400.

[59]*HFHD*, III, 115.

without mentioning them. The CCMH is attested early enough to convi[n]
me, at least, that Yang Hsiung wrote it.[60]

GENRE

Another question about the CCMH, but an easier one to answer, is
what genre it belongs. Since the *Wen hsüan* classifies it as a *fu-ming*, ma[ny]
scholars have concluded that it must have been a *fu-ming* written by Y[ang]
Hsiung as a means of obtaining employment under Wang Mang. Howeve[r]
exactly what Hsiao T'ung, compiler of the *Wen hsüan*, intended by [this]
category "*fu-ming*" is unclear, for in the same category he includes t[wo]
additional pieces, Ssu-ma Hsiang-ju's "Essay on the *Feng* and *Shan* Sacrific[e]
and Pan Ku's "Elaboration of the Canon." The label obviously is anachronis[tic]
for the Ssu-ma Hsiang-ju piece, for the term *fu-ming* did not gain curre[ncy]
until the Wang Mang period. Pan Ku, who wrote his "Elaboration of [the]
Canon" some time after the term *fu-ming* became firmly established, did [not]
refer to his piece, written in imitation of the other two, as a *fu-ming*. [Ap]-
parently the main reason Hsiao T'ung placed these pieces together is that th[ey]
share the common feature of being requests that the emperor perform [the]
Feng and *Shan* sacrifices. Thus, in the *Wen-hsin tiao-lung*, written in the fi[fth]
century, the pieces are discussed under the genre known as *Feng Shan*.[61]

The CCMH, therefore, should not be considered a *fu-ming* of the ty[pe]
that were presented in the Wang Mang period. These *fu-ming* were not litera[ry]
compositions, but portents that were used to support a recommendation [to]
the throne. The requests made were almost always specific and personal, a[nd]
the actual "text" consisted of only a few words. The famous *fu-m[ing]*
recommending that Wang Mang be made emperor was a white stone, rou[nd]
on top, square on the bottom, that had only eight vermilion characters o[n it]
that read: "Announce that the Duke Tranquilizing the Han, Mang, be ma[de]
Emperor."[62]

Strictly speaking, the CCMH is a special type of memorial. The auth[or]
himself calls it a *feng-shih* 封事, a "memorial of sealed matters," which wa[s]

[60]The earliest mention of it is by Pan Ku in his "Elaboration of the Canon" writ[ten]
in A.D. 74 some fifty years after the death of Yang Hsiung. It is also attributed to Y[ang]
Hsiung in the fourth century by Li Ch'ung (see the fragment of *Han-lin lun* quoted
WH 48.9a) and in the fifth century by Liu Hsieh (in *Wen-hsin tiao-lung chiao-chu* 文心
龍校注 [Taipei: Shih-chieh shu-chü, 1962], 156).

[61]This chapter has been translated by Vincent Yu-chung Shih, *The literary mind a[nd]
the carving of dragons* (New York: Columbia University Press, 1959), 121-25. Liu Hs[ieh]
claims that one of the purposes of this kind of writing was "to document the instituti[ons]
of the age." This definition would indeed fit the three pieces Hsiao T'ung calls *fu-ming*

[62]*HS* 99A.4079.

gnation for a secret memorial submitted to the throne in a black pouch.[63]
memorial observes many of the formal conventions theoretically stipu-
d for presentations to the throne, such as mentioning the author's name
title at the beginning followed by phrases such as *chi shou* 稽首 "knocking
head on the ground" and *tsai-pai* 再拜 "bowing repeatedly."[64]

INTERPRETATION

The CCMH is no ordinary memorial, however, for it is written in a
thmic prose that at times seems almost poetic. I have attempted to ap-
ximate this quality by indenting the text in the more rhythmic places.[65]
ne of these passages indeed seem highly reminiscent of the *fu*, such as the
ended metaphors used to describe the profusion of auspicious omens the
n has attracted:

> Swelling, spouting, roaring and raging,
> Like the flow of a river, welling of the sea,
> Movement of clouds, bending of the wind,
> Gathering of mist, scattering of rain,
> They extend to the eight limits of earth,
> And array themselves above in the court of Heaven.

ticularly artful is the "moisture metaphor" that depicts Wang Mang's
ral influence as a kind of "irrigator" that bestows increasing amounts of
isture the closer one gets to the capital:

> The capital was completely inundated;
> The imperial demesne was drenched;
> The vassal states were wetted or had to lift
>   their skirts;
> And the border areas were bathed and washed.

It is perhaps because of this poetic, even fictive quality, that Pan Ku
icized CCMH as "lacking the truth" (*wang shih* 亡實).[66] What Pan Ku may

---

[53] See Ts'ai Yung (A.D. 133-192), *Tu tuan* 獨斷 (*SPPY*), 5a-b and *Wen-hsin tiao-lung
o-chu*, 169.
[54] See *Tu tuan*, 5a, for a brief description of the various formal conventions of the
memorial.
[55] The prosodic patterns of the "rhythmic" parts include extended three and four-
ble lines as well as what can be construed as a prose modification of the "Sao-line"
/ ∪ / /). Hervouet has adapted this same technique of representing rhythmic prose in
Le Chapitre 117 du Che-ki.
[56] *WH* 48.21b.

mean by this remark is that the piece contains distortions of the truth, fa
ful metaphors, hyperbole, and other exaggerations, all of which are typica
the panegyrical style. Thus, CCMH employs a number of well-known paneg
cal conventions, such as the "outdoing *topos*" and the "matching *topos*.
The Hsin emperor is depicted as either surpassing or matching all previ
rulers in his deeds or virtue. For example, his portents are more valuable t
those of the past ("Such things as the white pigeon . . . are worthless compa
with these"). He is further "a partner with Heaven, a twin with Earth"
"Matches the Five Sovereigns/ Towers over the Three Kings," which all
common *fu* expressions.[68]

The CCMH surprisingly does not contain too many gross distorti
although the exaggeration about the Hsiung-nu khan (*shan-yü* 單于) decla
allegiance to the Hsin perhaps qualifies as an example of what Pan Ku wc
call "lacking the truth."[69] The same might be said for the slightly nega
treatment of the Han (at least a Han chauvinist might find this objectionab
but it does not match the hyperbole of the section on the Ch'in, itself a *top*
which I call the "disparagement of Ch'in *topos*." It has antecedents in e
Han literature, the most notable examples being "Finding fault with Ch'
(*Kuo Ch'in lun* 過秦論) by Chia I (*c.* 200-168 B.C.) and "Perfect wor
(*Chih yen* 至言) by Chia Shan (*fl.* 179 B.C.).[70] In its most common form,
writer denounces the Ch'in for its oppressiveness, citing its neglect of the r
and music, burning of the books, and suppression of dissent.[71] The CC
version of the *topos* is not especially original except for the addition of

[67]On the "outdoing *topos*" see Ernst Robert Curtius, *European literature and*
Latin middle ages, trans. by Willard R. Trask (1953; New York: Harper & Row rep
1963), 162-66. Curtius' Chapter 9, "Heroes and rulers," contains much valuable in
mation about the *topoi* of Western panegyrical literature.

[68]The *locus classicus* for the expression *ts'an t'ien erh ti* 參天貳地 is Ssu-ma Hsi
ju's "Objections by the elders of Shu" (*SC* 117.3051; see also Hervouet's note i
Chapitre 117 du Che-ki, 166, n. 3). *Ts'an t'ien ti* occurs in the "Fu p'ien" of *Hsün*
Hsün tzu yin-te [1950; Taipei: Ch'eng Wen Publishing Co. reprint, 1968), 26/11
Yang Hsiung's "Ho-tung rhapsody" (*HS* 87A.3538). The *topos* of the Five Sovere
and Three Kings is used by Yang Hsiung several times; see "Sweet springs rhapsody,"
87A.3523 and "Barricade hunt rhapsody," *HS* 87A.3542.

[69]See n. 38.

[70]Chia I's piece occurs in several versions, the earliest in *SC* 6.276-84 (for a transla
see *MH*, II, 219-36). An excerpt is quoted in *SC* 48.1962-5 as an interpolation by C
Shao-sun (see the translation in *Records*, I, 30-33). This excerpt was reprinted in
31.1820-5 and *WH* 51.1a-6a. Another "complete text" in a different order occurs in
Hsin shu 新書, a work attributed to Chia I; *Han Wei ts'ung-shu* 漢魏叢書 (Taipei: H
hsing shu-chü, 1966), 1.1a-7b. The Chia Shan essay is found in *HS* 51.2327-36.

[71]A complete study of all examples of the *topos* has yet to be done. One elem
that one would expect that is usually lacking is "burying alive of Confucian schol
(*k'eng ju* 坑儒).

w element, the list of evil portents that signified the impending fall of the ʼin.

The section on the Ch'in, however, is subordinate to the encomium for in. Even if one did not know that Yang Hsiung viewed the classics as the timate source of wisdom and morality, one could assume from the work elf that what he finds most laudatory about the Hsin is its promotion of assical learning. Some of the passages describing the Hsin encouragement of holarship read more like imaginary portraits of the ideal emperor than counts of Wang Mang's actual deeds. The following passage, in which the ughter of the hunting park and the extravagance of the palace garden have en replaced by the civilizing influence of rites and music, literature and egance (*wen ya* 文雅), closely resembles the didactic passages that conclude any Han *fu*.

> From afar, scholars collect in your park of
>   literature and elegance;
> They soar into your garden of rites and music.
> You continue the lost heritage of Yin and Chou;
> You carry on the vanished customs of Yao and Shun.

If the repetition of key words means anything in a literary composition, ιe virtue that Yang Hsiung seems to stress more than any other is the quality f *tien* 典. It is in fact this feature of CCMH that Pan Ku singles out for ιecial praise.[72] In its nominal sense I have translated it as "canon." The ord has a wide range of meanings in classical Chinese: "canon," "standard," norm," "rule," and as a verb "to take as a norm," "to regulate." It also has ι adjectival-adverbial use as "constant" or "constantly."[73] In the CCMH, en seems to represent a classical norm which serves as a link to the past and guide for the present. The Hsin emperor, for example, is praised for following the former canons" (*ch'ien tien* 前典), and the imperial tours of ιspection and sacrifices on Mt. T'ai and Liang-fu are considered the *tien yeh* 典業 or "standard duty of one who receives the mandate." The most nportant usage of *tien* is in the expression *ti tien* 帝典 or "Imperial Canon," ʼhich occurs three times in the piece. One of the defects of the Han rule was ιat "the Imperial Canon had gaps and was not repaired" but under the Hsin ιese gaps were filled in. In this usage *tien* need not refer exclusively to a ʼritten code or statutes, although the written tradition would be implied as a artial meaning of the term. Rather it seems to indicate a more abstract notion

---

[72] *WH* 48.21b.

[73] Professor Creel discusses the word *tien* in his *The origins of statecraft in China. ʼolume one: The Western Chou empire* (Chicago and London: University of Chicago ress, 1970), 125, 165.

of the norms, standards, even institutions, that have been handed down fr
classical antiquity, and that, if observed and maintained, will bring order
the world. The ultimate way in which to transmit the *tien*, however, is throu
a written text. Thus, Yang Hsiung urges that an additional "Imperial Cano
be written, which can serve as a supplement to the classical canons.

Implied in this suggestion is the assumption that each age, especially
glorious and prosperous age, based on the classical traditions of the past, m
write down its standards and norms (i.e. its *canon*), for transmission to futu
generations. The work will be particularly valuable for the futue as a guide,
as a restraining and moderating influence: "This will allow a myriad gen
ations to constantly/Wear 'lofty greatness'/Walk in 'awesome respect.' " T
terms *wei-wei* 巍巍 "lofty greatness" and *li-li* 栗栗 "awesome respect" see
to imply the necessity for caution. *Wei-wei*, besides being the famous epith
of praise used by Confucius for the sage emperors Shun, Yü, and Yao in *Lu
yü* 8.18 and 8.19, also means "precipitously high" or "dangerously lofty."
combination with the word *tai* 戴 "to wear on the head," and *li-li*, which al
means "to tremble," "to fear," it conveys a cautionary hint as well as praise

In connection with the transmission of classical traditions, one of t
most striking passages in the entire piece is the following ambiguous excerpt

> Sublime pitchpipes and excellent measures,
> Golden decrees and jade articles,
> Divine milfoil divination and sacred scapulimancy,
> Old texts on all of these have been discovered.

The term I have translated "old texts" is *ku-wen*, and if my translation
correct, this would be the first place that Yang Hsiung directly associates hi
self with the Old Text tradition. I do not want to insist on this renderin
however, for *ku-wen* can mean a number of things, even in this period. Earli
in the piece, for example, Ch'in is denounced for destroying *ku-wen*, whi
could mean *ku-wen* script, old texts, or even ancient literature. It is in th
multiple sense that one should probably understand the term. "Old text" ar
"ancient script" are relevant because of the promotion of "old text" versio
of the classics during the Wang Mang period, and it is for this reason that
translate it as I do.

Ku-wen in the sense of "ancient literature" is also appropriate, howeve
for it underscores Yang Hsiung's emphasis on classical norms. Even th
language of CCMH, which consists of numerous elegant phrases drawn fro
the classics, is consistent with this exaltation of the classical tradition. O
classic in particular, the *Book of documents*, provides the source for many
the epithets of praise applied to Wang Mang. Judging from the importanc
attached to the classical canons, one is not surprised at the number of tim

ang quotes from the "Canon of Yao," the most important of the *Shu*
nons. For example, the expression *ch'in ming* 欽明 ("reverent and en-
htened"),[74] and *ch'in chiu tsu* 親九族 ("to make affectionate the nine clans-
en")[75] are phrases attached to Yao in the "Canon of Yao." *Shu chi hsien
i* 庶績咸熙 ("their achievements all will be resplendent")[76] and *teng yung*
庸 (literally "to raise and to use"),[77] which Yang uses in a different sense,
ith have their *locus classicus* in the "Canon of Yao." Yang also uses several
rases from the Old Text "Canon of Shun": *yün se* 允塞 (literally "true and
cere"),[78] and *k'ou tse chien kuei* 寇賊姦宄 ("robbers, bandits, villains,
aitors").[79]

The emphasis on *tien*, on *ku-wen*, and the extensive quoting from the
nonical tradition all combine to reinforce the major theme of CCMH. If one
llows William Empson's principle that a key word "names the theme of a
em," the theme of CCMH in fact is summed up in the word *tien*.[80] Thus,
e major theme is not that Ch'in was particularly iniquitous and Hsin es-
ecially virtuous, or even that the material achievements of Wang Mang are
orthy of praise. All of these points of course are made, but they are
condary to the espousal of a kind of classicism,[81] in which the classics (the
en) are viewed as the embodiment of all ethical principles. Hidden beneath
e hyperbole, exaggeration, and panegyric, then, is a direct allusion to
assical ideals, contained in the ancient canons (the *tien*), which serve as the
uide to personal behavior and good government. It is to what Chaucer
ould call the "olde bokes" that Yang Hsiung looks for inspiration, and like
e Parson, he sees in the literary tradition of remote antiquity the basis for
l morality and wisdom:

> Stondeth upon the weyes, and seeth and axeth of olde pathes (that is to
> seyn, of olde sentences) which is the goode way,/and walketh in that

[74] *Shu* 1.1a.

[75] *Shu* 1.1b.

[76] *Shu* 1.3a, with another character for *hsi*. Bernhard Karlgren discusses this variant
1 "Glosses on the Book of Documents, *BMFEA*, 20 (1948), 58, #1229.

[77] Yang uses it in the sense of "to ascend to the throne," which seems to be a Han
nterpretation; see Wang Hsien-ch'ien, *Shang-shu K'ung chuan ts'an-cheng* 尚書孔傳參正
Hsü shou t'ang, 1904), 1.22a.

[78] See *Shu* 1.5b. Yang uses *yün se* in the sense of "to truly fulfill."

[79] See *Shu* 1.10a.

[80] See *The Structure of complex words* (Norfolk, Conn.: New Directions, n.d.), 84:
'If one wants to examine how a structure of meaning comes to be built up in a word it
eems natural to take the 'key word' of a long poem, in which the process might actually
e seen at work; and here the key word names the theme of the poem."

[81] The best discussion of Yang Hsiung's classicism is in Doeringer, pp. 141-79. I hope
hat Dr. Doeringer will publish his excellent study in the near future.

wey, and ye shal fynde refresshynge for your soules.

(Canterbury Tales, X, 77-78)

In this short study of CCMH, I have deliberately ignored the conve[n]tional question of the extent to which Yang Hsiung compromised himself [in] serving Wang Mang or writing this piece. Yang Hsiung's defenders, f[or] example, make much of the fact Yang Hsiung chose the Ch'in with which [to] compare the Hsin. To most of these scholars, Ch'in is supposed to be a co[de] word that actually stands for Hsin. Thus, whenever Yang Hsiung criticiz[es] Ch'in, he is really satirizing Wang Mang. Entire works have been analyzed this way, including Yang's *Fa-yen*, and even the *T'ai-hsüan ching*, writt[en] before the Wang Mang era.

I have ignored this question because it is not directly relevant to [a] literary interpretation. Instead, I have attempted a kind of New Criticis[m] which involves a close reading of the work, and pointing out some of t[he] terminological relationships, especially the multiple sense of words like *ti[en]* and *ku-wen*. I have then tried to show how these words contribute to t[he] general "meaning" of the piece. If in the process I have been able to conv[ey] something of Yang Hsiung's literary artistry, at least this work need not [be] discarded as a sauce jar cover.[82]

---

[82]This of course was a remark once made by Liu Hsin about the *T'ai-hsüan chin[g]* 太玄經: "You torture yourself in vain! Present scholars have salary and profit but still d[o] not understand the *Book of changes*. What about the *Hsüan*? I am afraid that later peopl[e] will use it to cover sauce jars." (*HS* 87B.3585)

Agricultural intensification and marketing agrarianism in the Han dynasty*

Hsü Cho-yun

this paper I shall argue that agricultural advancement in Han China 02 B.C.-A.D. 220) was closely related to population growth and that its ult, intensive farming, together with the market economy with which it s associated, formed in China a particular pattern of rural economy. We ill start with a discussion of the effect of the policies made by the political wer upon the conditions for agricultural development.

STATE AUTHORITY AND DEVELOPMENT OF AGRICULTURE

The Ch'in government, from its days as one of the seven states con-iding for dominance (4th-3rd cent. B.C.), developed steadily toward bureau-ıtization. The abolition of the feudal system was completed when Ch'in ıh-huang-ti (r. 246-210 B.C.) approved the proposal made by Li Ssu 280-208 B.C.) that the empire should be governed under the *chün-hsien* stem, with no prince enfeoffed as ruler of a vassal state.[1] This measure minated the intermediate strata of power holders between the Emperor d the mass of commoners. It was, indeed, the realization of the thought of

* This paper is a summary of one major part of my forthcoming book, *Han agricul-e,* to be published by the University of Washington Press, as part of its Han Dynasty story Project. I would like to express my gratitude to Professor Jack Dull of the Univer-y of Washington and Professor Evelyn Rawski of the University of Pittsburgh, both of om have extended great help and provided inspiration to improve the first manuscript. >we a great deal to my colleagues of the Peasant Studies Group of the University of tsburgh with whom I have tried out a number of ideas in our discussion sessions. This per is dedicated to my teacher Dr. H. G. Creel, to whom I am indebted for his guidance ring the happy years of my graduate training at the University of Chicago.

[1] Derk Bodde, *China's first unifier* (Leiden: E. J. Brill, 1938), 133-46; also *Shih chi ih chi hui-chu k'ao-cheng* ed.), 6/25-27.

Han Fei (c. 280-233 B.C.), the great master of the Fa-chia, who warned th
the powerful households could provide shelter for the ordinary citizens w
comprised the pool from which both producers and soldiers were drawn.[2]

The reforms carried out by Shang Yang (d. 338 B.C.) encouraged t
establishment of independent households as soon as males reached adulthoc
This development reduced the potential for the formation, particularly witl
kinship organizations, of another possible bloc between imperial author
and the individual common subjects.[3]

The Ch'in rulers made a successful effort to assert direct state cont
over the producers. Thus, in the stele inscriptions erected after the unificati
of China in 221 B.C., Ch'in Shih-huang-ti repeatedly stressed that he h
succeeded in mobilizing the people to engage in agricultural production.[4]
is obvious that Ch'in Shih-huang-ti viewed the farmers not only as manpov
to produce the only real goods in an agrarian economy but also as simple a
earth-bound subjects who lent stability to the state.[5]

The Han Empire, though it came into existence as a result of the ov
throw of the Ch'in dynasty, remained as bureaucratic a society as its p
decessor. The Han rulers continuously did their best to reduce the influen
of various groups in society in order to minimize their potential menace
imperial power.[6] By the time of Emperor Wu (r. 141-87 B.C.), the Han co

[2]Han fei tzu (SPPY), 17/13-14, 18/10-11, 19/8, 20/4.

[3]Shih chi, 68/8, 11.

[4]He visited the east coast area during 219-215 B.C. Long poems were inscribed
seven locations. The one inscribed in 219 B.C. at Lang-ya, for instance, includes su
sentences as: "The Emperor succeeded in making the people work for the basic p
duction (namely agriculture)"; "Agriculture is upheld, while the unimportant professi
(namely commerce) is discouraged, so that the common people are enriched"; "T
small and the big all exert their utmost effort, daring not to be lazy and negligent"; "T
production in all lines is plentiful and multiplies as the works are carried out at the ri
times and promptly." Or, the one in 215 B.C. inscribed at Chieh-shih includes the lin
"The male works happily in the field; the female fulfills her task"; "Everything is
order; the benefit is felt in all professions"; "People converge to cultivate the fields [as
subjects of the Empire] and all are satisfied with their lives." Shih chi, 6/34-46.

[5]Even though the Lü-shih ch'un-ch'iu 呂氏春秋 (LSCC) is not written by Lü Pu-v
(d. 235 B.C.) himself, a passage in LSCC does appear quite consistent with the Ch
policy of stressing the development of agriculture, which was first initiated by Shang Ya
A passage in the LSCC gives the reasons for encouraging people to engage in agricultu
(1) the profit from land, (2) farmers being useful for border defense (i.e. being go
soldiers), (3) farmers being law-abiding, and (4) farmers being attached to the real esta
The goal, as stated, consists of reverence to the ruler and the unity of the nation. Lü-sh
ch'un-ch'iu (SPPY), 26/4-11.

[6]Hsu Cho-yün, "The changing relationship between local society and the cent
political power in Former Han, 206 B.C.-8 A.D.," Comparative Studies in Society a
History, VII (1965), 358 ff.

d utilized the monopoly of crucial commodities, promotion of state enter-
ises, discriminatory taxation, and other financial measures, to extend
perial control into the economic sphere. These measures coincided with
e establishment of monolithic control over the whole society by means of
litical maneuvering.[7] Most enduring, however, were the constant attempts
the Han government to make a flourishing agriculture the very foundation
the bureaucratic empire.

During the Han dynasty, the law discriminated against the merchant in
vor of the farmer, and the land tax in the former Han dynasty (202 B.C.-
D. 8) was extremely light—only one-fifteenth of the produce in the early
riod and one-thirtieth after 166 B.C.[8] It is interesting to note, however,
at the favor extended to the farming population did not begin until at least
generation after the dynasty was founded. The edict issued by Emperor
en (r. 180-157 B.C.) in 176 B.C. is the earliest explicit declaration that
riculture was the foundation of the empire.[9]

For decades following this edict, a number of others were issued one
ter another. The one in 168 B.C. expressed grave concern over a shortage of
od reserves. It resulted in the reduction of the land tax to one thirtieth of
eld and, subsequently, the complete abolition of the land tax to provide
rmers with an incentive to return to the land.[10] Another interesting edict
ued in 163 B.C. inquired into the reasons for poor agricultural development
general, and the problem of insufficient food supply, in particular. It
estioned whether wine-making or animal husbandry had affected grain
nsumption, or if too many people had given up farming to engage in
mmercial activities.[11]

---

[7]Nancy L. Swann, *Food and money in ancient China: The earliest economic history
China to A.D. 25* (Princeton: Princeton University Press, 1950), 265-83. For discussion
such monopoly, see E. M. Gale, *Discourses on salt and iron: a debate on state control
commerce and industry in ancient China* (Leiden: E. J. Brill, 1930); Ch'ü Tung-tsu,
n social structure (Seattle: University of Washington Press, 1972), 196-201. For the
aracteristics of Han China and those of other ancient empires, see S. N. Eisenstadt, *The
litical systems of empires: the rise and fall of the historical bureaucratic societies* (New
rk: The Free Press of Glencoe, 1963), 121 ff.

[8]There were, of course, occasional fluctuations of tax rates. For instance, in the
riod 165-156 B.C., the land tax was totally abolished. For discussion on Han taxation,
e Yoshida Torao, *Ryō Kan sozei no kenkyū* 兩漢租税の研究 (Tokyo: Daian, 1966),
ff. For the status of Han farmers as the foundation of the Empire, see Ho Ch'ang-
ün, *Han T'ang chien feng-chien t'u-ti so yu hsing-shih yen-chiu*漢唐間封建土地所有形式
究 (Shanghai: Jen-min, 1964).

[9]*Han shu (Han shu pu-chu,* I-wen reprint), 48/9-10.

[10]*Han shu,* 4/14a-b.

[11]*Han shu,* 4/16a-17a.

POPULATION GROWTH IN THE FORMER HAN

The Han imperial edicts failed to recognize that the food shortage pro lem could have been the consequence of population growth after one full ge eration of relative peace following unification.[12] The population, howeve grew considerably. Ssu-ma Ch'ien (145-c. 90 B.C.) noticed that at the ve beginning of the dynasty, only 20-30% of the registered population remaine in their home areas. After less than one century, by Ssu-ma Ch'ien's own tim the population in various localities had increased twofold, threefold, or more. These rough estimates give very little help in drawing a demographic profile the first century of the Han dynasty. Fortunately, a small group of samples available. The *Han shu* gives the populations of nineteen marquisates at t time of their initial establishment around 200 B.C. and at the time when the were terminated by decree for various reasons.[14] The value and reliability these figures depend upon at least two variables: First, the number of hous holds in 200 B.C. may have been underestimated; and second, the increase population in the marquisates may have been the consequence of migratic and boundary changes as well as natural growth. Nevertheless, the possib significance of the first variable is diminished by the fact that the growth ra reflects the comparison of data from the same source. The dangers inherent the second variable are partially compensated for by the fact that the marquisates are distributed in virtually all the major regions of Han China, fact revealed by the wide range in population density. One is immediate impressed by the consistency with which most of these marquisates double or tripled their populations within the given periods. For the areas wi exceptionally high rates of growth, regional differentiation should be co sidered. Three other independent cases from the first century B.C. were al helpful in confirming the consistency of the possible growth rates.[15] T geometric mean of all the twenty-two cases is an annual growth rate of 1.6

Vagrancy is an indicator of excessive population relative to availab

[12]The edict of 163 B.C. explicitly ruled out the possibility of population growth saying that the census did not show an increase. *Ibid.*, 4/16b.

[13]*Shih chi*, 18/3-4.

[14]*Han shu, chüan* 16. Li Chien-nung, *Hsien Ch'in liang Han ching-chi shih-kao* 先 兩漢經濟史稿 (Peking: Chung hua, 1962), 236-37. The population density is taken fro Lao Kan, "Liang Han chün kuo mien-chi chih ku-chi chi k'ou-shu tseng-chien chih t' ts'e" 兩漢郡國面積之估計及口數增減之推測, *Bulletin of institute of history and philolo; (BIHP)*, V:2 (1935), 215 ff. The data Lao tabulated are those of A.D. 2, given in the *H shu, chüan* 28. The annual growth rate is determined according to the interpolatic method; *cf.* T. L. Smith and P. E. Zopf, *Demography: principles and methods* (Philad phia: Davis, 1970), 552-53.

[15]*Han shu*, 18/13-14, 76/14: Lao Kan, "Liang Han hu-chi yü ti-li chih kuan-h 兩漢戶籍與地理之關係, *BIHP*, V:2 (1935), 179-214; Smith and Zopf, *op. cit.*, 552-53.

ble land as the result of demographic growth. In addition to its mention
herding 725,000 poor people to the border provinces in 119 B.C. and the
oposal to move some two million unregistered vagrants to frontier land in
7 B.C., the *Han shu* recorded no less than twenty cases in the Former Han
which large numbers of people, often hundreds of thousands, wandered
und the empire. Over twenty citations of large scale vagrancy also appeared
the historical records of the Later Han period (A.D. 25-220).[16] Many of
se vagrants probably resettled in less crowded areas, such as the provinces
ng the northwest frontier or the sparsely populated areas in the southern
er valleys.[17]

Population increases, as well as the growth of administrative units in
th China, were prominent features of the Later Han. This population
vement began the perennial trend of southbound migration, which eventu-
y altered the center of gravity of population distribution in China.[18]

A good portion of the excessive population, however, was absorbed by
ans of opening the then unused land under government control. The
lowing are cases of the release of government land, which included pastures,
ks, land belonging to local administrations, etc., as registered in the annals
the *Han shu* and the *Hou Han shu*.[19]

Year	Categories of land released
Former Han	
140 B.C.	Pastureland belonging to the imperial stable
78	Imperial park at Chung-mou
69	Government land
67	Imperial ponds; Government land
48	Government land under the control of the Metropolitan Administration, the Ministry of Ceremonies, the local administrations in the provinces on the marquisate levels, and the imperial parks which could be spared.
47	Imperial game parks

[16] Wang Chung-lo, "Kuan-yü Chung-kuo nu-li-she-hui ti wa-chieh chi feng-chien kuan-
ti hsing-ch'eng wen-t'i" 關於中國奴隸社會的瓦解及封建關係的形成問題, in *Chung-kuo
-tai-shih fen-ch'i wen-t'i t'ao-lun chi* 中國古代史分期問題討論集 (Peking: San-lien,
57), 450-52.

[17] Lao Kan, "Liang Han hu-chi," *op. cit.*, 192-93, 208-14.

[18] Harold J. Wiens, *China's march toward the tropics* (Hamden, Conn.: Shoe String
ess, 1954); Hans Bielenstein, "The census of China during the period A.D. 2-742,"
lletin of the Museum of Far Eastern Antiquities, XIX (1947), 125-63.

[19] Amano Motonosuke, "Kandai gozoku no daitochi keiei shiron" 漢代豪族の大土地
營試論, *Takigawa hakase kanreki kinen rombun shū* 瀧川博士還曆紀念論文集 (Tokyo:
57), 8.

43	Government land
6	The land belonging to the Imperial Consort—Family Wang
A.D. 2	Prime minister, ministers, and other ranking officials presented their own property for the government to give to the poor.
2	A large imperial park on the northern frontier

Later Han

66	Land under the control of the commandery administrations and the administrations of the marquisates and prefectures.
70	Low land along canals
76	Imperial pond
84	Government land in the Empire
86	The land not reclaimed in the northern provinces.
107	Imperial game park at Kuang-ch'eng and the government land in the areas plagued by famine.

The land owned by the government, more commonly called *kung-t'ie* 公田 (government land), consisted of several categories. The largest of the consisted of uncultivated land, such as forests, marshes, dried river beds, tid land, etc., which the sovereign claimed as his reserved property. In the H. dynasty, land in this category was still regarded as a source of private incom for the imperial house, not as part of the state revenues.[20]

The second category was private property confiscated by the gover. ment because the owner was convicted of crimes. The largest amount of suc land in government ownership was seized in the reign of Emperor Wu durir the final quarter of the second century B.C. The third category was the lar assigned to government offices as a source of revenue for their maintenanc The income was in the form of rent collected from the tenants.[21]

The second and the third categories, however, were arable land alread under cultivation by tenants or government-controlled labor forces such slaves and convicts. It is obvious that if the land released to the poor in th cases given above belonged to these two categories, there would not be ar real increase of arable land to the total available for national production. Th list presented above shows that the Han government had exhausted i available uncultivated land by the mid-first century B.C. and the release o

[20]Masubuchi Tatsuo, *Chūgoku kodai no shakai to kokka*中國古代の社會と國 (Tokyo: Kōbundō, 1960), 265 ff.

[21]*Han shu*, 24B/16a-b; *Hou Han shu* (*Hou Han shu chi-chieh*, I-wen reprint), 29/12 11/14b, 80/11a.

nd thereafter was more of a political gesture than the actual opening of ptentially arable land. A similar pattern is repeated in the Later Han. As the st shows, after A.D. 86, the only really uncultivated land was that along the prthern border.

It seems clear that opening up uncultivated land could provide only a ry limited solution to the problem of excess population. If the population ew at the rate of a moderate one per cent per annum, a base population of)0 would be 128 after twenty-five years, 164 after fifty years, and 270 after he hundred years.[22] If the figure 59,594,978 from the census of A.D. 2 is ken to be the final registered population after 202 years of growth at an nual rate of 1.6%, then the registered population in 200 B.C. should have en about 2.5 million. The population pressure would be more acutely felt certain areas than in other ones as the consequence of uneven distribution. Han China, the areas where population was highly concentrated were the cinity of the capitals, the provinces located in the middle and lower reaches f the Yellow River, and a few enclaves such as the Red Basin in the present y province of Szechuan.[23]

Southbound migration through the whole period of the Han dynasty d spread population into the southern provinces. The most crowded centers the Former Han, nevertheless, remained in the north. The middle and lower aches of the Yellow River continued to be under population pressure.[24]

INTENSIFICATION OF AGRICULTURE

The reign of Emperor Wu was an eventful time characterized by foreign ars and expansion, construction of dikes and canals, etc. The grain stored om past surpluses was exhausted, and the food shortage appeared more rious than ever.[25] After trying to cope with the situation by resettling eople on frontier land and opening up government land, Emperor Wu, in the st years of his reign, turned his attention toward encouraging farmers to crease their productivity.[26]

[22]E. A. Wrigley, *Population and history* (New York: McGraw-Hill, 1971), 206; Table 2.

[23]Lao Kan, "Liang Han chün kuo," *op. cit.,* 216 ff. His calculation, however, can be isleading in the case of the metropolitan district, in which the density could be tremely high at limited localities in the capital and the counties near imperial tombs. f. Lao Kan, "Liang Han hu-chi," *op. cit.,* 197-201.

[24]Lao Kan, "Liang Han chün kuo," *op. cit.,* 216 ff. In comparing Lao's tables of opulation density in the Former and the Later Han, we see that ten of the thirteen ost crowded provinces in the Former Han were still among the seventeen top ones in e Later Han.

[25]Swann, *op. cit.,* 240-66.

[26]*Ibid.,* 267 ff.

In Malthusian theory, population should be stabilized at a given poi
until a major advance in material technology produces a more abundant foo
supply. The demography of a society in Malthusian terms is merely a variat
dependent upon its economic constitution. Yet, the relationship betwee
demographic characteristics and economic change is more complicated th
this. The appearance and diffusion of new technology through an econon
may often be stimulated by demand stemming from population change. *
E. A. Wrigley points out, the subtle and dynamic interrelationship betwee
these two may help to explain why in so many pre-industrial societies
Europe and elsewhere the agricultural base of the economy slowly ar
gradually broadened.[27]

Ester Boserup, in her provocative work on agricultural growth, bold
turned Malthusian theory around. She argued that population growth appea
to be the main force by which agrarian change is brought about. In typic
cases, cultivators would find it profitable to shift to a more intensive syste
of land use *only* when a certain density of population had been reached. Ai
if such a density were not reached, they might not use the intensive farmi
method, even if it were known to them, until the critical point of hig
population pressure were reached when the size of the population was suc
that they had to adopt labor-intensive methods, i.e., to accept a decline *
output per man-hour. Obviously, with abundant surplus population, lab
supply would not be a problem. What the farmer aimed at would be *
increase of yield per given area of land, namely, the increase of production.[2]

By the reign of Emperor Wu, the population density in the provinces *
the central plain along the middle and lower reaches of the Yellow River m
have been more than one hundred persons per km^2 and the "new" lan
opened up by the government was soon filled up. The demographic pr
requisite was there. In 85 B.C. Emperor Wu ordered Chao Kuo to promote
system of ridge farming known as the *tai-t'ien* 代田 system.[29]

As Boserup has suggested, no technical change would automaticall
follow the presence of the demographic prerequisite. The promotion of th
tai-t'ien method was preceded by government involvement in promotion *
agriculture in general, and by widespread knowledge of intensive farming :
early as the third century B.C., or even earlier. This government involveme
can be illustrated by a proposal made by Tung Chung-shu to persuade peop
to grow winter wheat in the metropolitan district in *c.* 100 B.C. This propos

[27]Wrigley, *op. cit.*, 46-50. *Cf.* T. R. Malthus, *First essay on population* (Londo
Royal Economic Society, 1798; 1926 reprint).

[28]Ester Boserup, *The conditions of agricultural growth* (Chicago: Aldine Atherto
1965), 41.

[29]Swann, *op. cit.*, 184-91.

s presented at a time when "the people departed from the fundamental
at is, agriculture)," and "the means for maintenance of the people was
ninished."[30] The essence of this proposal seems to suggest a shortening of
winter fallow period by adding one more crop. Thus, it can be viewed as
levelopment toward a multi-cropping system.

The level of agricultural technique in pre-Han times is best summarized
the last four chapters of the *Lü-shih ch'un-ch'iu*.[31] The techniques discussed
this agrarian treatise consist of seed selection, careful field management
ound-dressing, insect-control, etc.), rational adaptation to the conditions
the terrain and water supply, well-regulated alignment of plants in order to
ch optimum conditions of space-saving and good ventilation, and systematic
elioration of soil by using fertilizers, and crop-rotation.[32]

In the *tai-t'ien* method, Chao Kuo perhaps only organized the best tech-
ques of his time into an integrated system. The ridge and trench provided
pattern of spacing. The continuous leveling of the ridge by piling soil from
around the plant certainly would help the plant stand firm and deep-rooted.
nstant weeding would be much easier work, as the lines of plants were
atly arranged. The rotation of the locations of the ridge and the trench would
e each year's crop fresh soil. New implements were also used for improved
iciency. Among these new implements were the specially-designed weeding
e, ox-drawn plow, and seed-box which was attached to a light oxen-drawn
ow-digger. The yield per unit greatly increased.[33] Chao Kuo was assigned
e job of teaching this method to selected farmers, who, in turn, taught
hers. A special team of blacksmiths in the government foundry was also
ght to manufacture the implements designed for such a farming method.

---

[30] *Ibid.*, 177-79.

[31] These chapters on agrarian matters were not composed for the practicing farmers
read since most of them were probably illiterate. The style and the issues dealt with
these four agrarian chapters indicate that the author or authors intended to address
ruler and the officials who were concerned with the maximum use of land to yield
best agricultural productivity. Nevertheless, it is hard to imagine that a scholar could
ate all this applicable know-how from his own mind without some knowledge of the
l practice of agriculture in his own day.

[32] *Lü-shih ch'un-ch'iu*, 26/6-9. *Cf.* Hsu Cho-yün, "Liang Chou nung-tso chi-shu" 兩周
作技術, *BIHP*, XLII:4 (1971), 803-18. The best version of the text is in Hsia Wei-ying,
-shih ch'un-ch'iu Shang-nung teng ssu p'ien chiao-shih 呂氏春秋上農等四篇校釋 (Shang-
i: Chung-hua, 1956). For a good discussion of its value for agrarian history, *cf.* Wan
o-ting, "*Lü-shih ch'un-ch'iu ti hsing-chih chi ch'i tsai nung-hsüeh shih shang ti chia-
ih*" 呂氏春秋的性質及其在農學史上的價值, *Nung-shih yen-chiu chi-k'an* 農史研究集刊
(1960), 182-85.

[33] Swann, *op. cit.*, 58, 184 ff. Whether this *tai-t'ien* method was more suitable for
tivation of large pieces of land or for small farms is debated among scholars; *cf.* Itō
kao, "Daidenhō no ichi kōsatsu" 代田法の一考察, *Shigaku-zasshi*, 69:11(1960), 61-78;

Archaeological evidence indicates that the *tai-t'ien* method was rea
put to use. On the Han wooden strips discovered at the garrison settlement
Chü-yen, the terms *"tai-t'ien"* and *"tai-t'ien* granary" appear frequent
Within two years of the proposal's presentation to the court, this farm
method was established on the western frontier.[34] The light ox-drawn plc
seeder with three "legs," a new implement related to the *tai-t'ien* method
depicted on a Han tomb mural painting. The excavator of this first century to
reports that the three "legs," i.e. the plowshares, are unmistakably visible.

A further elaboration based on the *tai-t'ien* method is that called c
chung 區種, or pit farming. This method, attributed to Fan Sheng-chih (*fl.*
cent. B.C.), consisted of intensive concentration of labor and fertilizer wit
very small spaces, known as pits, which were evenly spaced either besid
long strip or in an area arranged as a matrix. The size and depth of the
varied according to the needs of different crops. It required that the farm
constantly keep the pits well-irrigated and fertilized. The purpose, as given
the text, was to utilize marginal land which was too small or inconvenient 1
regular plowing.[36]

As Shih Sheng-han points out, in the pit method of cultivation, F
Sheng-chih advocated heavy utilization of fertilizer and maintenance
moisture.[37] To raise the per unit yield, this method of labor concentrati
in diligent husbandry and application of water and manure, was definit
superior to the practice of extensive broadcasting which produced poor yiel
Only in certain localities, such as mountainous districts with little level grou
and heavy erosion, where ample manpower was available while man
resources were scanty, would this method be advantageous. Otherwise, t
forbiddingly high labor requirement would cancel out its advantages. T
alleged per unit yield, as given in the text, was incredibly high. It is stat

---

and Nishijima Sadao, *Chūgoku keizaishi kenkyū* 中國經濟史研究 (Tokyo: Tokyo Univ
sity, 1966), 166 ff. The two opinions are not incompatible since this method of rid
farming is adaptable to both large and small farms.

[34] Chang Chun-shu, "The Han colonists and their settlements on the Chü-y
frontier," *Tsing Hua Journal,* new series, V:2 (1966), 161-215.

[35] Shan-hsi Sheng Wen-wu Kuan-li Wei-yüan-hui, "Shan-hsi P'ing-lu Tsao-yüan-ts
pi-hua Han mu" 山西平陸棗園村壁畫漢墓, Kaogu, 1959.9, 463; Plate I, 4.

[36] Shih Sheng-han, *Fan Sheng-chih shu chin shih* 氾勝之書今釋(Peking: K'o-hsi
1959); Ōshima Riichi, "Han Sho-shi sho ni tsuite" 氾勝之書について, *Tōhōgaku
Kyōto),* 15:3 (1946), 86-116.

[37] Pig excrement was a main source of fertilizer. Terra-cotta molds of buildings fou
in Han tombs always include a pig-pen connected to a toilet outlet leading to a dep
pit. *Cf.* Okazaki Takashi, "Kandai meiki deizō to seikatsu yōshiki" 漢代明器泥像と
活樣式, *Shirin,* 42:2 (1959), 39-78. In Han village sites the same set-up is also found.
Tung-pei Po-wu-kuan, "Liao-yang San-tao-hao Hsi-Han ts'un-lo i-chih" 遼陽三道壕西
村落遺址, *K'ao-ku hsüeh-pao* 考古學報, 1957.1, 124.

t two persons working on ten *mou* 畝, using the *ou-chung* method for one
ar, would be able to feed themselves for twenty-six years! However, there
discrepancies between the figures given in different parts of the text.[38]

In spite of the rather dubious high productivity claimed for the *ou-chung*
thod, the general principles adopted in the *ou-chung* method and the *tai-
n* method appear reasonable and consistent. The basic concepts of these
methods can be categorized into six groups as shown below.

I. Field Preparation
    1. Planting in patterns rather than broadcasting seed
    2. Fairly deep cultivation
    3. Consideration of local terrain features
II. Seed
    1. Careful selection of the best specimens
    2. Some treatment of seed before sowing
III. Cultivation
    1. Precise timing to take advantage of optimum atmospheric
       conditions
    2. Constant and diligent weeding and insect control
    3. Irrigation to keep adequate moisture
IV. Soil Amelioration
    1. Using manure to fertilize the soil
    2. Rotating crops to shorten or to avoid fallow
    3. Using leguminous plantings to improve soil quality
V. Land Utilization
    1. Multi-cropping; or even interpolated crops
    2. Growing vegetables on marginal land
VI. Implements
    1. Using animal power
    2. Using specialized tools for various functions

It is clear that the Han farmer did command technical knowledge of
ensive farming at the level of continuous and rational utilization of land,
hough some regional variations in the actual level of practice should be
pected. In the first century B.C., plants cropped included spiked and
tinous millet, winter and spring barley and wheat, soya and other beans,

[38] Shih Sheng-han, *op. cit.,* 64. There have been numerous attempts to apply the *oung* method with certain modifications. Ten records, mostly done by "gentlemen
mers" of the 17th-19th centuries were collected by Wang Yü-hu in a single volume
itled *Ou-chung shih chung* 區種十種 (Shanghai, 1955). For experiments in 1958 in
pei and Honan, *cf.* Wan Kuo-ting, *Chung-kuo nung-hsüeh shih* 中國農學史 (Peking:
-hsüeh, 1959), 178.

hemp, melons, gourds, taro, waterdarnels, paddy rice, perilla, sesame, alfal█
and peas. Fertilizers included human night soil, and the excrement of anim█
such as sheep, goats, pigs, oxen, horses, domestic fowl and silkworms, █
addition to green manures. The water supply was under control, as can█
ponds, and wells facilitated the change from rain-fed to irrigated agricultu█
These conditions definitely helped the development of a sophisticated inte█
sification of the farming system.[39]

NON-AGRICULTURAL ACTIVITIES AND MARKETING AGRARIANISM

Intensification of farming could reduce seasonal underemploymer█
especially that of female and minor laborers, who could be helpful at l█
toilsome jobs, such as weeding.[40] The practice of multi-cropping shorten█
the length of the idle months. Nevertheless, the long frost season in Chir█
specifically in the north, the heartland of the Han empire, still put the H█
farmer through a prolonged winter period. Accordingly, the labor distributi█
for agricultural work tended to be uneven, with the largest amount of lab█
required in the peak periods, i.e. the growing season and the harvest season.█

Non-agricultural work carried out in the dead season by men and in t█
busy season by women and children would absorb some of the underemplo█
ment. The result could either be of logistic value or could be translated in█
market value. Such activities are grouped under one name by some economi█
as "Z" activities.[42]

In a semi-humorous mock contract between a master and his sla█
written in 59 B.C. Wang Pao listed the work assigned to the latter. T█
activities cited appear to be an inventory of all the daily tasks on a far█
instead of the work done by a single individual. The entire list included pure█
agricultural activities (such as cultivation, vegetable growing, fruit-tr█
planting, etc.), repair jobs (of the house, irrigation system, implements), fo█
gathering (such as fishing, hunting), husbandry (of domestic animals), tradi█
(in near-by, as well as distant, market places), and manufacturing (of fabri█

[39]Cf. Shih Sheng-han, op. cit., 48-49.

[40]Mention of female and minor laborers working in the field is quite common in █
Han sources. For instance, as P'ang Kung was tilling the land, his wife and childr█
weeded the field, see Hou Han shu, 83/15.

[41]Cf. Boserup, op. cit., 51-53. This note merely serves the purpose of calling att█
tion to the patterns of labor distribution under intensive farming. I do not mean █
imply that her discussion of conditions in 20th century China can be applied retroactiv█
to those of the Han.

[42]Stephen Hymer and Stephen Resnick, "A model of an agrarian economy with n█
agricultural activities," American Economic Review, 59 (1969), 492.

›es, mats, and other wooden and bamboo artifacts).[43]

Goods produced by such non-agricultural activities could easily be ›verted into marketable items. This situation conforms to the nature of Z activities in the Hymer-Resnick framework.[44]

Such domestic production on the farm would encourage development a marketing agrarianism by which transactions were carried out along a ›-like structure that tied the scattered settlements (such as villages, towns, .) into a marketing network.[45] Indeed, as in the mock contract cited above, geographic area covered by the farmer-trader could be fairly extensive. As ›unomiya has pointed out, transactions were conducted within two circles: arge one with a radius of two hundred kilometers, and a small one with a ius of fifty kilometers.[46] Even in the text of the mock contract itself, ›re is mention of cities, marketing towns, small markets, and side markets, ıs denoting the development of a hierarchical network of trading posts.[47]

Under marketing agrarianism, some market speculation becomes feasible. :cording to a mid-second century work, the *Ssu-min yüeh-ling* [Monthly linances for the four categories of people], the farmer could engage in ing and buying grain several times a year, not for the purpose of acquiring ›plies for consumption, but rather for making profit. Meanwhile, the pro- ction of preserved food, wine, vinegar, medicine, silk and silk fabrics, ›es, and so on, in the farming household was compatible with both home ısumption and marketing.[48] There were similar works in ancient times ıtaining calendars of activities. Yet, the *Ssu-min yüeh-ling* is the first one which commercial activities were cited. It thus reflects the significant point ıt it is in the Han period that marketing agrarianism becomes integrated

---

[43] A translation is included in C. Martin Wilbur, *Slavery in China during the Former Han ıasty* (New York: Russell and Russell, 1967 reprint), 382-92. For a thorough study of s document, see Utsunomiya Kiyoyoshi, *Kandai shakai keizai shi kenkyū* 漢代社會經 史研究 (Tokyo: Kōbundō, 1967), 256-38.

[44] Hymer and Resnick, *op. cit.*, 492-97.

[45] John C. H. Fei and Gustav Ranis, "Economic development in historical perspec- ›s," *American Economic Review*, 59 (1969), 386-95.

[46] Utsunomiya, *op. cit.*, 349-53.

[47] Wilbur, *op. cit.*, 385-87.

[48] The present day text of the *Ssu-min yüeh-ling*, attributed to Ts'ui Shih of the mid- ›ond century, is reconstructed from various quotations. The best existing version is › one worked out by Shih Sheng-han, *Ssu-min yüeh-ling chiao-chu* 四民月令校注 king: Chung-hua, 1965). Ts'ui Shih (*fl.* 145-167), an official himself, tried in this ıume to establish a model for contemporary gentry on how to make a livelihood of ming, supplemented by income from business adventures, as well as some manu- turing. Thus, the title is "Monthly ordinances for the four categories of people" .mely gentry, farmer, merchant, and artisan). The reconstructed text is not complete, ıch is missing. Nevertheless, it is one of the most valuable sources for the study of the

into the rural economy.[49]

The notion of growing cash crops for profit is included in the *F Sheng-chih shu*. For example, gourds were grown, not only for fodder and make dippers, but also for making candles. The income from such items v calculated in terms of cash value at the market.[50] Commercialization linked local economy to an integrated regional and, ultimately, national econon system. This, in turn, facilitated interregional product specialization.[51] In t time of Ssu-ma Ch'ien, around the first century B.C., there were staple goo such as chestnuts of Yen and a number of other areas, dates of An-i and Ch' citrus fruit of Shu, Han, and Chiang-ling, catalpa of the region between t Huai, Chi, and Yellow Rivers, lacquer of Ch'en and Hsia, mulberry trees a hemp of Ch'i and Lu, bamboo of the Wei valley, ...[52] These all appear products in national markets.

Though the historical sources do not provide us with any nation-wi data for the Later Han period, Chao Ch'i (*fl.* A.D. 110-201), in a casual obs vation, reported that one county in Ch'en-liu (in the eastern part of the prese province of Honan) planted no crop other than indigo. According to Ch Ch'i, the indigo field stretched to the horizon![53] Among the Han strips c covered at Chü-yen and Tun-huang (in the western part of Kansu province) a inventories which mention clothes described as being from Ho-nei (northe part of Honan), Kuang-han (northern part of Szechuan), and Jen-ch'e (southern Hopei). This indicates that staple goods from the above-mention areas could be shipped one thousand miles away and still be labeled as t products of their places of origin. And these clothes were only ordinary ones.

---

history and economy of Han rural life. I have made a full English translation of t Shih version. It is to be included in my forthcoming volume, *Han agriculture*, to published by the University of Washington Press. For the study of this text in relation mercantile activities, *cf.* Yang Lien-sheng, "Ts'ung Ssu-min yüeh-ling so chien-tao ti H tai chia-tsu ti sheng-ch'an" 從四民月令所見到的漢代家族的生產, *Shih-huo*, 1:6 (193 8 ff., and Shih Sheng-han, *op. cit.,* 89.

[49] Moriya Mitsuo has compared *Ssu-min yüeh-ling* with other calendars such as *Yüeh ling* in the *Li chi* and the *Hsia hsiao cheng*, etc. He finds that the only parts wh are not comparable relate to commercial activities and non-ritualistic routines; see Mor Mitsuo, *Chūgoku ko saijiki no kenkyū* 中國古歳時記の研究 (Tokyo, 1963).

[50] Shih Sheng-han, *op. cit.,* 4.10-4.10.4.

[51] Fei and Ranis, *op. cit.,* 393.

[52] Swann, *op. cit.,* 432-33.

[53] Yen K'o-chün, *Ch'üan Hou Han wen* 全後漢文 (Taipei: Shih-chieh, 1961 repri 62/5. Around the beginning of the second century, Yang Chen (54-124) also ren fields to grow indigo at a place not far from Ch'en-liu; *Hou Han shu*, 54/1 (a quotat cited from *Hsü Han chih* 續漢志 by the commentator).

[54] Ch'en Chih, *Liang Han ching-chi shih-liao lun-ts'ung* 兩漢經濟史料論叢 (Sian: J min, 1958), 68.

The recent discovery of a Han village site provides a close look at the
age economy. In this village, San-tao-hao, dated 200 B.C.-A.D. 25, residency
as have been excavated. In addition to evidence of common agricultural
ivities at least seven brick kilns have been discovered. The productive
acity for each kiln was about 1,800 bricks. The excavator reports that two
the kilns were designed to operate in alternation with each other so that
cks could be produced continuously. The bricks produced in this village
found not only on the building-sites in that village but also in the whole
ion of Liao-yang. Leading away from the village is the foundation of a
l-pounded road with three or four layers of pebbles built to a height of
5 meters. On the road surface, two wagon tracks are clearly visible. The
d has a width of seven meters, broad enough to take two lanes of traffic.[55]
e San-tao-hao discovery indicates that even a village in an economically
ignificant commandery close to the frontier had received the impact of
nmercialization to such a degree that its inhabitants engaged in the pro-
ction of bricks in sufficient quantities to supply not only village needs but
o the market of neighboring areas. And the wagon track on the heavily-
lt road indicates the busy flow of inbound as well as outbound shipments.

A commercialized agrarian society knit the individual farmer into a
ssive economic network. The situation, therefore, did not correspond to the
nmonly held image that ancient Chinese agrarian society was made up of
ttered, isolated, self-sufficient cells, which were the farming households.[56]
mmercial urban centers had been stimulated to grow to a remarkable level
prosperity, as indicated by the fact that at least twenty-six important urban
aters had been formed along major transportation routes in the Former Han
riod.[57] Yet the merchant-entrepreneur class was nipped in the bud, first, by
aperor Wu, who, engaged as he was in strengthening the authority of the
narchy, was jealous of any potential challenge to his sovereign power.[58]
d, thereafter, the bureaucracy of the empire had become so well-established
at its members, i.e. the bureaucrats and the local leaders, were able to mon-
olize not only political power, but also great wealth. The full development
commercialization, therefore, was never permitted to take place.[59]

[55]Tung-pei Po-wu-kuan, "Liao-yang San-tao-hao Hsi-Han ts'un-lo i-chih," *op. cit.*,
9, 125-26.

[56]For instance, Etienne Balazs, *Chinese civilization and bureaucracy,* translated by
M. Wright (New Haven: Yale University Press, 1964), 15-16.

[57]Utsunomiya, *op. cit.,* 109-19.

[58]Hsu Cho-yün, "The changing relationship between local society and the central
litical power in Former Han, 206 B.C.-8 A.D.," *Comparative Studies in Society and
tory,* VII (1965), 364.

[59]*Ibid.,* 367-70; Balazs, *op. cit.,* 15-18, 41-42.

The level of commercial activity fluctuated with the stability of political order. When the empire was unified, when roads were good, wl travel was safe, inter-regional specialization would pull individual farmers the village into participation in a gigantic marketing network. When everyth went wrong, the empire was divided and the central government failed to r effectively, and, in more practical terms, when former special export produ could not be shipped out and staple goods from outside became too expens to acquire, the farmer had to change his habits of production. Local figu who already occupied prominent positions would lead the local area to cl in upon itself. The non-agricultural Z activities would then be shifted fr producing marketable goods back to producing goods and services for th own consumption. There emerged, therefore, a self-sufficient rural communi Since such a small community was often under the dominance of local lead(the self-sufficient economy exhibited the characteristics of a manorial syste Fan Hung, the maternal uncle of Emperor Kuang-wu (r. 25-57), managed organize a whole community around himself for self-defense and self-sufficien during the turbulent years at the time of Wang Mang's (45 B.C.-A.D. fall.[60] At the end of the Former Han as well as at the end of the Later H such communities were numerous.[61] Nevertheless, their isolation and self-s ficiency were temporary phenomena. Like a sea-urchin, the framework wh underlay marketing agrarianism and intensive farming expanded during peri of security and contracted at times of danger.[62]

In summary, agricultural development during the Han period seems have occurred largely in the areas of improved methods of intensive farm as a response to the relative increase of population pressure on arable la especially within the most well-developed regions. The uneven seasonal (tribution of labor characteristic of intensive farming was compensated for means of non-agricultural productive activities which, in turn, made it possi for the farmer to develop market-oriented economic behavior. Neverthel(if the market became inaccessible, the farmer could still readjust his behav in the direction of greater economic self-sufficiency.

---

[60]*Hou Han shu,* 32/1.

[61]Chin Fa-ken, *Yung-chia luan hou pei-fang ti hao-tsu* 永嘉亂後北方的豪族 (Tai 1964), 11-12, 28-31.

[62]William Skinner observed the same phenomenon of recurrent cyclical trends ba on studies in eighteenth century China; *Cf.* G. William Skinner, "Chinese peasants a the closed community: an open and shut case," *Comparative Studies in Society* (*History,* XIII (1971), 270 ff. It should be noted, however, that the two millennium s between the period covered by this paper and that of Skinner should create some parity in levels of development, if not in basic pattern.

The enjoyment of life in the Han reliefs of Nanyang*

Richard C. Rudolph

.ough formal banquets, intimate parties, drinking bouts, and hunting
ts of early China are all described in wordy detail in the *Wen hsüan*, it is
ossible to tell where fact leaves off and poetic license takes over. But
rtainment scenes portrayed in some Late Han bas-reliefs of an unusual
: uncovered around Nanyang must be quite factual. They are not the
t common motif among these reliefs, nor the most impressive in execution,
they are of interest in that they provide vivid pictorial representations of
aspect of life among the aristocrats of that time and place. Before de-
·ing some of them, however, something must be said about the discovery
characteristics of the reliefs in which these scenes occur.

For over one and one-half millennia, residents of the Nanyang region in
hwestern Honan found a convenient source of building material in the
f-decorated stone slabs taken from ancient tombs that abound there. One
tomb in this area, for example, was cannibalized shortly after it was built
naterials to build a second one, and another was the source of twelve
rated slabs for a tomb built about a century later.[1] This practice was not
icted to the Nanyang area, of course, but was perpetrated throughout
a in spite of the alleged veneration of the past and respect for one's own
others' ancestors. The deliberate destruction of historic objects had been

The first four words of this title are those of a chapter title in Professor Creel's well-
n *Birth of China* which I first read when I joined him as an assistant at the Univer-
·f Chicago just forty years ago. I recently went through his book again, recalling
.nt memories of those early days, and now I use this opportunity to offer him
e wishes for the continued enjoyment of life.

Vang Ju-lin, "Ho-nan Nan-yang Hsi-kuan i tso ku mu chung ti Han hua hsiang shih"
洞陽西關一座古墓中的漢畫象石, *Kaogu* (K'ao ku), 1964.8, 424-26, and Wang Pao-
˛, "Ho-nan Nan-yang Tung-kuan Chin mu" 河南南陽東關晉墓, *Kaogu*, 1963.1,

decried as early as Chin and Sung times,[2] but obviously those who vandali‹ early monuments were neither avid readers of such sources nor firm suppor‹ of such attitudes. As late as 1915, when Lo Chen-yü first visited the sit‹ the last Shang capital, he also lamented the degrading use of inscribed sto for building materials and weights.[3]

In the Nanyang region, through the course of the centuries, a l‹ number of stones from Han tombs for the dead were used for various pract‹ purposes by the living, but they were most commonly used in the construc‹ and repair of bridges. Although the defacing of any ancient artifact is dep‹ able, it is especially so in the case of these stones because most were decor‹ with reliefs in a specific regional style. The predilection of the traditi‹ Chinese antiquarian for inscriptions—reverence for the written word appreciation of calligraphic style—is undoubtedly responsible for the that these highly important but uninscribed stones went unrecorded unappreciated until some fifty years ago.[4]

In 1923 and 1924, the late Professor Tung Tso-pin, Kuan Po-i, others searched out and made rubbings of a number of these stones which been scattered about the countryside, and this resulted in the first publica of reliefs executed in this style.[5] The forces of nature, so often respons for archaeological discoveries, brought to light an important group of t‹ reliefs in the autumn of 1932 near the village of Ts'ao-tien about six n southwest of Nanyang. Heavy rains flooded the Yü River which mean‹ through this region and caused part of its west bank to collapse. This reve‹ the remains of a Han dynasty stone and brick tomb which was prom‹

---

[2] *Sui shu* 隋書 (Wu-ying tien ed.), 45/13a. Ch'en Yu, *Fu hsüan yeh lu* 負喧 (*Ts'ung shu chi ch'eng* ed.), Vol. 1552, p.3.

[3] For the establishment of the date of 1915 for Lo's first visit to Yin-hsü, after se‹ his younger brother there in 1911, see Richard C. Rudolph, "Lo Chen-yü visits the ‹ of Yin," in Frederic Wakeman, Jr. (ed.), *"Nothing concealed" essays in honor o,* Yü-yün (Taipei, 1970), n. 4. In his diary of his visit to the last Shang capital, *Wu sh‹ meng hen lu* 五十日夢痕錄, p. 31a, where he denounces the misuse of early monumen‹ seems to be paraphrasing the *Sui shu* statement noted above. He was very sensitive a the loss of China's early artifacts and in an essay, "Hai wai chen min lu" 海外貞‹ *Kuo hsüeh ts'ung k'an*, Vol. 20, maintained that stones with inscriptions and reliefs "buried a second time" when they went into foreign collections.

[4] This is basically true but there were some exceptions.’ A few slabs with characte‹ Nanyang decoration were placed in temples and public buildings for preservation. one large stone bearing an astronomical relief (Sun Wen-ch'ing, no. 4) was found in times and put in a place of safety according to a note pasted on the rubbing of it Tung Tso-pin's collection of these in Academia Sinica. This is not to say that no reliefs were collected and studied at earlier times; it is well known that they were.

[5] Kuan Po-yi, *Nan-yang Han hua hsiang chi* 南陽漢畫象集 (Shanghai, 1930). reproduced, unfortunately, only thirty-nine rubbings on a very small scale.

ted and partially demolished by the villagers, but the stone part of it
ained intact. It was a post and lintel structure, apparently an offering
ne, measuring about 5 m. long, 2 m. wide, and 2.6 m. high. The first in
area to be studied by scholars, it was built with twenty-seven pieces of
ssed stone decorated with forty-four reliefs. There was a carefully planned
consistent placement of different motifs throughout the structure, and
parison of them with those on many of the scattered stones helped to
ermine the original structural function of the latter. The discovery of these
y-four reliefs led to a second publication, this one containing repro-
tions of 145 rubbings.[6]

The term Nanyang relief (or Nanyang style) as used in this paper, does
include all Han reliefs from this area. It refers only to those executed in a
que regional style in which representational art is characterized, generally
aking, by much freedom in composition, spontaneity in drawing, and an
ependent stock of motifs.

There is much difference between the Nanyang and the more "coven-
al" Han style mentioned below, but the greatest contrasts are to be seen
he Nanyang reliefs depicting animal combat—men fighting animals or
nals fighting each other. In these scenes the free and dynamic style of
ving and composition imparts a feeling of kinetic energy, and one is acutely
re of the motion and power of the combatants. In some cases it is obvious
the artist had a genius for depicting movement. This is true to a lesser
ree in scenes that do not represent such vigorous action, but a feeling of
ion and strength is still apparent, and this feeling even extends to some of
static figures. In short, this style differs greatly from what may be loosely
d the conventional style which is well known from early Western publi-
ons of reliefs and stamped tiles from Shantung, Honan, and other places.[7]
best known, through early and wide publication, are those from the

Sun Wen-ch'ing, *Nan-yang Han hua hsiang hui ts'un* 南陽漢畫象彙存 (Nanking,
7). He also published at least two preliminary reports which need not concern us
except for the fact that he fails to report on the type of stone used for these reliefs.
nay infer that it was sandstone from the report of Wang Pao-hsiang cited in n. 1.
s publication was by no means comprehensive for Tung Tso-pin made a collection of
300 rubbings of reliefs from the Nanyang area before he left the mainland for
an. He kindly made these available to me at Academia Sinica from 1959-1960 and
, plus later finds, will appear in a forthcoming publication. For recent Nanyang
see the very useful work by Käte Finsterbusch, *Verzeichnis und Motivindex der
Darstellungen*, 2 vols. (Wiesbaden, 1966, 1971), hereafter *VHD*.
Edouard Chavannes, *La sculpture sur pierre en Chine au temps des deux dynasties*
(Paris, 1893), and *Mission archeologique dans la Chine septentrionale*, I, 1, *La sculp-
a l'epoque des Han* (Paris, 1913). Victor Segalan, Gilbert de Voisins, and Jean
gue, *Mission archeologique en Chine* (Paris, 1923-24). W. C. White, *Tomb tile
res of ancient China* (Toronto, 1939).

offering shrines at the Wu family cemetery in Shantung.[8] Here, as in s
other places, figural representation is stereotype and static, and the art
attempts at representing action are not very convincing.[9] But while tl
shrine reliefs are in what I call the conventional style, they are, of course,
in a regional style. In recent years it has been possible to define sev
regional styles in Han reliefs, and more are coming to light through
intensive archaeological program being carried out in the People's Republi

Generally speaking, there is also considerable difference between
motifs in the Nanyang reliefs and those found in other areas. In the fo
are lacking popular Confucian subjects, such as the model emperors,
paragons of filial piety and related figures; and the numerous procession
chariots and horsemen and files of standing officials, so common in Shant
are rarely if ever seen. More conspicuous by their absence are some of
larger scenes in the reliefs from Shantung and other places: the attem
assassination of Ch'in Shih Huang Ti, the battle on the bridge, the solar
the formal banquets taking place in two stage structures, and the attem
recovery of the legendary *ting* 鼎 from the Ssu River. Also missing in
Nanyang reliefs, unfortunately, are those interesting illustrations of
technology, although some do occur on the pressed clay tiles found in ne
Szechwan. The Nanyang motifs may be roughly grouped into five catego
combat, entertainment, constellations, animals, humans and monsters.

One constant characteristic of the Nanyang style is the treatment o
recessed background. This invariably consists of fairly coarse striations run
at right angles to the longitudinal axis of the scene. They are always pai
and very regular, with three or four to the inch, and generally appear
they may have been made by the use of a multiple-toothed claw chisel.[11]

[8] See Wilma Fairbank, "The offering shrines of Wu Liang Tz'u," *HJAS*, VI (1941).
[9] For juxtaposed illustrations of the static Shantung and dynamic Szechwan ver
of the attempted assassination of Ch'in Shih Huang Ti, see Richard C. Rudolph,
tomb reliefs from Szechwan," *Archives of the Chinese Art Society of Americ*
(1950), 32.

[10] In Richard C. Rudolph and Wen Yu, *Han tomb art of West China* (Berkeley, 1
hereafter *HTA*, different styles were found to exist in a relatively small area in Szech
See the excellent study on a regional style of northern Shensi in Hsio-yen Shih,
stone reliefs from Shensi Province," *Archives of the Chinese Art Society of Am*
XIV (1960), 49-63.

[11] This is in sharp contrast to the various and often distracting patterns of backgi
striations in the Szechwan reliefs. See, for example, four different types with i
variations from the Hsinchin area alone, in *HTA*, Pls. 37, 38, 40, 52, 54, 55; 42, 4
59; 49, 50. There must be some implication in the consistency of the Nanyang m
in such a large number of reliefs. In a study of some medieval Italian reliefs it is i
that the background striations were made by a four-toothed claw chisel, and
specialists were used for different degrees of detail and complication. See John V

iations rarely run through the figures which are in low relief.

A peculiar device seen in some of the reliefs is that of a man or an
imal stepping out of the frame which surrounds an individual scene. It is
possible to say whether this occurs through accident or design, but it does
e the impression of depth and enhances the feeling of movement. In one
e where a man is fleeing from some rampaging animals, the lower border
rounding the scene forms a base line upon which the animals are moving in
efinite two-dimensional context, but the running man's extended near foot
below and in front of this base. This gives him the appearance of moving
ward from the plane of the picture and creates an illusion of three-
nensional space.[12] In other cases where a part of a figure protrudes beyond
: frame of the scene, it seems clear that it was unintentional. Such a mistake
not likely to happen if the subject is first drawn upon the stone, but it
uld result from tracing a pattern which was a bit too large for the panel
ing used. T'ang sources tell of pattern books used by mural painters, and
: transfer of designs by pouncing or tracing.[13] It is possible, and indeed
obable, that pattern books were also used by the artists who designed many
the Han reliefs.

Of the more than twenty reliefs representing entertainment, only five
ve been chosen for discussion here because they contain most of the
ments that occur in the others. Unfortunately, these are not the best
amples of the dynamic Nanyang style referred to above.

Figure 1. A scene in two registers, 68 x 153 cm., showing entertainment
ove and a bullfight below. In the upper one five seated people and two
ncers are shown in frontal view. The two people on the right appear to be
est and host seated near a round tray with dishes on it. What looks like a
y table between them is shown in elevation, but the tray is shown in plan.
the left of them are three people playing musical instruments. Only one
trument can be clearly identified in this relief in which broad vertical
iations go through the figures; it is a *p'ai hsiao* 排簫 or panpipe held by the
sician on the left. From the position of his hands, the one in the center
y be playing a vertical flute. The last two figures on the left are engaged in
animated dance. The one on the right appears to be fully clothed and has a

---

e reliefs on the facade of the duomo at Orvieto," *Journal of the Warburg and
rtauld Institutes*, XXII (1959), 279 and 254 respectively. The older and softer
ayang reliefs, unfortunately, do not offer such specific evidence.

[12] As only one example of several, see Richard C. Rudolph, "Notes on the Han
nasty reliefs at Nanyang," *Symposium in honor of Dr. Li Chi on his seventieth
hday*, I (Taipei, 1965), Fig. 1.

[13] Hsiang Ta, *T'ang tai Ch'ang-an yü hsi yü wen-ming* 唐代長安與西域文明 (Peking,
7), 405-407.

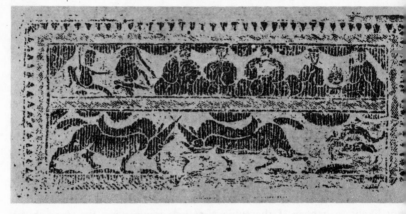

Figure 1

scarf or long sleeves and an elaborate headdress, while the potbellied clowr
acrobat seems to be stripped to the waist. On the floor underneath the lat
figure is an unidentifiable object which may be a small drum, sometimes s∈
in association with these dances. The border of triangles and the obje
above the people, generally assumed to be hangings or drapes, are comm∈
features of the Nanyang reliefs. The objects protruding from the top ₃
bottom borders of the lower register may represent configurations in the la
they are more realistically represented in the following illustration.

In the lower register two taurine beasts are clearly shown charging e∂
other, but the figure in the lower right corner is illegible because of damage
the stone. Six near-identical pairs of fighting beasts, and several sir
examples of the same type fighting with normal animals also occur in th
reliefs. In all cases the artist has endowed them with wings and what appe
to be a single horn. That only one horn is shown (as is also one wing) may
the result of profile drawing. On the other hand, these beasts do have so
resemblance to the supposed appearance of the *pi hsieh* 辟邪, the myth∃
apotropaic animal; but one would hardly expect two creatures whose purp
it is to guard tombs to attack each other.[14] Because of the prevalence
these scenes, and the association of these animals with perfectly nor₪

[14] On the origins and appearance of this mythical animal, see Schuyler Camma
"The lion and grape patterns on Chinese bronze mirrors," *Artibus Asiae*, XVI (19.
270. For those partial to unicorns, it should be pointed out that a bronze one 75
long was found in a Han tomb in northern Kansu in 1956. It is illustrated in *Wen*
文物, 1959.10, 77, Fig. 9, and its horn is quite unlike those in this relief. Again, as ₪
the *pi hsieh*, why should unicorns attack each other? See A. Bulling, "Notes on
unicorns," *Oriental Art*, XII:2, 1-5, where this illustration is reproduced and informa
is given on various aspects of the unicorn in China.

s, we must conclude that this scene simply represents a bullfight.

It is common in Shantung and other places to find Han reliefs in two or a more registers, but of the 300 rubbings of reliefs in the Nanyang style I have examined, only this and one other of identical composition appear wo registers. Do these two exceptions in such a large number mean that artist intended them to form a single scene, using the border between n as a spatial device? If this is indeed the case, then we have an illustration eople being regaled with food and entertainment in some sort of shelter, ably an open balcony, while watching a bullfight in a courtyard or arena w. That bullfighting, and animal fighting in general, were spectator sports Ian times has been discussed elsewhere.[15] Bullfighting with ritualistic ciations has continued down into modern times in some parts of China. s difficult, if not impossible, to pinpoint the introduction of the cult ient in bullfighting or bull and buffalo sacrifice in China, but it must go to pre-Han times.[16]

Figure 2. Detail of a relief measuring 36 x 269 cm. Another type of fighting practiced in Nanyang was that of man versus animal—of dubious yment for the man but undoubtedly exciting sport for the spectators. In relief a man and a realistic and powerful bull are rushing forward to ck each other. The man is running toward the bull and has seized one of horns with his left hand, certainly a preliminary step in an attempt to lue the animal or some type of acrobatic trick.[17] Men attacking bulls in

[5]Richard C. Rudolph, "Bull grappling in early Chinese reliefs," *Archaeology*, XIII 0), 241-45, and "Notes on the Han dynasty reliefs at Nanyang," 102-103. It is of est to note that damaged murals found at Knossos in Crete apparently showed tators in balconies watching bullfights and other contests below; see Arthur Evans, *Palace of Minos*, I, 527-28, III, 47-62, *et passim*.

[6]C. W. Bishop, "The ritual bullfight," *China Journal of Science and Arts*, III (1925), 37. Chang-kong Chiu, "Die Kultur der Miao-tse nach älteren Quellen," *Mitteilungen lem Museum für Völkerkunde in Hamburg*, XVIII (1937), 12-14. M. Portia Mickey, e Cowrie Shell Miao of Kweichow," *Papers of the Peabody Museum of American aeology and Ethnology*, XXXII:1 (1947), 76-80. Inez de Beauclair, "Culture traits on-Chinese tribes in Kweichow Province, South-west China," *Sinologica*, V (1956), 1. Additional information on the cult aspect may be found in Derk Bodde's vals in Classical China (Jointly published by Princeton University Press and The ese University of Hong Kong, 1975), 201-209.

[7]Although no Cretan connection is implied, there is a certain resemblance between Nanyang scenes and the well-known bull-vaulting fresco from Knossos dating 00 B.C. Evans, III, 212-15, *et passim*. Closer to the Knossos fresco in spirit and time ome scenes cast into a bronze *hu* vase dating from the Warring States period. One s a man leaping over or onto a bull while holding onto a horn and another shows a astride a bull (?) and holding onto a horn, but in both cases the beasts are being acted by armed men. See *K'ao-ku hsüeh-pao*, 1953.1-2, 84-86; better illustrations be found in Cheng Te-k'un, *Archaeology in China*, III (Cambridge, 1963), Fig. 25,

these reliefs generally have common characteristics: they are always
vigorous motion, they have bulky sleeves or clothing or both, many have
"un-Chinese" look or appear to be wearing masks, they wear a peculiar t
of headdress or have their hair arranged so that it projects from the top of
head, and they are unarmed. Here the bullfighter appears to be holding so
thing in his right hand, but in six other similar scenes he is empty-handed
scene almost identical to this one is on the side of a Han clay funerary cook
stove. Here the man is unarmed, has an upright hairdo, prominent whisk
and bulky sleeves. He has seized the bull by one horn and is in a stance sim
to that of the Nanyang man but the action is not portrayed in such a dyna
manner. No provenance for the object is given, but the presence of this m
suggests that it was manufactured in this region.[18]

It is fortunate that we have what is presumably an eyewitness acco
of this sport in the writings of a native of this region, the famous mathe
tician-astronomer Chang Heng (A.D. 78-139). In his "Description of
Western Capital" (Changan), he says that animal fighters "roll up their l
with red cloth so that it stands up like a stick."[19] which is exactly what
man must have done. And other contemporary writers tell of "barbar
from the North" being invited to attack ferocious animals barehanded
prove their bravery.[20]

Figure 3. This lively entertainment scene with five musicians and th
performers measures 39 x 151 cm. but it must be incomplete because
audience is shown. The first member of the orchestra on the right is holdi
bronze bell and striking it with a mallet. The second and fourth are si
taneously playing panpipes held in their left hands and twirling clapper dr
with their right hands, and the one between them appears to be playi
vertical flute or an ocarina. The fifth is playing a zither (ch'in 琴), maki
total of seven instruments being played at the same time. One of the
formers is doing a handstand or handspring near some undefinable obj
This may be a table with food and drink or a stand for the performer; t
are often shown performing on a stand or table, as in the next illustratior
even on a stack of them.[21] A juggler, stripped to the waist, is balancing a
on his right forearm, and balancing a ball or twirling a clapper drum with
left hand. He has an unusually large face and is probably wearing a mask,

and Charles D. Weber, *Chinese pictorial bronze vessels of the Late Chou period* (Asc
1968), Fig. 62.

[18] Lo Chen-yü, *Ku ming-ch'i t'u-lu* 古明器圖錄 (1916), Ch. 2, 14a.

[19] "Hsi ching fu" 西京賦 , *Wen hsüan* (Taipei: I wen yin shu kuan ed., 1959), 33.

[20] Yang Hsiung, "Ch'ang yang fu" 長楊賦 , *Wen hsüan*, 91.

[21] *VHD*, II, 191, 206. Details on many aspects of Han entertainment can be fou
Sun Tz'u-chou, "Lun Nan-yang Han hua hsiang chung te yüeh wu" 論南陽漢畫像
樂舞, *Li-shih yü k'ao-ku*, No. 3 (1937), 9-14.

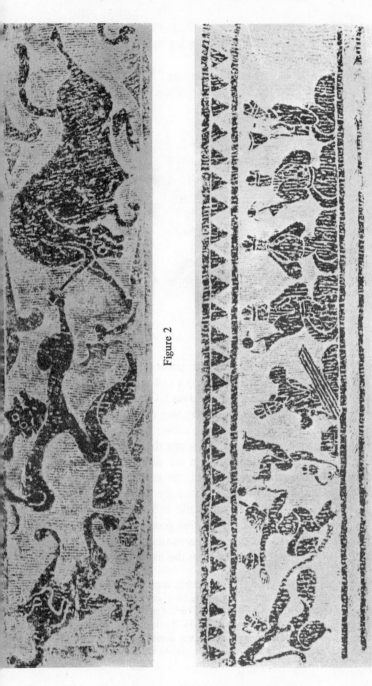

Figure 2

Figure 3

his hair is done in a vertical form like that of the bullfighters. He is exhibit
his juggling skill while dancing or jumping over a long scarf being swirled
the leaping dancer on the far left.

     Figure 4. Detail of a relief measuring 25 x 150 cm. The combination
dancers, acrobats, and musicians is a popular one in the Nanyang reliefs, a

Figure 4

to this one has been added a clown or jester. The dancer on the right has t
usual long sleeves and seems to be using a ball as a prop, unless this is a scar
the stone or a fault in the rubbing. To his left an acrobat, perhaps a dwarf
is performing the difficult feat of standing on the one hand on a low tal
and holding an object out toward the clown with his other. Long scarves a
attached to his feet or legs and he swings them around as he performs. F
waist and legs are barely discernible in this picture due to an attempt at fo
shortening. Because three or four of the striations next to the arm up
which he is standing have been very heavily inked in this rubbing, it alm
appears as if he is seated upon this stand and waving two scarves, but thi
not the case. A clearer example of this pose can be seen in another rel
which is a mirror image of this one, indicating that it was a popular type
entertainment.[23] The third figure from the right, a jester, is either kneeling

---

[22]Undersized people appear in Han reliefs, and dwarfs were probably kept in
homes and courts of members of the ruling class as entertainers. For dwarfs in Chin
figurines and literature, see Kobayashi Taichirō, *Kantō kozoku to meiki dogu* 漢唐さ
と明器土偶 (Kyoto, 1947), 245-47, Pls. 55-56. Their roles as entertainers, gladiators, a
lovers in the early Mediterranean world are described in Jean Boullet, "Les Nain
Aesculape, XLI:9, 3-61, and they must have played similar roles in China.

[23]*VHD*, II, 719a.

:ing on some object; in any case he is much taller than the others. He has
oversized head, probably a mask, and a bulging belly.[24] He has assumed a
nic pose and seems to be gesturing toward his long, extended tongue;
iind him are four seated musicians. A grotesque figure and extended tongue
common attributes of other jesters in Nanyang entertainment scenes.[25]

Figure 5. Detail of a relief measuring 30 x 124 cm. in which two men,
:h an attendant, are playing *t'ou hu* 投壺 or pitch-pot. They wear different

Figure 5

'le hats, perhaps indicating host and visitor, and are kneeling on either side
a *hu* vase and pitching (*t'ou*) arrows into it. Between the elderly-looking
ıyer and the vase is a *tsun* 尊 wine vessel with a ladle. Some arrows have
eady been thrown into the vase and each man is holding three arrows in
e hand and is ready to toss one with the other.[26] One would normally

[24]These are descendents of the type of Chou jester discussed in H. G. Creel, *The
:h of China* (New York, 1954), 320-21. The grotesque aspect of the jesters may
licate that they are foreigners. It is well known that entertainers, including dwarfs and
glers, as well as strange animals, were imported or sent to Han China as tribute gifts.
: Ying-shih Yü, *Trade and expansion in Han China* (Berkeley, 1967), 196-97, and
seph Needham, *Science and civilisation in China*, Vol. I (Cambridge, 1954), 197-98.

[25]The extended or long tongue motif in humans or deities is rarely found outside the
ı Ch'u domain, in which the Han Nanyang commandery was situated, but it is com-
ınly seen on wooden artifacts from Ch'u tombs. See Alfred Salmony, *Antler and
ıgue: an essay on ancient Chinese symbolism and its implications*, *Artibus Asiae*,
pp. 13 (1954), and "With antler and tongue," *Artibus Asiae*, XXI (1958), 29-35.

[26]Three papers on this game have approached it from different angles. Gosta Montell,
'ou hu—The ancient Chinese pitch-pot game," *Ethnos*, V (1949),70-83, used literary
ırces. Richard C. Rudolph, "The antiquity of *t'ou hu*," *Antiquity*, XXIV (1950), 175-
, used this relief and a similar one from Nanyang plus additional historical sources.
bert J. Poor, "Evolution of a secular vessel type," *Oriental Art*, n.s. XIV (1968), 98-
6, made a detailed chronological study of the development of the *hu* vases used in the
ne.

expect both men to be holding their reserve arrows with the left hand a tossing with the right, but the artist, probably for the sake of symmet makes one right-handed and the other left-handed. The alternative, of cour is that the latter actually was a sinistromanual player of note and was th intentionally represented. In any event, we have in this relief a very ea Chinese illustration of this phenomenon.

T'ou hu seems to have been commonly played from late Chou un modern times, and some devotees claimed there were certain moral values be derived from the game. The Li chi, compiled in the Early Han, has a whe section devoted to the elaborate rules of play and counting for this game.[27] is also mentioned in the earlier Tso chuan and various other sources anc half-dozen books were written on it, two of them by the famous Sung h torian Ssu-ma Kuang. It is indeed a strange coincidence, in view of its appare popularity and the many extant entertainment scenes of this period, that tl game is found on only two of the many hundreds of known Han reliefs a that both of them come from Nanyang.[28]

This rubbing has been reproduced in Needham's monumental work a he describes the object near the hu as "a small ladle something like the lo stone spoon, standing free upon a small table . . ." and relates it to the m netic compass and diviner's board.[29] Although this interpretation may true for similar objects in other reliefs, it appears to be untenable for tl particular one.

Many Han illustrations of games or entertainment also include vessels different sizes and styles with ladles, presumably containing drink for t players and spectators. In this relief, among others, a small, three-legged ves is shown in profile with a ladle above it. In other reliefs executed on a larg scale, and where the observer has something approaching a bird's eye view, looks down into the containers and sees ladles inside them with handl protruding over the edge.[30] In such scenes there is nothing that resembles t three-legged object and ladle in this game of t'ou hu. In other words, the objects are one and the same, and proper interpretation may depend, literall upon one's point of view. In the present case, of which there are numero examples, the artist wanted the observer to recognize without question tl object represented, so he showed the entire ladle above the silhouette of tl container. Moreover, drawings of forty-eight tsun from Han reliefs inclu

---

[27] Li chi 禮記, ch. 37, t'ou hu.

[28] Finsterbusch's VHD is a detailed index to all Han pictorial art published throu mid-1966 and lists only these two examples of t'ou hu.

[29] Needham, IV:1 (Cambridge, 1962), Fig. 350.

[30] HTA, Pls. 57, 77-79; these were noted by Needham, 267, but he did not rela them to the object under discussion.

ral with the ladle above the container, as in this case, but they are also
mpanied by drinking cups which remove any doubt about their function.[31]

That this object is merely a container and ladle is also supported by
literary references to the game. In the regulations concerning *t'ou hu* in
Li chi, a player's turn is determined not by lot (which apparently would
he purpose of this object according to Needham) but by rule; more
ortant, these regulations show that drinking was an integral part of the
e, and supposedly a container of wine would be kept near at hand.
lly, the Warring States sophist Shun-yü K'un clearly associated wine
king to the games of *t'ou hu* and *liu po* 六博 in a speech to the King of
[32]

The occurrence of the conventional and the markedly different Nanyang
fs in the same area at the same time is puzzling. It is especially so when
considers the dynamic portrayal of motion, the absence of traditional
ifs, and the unusually large number of combat scenes: the Nanyang reliefs
appear, so to speak, as an island surrounded by a sea of reliefs in the con-
ional style, including variations on the latter.[33] Similar situations in medie-
European sculpture resulted from the distinctive styles of wandering arti-
, but is that the case for Nanyang in Han times? Did influence come from
animal style so common in the vast areas far to the north and west of China?
rom the southwest where animal art, and especially the bull, preoccupied
bronze craftsmen of Shih chai shan in what is now Yunnan? Expatriate
aese artisans worked on Khmer reliefs, at a much later date, and carved their
motifs on some of them.[34] Did something comparable happen at Nanyang?

Liu Hsiu, founder of the Later Han dynasty, was born here and Nanyang
ame famous for its aristocratic and influential families.[35] It was advan-
ously located on important arteries of communication, and many families
aired great wealth from salt and iron manufacture and commerce in

[1] *Wen wu*, 1963.4, 2-3.

[2] *Shih chi* 史記, *ch*. 126.

[3] By this I mean some reliefs that are "semi-Nanyang" in style. These have some of
Nanyang spirit in them, but on the whole they contain much more of the conven-
al style. Perhaps this mixture is the precursor of the Nanyang style at its most
ous, and therefore somewhat earlier. For an example of this mixed style, see An
a-huai, "Ho-nan Nan-yang Yang-kuan-ssu Han tai hua hsiang shih mu fa-chüeh pao-
' 河南南陽楊官寺漢代畫象石墓發掘報告, *K'ao-ku hsüeh-pao*, 1963.1, 111-39. Unfor-
ately the tombs in this region do not have dated inscriptions, but this tomb has been
d to the early part of Later Han because of its structure and the grave goods found
t. Tombs decorated in the more advanced Nanyang style of reliefs are generally
sidered to date from the latter part of this period.

[4] V. Goloubew, "Artisans chinois à Ankor Vat," *BEFEO*, XXIV (1924), 513-19.

[5] Hans Bielenstein, "The restoration of the Han dynasty," *BMFEA*, 82-165, and
aur Waley, "Life under the Han dynasty," *History Today*, 1953, 91-92.

general.[36] Chang Heng's *fu* on the Southern Capital, a poetic descriptio his native Nanyang, paints it as a pleasure garden, and wealth is the domi color in this picture. Was the prevailing affluence, well attested in these re and a consequent compulsion to outdo the Wangs, responsible for a new of relief that reflected the spirit of the times for those who enjoyed the life? If so, how was this brought about? The excavation of more tombs in region, and the study of other regional styles, should eventually solve m of these questions.

[36]Nancy Lee Swann (tr.), *Food and money in ancient China* (Princeton, 1950), 448, 454. In 1959 the remains of a large Han iron foundry covering 120,000 sq. m. all its equipment was excavated near the old Nanyang city of Wan; see P'ei Ming-hs "Nan-yang Han tai t'ieh kung-ch'ang fa-chüeh chien-pao" 南陽漢代鐵工廠發掘簡報, *wu*, 1960.1, 58-60.

An "old rubbing" of the Later Han *Chang Ch'ien pei*

Kenneth Starr

INTRODUCTORY NOTE

hinese rubbings are ink-on-paper copies of engraved or cast inscriptions and ecorative elements found on a wide range of ancient and modern cultural bjects fashioned of stone, metal, and other hard substances. Most rubbings present only length and breadth, are two-dimensional in effect, and can be alled "simple rubbings." The most common examples of these are rubbings f stone-tablet inscriptions of the kind used to illustrate the present article. ubbings also occur as representations of objects in the round, as most often e early ceremonial bronze vessels. Such rubbings make an effort to capture epth, are three-dimensional in quality, and can be called "composite rubings." The terms *simple* and *composite* speak of both visual effect and the chniques of achieving those effects.

Traditionally the Chinese have used two variant techniques to make bbings. With each characterized by its own materials and methods these chniques can be distinguished by the names, "wet technique" and "dry chnique." The differences between the two techniques center in the way in hich the paper is applied, wet or dry, the manner in which the paper is anipulated, and the state in which the ink is applied, in moist or in solid orm. The wet technique is the more standard of the two methods, and istorically and culturally is more significant than the dry technique. Described quintessential manner the basic wet technique, which is used to make imple rubbings and which constitutes one of two main phases in the process f making composite rubbings, consists of the following steps: laying the ppropriate paper on the surface of the object being copied; wetting the paper done either before or after the laying, according to the artisan's preference); amping the wetted paper with brush or pad until the paper is tight against he relief and almost totally dry; daubing moist Chinese ink on the high urfaces of the paper; and then carefully stripping the finished rubbing from the relief.[1]

According to our best knowledge the Chinese invented the rubbi?
technique sometime in the last part of the fifth or the first part of the six?
century, with A.D. 500 being a convenient date. The earliest known exta?
rubbing dates from the first decade of T'ang, in the mid-seventh centur?
The rubbing technique was the first means the Chinese had of mechanica?
copying a longer text from engraved or cast materials, and the only means ?
doing so until the invention of wood-block printing some two hundred yea?
after the innovation of the rubbing technique. It has been the need to ha?
one-to-one copies of culturally valued engraved or cast inscriptive and, ?
lesser measure, pictorial materials that has maintained the technique over ?
period of a millennium and a half, despite the subsequent invention an?
dominance of such other graphic techniques as the various more sophisticate?
forms of printing and illustration. The initial applications of the techniq?
were to copying stone inscriptions, especially the Confucian stone classic?
and, somewhat later, bronze inscriptions. Through the centuries, howeve?
culminating in the Ch'ing and modern periods, the Chinese extended th?
technique to include an ever wider range of substances, cultural objects, an?
subject matter, in keeping with the ever broadening concerns of Chines?
scholarship.

Collectors call rubbings "black tigers" (*hei lao-hu* 黑老虎) or "in?
tigers" (*mo lao-hu* 墨老虎), by way of reference to the fact that the lust fo?
fine rubbings or the losses stemming from uncritical purchases can devour ?
collector and his money. Apart from the basic distinction between *pei* 石?
(rubbings of original inscriptions, especially stele inscriptions) and *t'ieh* 帖
(rubbings of calligraphic models), connoisseurs distinguish special categorie?
of rubbings, of which the two most common are "old rubbings" and "qualit?
rubbings." To be counted as an "old rubbing" (*chiu t'a-pen* 舊搨本, or *t'?
pen* 拓本),[2] a rubbing generally must date at least from the Ch'ing dynasty?
When evidence permits, students assign dates to rubbings, even if only broa?
dynastic dates, as "Sung rubbing" (Sung *t'a* 宋搨) or "Ming rubbing" (Min?
t'a 明搨). More often than not, however, in part because rubbings traditionall?
have been considered craftwork rather than art, and so commonly have no?

[1]The writer is readying a monograph on traditional materials and techniques that ar?
used in making rubbings. The present article is largely derived from one of the chapter?
on connoisseurship in that work. I am much indebted to Dr. Tchen Hoshien, Professo?
Tsien Tsuen-hsuin, and Professor Su Ying-hui, for all of whom I have deep feelings o?
respect, affection, and gratitude. I also acknowledge the generosity of the Wenner-Gre?
Foundation for Anthropological Research in providing me with a grant to enable me t?
carry out this and other related writings.

[2]The terms *t'a-pen* and *t'o-pen*, "rubbings," generally are interchangeable, as also ar?
t'a and *t'o*, "to make rubbings."

en documented, such evidence of date is wanting, in which case it is possible
ly to designate the piece as a *chiu t'a-pen,* an "old rubbing." A "quality
bbing" (*ching t'a-pen* 精搨本) is marked by an aura of excellence. Such an
ra in some measure derives from the intellectual or esthetic attributes of the
iginal object or subject matter, with calligraphic value a particular point of
terest. The essential focus, however, is on the quality of the rubbing and
e manner in which it has been mounted and preserved. The rubbing proper
ould be a cut above the average, with the materials of appropriate type and
ality, and the technique sound. The mounting and other related protective
mponents should be tasteful and pleasing, enhancing the rubbing for which
ey are vehicles and preservers.

My primary interest here is not the contents of the rubbings or the
iginal object of which the rubbing is but a reflection. Rather, the chief
phasis is on those aspects of rubbings and rubbings lore that represent the
stinctively and often subtly Chinese qualities that make the study and
nnoisseurship of black tigers an absorbing and satisfying pursuit, and an
traordinary vehicle for gaining insights into China's long history and intel-
ctual and esthetic traditions. As Chiang Hsüan-i observes, "a love of metal-
d-stone [inscriptions] is like turning toward the ancients, like going back
o the [cultural] memory...."[3]

THE CHANG CH'IEN STELE

The above remarks about the manner in which a rubbing of a stone
scription is prepared and mounted in album form relates to works of high
ality. By way of illustrating that the mounting often can be of lesser quality
is instructive to note the manner in which an old rubbing of quite good
ality has been album-mounted in shoddy fashion. I refer to a rubbing of
e Han-period stele erected to Chang Ch'ien.

The Chang Ch'ien tablet, known as the *Chang Ch'ien pei* or, in fuller
rm, the *Han Tang-yin ling Chang Ch'ien piao-sung* 漢蕩陰令張遷表頌, was
ected in tribute to Chang Ch'ien, a Han-period civil servant. Chang, who
as magistrate of ancient and historically rich Ku-ch'eng, now Tung-o Hsien
west-central Shantung Province, and then subsequently magistrate of Tang-
n Hsien in Honan Province, was known for his fine personal qualities and
s virtuous administration, and so in good traditional fashion was remembered
stone by his former subordinates. The tablet was preserved at the district
hool in Tung-p'ing Hsien, Shantung Province. The main text, which consists

---

[3]Chiang Hsüan-i, "Mo-t'o shu" 墨拓術, *Shuo-wen yüeh-k'an* 說文月刊, I:12 (1939),
.

of sixteen columns of forty-two characters each in the cases of the fo
columns, is both complete and fully legible, a condition that does not alwa
obtain in the cases of such old stone inscriptions. The *li* 隷 script in which
is written is considered to be elegant, marked by a flavor of the life and tim
characterizing the Later Han capital of Lo-yang. Connoisseurs for centuri
have appreciated the writing for its simplicity and strength, and have co
sidered it an excellent example of Han *li*.[4] The *Chang Ch'ien pei* is dated tl
third year of the Chung-p'ing reign period of the Later Han dynasty, corr
sponding to A.D. 186.

Among numerous catalogs providing such information the *Chin-sh
ts'ui-pien* gives a brief physical description of the stele and a full statement
its text, as follows:

> *Tang-yin ling Chang Ch'ien piao.* The stele is nine *ch'ih* 尺 [Chine
> feet] and five *ts'un* 寸 [Chinese inches] high, three *ch'ih* and two *ts'u*
> wide. [There are] sixteen lines [of characters, and] each column [ha
> forty-two characters. The fourteenth line is blank [and] has only or
> character. The heading is inscribed with twelve characters in seal scrip
> *Han ku Ku-ch'eng chang Tang-yin ling Chang chün piao-sung.* [Tl
> stone] now is [on the grounds of] the district school at Tung-p'in
> [The inscription reads as follows:]

> "The Master's name was Ch'ien, [his] style was Kung-fang, and [he
> was a native of Chi-wu in Ch'en-liu [*chün*]. The Master's ancestry ca
> be traced back to the Chou [dynasty]. During the time of [the emperor
> Hsüan Wang of Chou there was Chang Chung, who was known for h
> filial piety and [spirit of] brotherly harmony. Reading through tl
> *Hsiao-ya* in the *Shih ching* one will get a clear understanding of th
> ancestor. [When] like a dragon [the Former Han emperor] Kao '
> ascended there was Chang Liang, the master of strategy who [whi
> remaining] at headquarters could determine the outcome [of battle]
> thousand *li* away. He was enfeoffed at Liu. In the reigns of [the Form
> Han emperors] Wen [Ti] and Ching [Ti], there was Chang Shih-chi
> who provided loyal assistance. [On one occasion] the emperor visite
> the [imperial] Shang-lin [Park] and asked how many [captive] bir
> and animals there were. The superintendent could not give the answ
> [and so the emperor] further asked a custodian, who replied correcti
> [to every inquiry]. Thereupon the emperor promoted the custodian 1

---

[4] It was to demonstrate the qualities and excellence of the script that I included
rubbing of the Chang Ch'ien stone in the section devoted to language and scholar
pursuits in the Chinese exhibit at the Field Museum, "China in the Ch'ing dynasty
which opened in 1964.

superintendent and demoted the superintendent to custodian. Shih-chih questioned this [action, arguing that] the superintendent had the talents of a minister, whereas the custodian was only a talkative underling who could not be trusted with the grave responsibilities of the state. The emperor acted in accordance with his words. During the reign of Wu Ti there was Chang Ch'ien, who established contact far and wide with [peoples of different] customs and opened up new lands for the sovereign. In the south [the Chinese] embraced the eight *Man* [tribes]; in the west [they] restrained the seven *Jung*; in the north [they] repressed the five *Ti*; and in the east [they] pacified the nine *I*. When the distant peoples had capitulated, each brought its products as tribute.

"The Chang clan has supported the Han [imperial house, and] successive generations record its virtue [in this respect], and this distinguished tradition continued in the Master. Successively holding various local administrative posts, he never let his high reputation be tarnished. [He] showed filial piety and brotherly love at home [and] was fair and outspoken in office. He studied the *I ching* according to [the school of] Ching [Fang]. He was intelligent, elegant, resourceful, and adept in administration. In his youth he was a clerk in the provincial government, [and] being reliable and efficient he always was an indispensible aid to his superiors. On several occasions he served as an administrative assistant, and there was never the slightest question about his reputation. He was summoned to be a board secretary, [and subsequently] was appointed magistrate of Ku-ch'eng. In the months of sericulture, he did not close the four [city] gates, [but let the people move freely]. [At the time of] the winter solstice sacrifice he furloughed the prisoners and let them return [to their families] to celebrate. [At the time of] the poll-tax assessment in the eighth month there were no disturbances in the countryside. He went out to the markets and villages, and inquired after the elderly. Along the roadsides no one picked up things [that had been left], and [the people] could leave their ploughs and seeds in the fields overnight [without fear of their being taken]. When the Yellow Turbans first rebelled, [they] burned down many towns, [but] Ku-ch'eng alone was left intact [out of respect for Chang Ch'ien].

"When Tzu-chien was first given authority over a small place his principles gradually spread. [Among] the five doctrines of the *Shang shu* the Master revered leniency. The *Shih ching* speaks of grace and courtesy, and the Master exalted its kindness. [Tzu-ch'an of] Tung-li was [noted for being] benevolent, [and] the Master carried on this virtue. Shao Po [Shao Kung] opened up Shensi [in early Chou times],

and the Master [similarly] was exemplary in nobleness. [Tung An-
of] Chin-yang [in the State of Chin in the Spring and Autumn perio
wore a leather girdle [to restrain his rash temper], [whereas] Hsi-m
Pao [of the State of Wei in the Warring States period] used a bowstri
[to vitalize his slow action], [but] the Master's nature was even a
was marked by both these qualities.

"After guiding the people [of Ku-ch'eng] for eight years, [t
Master] was appointed Magistrate of Tang-yin. [Both his] subordina
and the common people [of Ku-ch'eng] came to see him off, followi
him like a cloud. When Chou Kung was on eastern expedition [in ear
Chou times], the people in the west were unhappy [about his absenc
and thought of him. Hsi Ssu eulogized [the state of] Lu, [and] Hsiao
praised Yin. [With respect to] the works of former sages, if accomplis
ments were not written down posterity could not know about the
Consequently we have cut a stone, erected [this] tablet, [and] ha
made an engraving [that will endure] for ten thousand years. Events
the Three Dynasties, although remote still are familiar. The *Shih chi*
speaks of an old country, but its mandate is new.

"Our esteemed Master was both sincere and honest. [He had]
snow-white character [and] filial and brotherly virtues. In recordi
deeds, one starts with basics. Orchids have fragrance, [and] there we
omens at the time of the founding of the Chou [dynasty]. Governi
requires virtue to win the people; without the proper equipment [on
cannot draw fish from the deep. The bounty of this pillar of t
kingdom is a legacy for the people. The shading tall pear tree is m
and respectful to people. The Way of Heaven does not err, [but]
intimate only with the virtuous. Having been much blessed [may Mast
Chang] eternally enjoy the Southern Mountains, receive honor witho
end, and [be blessed with] children and grandchildren. [There follo
next a blank column, at the bottom of which stands an unidentifi
character.]

"In the first ten days of the second month of the third year [A.
186] of Chung-p'ing, the *she-t'i-ko* year [cycle], the positive eleme
of nature abounds. Thinking of our erstwhile Master, Former Clerk W
Meng and others unanimously agreed [upon this course and] hired the e
pert Sun Hsing to carve the stone and erect this tablet to inform posterit
[May] everyone enjoy heavenly blessings for ten thousand years!' "[5]

[5] The translation is based on the text of the stele as given in Wang Ch'ang, *Chin-sh
ts'ui-pien* 金石萃編, 18/16b-18b (in *Shih-k'o shih-liao ts'ung-shu* 石刻史料叢書. Taip
I-wen, 1966). I thank Professor T. H. Tsien and Mr. Ma Tai-loi for their very considerat
assistance in the translation.

The present account includes reference to three rubbings of the Chang
'ien stone, all in the collections of the Field Museum. Two of these are in
eet form, unmounted and unbacked, and are duplicate copies of the front
ce of the stele only. The third rubbing, the piece under specific consideration
re, is mounted in the form of an accordion album with board covers, and
cludes both the front and rear faces.[6]

Although the focus here is on the album copy comparative purposes
ggest a brief description of the sheet rubbings. As was noted, these rubbings
present only the main text cut on the front face of the stone. One of the
eces (244611/1) also includes the *pei-e* 碑額, or heading, consisting of twelve
aracters, two columns of six characters each, written in the customary seal
ript (Plate I). The heading reads *Han ku Ku-ch'eng chang Tang-yin ling
ang chün piao-sung*, "eulogy to Master Chang, former magistrate of Ku-
'eng [and subsequently] magistrate of Tang-yin [Hsien] under the [Later]
n [dynasty]." The *pei-e*, interestingly, is not centered at the top of the
ne, but stands slightly to the left of center. The materials and techniques
ed in making the two rubbings are of but what might be called commercial
ade. The paper is of very modest quality, grayish in cast, rather than white,
d now extremely brittle, breaking with even normal handling. The rubbing
chnique is of the same commercial grade, with the tamping well enough
ne, but with the ink laid on unevenly, very densely in some places, much
ss so in others.

It is of interest to note that in the case of the rubbing that carries the
i-e the *t'o-kung* 拓工, or "rubbing artisan," has rubbed both *pei-e* and text
one time, rather than rubbing the two separately, as sometimes is done.
e artisan did not use a single sheet of paper in accomplishing this, however,
t for sake of economy of material cut a separate small piece of paper to
commodate the heading. He first applied the smaller piece to the *pei-e*, then

---

[6]The two duplicate sheet rubbings carry Field Museum catalog numbers 244611/1
d 244611/2, and each measures 189.0 x 77.0 cm. Rubbing 244611/2 (Pl. I) also
cludes the *pei-e*, or heading, which measures 35.0 x 26.5 cm. (In keeping with estab-
hed practice measurements are given in the order of height, width, and thickness.) The
o rubbings are of modern manufacture and as with the majority of others in the
llection, came to the museum through the keen perception of Berthold Laufer, who
cording to the accession information acquired the two pieces about 1904, while he still
s at the American Museum.

The album-mounted edition is numbered 244122, and closed it measures overall
.5 x 16.0 x 2.5 cm. (Pl. II). The present writer purchased the album from Mr. Liu
n-sheng for the Field Museum in 1967 because of its interesting relation to the sheet
bbings already in the collection. The photograph of the full sheet rubbing (Plate I) is
ovided through the courtesy of the Field Museum. The remaining illustrations were
ken by the present writer with permission.

laid the larger main sheet on the body of the stone, overlapping the small
heading piece slightly in established fashion, felted them together in the
tamping process and, finally, laid on the ink. Both of the sheet rubbings are
of modern manufacture, presumably made in the first years of the present
century.

THE ALBUM OF CHANG CH'IEN PEI

The Chang Ch'ien album merits greater consideration in terms of the
rubbing, the manner in which it has been mounted, and the elements of
connoisseurship associated with both (Plate II). With respect to its general
features the album is plain in appearance, fronted and backed with simple
wooden boards, the front one of which carries an inscribed paper title-label.
The mounted rubbing within includes not only the main text on the front
face of the stone, but also the related text on the rear face, the latter consisting solely of a list of those who sponsored the erection of the tablet, their
official titles, and the amounts of their contributions.

The boards are of plain pine, soiled by handling and spotted with honey
vermiculations. At its upper left the front board carries a worn, ragged, dis-
colored, and heavily vermiculated title-label bearing the brushwritten main
inscription, *Chiu-t'a Chang Ch'ien piao* 舊搨張遷表, "old rubbing of the Chang
Ch'ien eulogy." Just below, off center to the right and in slightly smaller
script, is the writer's signature, *Ch'eng-chai* 澄齋, studio name of Yün Yü-tir
惲毓鼎 (1863-1918), a past owner of the piece. Such labeling is typical.
Rubbings protected by wood or paper boards, in the form of either a packet
of separate rubbings sandwiched between two loose boards fastened with ties
or an accordion album more permanently faced with attached boards, as here
generally are labeled in one of two ways.

The top (front) board carries the title information either brushwritten
on a separate paper title-label pasted on, as has been done in the case of the
Chang Ch'ien album, or engraved directly on the board proper, as sometimes
is done in the case of wood boards. If the label is separate, it usually is made
either of plain white paper or of the mottled yellow "Buddhist sutra paper
(*tsang-ching chien* 藏經牋). The label is inscribed with brush and ink and
pasted along the left side of the upper board, running downward from the
top. The content and elements of connoisseurship usually are simple, with the
caption information limited to the name of the cultural object represented
by the rubbing and, normally in smaller character, the name and sometimes
the seal of the calligrapher, owner or other, who penned the label inscription.
Often, however, there will be more, in such measure as the rarity, excellence
or interest of the piece warrants. If the information is engraved, then the title

nerally is done in larger characters down the center line of the board, with y additional information, such as the name of the calligrapher and his seal, t in smaller characters below and slightly off to the right of the center line.

The rubbing, portions of which are illustrated in the accompanying ates, is quite well done, as marked by the qualities of both the materials and e technique. The paper is off-white in color, at least in part by reason of ne, and obviously is of good quality, for despite its age it still has resilience. te care taken in making the rubbing is evidenced both in the characteristic tpressions and surface wrinkles remaining from the tamping process and in e inking, which is crisp of line and even of tone. The rubbing is in very good ndition and is said to be of Ming date, an attribution that I shall examine low.

The materials and technique used in mounting the rubbing unfortunately e not of comparable quality, by reason of which the album is in an extremely or state of preservation. The piece is put up in accordion style, but because ` the poor quality of the paper and paste used in the mounting the album is disintegrated to such a degree that most of the folds have worn through, deed, to a point where the original form can hardly be recognized (Plates I, IV, VII, VIII). Such a situation is not without decided advantage to the adent, however, for the extreme state of disintegration affords abundant portunity for examining the manner in which the mounting work was done. deed, although the text of the rubbing is informative and the calligraphy is cellent the rubbing itself and the album into which it has been mounted e both quite ordinary, and in terms of connoisseurship call particular tention to themselves mainly by reason of their condition.

Turning the front board and opening out the album one sees facing les of the paper that presumably once was white or off-white, but that now buff with age and darkened further here and there by stains. On the right lf of the double face, now parted from the left half, one notes several structive features. First, the paper is not single, but double, two sheets of fferent paper laminated. The upper sheet, the sheet that one sees, is buff d of better quality, and apparently was intended to introduce the album. he use of better paper at fronts and backs of albums is a common practice, course, inspired both by desire for pleasing appearance and by need of oper ground for brushwritten commentary. The lower sheet is darker buff d of coarser quality. It is this lower sheet, formed by joining lengths of the per as dictated by the length of the album, that constitutes the running dy of the album. The bordering edges on the back of this lower sheet, pecially those opposite [the *t'ien*, or] the upper framing border, on the bverse, are appreciably darker brown, a product of the bleeding effect of the ye in the paper used to frame the rubbing panels and the glue used to attach

them to the running body.[7] Second, this laminated sheet is attached to t
back of the front board, with about 4.0 cm. of the right end of the st
pasted to the right edge of the back of the board, approximately opposite t
area taken up by the title-label on the front left side of the board. T
remainder of the paper on this right half of the double face is free from t
board. Third, the lower sheet of the laminated running strip, the sheet th
lies against the back of the front board, is heavily stained from long a
tight contact with the board. Indeed, so intimate has been the contact th
the paper even shows the veining of the wood. Fourth, both papers st
maintain life.

The left half of the double face is of similar physical makeup, with t
exception that it it not attached to the board, but rather constitutes the fi
free half fold of the running body of the album. In the area of connoisseurshi
this left face carries along its left edge a brushwritten inscription in regul
script and an accompanying seal. The inscription is composed of two par
The more important part, placed on the upper half of the page and in larg
script, reads *Ming-t'o Chang Ch'ien pei*, "Ming [period]-rubbed Chang Ch'ie
stele." Below, on the lower half of the page and in smaller script, is a two-li
inscription that describes the circumstances of the writing, *jen-ch'en ch't
chieh/ Hsüan-ko chih yü Tung-tu* 壬辰秋節宣閣識於東都 "the fifteenth of t
eighth month of the *jen-ch'en* year, recorded by Hsüan-ko in Tokyo." *Hsüa
ko* is the *hao* of the former owner of the album, Liu Lin-sheng 劉麟生, wh
orally provided the information that he had penned the inscription in Toky
in 1952 when he was serving there in the Chinese embassy. The red-oran
seal imprint below is in *li* script and reads *Liu Lin-sheng*.

The turn of the fold brings one to the first double face of the mount
rubbing, the first of two such double faces carrying the heading of the Cha

---

[7]The frame of a mounted painting, rubbing, or other similar piece includes the to
bottom, and two side borders. The two side borders are the same width and common
are narrower than either the top or bottom borders, which traditionally are treat
distinctively. Thus, the top border is called the *t'ien*, or "heaven," and is the widest
the four surrounding borders; while the bottom border is called the *ti*, or "earth," a
is narrower than the top border, but customarily slightly wider than the side borders.

Tangentially, I find considerable interest in the resemblance between the proportion
relationships of the traditional *t'ien* and *ti* of framing and what could be interpreted
the *t'ien* and *ti* of the coffin complex of the Former Han tomb at Ma-wang-tui of th
remarkable lady, the ageless wife of the Marquis of Tai. The similarities of the pr
portional relationships of the top, bottom, and side spacings to those adhered to
framing are striking, as also are the general format and the dominance of the horizont
elements over the verticals. See the illustration in the report jointly published by t
Hunan Provincial Museum and the Institute of Archaeology of Academia Sinica, *Ch'an
sha Ma-wang-tui i hao Han mu* 長沙馬王堆一號漢墓 [The number one Han tomb at M
wang-tui, Ch'ang-sha], II (Peking, 1973), Plate 8.

'ien stele (Plate III). Before embarking upon a journey through the album, wever, I consider it relevant to review briefly the general method followed cut-mounting a rubbing and to describe the manner in which the present bing has been treated. The mounting process generally involves backing e original sheet rubbing, cutting it into strips of a length appropriate to the ended size and shape of the album page, fitting the strips together and sting them down on the support paper in such a manner as to reflect curately the original aspect, sequence, and spacing as closely as possible, d finally, adding the various and sundry mounting accouterments to give whole a proper and pleasing appearance. The mounter has followed that ttern here, but the poverty of the materials and techniques that he used, gether with the adverse effects of time, have combined to produce a dis- ssing present result.

Broadly viewed, the Chang Ch'ien album includes three different in- iptive components, mirroring those composing the original stone: the *pei-e*, heading, the main text of the stone, and the list of donors who contributed the erection of the stone. The *pei-e* and the text, it was noted, made up the nt face of the original stone, and the list of contributors, the rear face. ngentially, this accounting of the several inscriptive components occasions e observation that in purchasing rubbings one must have a good knowledge the original object and its inscription or he risks coming away with a bbing of but a portion of it. The matter calls for some degree of care and phistication, for there are not only headings and front and rear faces to nsider, but also sometimes edges, bases, and other elements as well. Prior erence to descriptive catalogs is essential.

Let us return to the three components of the Chang Ch'ien stone and e treatment that each required in the mounting process. The *pei-e*, it will be alled, consists of twelve large characters, with six characters in each of the o columns. The characters are in seal script and are irregular in size, but th each averaging about 7.0 x 9.0 cm. The text and donor list are formed many columns of smaller characters in *li* script, with these smaller charac- s running about 3.0 cm. square. By reason of the differing nature and e of the two different types of inscriptions, therefore, the mounter had deal with them in different ways. On the one hand, having considered e nature of the *pei-e*—its titling function, and the size and style of the aracters—he cut the two columns apart vertically and then further cut ch of the two resulting vertical strips in half horizontally, thereby pro- cing four groups of three characters each. These he placed in order and ounted on the first two double faces of the album, with three characters each of the four single sides, or pages. Thus, side one, the first page the right that one sees in opening the album, holds the first three charac-

ters; while page two, the second or left side of the first double face, ho
the second group of three characters. The second double face then carr
the third and fourth groups of three characters on sides three and four. W
slash marks to separate them, the order of the four groups of characters
the four sides of the two double faces is as follows: *Han ku Ku-/ ch'e
chang Tang-/ yin ling Chang/ chün piao-sung.* Comparison of this orderr
with that indicated in the writing of the title in the original heading sho
that the mounter was not troubled by having to break up some of the wc
units, as the place names, Ku-ch'eng and Tang-yin, and the personal nar
and associated honorific, Master Chang.

Each of the cut strips of rubbing, with its three characters, measu
from 17.0-19.0 cm. long by about 4.0 cm. wide. Each of the four sides
pages, consisting of two juxtaposed rubbing strips and the necessary bits a
pieces used as filler, measures about 22.0 x 14.0 cm. On the other hand, t
mounter has cut the rubbing, put the cuttings in order, and mounted t
pieces of the text and the donor list, with their smaller *li* characters, in su
a manner that normally there are three columns of five characters each o
side, or page, thus making six columns of five characters each, or a total
thirty characters on a double face, as the album lies open (Plate IV). By t
nature of its contents the donor list is less regular, with the columns genera
composed of five characters, but often with fewer (Plate VII). Each c
rubbing strip measures about 22.0 x 4.5 cm., and each group of three str
forming a unit or panel on each side or page measures about 22.0 x 14.0 c
The mounter's basic approach thus is standard.

THE CONNOISSEURSHIP OF THE RUBBING

Having given passing attention to the broad manner in which t
mounter converted the original Chang Ch'ien sheet rubbing into album for
let us return to the first double face whence we strayed and proceed throu
the album, recording some observations on the connoisseurship of the rr
bing and the manner in which it is mounted.

The first double face carries the initial six characters of the headir
Han ku Ku-/ ch'eng chang Tang-. Examining the rubbing one notes th
although the uninked areas are off white, presumably through the effects
age, the paper still is in excellent condition, manifesting its continuing vitali
in the fact that none of the edges has flaked away. The rubbing technique w
standard or better, with quite good tamping as evidenced by the still clear
evident tamping impressions and wrinkles created originally by the *t'o-ku*
in the rubbing work and maintained by him in freeing the rubbing from t

ne, and then maintained by the mounter in his turn.[8] The inking also is
rage, clean of line and reasonably even of tone. The mounting work, how-
r, in terms of both materials and techniques, is of appreciably lesser
ality than that manifested in the rubbing.

First, the mounter did not back the original sheet rubbing before cutting
nto strips. Second, and immediately apparent, he carried out the cutting,
ing, and patching with little care and esthetic judgment, as evidenced by
uneven cutting and the clumsy patching and filling (Plate III). The cutting
irregular, especially along the bottom edge of the three characters on the
ht half of the double face carrying the *pei-e* and along the top edge of the
ee characters on the left half. The unevenness here, it must be allowed, is
t wholly the product of carelessness, for in studying the inscription as it
sts in uncut sheet form one sees that the irregularity and the closeness of
seal characters combine to make it impossible to make a straight horizon-
cut between the characters *ku* and *ch'eng*. The poor match between the
o strips of characters centered in their respective sides of the double face,
d the consequent patching with pieces fitted in at top and bottom to fill
t the faces also is explainable, in that the heading is so compact or the
bing of it so tightly done that there is no empty space around that could
used for such patching. For this reason the mounter has had to fill out the
nels with patch paper taken from uninscribed areas of this or some other
bing. The chief criticism that one can level against the mounter here is
t he could have used more care in his choice of patch paper, selecting
ces of rubbing whose textural and tonal qualities more closely matched
paper carrying the heading inscription (Plate III). Such subtleties are
portant to the connoisseur. Third, the artisan pasted the rubbing strips too
ntly on the running body of the album, for the rubbing strips have lifted in
ny places, and will drop away and be lost or damaged, if the rubbing is not
n remounted. Fourth, the framing of the rubbing strips is badly done
ates III, IV, VII, VIII). The mounter has framed the rubbing panel all
nd and has maintained the traditional proprieties by keeping the proper
tial relations at top and bottom, but he chose paper of the worst possible

[8]In removing a finished rubbing a maker of rubbings must be particularly careful
t to stretch the still damp paper, but rather to peel the rubbing carefully and then to
it flat to dry just as it came off the object. The reason for this care, especially
portant in the rubbing of inscriptions, is that stretching the damp and still plastic
per causes distortion, with the result that the characters become "fat," especially
ticeable in the horizontal plane, and so lose the essence of their calligraphic quality.
ose who mount rubbings also need to pay attention to the same aspect of the situation.
leed, more serious collectors of black tigers take their rubbings only to mounters who
cialize in rubbings, so different do they count the demands of mounting rubbings, as
inst paintings.

quality for his framing purposes. As a result, this edging long since has l
its life and has become so dry and brittle that it flakes literally at the tou
Indeed, it is impossible even to turn one of the leaves of the album with
losing a bit of the framing paper. That age alone is not the cause of the p
condition of the framing paper and, in lesser measure, of the paper that for
the running body of the album is indicated by the fact that the origi
rubbing paper still retains its vitality. In sum, it is obvious that a deservi
rubbing has been given undeservedly bad treatment.

The framing sequence seems to have been standard, for it appears fr
the manner in which the overlaps of the frame occur that the entire dou
face was treated as a unit. The vertical elements of the framing (the cen
strip dividing the right and left sides, and the left and right borders, whi
later continue around the respective edges and form the side borders of t
panels on the preceding and following pages) were applied first, and then t
horizontals were laid across the vertical strips. The side borders avera
slightly less than 1.0 cm. wide, the upper is about 3.5 cm. wide, and t
lower, about 2.8 cm. wide. These borders also have been but lightly past
for they too have lifted in many places.

Two elements of connoisseurship here are worthy of mention. First
is important to note that despite his modest approach in other aspects of
work the mounter was quite attentive to maintaining the proper proportio
of the characters as they were captured in the rubbing. He pasted down t
rubbing paper just as it came off the stone, as is indicated by evidences of t
original tamping, showing that he did not stretch the rubbing in the mounti
process. Second, stamped in red orange in the lower left corner of the l
side is the seal of the last owner, Liu Lin-sheng (Plate III).

The second double face of the album carries the final six characters
the heading, -yin ling Chang/ chün piao-sung. The same features occur, so
as materials and techniques of rubbing and mounting are concerned, and the
are no noteworthy elements of connoisseurship save for a seal in the low
left corner of the left face (Plate III). The inscription is in seal character a
reads Ch'eng-chai shou-ts'ang shu-hua澄齋收藏書畫, "books and paintin
collected by Ch'eng-chai." The imprint is that of Yün Yü-ting, the origin
collector of the rubbing.

The text proper begins on the following page and continues for ninete
double faces, making a total of thirty-eight single sides or pages. As describ
above, each side or page carries three rubbing strips, with each strip norma
carrying five characters. Although there is nothing distinctive as regards t
materials and techniques used in the rubbing and mounting work there a
three noteworthy elements of connoisseurship that invite attention. Two
these are particularly significant and so deserve emphasis. First, it is of hi

erest to note that in one instance the mounter has pasted the rubbing strips
incorrect sequence. Thus, on page one of the text he has transposed lines
ɔ and three, as compared with the original rubbing (Plates I, IV). Reference
the uncut sheet rubbing shows the proper sequence, in which the sixth and
venth characters are *fang* 方 and *jen* 人 , rather than the other way around.
is situation speaks clearly of the haste and carelessness of the mounting
rk and, more important, also confirms the traditional counsel that when-
r possible a serious collector of rubbings should maintain an uncut copy
hand for sake of reference, so that intellectually and esthetically important
ects of the cut-mounted rubbing can be checked in case of question as to
authenticity or date of the rubbing. Ready access to an uncut copy also
ps one better to visualize the shape and size and general appearance of the
ginal object, and the composition of the text or pictorial elements on its
face or surfaces. Yeh Ch'ang-ch'ih (1849-1917) expresses the traditional
w:

> [When] former people obtained a fine tablet [rubbing, they] liked to
> whole-mount [it in its full uncut form], thus avoiding [the risk of
> pieces of the rubbing] falling off [and being lost]. Moreover, [they]
> did not lose track of the original dimensions of the tablet. [It] certainly
> is a good method [to have a rubbing in uncut form], but unless [one]
> spreads [the rubbing] out on a table [or] hangs it on the wall, [it] is
> not easy to unroll and examine. I say that to collect stele rubbings [in
> the proper way, one] must have two copies [of a given rubbing], with
> the master copy whole-mounted to preserve the format of the original
> stone, [and] with a duplicate copy cut-mounted ... for the sake of
> convenience in handling it.[9]

Chiang Hsüan-i echoes these comments, noting that access to an uncut
sion often prevents mistakes in scholarship.[10] Having the full uncut rub-
g at hand permits the student to observe such important features as the
pe of the original stone, the gradual disintegration of the surfaces and
cription, the locations of colophons, and minute differences as compared
h re-cut editions.

It is with these considerations in mind that cut-mounted editions,
ether in album or in book form, sometimes carry at their beginning a
niature version of the full uncut rubbing, done traditionally by cutting a
niature woodblock of the original text and then, depending on the nature
the cutting, positive or negative, making a rubbing or a print of the small

[9] Yeh Ch'ang-ch'ih, *Yü shih* 語石 (Taipei: Commercial Press, 1956), 316-17.
[10] Chiang Hsüan-i, 52-53.

block. Plate V shows such a miniature rubbing, included at the front c
book-mounted rubbing of the *Chiu-t'o Lang-ya t'ai pei* 舊拓琅琊臺碑, a r
inscription cut in the late 3rd century B.C. by order of Ch'in Shih Huang
First Emperor of Ch'in (r. 221-209 B.C.), and in the famous small-s
calligraphy of Li Ssu (d. 208 B.C.).[11] Van Gulik also refers to this practi
although in a slightly different context: "During the Ming dynasty epig
phists had a large number of Han inscribed tablets re-cut in wood on a sma
scale, about one-sixth of the size of the original. As many of the origi
stone tablets and rubbings thereof have since then disappeared, such miniat
Ming rubbings are now much sought after."[12]

The second significant feature relates to the character *hsien* 先 on
same initial page, which by reason of the transposition just described is
last character in line two, but that should be the last in line three. T
character, whose lower strokes bleed into a fractured area of the tablet a
are so reflected in the rubbing, has a distinguishing characteristic that ser
as an important criterion in the relative dating of the present album-moun
edition. I shall defer speaking of the details here, but will include considerat
of the point in discussing the datings of the rubbing and the album. The th
element of connoisseurship is the seal that stands at the bottom of the ri
face, astride the cut between the first and second lines of characters. This s
which was positioned there to mark the dating feature of which I have j
spoken, reads *Wei-sun* 薇蓀 and is the *hao* of Yün Yü-ting (Plate IV). Noth
else is noteworthy on this double face, save in negative vein the gross use
cellulose tape for repair at the upper right corner of the right side, a technic
used frequently throughout the album, and always with the usual unfortun
results.

Other elements of connoisseurship scattered throughout the text inclu
Yün's seal, *Ting yin* 鼎印, on page twenty-seven of the album, marking t
other characters that have meaning for the dating of the rubbing. It
instructive in passing to make note of the difficulty that is involved in read
such old and much eroded stone inscriptions. One has only to study some
the more heavily eroded portions of the Chang Ch'ien tablet, especially
mirrored in the modern sheet rubbing (Plate I), to see the manner in wh
damaged characters ultimately disappear, either through spalling or throu

[11]Along with a series of other rare old and quality rubbings I acquired this rubb
(PM233919) of the Lang-ya stone while on a research trip to Taiwan in 1960.
rubbing is said to date from early Ch'ing and in its present book-mounted form deri
from the collection of Viceroy Tuan-fang (1861-1911), the well-known late-Ch'
official and collector, who had a preference for this style of mounting.

[12]R. H. van Gulik, *Chinese pictorial art as viewed by the connoisseur* (Rome, 195
99.

ouflage produced by the pitting of the surface of the stone. Were it not the careful records kept through the long centuries there would be no ns of documenting the relentless attrition that ultimately destroys these eless records of China's past. The extremities of this wearing process are illustrated in the early Ch'ing rubbing of the Ch'in-period *Lang-ya t'ai* referred to above (Plate VI). The rubbing of an inscription in such dissed condition is an indication of the keen interest that Ch'ing scholars ntained in early stone inscriptions, and the reverence that they held for calligraphic hand of Li Ssu. *Wei-sun*, Yün Yü-ting's *hao*, appears again on e thirty-six, marking another key dating character. The text ends with the e of the cutting of the stone, *Chung-p'ing san nien*, the third year (A.D.) of the Chung-p'ing reign period of the Later Han. Following the last racter of the text Liu Lin-sheng has affixed his seal, *Liu yin Lin-sheng*.

The turn of the album page brings one immediately to the list of those o contributed to the cutting of the tribute to Chang Ch'ien. Although re is no break in the album, or any variation in the style or size of the pt, the difference of the content is mark enough of the change from the nt face of the stone to the back. The donor list fills thirteen and a half ble faces, or twenty-seven single sides of the album. The pattern is clear simple, with the entry generally giving the title and name of the donor, the amount that he has contributed. A typical entry reads as follows: *ku Wei Yüan-hsü ch'ien ssu pai* 故吏韋元緒錢四百, "former clerk Wei Yüan-, four hundred cash" (Plate VII).

Each of the entries is preceded by the term *ku*, "former." The title nes next, with these including the following: *chang* 長, magistrate; *ts'ung- 從事*, administrative assistant; *shou-ling* 守令, county prefect; *li* 吏, clerk; *tu-yu* 督郵, commandery investigator. Then comes the name, with surne followed by given name. The list of donors includes forty surnames, but names Wei, with twenty-three entries, and Fan, with thirteen, predomi-e, making up thirty-six of the total. The remaining four surnames are resented by one name each. It is interesting to note that the surname ang is not among the list of donors.

Finally, the range of the contributions is from a thousand cash down two hundred, in units of even hundreds, and with the average contribution ging between three hundred and five hundred cash. Thus, thirty of the ty donors gave either three hundred (thirteen donors), four hundred (six ors), or five hundred (eleven donors) cash. Of the remaining contributors, prosperous donor gave a thousand cash, three gave eight hundred, four e seven hundred, and one could afford to give but two hundred.

The last page or side of the donor list carries two seals (Plate VIII). e, in the center of the page, reads *Ch'eng-chai shou-ts'ang shu-hua*. The other is at the lower left corner of the page and reads *Liu yin Lin-sheng.*

DATING OF THE RUBBING

Rubbings are dated in one of two ways, either absolute or relat
Absolute dating of rubbings, especially old rubbings, is rare. Rubbings are o
occasionally signed or datable in other ways, either precisely or wit
reasonably narrow limits. Much more often, rubbings can be assigned o
some form of relative date, a broad date relative to a dynasty, a reign peri
or another rubbing. Various types of evidence are used to assign such a rela
date, among them the following: physical characteristics, associated corr
orative data, bibliographic references, shapes and proportions of charac
and strokes remaining, and surface features aside from those relating to
inscription or design.[13]

Opposite the final face of the donor list, on the last page of the rubb
proper, there is a colophon by Yün Yü-ting bearing on the conditions
several characters in the text and the importance of those conditions for
dating of the rubbing (Plate VIII). Yün focuses on four characters, which
marked by seals at the points where they occur in the text: the charac
hsien 先 (line one, fifteenth character); the two characters *jun* 潤 and *se*
(line eight, fortieth and forty-first characters); and the character *yüan*
(line twelve, fortieth character). Examination of the reasons for Yün's inte
in these characters as they relate to the dating of the rubbing is informat
Yün bases his observations on comments penned by Weng Fang-kang 翁 ﬤ
(1733-1818), the eminent scholar, official, and antiquarian, on another
rubbing of the Chang Ch'ien text that Weng had examined and annotate
his time, a rubbing in the possession of one Mr. Yen, a native of Ch'ü-fu.
way of a relevant aside relating to connoisseurship one should note that
traditional mode Yün refers obliquely to Weng as "Mr. T'an-ch'i 覃溪,"
of Weng's *hao*. According to Weng's notes set down on the Yen rubbing,
original stone, as reflected in Yen's rubbing, was in much better conditior
the time that the Yen rubbing was made than it was in Weng's own time, tl
suggesting that the Yen rubbing was somewhat earlier than Weng's time. 7
extent of the difference, however, was not specified. Yün then uses

---

[13]Before leaving the subject of relative dating the writer is moved to refer t
practice darkly said to be followed by unprincipled collectors. Having made a rubbing
a particular stone inscription, and in order to assure the relative position of his rubt
in time, an unscrupulous collector may deface the stone in some small way, as
minutely nicking the surface or, even more despicably, by chipping the edge of a str
of one of the characters in the inscription. Needless to say, to a collector of conscie
such a practice is in the nature of a mortal sin.

rmation provided by Weng to date his rubbing, the present album. Yün
necessity relies on relative dating—and broadly so at that—as against
lute dating. Given the circumstances, however, Yün could take no other
se than to use broad relative dating, for there are no certain dates of any
involved in any of the three Chang Ch'ien rubbings that he was consider-
proceeding from the earliest to the most recent, Yün's album-mounted
ing, the Yen rubbing seen by Weng, and rubbings made during Weng's
. We, of course, have the advantage of even greater time depth by way of
ence to the sheet rubbings dating from the beginning of the present
ury.

The first character referred to by Yün as having been mentioned by
g Fang-kang is the character *hsien*, the fifteenth in line one of the text
the most important of the four characters in the relative dating process.
is own colophon at the end of the album Yün Yü-ting observes that he
seen a notation written by Weng Fang-kang on a rubbing of the Chang
en stone in the possession of Mr. Yen. In that colophon, according to
, Weng specifically remarked upon the condition of the character *hsien* in
Yen rubbing. Citing Weng, Yün states that in the Yen rubbing "the small
protrusion in the left downward stroke at the point of fracture in the
still exists" (Plate IX). Having compared the two rubbings—his own
the one owned by Yen—Yün judges that in his own rubbing the pro-
on is longer, thus indicating that the stone was less worn when his
ing was made, as compared with the condition of the stone when the
rubbing was made. As we do not have access to the Yen rubbing we
no means of verifying Yün's conclusion and so tentatively must accept
the while hoping that Yün's analysis was objective. We do, however,
at hand the uncut rubbing in sheet form, dating from the beginning of
present century, and comparison of the character *hsien* as it appears in
s album-mounted edition and in the uncut sheet rubbing shows clear
rences between the conditions of the stone as mirrored in the two, with
modern uncut rubbing reflecting a much greater degree of wear, and so
asizing that the cut-mounted edition is relatively much older. The
itions of the two are manifested in the illustrations of the two rubbings
n in Plate IX.

The second and third characters involved in the relative dating are *jun*
se, which follow each other as characters forty and forty-one in line eight
e original uncut text. Weng does not mention these two characters, but
notes that the *jun* is in better condition in his rubbing, while the *se* is in
r state in the Yen rubbing. Here, also, the uncut rubbing from the turn
e century shows the stone to have deteriorated noticeably from the time
the Yün rubbing was made. Incidentally, as is clearly indicated by

reference to the uncut rubbing in sheet form the weathering on the lo
portion of a stone normally is much greater than it is on the upper
(Plate I).

The fourth character cited by Yün as having been mentioned by W
is the character *yüan*, the fortieth in line twelve of the uncut text. H
Weng observes only that the character *yüan* is still legible, a condition
Yün notes also obtains with respect to his rubbing here. The character y
also still exists in the uncut rubbing dating from the turn of the century,
deterioration over the century or so has progressed to such a degree th
would be extremely difficult to recognize the character in the modern rub
if one did not know the character and its location. Here also, it is eas
place the two rubbings—the one in the Yün album and the modern u
rubbing—into relative temporal relationship with one another.

As a result of Weng's observations and his own studies Yün in
colophon concludes that his rubbing of the *Chang Ch'ien pei* is "unq
tionably" of Ming date. His statement inspires several comments. First, t
is no certain proof that his rubbing is of Ming date. On the basis of
observations made by Weng Fang-kang, however, one comes to feel that
album edition here under study, indeed, is earlier than the Yen rubbing
by Weng in Ch'ien-lung (1736-1795) times. It is extremely difficult to
exactly how much earlier the Yün rubbing is, but as Weng considered
even in his own time the Yen rubbing had some age, it certainly is poss
perhaps even likely, that the Yün rubbing had its origins in the Ming.
down in stratigraphic fashion the four rubbings referred to here thus ap
to have the following temporal relation relative to one another:

         Laufer sheet rubbing . . . . *c.* 1900
         [Rubbings made in Weng's time] . . . . *c.* 1800
         The Yen rubbing (with Weng's notes) . . . . . pre-Ch'ien-lung
         The Yün album rubbing . . . . Ming (?)

The mounting, as distinguished from the rubbing, presumably dates t
Yün's time. There is no information on the matter, but several facts lead
to such a conclusion. First, Yün wrote the inscription on the title-label,
such a contribution generally is made at the time of the mounting. Sec
the rubbing seems not to have been mounted before, but to have been fre
mounted here. Third, the album contains no components carried over fro
earlier mounting. Remountings commonly retain title-labels, paper sam
inscriptions, seals, and other memorabilia from earlier mountings, o
reverence for the old and by way of enhancing the impressions of age
quality that the new mounting communicates about the rubbing it carries

For such value as the observations may have, one notes three features
the album itself that speak of a certain amount of age. One, the wood
ler the title strip on the front board of the album is cleaner than the
osed board surface, a phenomenon that suggests that the title-label and
board, and with them almost certainly the album inside, are of the same
(Plate II). Two, as was described above, the under side of the running
ly of the album paper, the side that lies against the back of the board
er, is deeply stained, a condition that speaks of long contact with the
od. Three, the disintegrated condition of the album also speaks of its age,
vell as of the poverty of its materials (Plates III, IV, VII, VIII). Although
re is no necessary correspondence among the ages of the rubbing and of
several components of the mounting, it is useful to note such age-related
ures.

Yün concludes his colophon statement with an inscription that includes
date of the writing, the place, and his name: *Wu-wu san yüeh Pei-p'ing
* *Yü-ting chih* 戊午三月北平惲毓鼎識, "recorded by Yün Yü-ting in Pei-
g in the third month of *wu-wu* [the seventh year of the Chinese Republic,
esponding to 1918]" (Plate VIII). Two of Yün's seals complete the
phon, positioned along the lower left margin of the page. The upper one
s *Yü-ting*, his name, and the lower one, *Wei-sun*, his *hao*.

The final double face of the album, the tail end of the running body,
ies a small group of informally scribbled inscriptions, evidently meant as
cord of the latest collector. The first line simply states that *Ch'eng-chai* is
pieh-hao, or alternate style of Yün Wei-sun. The succeeding lines, all in
same hand, are but a series of dates, set down in traditional Chinese
ner, with cyclical symbols for the years and special terms for the seasons
'grain in ear" (early June), "frost descends" (late October), and the like.
owing each of these dates is one or another of the two terms, *lin* or *lin-*
語畢, indicating that the writer had copied the text, presumably using it as
lligraphic model.

The cyclical symbols represent a spread of eighteen years, from *chi-*
u to *ping-wu*, but with the location of the spread undefined in terms of
er Chinese history or the calendar. The history of the album, however,
ests that the spread is over the years 1949-66. There also is no signature,
judging from the fact that the calligraphic style of the notes agrees with
of Liu Lin-sheng's signed prefatory inscription, one concludes that Liu
the studious copier.

We have now completed our serpentine course through the Chang
en album, with its very instructive features bearing on the physical aspects
the connoisseurship elements involved in a rubbing mounted in album
n. The Chang Ch'ien album is but one very modest example of mounted

rubbings that collectors prize by reason of their age, rarity, and excellen
Most such rubbings share basic features, but each further manifests distinc
physical and connoisseurship qualities, the product of its own particu
history. It is the almost endless number of permutations of these shared a
unique features that makes the study of rubbings so very challenging a
satisfying, and that so nicely both explains and justifies their alterna
name, "black tigers."

Plate I *Chang ch'ien pei:*
uncut modern sheet rubbing

Plate II *Chang ch'ien pei:*
album-mounted "old rubbing"

Plate III *Chang ch'ien* album:
first two double faces with tablet heading

Plate IV *Chang ch'ien* album:
first double face of text showing format, transposition of lines, and other connoiss
ship features

Plate V *Lang-ya t'ai pei:*
rubbing of miniature copy of boulder inscription

秦石僅存孤刻海魚又至琅邪
安得靈鞭一掃再令丞相磨沙

癸卯三月閻運題

Plate VI *Lang-ya t'ai pei:*
portion of book-mounted early Ch'ing rubbing, showing heavily eroded nature of sto

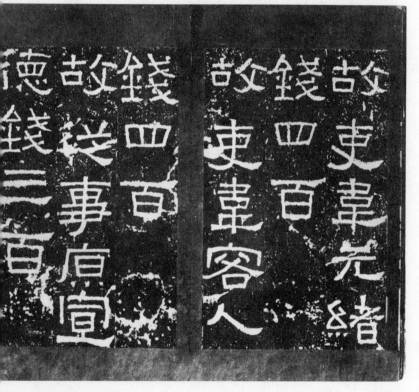

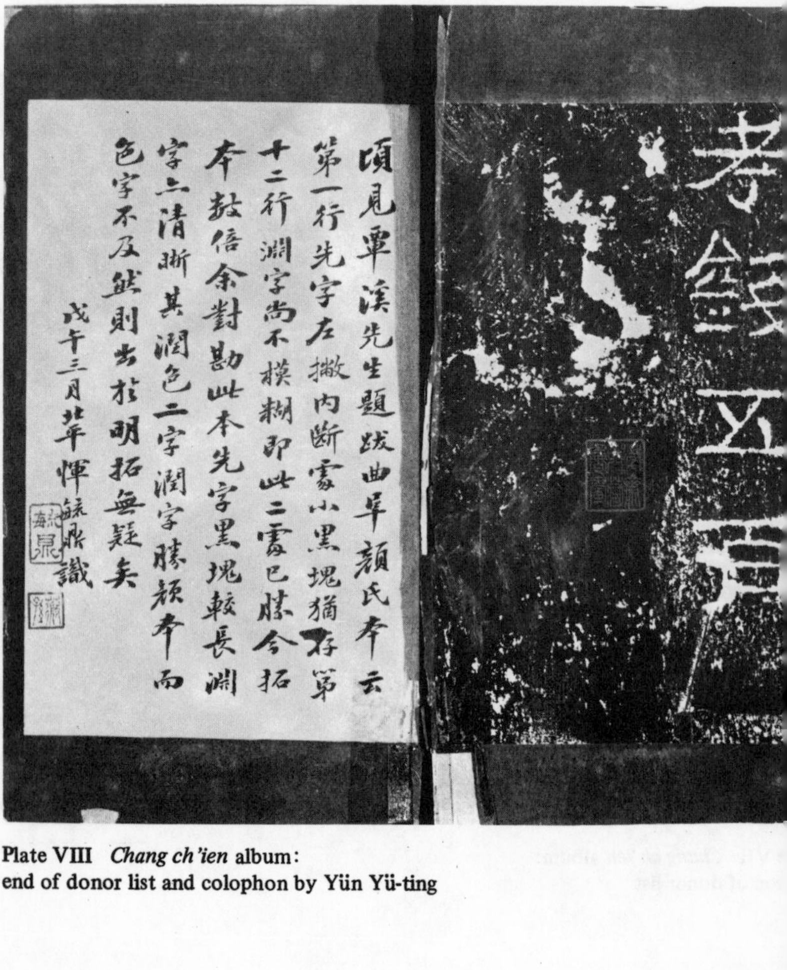
頃見覃溪先生題跋曲阜顏氏本云第一行先字左撇內斷處小黑塊猶存第十二行淵字尚不模糊即此二處已勝今拓本鼓信余對勘此本先字黑塊較長淵字亦清晰其潤色二字潤字勝顏本而色字不及然則出於明拓無疑矣

戊午三月北平惲毓鼎識

Plate VIII *Chang ch'ien* album:
end of donor list and colophon by Yün Yü-ting

te IX *Chang ch'ien pei:*
(top). *hsien* character in album-mounted "old rubbing"
bottom). *hsien* character in uncut modern sheet rubbing

Managing heaven's mandate:
ded communications in the accession of Ts'ao P'ei, A.D. 220*

Carl Leban

"You all did see that on the Lupercal I thrice presented him a
kingly crown which he did thrice refuse. Was this ambition?"

INTRODUCTION

en the tough Chou warriors of northwestern China overthrew their Shang
decessors on the central plains in the twelfth or eleventh century B.C., they
med,[1] like the Children of Israel coming out of Egypt, to be acting under
pecial relationship with their deity. Their deity, *T'ien* or Heaven, they
med, was universal, with power over all the world, but they alone were its
sen instrument of immediate action, and that special status was defined in
ontractual relationship or covenant specifying the obligations of both
ties:

1. Rule over the conquered territory is given to the chosen people, on
   condition that they reverently attend to their virtue, otherwise
2. Failing reverently to attend to their virtue, their rule shall be terminated and given to yet another.

*The major component of this paper was originally presented in brief form and under
er title at the Annual Meeting of the Association for Asian Studies in New York,
ch 1972. I am grateful for comment from Professor Creel and from my friend Pro-
or Lyman P. Van Slyke, and for a fellowship from the National Endowment for the
nanities, all of which stimulated me to rework thoroughly both the front matter and
clusions. The new import which results now requires the more accurate description of
revised title.
[1] See *Shang shu* [Book of documents], "Shao kao" [Announcement to the Duke of
o].

While this theocratic rationale provided both an effective propagan
justification for the Chou conquest and a neat and high-sounding explanat
of the course of national history, it also provided a proto-constitutional p
cedure for effecting dynastic change. I call it "proto-constitutional" becaus
took almost a millennium of philosophical and syncretizing developm
before the phenomenological manifestations of Heaven's will could be sa
fyingly delineated, related to politics, and finally form a functional article
the unwritten constitution of the imperial Chinese order. The ultimate triun
of Confucianism in the Han and its application to politics, particularly
Mandate of Heaven concept, brought about an understandable retrospect
tendency; that is, previous history and legend was reinterpreted and syncreti
in the light of this "new" knowledge. The Former Han dynasty, its predeces
Ch'in, the Chou, and even the ancient legendary rulers were all assigned p
itions in the cycle of dynasties, and these assignments were the subject of m
diverse scholastic debate before a satisfactory description was finally accep
midway through the Former Han dynasty.

The important fact to remember is that the assignment of position in
dynastic cycle was retrospective. In fact, the question of Heaven's Mand
was *not* an issue in either the Ch'in unification or the Han triumph wh
supplanted it, but this fact is often obscured, if not occasionally forgotten
the tendency to view the past from the Han point of view: that things l
always been as they appeared to be in the Han and later. Most easily obscu
from the view of very late observers, modern observers, is the high degree
sophisticated political cynicism which saw in the "new" Mandate of Heav
(as opposed to the "old" Chou concept) an effective weapon of psychologi
warfare compounded of popular superstitious belief and theocratic schol
ticism.

That sophisticated cynicism had developed as early as the third centu
B.C. is apparent in the writings of the "right-wing" Confucian, Hsün Tzu (b
c. 312 B.C.), who, in his discussion of Heaven,[2] wrote:

Are order and disorder due to the heavens? I reply, the sun and mo
the stars and constellations revolved in the same way in the time of Yü
in the time of Chieh. Yü achieved order; Chieh brought disorder. He
order and disorder are not due to the heavens .... When stars fall
trees make strange sounds, all the people in the country are terrified a
go about asking, "Why has this happened?" For no special reasor
reply. It is simply that, with the changes of Heaven and earth and
mutations of the yin and yang, such things once in a while occur. Y

[2]Burton Watson (tr.), *Hsün tzu: basic writings* (New York: Columbia Univer
Press, 1963), 82-85.

may wonder at them, but you must not fear them. The sun and the moon are subject to eclipses, wind and rain do not always come at the proper season, and strange stars occasionally appear. There has never been an age that was without such occurrences. If the ruler is enlightened and his government just, then there is no harm done even if they all occur at the same time. But if the ruler is benighted and his government ill-run, then it will be no benefit to him even if they never occur at all . . . . You pray for rain and it rains. Why? For no particular reason I say. It is just as though you had not prayed for rain and it rained anyway. The sun and moon . . . undergo an eclipse and you try to save them [by beating drums]; a drought occurs and you pray for rain; you consult the arts of divination before making a decision on some important matter. But it is not as though you could hope to accomplish anything by such ceremonies. They are done merely for ornament. Hence the gentleman regards them as ornaments, but the common people regard them as supernatural . . . .

Hsün Tzu's most distinguished students, Han Fei and Li Ssu, both identified with the Realist or Legalist school, were closely involved in the Ch'in tory. That they did not employ the Mandate of Heaven concept as a weapon psychological warfare (though there is evidence of the contemporary use of er propaganda techniques[3]) may be due partly to the influence of their cher, partly to their own hard-headed practicality in politics, for which they identified as Legalists, but is most likely due to the absence of a general lief in the Mandate of Heaven concept itself. For if there were a general be-f in the concept, it seems inconceivable that the practical politicians of Ch'in uld not have employed it, as they employed every other political weapon ilable.

Further, the vigorous Ch'in attempt to extirpate all competing ideologies burning their texts and liquidating their exponents, could only have weaked the Mandate of Heaven concept. The *Shang shu* [Book of documents], ich contained the story of the Duke of Chou's announcement of Heaven's ndate, was probably the most severely endangered text; at least it was the st difficult to recover. It is not surprising then, that when the Ch'in were erthrown and civil war ensued among the victors, the concept of a Mandate Heaven could only have been a vaguely antique idea committed to the mem- y of a few dedicated scholars, which did not exist in any generally accepted stem of belief to make it a useful weapon of psychological warfare.

[3] As in Ch'en She's enlistment of "supernatural" aid in his initial uprising, recorded in ih chi 48, translated by Burton Watson, *Records of the grand historian of China*, I ew York: Columbia University Press, 1961), 20 f.

Ironically, the combination of Ch'in's attempt at extirpation and '
ultimate success of Confucianism as state doctrine under the Former Han p
bably served not only to rejuvenate the moribund concept, but to imbu(
with a vigor it had never seen before. Once the Han Confucians had recove
all they could of the texts Ch'in had sought to destory, they set about
embellishment and elucidation of those texts by parallel compilations of th
own. One particularly important group of new writings were the mystical ı
緯 or "weft" texts, originally written to complement the "warp" or *ch*
[classic] texts, but soon combined with *ch'an* 讖 [originally prognosticatic
texts to produce a mystically oracular hybrid, the apocryphal *ch'an-wei* t
dition.[4] The apocryphal works, many of which seem on internal evidence
have been compiled to order during periods of active struggle for the thro
drew the prestige of the Confucian classics over the dubious art of progn
tication, while at the same time providing a rationale for determining the p
itical will of Heaven in observed phenomena.

Most prestigious of the apocrypha, and for that reason probably the or
such work to escape intact the literary persecutions which by Sung times
but obliterated this tradition, was the *Ch'un-ch'iu fan-lu* [Deep significance
the Spring and Autumn Annals] by the great scholar Tung Chung-shu (17
104? B.C.). In this highly syncretic work of cosmology and politics Tu
wrote:

> The creatures of Heaven and earth at times display unusual changes a
> these are called wonders. Lesser ones are called ominous portents. T
> portents always come first and are followed by wonders. Portents :
> Heaven's warnings, wonders are Heaven's threats . . . . The genesis of
> such portents and wonders is a direct result of errors in the state . .
> If we examine these wonders and portents carefully, we may discern t
> will of Heaven.[5]

Tung Chung-shu and the Han Confucians thus adopted views complete
opposed to those elaborated by Hsün Tzu little more than a century earlier.
Confucianism gained the force of state doctrine from 135 B.C. on, these apoc
phal theories also were informally codified and accepted in the unwritten cc
situation of the Han state.

The effect, I suggest, was two-fold: On the one hand doctrinal prest
now legitimized the customary practice by which officials submitted memori
reporting selected natural phenomena. This practice enabled them indirec

[4] For an excellent review of the apocrypha see Tjan Tjoe Som, *Po hu t'ung: The co
prehensive discussions in the White Tiger Hall*, I (Leiden: E. J. Brill, 1949), 100-20.

[5] Burton Watson tr., in Wm. T. deBary *et al, Sources of Chinese tradition* (New Y(
Columbia University Press, 1960), 187.

safely to pass judgement on and attempt to influence actions taken by the
ereign or others in his name.[6] On the other hand the concept of the Man-
e of Heaven was officially revived and doctrinally sanctioned.

The new Han Mandate of Heaven here hypothesized differed from the
ient and half-remembered Chou theory in four crucial aspects:

(1)   The new system was to be the *a priori* rather than merely the
t hoc justification of dynastic change.

(2)   Precisely because the new Mandate had now to be elucidated *be-
e* dynastic change could occur, it provided a valuable alternative to violent
flict. Competition for the throne could now be attacked with psychological
fare or, failing that, a combination of psychological warfare and armed
nbat.

(3)   Centuries of traditional belief and the new codification provided
Han apocrypha served to define the scope of phenomena and the manner
nterpretation which might be adduced in propaganda conflict, thus placing
ell-understood means of competition, as it were, in the public domain.

(4)   Because of the three foregoing factors and the customary use of
tentous memorials for upward criticism, a symbolic jargon was readily avail-
e for a two-way testing of opinion on any proposal to change the Mandate.
s testing, which constituted a disguised opinion poll of the principal's own
al constituency, permitted an open but safe discussion of the dangerous
all-but-forbidden subject of dynastic change. Responses to a symbolic but
dentiary suggestion for dynastic change could cover a broad range from (*a*)
right rejection as treasonous fabrication, through (*b*) interpretations sym-
ically questioning such political realities as the candidate's personal fitness,
timeliness of the act, and the likelihood of general acceptance outside the
al constituency, to (*c*) ratification of the proposal, not only by acceptance
its validity, but by augmentation of its evidence, amplification of its ar-
nent, and broadening of its appeal.

Certainly this last factor and its operation would be the most interesting
observe, since it would reveal the balance of political forces and their inter-
ion in a sophisticated and complex decision-making process of the highest
sonal and national political moment.

Wang Mang (d. A.D. 23), who had already become virtual ruler as the
ent for a puppet sovereign, was the first to employ the new system as a
chanism for effecting dynastic change. In the process, as in many of his

---

[6] See especially Hans Bielenstein, "An interpretation of the portents in the Ts'ien Han
," *Bulletin of the Museum of Far Eastern Antiquities*, XXII (1950), 127-43, and
fram Eberhard, "The political function of astronomy and astronomers in Han China,"
. K. Fairbank (ed.), *Chinese thought and institutions* (Chicago: University of Chicago
ss, 1957), 33-70.

other efforts, he developed influential and lasting innovations. The first these was the compilation to order of auspicious propaganda favorable to h self. The second and probably more significant innovation was the use of al cation as the final element in the drama, achieving in the same act and inst both succession and the transfer of legitimacy.

So with the very first cycle of the newly defined Mandate of Heave novel ideal had also been created: non-violent dynastic succession and leg macy transfer by adbdication. For abdication to be significant, however, quired a universally, or nearly universally recognized vessel of legitimacy fr which to transfer power. In periods of the greatest stress and disorder, wl rapid change had obliterated even a symbolic national authority, it was possible of course to find such a vessel, and competition could only be resol by resort to violence..

Such was the situation when Wang Mang was killed and prolonged c war broke out in contention for the throne. All parties turned to armed cc bat augmented with extensive use of the newly developed propaganda weap in sophisticated psychological warfare. The best documented of those eff is quite naturally that of Liu Hsiu, who became the founding "Brillian Martial" Sovereign of Latter Han, and his partisans.[7]

A tangential question arises: To what extent were these contestants cere believers in the dominant ideology of their time, acting out their desti as they believed them to be determined by Heaven, and to what extent w they simply cynical and practical politicians, employing a generally-held syst of belief as a means to determining their own destinies? In the terms used Hsün Tzu, did they understand their auguries and portents as useful politi "ornaments," or did they join the common belief that they were really "sup natural" and not of their own making?

Homer H. Dubs[8] seems almost convinced of Wang Mang's sincere (dence in his own propaganda, while Hans Bielenstein,[9] writing of Liu Hsiu a his competitors, says, "Those who spread prophesies, even though of rec manufacture, seem as a rule to have convinced themselves of their trut. Arthur F. Wright[10] too, in his discussion of Yang Chien's ideological ca paign to secure his throne as the "Cultured" Sovereign of Sui, seems simila convinced of a sincere belief in the authenticity of the very measures fabrica

---

[7] See Hans Bielenstein, *The restoration of the Han dynasty*, II, "The Civil W; BMFEA XXXI (1959).

[8] Homer H. Dubs (tr.), *The History of the Former Han dynasty*, III (Baltim Waverly Press, 1955), 104.

[9] *Restoration*, II, 235.

[10] "The formation of Sui ideology, 581-604," in *Chinese thought and institutic 71-104.

ng that campaign. Yet it seems paradoxical, if not completely inconsistent, these men could maintain a sincere belief in any ideology while simul-eously cynically manipulating that ideology for their own ends. The issue irther complicated by the difficulty of determining which propaganda was duced by or on direct order of the principal, and which was produced by partisans on their own initiative.

For the cases cited at least there seems little chance of getting at the true ivation of the involved personalities and therefore the locus of any cyni-ı which may have existed, except by extremely indirect evidence. This dif-lty obtains partly because the sources were compiled by historians who e themselves proponents of the dominant ideological tradition, but more ause the historiographical imperatives of those compilers led them generally mphasize recording documents which themselves constituted an historical ent" rather than those which revealed the mechanics which produced the ent." Politicians being what they are, motivation is carefully hidden, even ipletely inverted, in the "documentary event," while office memoranda, mechanical documentation of the actual happenings, are kept secret and pressed if possible.

In this paper I will briefly treat the case of Ts'ao P'ei, who accepted the dication" of the "Proffering" Sovereign of Latter Han and acceded to the ne as the founding "Cultured" Sovereign of Wei in the tenth moon of A.D. . The documentation of Ts'ao P'ei's accession is unique by the inclusion in sources of a remarkable file which seems to contain both "documentary its" and office memoranda. Through analysis I hope to be able tentatively upport the hypothesis that the use of portentous propaganda in claiming Mandate of Heaven was implemented, at least in one case, with enough histicated cynicism as to raise doubts about the relevance of questions con-ing the principal's belief in the ideology. Most important, I hope to dem-trate the manner in which the new Mandate of Heaven was consciously ipulated in the four crucial aspects defined above, thereby to elucidate actual operating mechanism for effecting the essential "ornament" of early stitutional dynastic change.

HISTORICAL BACKGROUND

Following a long period of declining imperial vigor which resulted in ere inability to control self-aggrandizing factions both in the capital and onally, in 184 the Han was finally shaken irrevocably by a violent paroxysm peasant rebellion. Though the rebels of 184, known to history as Yellow bans, were suppressed within the year, the effort was the last effective act national policy by the Han house. Rent within by factional strife among

distaff relatives, eunuchs and officials, and without by the transfer of
power to local military leaders, the facade of national unity soon crumb
into a wildly confused pastiche of competition among local warlords, la
and small.

By 190 the person of the nine-year old "Proffering" Sovereign was h
self hostage to the ambitious warlord dictator Tung Cho, on whose assas
ation he passed like some prized item of booty through the hands of a s
cession of like opportunists. In 196 the brilliant general Ts'ao Ts'ao gamb
successfully on a sudden opportunity, captured the Sovereign for his own p
pet and, posing as defender of the Han, began the step-by-step eliminatio
his competitors. Over the next twenty-five years Ts'ao Ts'ao succeeded in
fying all of northern China under his sway, but his state of Wei could not c
quer the two competing separatist states of Wu in the southeast and Sh
the southwest. At his death in the first moon of 220 (on the *keng-tzu* day,
23rd, March 15), the house of Han still stood, but only nominally. In fact,
empire was locked in a three-way split that alternated cold diplomacy and
war among three states so nearly equal in power and strategic position t
none could gain any lasting advantage over the others.

Throughout this period of decline the psychological war raged in
tangled with diplomatic jockeying and armed struggle. Pretenders rose a
fell, a few to have their careers preserved in some detail by the historia
some to have no more than their claims recorded, some perhaps ignored
together, but all contributing to the store of portentous evidence that
Mandate of Heaven had passed from the Han. Still, the three main contend
hesitated to claim that Mandate as their own. Though they were actually o
nipotent monarchs within their own domains, for whatever reasons of fear
prudence they yet maintained their nominal status as subjects of Han. T
situation changed suddenly and radically with the death of Ts'ao Ts'ao.

Ts'ao Ts'ao's passing was in every way as shattering an event as the de
of any world-bestriding ruler; both within the state of Wei, which ruled
north in all but name, and throughout the nation, the impact must have be
tremendous. It was a moment fraught with ambivalence and danger, and p
cisely because everyone must have realized that an epoch had ended, t
things could never again be the same, it was a moment charged with opp
tunity: the farce had ended, and when the final ornaments had been display
the Han too had ended.

There was, however, some little difficulty in arranging the display
those final ornaments. Ts'ao Ts'ao, returning from campaigns in the sou
west, had died in Lo-yang, but his designated heir, P'ei, then thirty-four a
the eldest son by Ts'ao's principal wife, was in Yeh, the capital of Wei sta
some seventy-five miles to the northeast. The situation was far from cal

ere was popular unrest due to recent heavy corvee, an epidemic was raging,
d the army was clearly restive. Some officials, fearing the possibility of a
up or even open rebellion, wanted to hush up Ts'ao's death to gain time for
unter-measures. Someone also proposed replacing all local officials with
usted men from the Ts'ao family's home region. Both of these proposals
re rejected,[11] the death was announced and mourning begun.

At that point, the Ch'ing Province troops, remnants of a vast body of
ellow Turban rebels captured by Ts'ao in 192 and personally loyal to him
one, deserted *en masse*, creating a new crisis. Open conflict was avoided by
ecting proposals to restrain these troops by force; instead they were granted
e conduct home and their needs were supplied *en route*. Meanwhile Ts'ao
ang and Ts'ao Chih, P'ei's surviving full brothers and his active competitors
r succession, had arrived in Lo-yang to attend Ts'ao's funeral. Chang im-
ediately asked for Ts'ao's seals of office, the tangible symbols of his auth-
ity, and though he was rebuffed by P'ei's partisans, the request probably
creased P'ei's sense of danger. P'ei promptly ascended the throne of Wei as
'ao's successor, even before his partisans could draft an edict of the Han
vereign and send him Ts'ao's seals as Chancellor of State, King of Wei, and
epherd of Chi Province. All of these events must have occurred within
ys, and to forestall any further sudden crises P'ei quickly installed his own
en at the very top of the national administration. When Ts'ao Ts'ao's corpse
s finally interred on the *ting-mao* day of the second moon (the 21st, April
, 220) P'ei was able to send all of his younger brothers separately to their
vn fiefs, and for the moment things began to appear finally stabilized.

In the fifth moon minor but open rebellion broke out in Liang Province
reatening P'ei's control of the strategic northwest, but was immediately sup-
essed. Toward the end of the sixth moon, P'ei personally led his army on an
spection tour of the south. This tour doubtless had several purposes:

1. To demonstrate real confidence in the stability of state and government, by reason of which P'ei could so easily leave his capital for the
   provinces.
2. To overawe local officials by personal visits and a show of power, as
   well as to renew and establish personal loyalties in the provinces.
3. To visit P'ei's bases of real power, particularly his own home region,
   to sound out feeling for and support of his plans to take the throne,

[11] By two highly placed advisers who were concerned with avoiding any sudden and
sruptive changes in policy, thereby to maintain the solidarity then existing among
'ao's adherents. See *San Kuo chih* (*SKC*) Wei 15:26b commentary citing Wei lüeh 魏略
d Wei 22:22b. (The edition cited is Lu Pi, *San Kuo chih chi-chieh* (*SKCCC*)三國志集解
'ollected commentaries for *San Kuo chih*], preface dated 1936, Peking: Chung-hua shu-
ü, 1957.)

and to build that support by remission of local taxes *en route*.
4. To "show the flag" to the southern enemies of Wei, making cl⬛
that the Wei state was in strong and steady hands and that there wo⬛
be no weakening of Wei military posture.

Whether owing to the success of P'ei's martial gestures or perhaps beca⬛
others saw their own advantage consonant with Wei's in the ambivalence ⬛
the moment, in the seventh moon three fortuitous events occurred wh⬛
augured well for P'ei. First, Sun Ch'üan, ruler of the southeastern competi⬛
state of Wu, sent tribute to the Wei court. Then an important general of t⬛
southwestern Shu state, Meng Ta, surrendered with 4,000 of his troops. Af⬛
that, the king of the Ti barbarians of Wu-tu in a contested area along the W⬛
Shu border led his people in adhering to Wei. They were resettled furt⬛
north in Han-yang commandery, probably as a buffer against Shu incursio⬛
It thus appeared that a stable situation existed internally, while Wei's enem⬛
if not completely off-balance, were at least unsure enough to prevent a⬛
effective interference from outside.

It was at this point, probably about the beginning of the tenth mo⬛
that P'ei's partisans began the final culminating propaganda effort to char⬛
the Mandate of Heaven.

SOURCES

Information on the change of Mandate in the official histories is e⬛
tremely scanty. *Hou Han shu*[12] [History of the Latter Han Dynasty] (A9:11⬛
supplies only a single sentence:

> The Sovereign relinquished the throne and the King of Wei, P'ei, p⬛
> claimed himself Son of Heaven.

San Kuo chih [Three States treatises] (Wei 2:13a-14a, 35b-36a) offers b⬛
little more:

> On the *ping wu* day [of the tenth moon, the fourth day, November ⬛
> 220], the march [of P'ei and his army] reached Ch'ü-li (Honan Provin⬛
> northwest of modern Lin-ying hsien). The Han Sovereign felt that t⬛
> hope of the masses lay with Wei, so summoning the many dukes a⬛
> ministers he announced [his intentions] in sacrifice at the High [Pr⬛
> genitor's] Temple, and sent the concurrent Grandee Secretary [*yü-s*⬛
> *tai-fu*] Chang Yin with Special Commission [*ch'ih-chieh*] to present t⬛
> imperial seal and cord and abdicate the throne [to Ts'ao P'ei]... [t⬛

[12]The edition cited is Wang Hsien-ch'ien, *Hou Han shu chi-chieh* (*HHS*) 後漢書集
[Collected commentaries for *Hou Han shu*], reprint of 1915 Changsha edition.

edict is omitted here] . . . So they made a platform at Fan-yang [Hamlet in Ch'ü-li], and on the *keng-wu* day [the 28th day, December 10, but it was actually *hsin-wei*, the 29th day, December 11] the King [of Wei, P'ei] mounted the platform and ascended the throne. All the officials were in attendance, and when the affair was ended they dismounted the platform, watched the sacrificial flames [carry news of the event to Heaven] completing the ceremony, and returned [to their encampment].

The official histories thus supply no information on the events tran-ring between the *ping-wu* and *hsin-wei* days, the twenty-five days between e time (we are told) the Han Sovereign first conceived the idea of abdicating d the time the Wei Sovereign actually ascended the imperial throne. To help l in this gaping lacuna in the histories, P'ei Sung-chih (372-451), who compiled e masterful original commentary to *San Kuo chih*, added a long passage from vork no longer extant. That quotation, which is more than 8,000 characters ng and may well be the longest quotation in Chinese historical commentary, drawn from a work of the Three States period called *Hsien-ti chuan* [Bio-iphy of the "Proffering" Sovereign] completed probably about the year 4.[13]

The *Hsien-ti chuan* quotation in question is really quite remarkable. It ms to be an actual file of documents dealing with the entire abdication fair, forty-two discrete documents in all, only a very few of which are re-rded elsewhere. Needless to say, those that are recorded elsewhere are the ocumentary events" discussed briefly above. Those documents are flowery ings, oozing with obvious sycophancy and tedious propaganda, and since ey predominate by far it is very easy to skim them quickly and condemn the tire record as dull historically and useless historiographically. For example, passing over them Achilles Fang[14] remarks:

> P'ei sung-chih's commentary in *SKC* reproduces practically all the docu-ments relating to the farce called *shan-tai* (Handing over the Throne) as given in the *Hsien-ti chuan.* . . . From the modern point of view they possess no historical value whatsoever. Ssu-ma Kuang was probably of the same opinion; his three sentences given here [in Fang's translation of the Wei chapters from *Tzu-chih t'ung-chien*] do ample justice to the verbose account.

[13] The compiler of the *Hsien-ti chuan* 獻帝傳 is unknown, but he was probably a Wei bject. The reason for assuming completion after the year 234 is the recording of the yard of the posthumous agnomen "Proffering" to the deceased Han Sovereign in that ar. See Yao Chen-tsung, *San Kuo i-wen-chih* 三國藝文志 [A bibliographic treatise for e Three States], in *Ehr-shih-wu shih pu-pien*, III, 3222a.

[14] *The chronicle of the Three Kingdoms*, chapters 67-78 from the *Tzu-chih t'ung-ien* of Ssu-ma Kuang (Cambridge: Harvard University Press, 1952), 36 f.

In the description and analysis to follow, I hope to show that some
these documents not only possess historical value, but that they supply r
historical and historiographical insights relevant not only to an import
event but to the making of that event and the thinking of the actors in it.

DESCRIPTION AND ANALYSIS OF THE ABDICATION DOCUMENTS

The *Hsien-ti chuan* quotation consists of forty-two documents arran
in chronological order, though only eleven of them are precisely dated (
Table I). They were all prepared or recorded within the tenth moon of 2
but the corpus is quite varied, ranging from purported formal edicts a
memorials in flowery archaic style, through oral presentations of carefu
prepared material in balanced argument, to off-hand, informal, almost c
loquial orders, both written and oral. In length they range from as long
several hundred words down to a single word, while the subject matter ran
from the most elevated cosmological speculation to expedient day-to-c
political jockeying. Their most obvious feature is this lack of homogenei
which strengthens my conviction first of their authenticity, and second th
they are in fact a transcription of an actual archival file not originally
tended for publication in this form.

The scope of this paper precludes extended translation of the entire c
pus; indeed the esoteric speculations of the propagandistic documents can
be understood at all without very extensive, often highly speculative annotati
Further, this very corpus is a primary source for apocryphal quotations fr
lost and destroyed *ch'an-wei* texts, the very titles of which are often incomp
hensible, separated as they are from an almost extinct tradition. In this descr
tion, then, I will translate in full only those documents which seem to reveal t
political process, and only supply occasional examples of the propaganda i
summary account of the esoteric items. The tabular display accompanying t
description provides an additional easy reference for viewing the entire cor
and supplies the loci of individual items for further reference.

The file opens with a memorial (*piao* 表) from a nominally Han offic
the Left General of Gentlemen of the Household, Li Fu, recounting a p
diction of change of Mandate made by a certain Chiang Ho (d. 219) in 2
when Ts'ao Ts'ao first made himself Duke of Wei. Portents of change a
rehearsed only in non-specific terms, but this memorial (doc. 1) inclue
some significantly revealing aspects of motivation among the Wei offici
Li Fu remarks:

Since I have been at [the Han?] court, I often spread word of [t
prediction] among my intimates, but since the time seemed imprope
dared not openly state it. This year the Prince has ascended the thro

[of Wei], and numerous lucky omens and auspicious portents arrive daily and monthly. It is clearly to be seen that there is a Mandate from Heaven: Your sage power reaches everywhere, the harbingers manifest your future glory, in truth Heaven and Earth congratulate you, the myriad states put their faith in you. Every time I rejoiced in congratulating you I wanted to speak [Ch'iang] Ho's prediction. If one exhausts the rites in serving one's prince, others will take it to be sycophancy. How much more when my reputation and conduct are low and base and I have been at court only a little time: to speak was to commit an offense, so I merely repressed myself. Now your vast favor has fallen over all quarters, your lofty grace moves Heaven and Earth, your majesty flourishes within the seas and foreign quarters turn to you in submission. Harbingers and foretokens gather to signal that the fortunate Mandate is truly auspicious. I cannot contain my happiness and respectfully memorialize all of this to inform you.

As Dubs has pointed out in his work on Wang Mang, it is not necessary assume that the compilation of flattering and subservient documents was lered. The sophisticated officials of the usurper's court and coterie were ubtless well aware what kind of documents would be welcomed. Li Fu's morial is even more explicit than needed in explaining that conditions now ripe for speaking up clearly and loudly on the change of Mandate. Though own letter's contribution is really trivial, its appearance, whether prompted design or coming by coincidence, provided the opportunity for calling forth velter of portentous reports and employing them in propaganda. No wonder King's order (doc. 2), while attributing the auspicious signs to his father's tue and disclaiming his own, opens that order with the words: "Show [Li 's memorial] abroad."

The effect of publishing Li Fu's memorial was immediate, because the xt item (doc. 3) is a record of an oral statement (*yen* 言) by at least eight mbers of the Wei court. This record is presented in the usual Chinese fashion a single statement, but is probably synthesized from the secretarial record a discussion before the King's court. Not surprisingly, the Wei officials agreed th the nominal Han official's view, but their discussion centered on pre- lents and ground rules for the ritualistic propaganda to follow. One par- ularly interesting sentence is worthy of quotation:

These [precedents we have cited] are the manner by which Heaven's Mandate is made clear to the sage and wise: It has neither sound of word or speech nor odor of sweet blossoms that it may be known. [Heaven] merely dangles symbols to show men, using the tiniest of things to effect its will.

The ground rules thus laid out, the King issued an order (doc. 4) e
pressing reservations about the interpretation of current signs, and the Sup
visor of the Masters of Writing "proclaimed [the order and discussion] to
officials and had them hear and know [the import thereof]." This probat
had the effect of bringing forth the first truly propagandistic item of this fi
"On the *hsin-hai* day [the ninth of the tenth moon, Nov. 21, 220] the Clerk
the Grand Astrologer, Hsü Chih, laid out for the King of Wei those apocrypl
texts [which prophesied that] Wei replaces Han."

Some of the evidence cited by Hsü Chih was, so to speak, comm
apocryphal property including the *Book of changes*, and had been used l
other pretenders in pressing their own claims to the throne. Other eviden
was newly created to meet the needs of the Wei propaganda. An example
the former:

The *Ch'un-ch'iu tso-chu-ch'i* 春秋佐助期 [Helpful forecasts from t
Spring and Autumn Annals] says, "Han by Hsü [the capital establish
by Ts'ao Ts'ao on capturing the Han Sovereign in 196] rising will lose t
world." The former Prefect of Po-ma, Li Yün, reported, "In Hsü a risi
aura was seen at 'High-on-the-road 當塗高 .' [There was a well-knov
prophesy that "the one who replaces Han is high-on-the-road."] O
who is high on the road will rise in Hsü." "High-on-the-road" is Wei; it
[the *wei* of] *hsiang-wei* 象魏, a gate of two pavillions [anciently a hi
gate of the capital city where laws were displayed and announced]. T
one who is great and high in the Way [a pun on *tao*; as in Englis
way=road] is Wei. Wei shall replace Han. Wei bases its rise in Hsü; H
proves its end in Hsü. Now these things are seen in effect according
Li Yün's words, and the rising [aura] in Hsü is a corresponding foretoke

An example of some fairly obvious forgery is the following:

The *Hsiao-chiang chung-huang-ch'an* 孝經中黃讖 [Median yellow pr
gnostications of the Classic of filial piety?] says, "When the sun 日 carri
east 東, it cuts off the light of fire; when 'not' 不 carries 'one' 一 acro
sage acuity is illumined." ... This is the surname 曹 (曺) and taboo
personal name 丕 of the King of Wei seen in the diagrams and prognos
cation [texts]. The *I yün-ch'i-ch'an* 易運期讖 [Prognostications foreca
by mutations in the *Book of changes?*] says, " 'Speech' 言 resides to t
east; there is 'noon' 午 in the west. Two suns 日 shine together. [That]
sun resides below [means] who was chief turns to be subject. Five eigh
[are] forty, a yellow aura is received a true man appears." "Speech" ai
"noon" form a Hsü 許 logograph; "two suns" form a "rising" 昌 log
graph. Han shall be lost by Hsü. Wei shall rise by Hsü. Now the foreca

of this event is in Hsü and this is the great effectuation [of the prophesy]. The *I yün-ch'i* further says," 'Demon' 鬼 in a 'mountain' 山, 'millet' 禾 and a 'girl' 女 joined; [this] will rule the world. [The combined logographs make an archaic *wei* 巍 logograph.] "

While the first example drawn from Hsü Chih's list of prophesies shows w commonly-held belief was applied to the Wei case, the second perhaps ws very explicit forged prophesy. It is possible that some vaguely oracular terial, which might be commonly known, is also here combined to lend more dibility. The numbers "five eights are forty" are variously interpreted, but m most likely to be included in Hsü Chih's discussion because they point the end of the Han's 400-year reign. Moreover, since everyone knew that n ruled by virtue of the fire element, and that the earth element, its yellow or and other attributes were next in the cycle, it is almost certain that conerable prophetic effort had earlier gone into apocrypha aimed at proving endance of the earth element in behalf of Wang Mang. It was necessary, erefore, only to make it apply specifically to the claims of the Wei King and the moment at hand.

Hsü Chih's long listing drew forth a flowery demurrer (doc. 6) from the i King, which ordered again that the above documents be published abroad cause those far and near to reflect red [loyal] hearts." Thereupon, nine icials of the Wei court, including seven who had participated in the earlier cussion, memorialized (*tsou* 奏) (doc. 7), insisting on the authenticity of prophesies, that "these texts were all well known in former ages and also n under the Han,[15] from which it may be said that [Wei's] Mandate of aven has been [proclaimed] for a long time." The King's order in response c. 8), "Send this to the four quarters to make clear my sincere heart," was claimed on the *kuei-ch'ou* day (the 11th, Nov. 23, 220).

Document 9 is a record of discussion by at least five officials bearing es of the Han court specifically recounting the errors and defects of the Han vereigns and assuring the Wei King that "nine out of ten have entrusted themves [to Wei.] " Document 10 is the Wei King's order rebutting the discussion a listing of alternative historical precedents, but apparently he felt that such paration had gone far enough. There is no indication of extensive publication either of these two documents, and they are followed immediately by the t edict of abdication (*ts'e-chao* 册詔) (doc. 11) from the Han Sovereign. We ow this and subsequent such edicts were drafted by Wei men,[16] and they filled with self-criticism, historical precedent, and acknowledgment of the

---

[15] Possibly from the time preceding Wang Mang's accession.

[16] Our sources tell us that the edicts were drafted by one Wei Chi, a Master of ting in the Wei court who had been transferred to the Han court as a Gentleman in

will of Heaven as evidenced by prophesy and portent. This first edict is da▮
the *i-mao* day (the 13th, Nov. 25, 220).

When the edict of abdication arrived, even before it was opened, it ▮
off a flurry of excitement among officials who were not privy to the high
level planning of the farce. Document 12 is an enthusiastic memorial (*tsɔ*
from a group led by the Wei Prefect of Masters of Writing, Huan Chieh, w▮
participated in the discussion in document 7 and is elsewhere reported earl▮
to have urged Ts'ao Ts'ao to take the throne with equal enthusiasm.

> The Han clan yields its position as Sons of Heaven to Your Highn▮
> [Here Huan Chieh addresses the Wei King by the imperial form, *pi-h*
> 陛下]. Your Highness by sage and brilliant virtue and the [prop▮
> order of destined sequence succeed to the yielding of Han in acc▮
> with the will of Heaven. Now, Heaven's Mandate cannot be begged ▮
> the hope of the myriad peoples cannot be contraverted. Your subje▮
> now beg to convene the ranked marquises, all the generals, the ma▮
> ministers, and attendant clerks, to open the [Sovereign's] personal let▮
> and comply with Heaven's Mandate. [When] all rites and ceremon▮
> [have been prepared] we will memorialize them item by item.

Chieh must have assumed quick acquiescence in the Sovereign's "edi▮
and in his own suggestions, but clearly the assumption was premature. The K▮
issued a blunt and terse order (doc. 13):

> You should discuss [only] my intention all along not to accede to [▮
> abdication] and that's all. I am still [away from camp?] on a hunt, a▮
> I will issue [further] orders on my return.

But Huan Chieh and his fellows apparently did not understand or co▮
not contain their excitement. They memorialized further (doc. 14):

> Of old Yao and Shun handed over [their Mandates] in the ancest▮
> temple. Coming to the Han clan, [the High Progenitor] received t▮
> Mandate while the army was on campaign, [and since] one dare not▮
> dilatory in fear of Heaven's majesty, he ascended the throne in the pl▮
> where he happened to be. Now [you too] should receive the Mand▮
> handing over [the throne]. It would be proper to assemble all offici▮

Attendance (*shih-lang* 侍郎). He is reported to have urged the abdication on the ▮
Sovereign and drafted the edicts of announcement to Ts'ao P'ei (*SKC* Wei 21:34▮
K'ai's tombstone biography records that he also drafted Ts'ao P'ei's announcement▮
acceptance which was carved in stone. See the supporting quotation from *Wen-hsin ti*
lung 文心雕龍 and Yen K'o-chün's comments appended in *SKCCC* Wei 21:34a. The t▮
of the inscription (with a few gaps) has been preserved by Hung K'ua in his *Li-shih* 隸▮
[Explication of (ancient) inscriptions], appended by Lu Pi at *SKCCC* Wei 21:36b-3▮

the many officers, and the troops of the six armies, and to cause them all
to take up position and observe the [implementation of] Heaven's Mandate. [If] the encampment is too restricted, we can set up a platform in
some [appropriate] level place [where you may] receive and respond to
the Mandate. We will, then, meet with the Palace Attendants and Regular
Attendants to discuss the rites and ceremonies, and [ask] the Grand
Astrologer to select a lucky day. When [these things] are done we will
again memorialize.

The Wei King again issued a terse and blunt order to stop this premature
ivity on the part of his loyal but over-zealous officers (doc. 15):

Besides that I very much do not [yet] dare to accept [the Mandate],
why are you anticipating [matters]?

The King's order may have been too late to stop the enthusiasts, because
next item is a memorialized discussion (*tsou-i* 奏議) (doc. 16) from the
ace Attendant Liu I, the Regular Attendant Wei Chen (who had also taken
t in the court discussion in document 7) and others, doubtless the persons
an Chieh had consulted on the mechanics of the abdication arrangements.

The Han clan follows respectfully the righteousness of T'ang Yao in
[holding] the world in common (*kung* 公). By sage virtue Your Highness
will respond to this turn of the cycle of destiny, there being nothing
which is not in proper compliance with the harbingers of the spirits, by
speedily ascending the august throne. [We have asked] the Clerk of the
Grand Astrologer Hsü Chih [to select a day and he responded that] the
17th day of the present moon, the *chi-wei* day, is a day of auspicious
"upright achievement" (*ch'ih-ch'eng* 直成), on which you may receive
the Mandate handing over [the throne]. So we will prepare the place of
the [abdication] platform, and when that is carried out we will separately mamorialize [that matter].

It was clear that things were rapidly getting out of hand, and that the
g's officers were running away with matters on their own. The King took
:ters into his own hands again by making a personal check of what was
ng on, then issued another order (doc. 17):

I just went out [of the camp] and saw that you are [already] setting up
the [abdication] platform. What is the meaning [of this]? Presently, I
should [only] make excuses and refuse, and not accept the edict. I will
merely open the [Sovereign's] personal letter before my tent, [main-
taining] the rites of respect as usual. Moreover, the weather is cold; stop
building the platform and send the soldiers back [to the encampment].

So it was necessary for the Wei King to finally lay it out clear and squ[are]
for his over-zealous subordinates: There was a plan and a schedule for t[he]
affair, and he intended to carry it out without being rushed. After fina[lly]
opening the Sovereign's edict, the contents of which could not have been v[ery]
surprising to him, P'ei issued a florid order (doc. 18) announcing his intent[to]
refuse the Mandate, and this order was proclaimed to all officials, to Wei a[nd]
to the rest of the world on the *chi-wei* day, the 17th, Nov. 29, 220. That v[was]
the same day Hsü Chih had chosen for the abdication, supplying a rough me[ans]
of dating the documents between the 13th and 17th days of the moon.

There followed then an exchange of memorials and orders between [the]
Wei King and 120 officials who were apparently anxious for inclusion in [the]
group urging the abdication (docs. 19-22). The last of these, P'ei's order [to]
draft a letter of refusal and return the imperial seal and cord, lists a number [of]
auspicious signs that are absent, quite as if he were suggesting their inclus[ion]
in future urgings. Document 23 is a memorial from the Palace Attendants p[ro]
testing this latest rebuff, but agreeing to draft the refusal letter. That lett[er,]
the first formal refusal to accept the Mandate of Heaven (doc. 25) was da[ted]
on the *keng-shen* day, the 18th, Nov. 30, 220.

It was P'ei's plan to refuse three times and then accept, as was the cust[om]
dictated by historical and legendary precedent; he makes this clear in a br[ief]
order (doc. 24) reassuring his officers. All the refusals of his own partis[ans]
do not count in the working out of this elaborate ballet, which required th[ree]
formal refusals of three formal commands from the incumbent Sovereign. T[he]
waiting must have been hard on the more naive of P'ei's subordinates.

Dcoument 26 is another memorial (*piao* 表) dated *hsin-yu*, the 1[9th]
Dec. 1, 220, from two of the nine Wei officials who had submitted docum[ent]
7. Their intent seems to be to fill in the missing evidence which P'ei had m[en]
tioned in his order to draft the first letter of refusal. Most of the documen[t is]
concerned with abstruse astrological portents. This probably was just w[hat]
P'ei wanted, because his subsequent order (doc. 27) admits the authentic[ity]
of the evidence for a change of Mandate, but demurs on the basis that he h[im]
self cannot be the person intended.

On the *jen-hsü* day, the 20th, Dec. 2, 220, the second edict from [the]
Han Sovereign arrived, again ordering P'ei to accept the throne. Once aga[in]
the enthusiastic Huan Chieh and his fellows got out of hand. Apparently t[hey]
were either completely naive about what was happening, or so fearful t[hat]
something might throw the plans awry, that they could not check their [en]
thusiasm in urging an immediate accession. Their memorial (doc. 29) argu[es]

Now the Han have [again] sent [Chang] Yin to us with a personal let[ter]
[from the Sovereign]. We, your subjects consider that the Mandate

Heaven may not be delayed, the holy vessel [of state] may not be turned aside. The "Martial" [King] of Chou had the omen of a white fish in the midst of a stream, and without awaiting the outcome of his military hopes already established his grand summons. When Shun was made Grand Recorder [This is from an obscure passage in the *Book of documents*], before the shade of the mulberries had shifted he already ascended the Sovereign's throne. The respect with which they accepted Heaven's Mandate was as rapid as this. Consequently, there was no [small] righteousness of firm refusal; they did not take preserving their [individual] integrity as noble, [but] merely had to trust in the Way of the spirits and accord with the omens of Heaven and Earth. The [*Book of*] *Changes* says, "He receives the Mandate like an echo, without regard to distance or depth, and so [may] know what is yet to come." If this is not the ultimate essence of the world, what then could stand with it? Now, Your Highness in response to the order of destiny is made a son by august Heaven and yet delays in refusing by excuses, vaccillating regarding the grand summons. This is not whereby to exemplify the Way of Heaven and Earth and assist the hopes of the myriad states. We, your subjects, dare risk death to beg you immediately to order those concerned to prepare the [abdication] platform, select an auspicious day, and so accepting the Mandate of abdication, open [the package containing the Sovereign's] seal and cord.

Ts'ao P'ei had to be even more explicit in responding to these latest ▸ortunities. His order (doc. 30) reads:

I hope to refuse three times and am not obeyed [by you.] What is the rush in this [matter]?

▸ even so, his plans were moving along pretty much on schedule. On the ▸-tzu day, the 22nd, Dec. 4, 220, P'ei delivered up his second formal re-▸l, and returned the Sovereign's seal and cord. Then the Palace Attendants ▸ up yet another recitation of arguments, still aimed at the Wei King and ▸ very useful as propaganda. Their memorial (doc. 32) reads:

We, your subjects, have heard that a sage Sovereign does not violate [the requirements of an opportune] moment, that an enlightened chief does not go against his people. Consequently, the [*Book of*] *Changes* praises putting through the will of the world and cutting off the doubts of the world. We humbly consider that Your Highness embodies the superior sageness of Yu-yü [Shun] and succeeds to the cyclical fortune of the earth power. We are at an occasion when [the five-element cycle]

is about to change, when [the virtue of] a subject exceeds his rul
when [there are clear] signs that the fortune of the Han clan is exhauste
[Your Highness] matches the most august, accords with Heaven a
Earth. This is why sage auspices are evidenced and the world all respon
The rise and fall of the cycle is extremely clear: if [one] discusses [yc
accession] with respect to the Mandate of Heaven there is none [else]
speak of; if one measures [your accession] against the appropriaten
of the moment, there are none to compete with you. Consequently, t
moment to receive the Mandate is now. The weather is clear, the d
bright, the sun spreads his light and a fortunate aura rises to the clou
This is because Heaven is pleased and the hearts of the people rejoi
If you still close [yourself] and reject them, what basis can it have
rites? Moreover, the masses cannot be without a chief for [even] a d
the sacred vessel may not lack continuity by hesitation. So, your subje
go against their prince to achieve his enterprise, subordinates have be
false to superior to establish the [grand] affair. Can we, your subjec
dare not again risk death to plead for [your accession]?

By this time, Ts'ao P'ei was a bit more lenient with these zealots, a
his rejection was couched in kinder terms, rather letting them join in the gar
but still making the rules clear to them. His order (doc. 33) reads:

The world is a weighty vessel, one joins the proper succession of rul
by sage virtue. I still have a fearful heart. What kind of person am I
to presume]? Further, you gentlemen have not yet come to [the po
that you] lack a chief. Is this some small matter? Also it would be prop
to wait until after I have firmly refused [three times] and only th
should you begin discussing the possibility [of accepting].

Document 34 is the third edict from the Han Sovereign, dated *ting-m*
the 25th, Dec. 7, 220, and followed by a statement from all the high offici
of the nominally Han court (doc. 35). That longish piece of pure propagar
drew an equally false response from P'ei (doc. 36), after which a third forr
refusal (doc. 37) was sent up on the *chi-ssu* day, the 27th, Dec. 9, 220. T
Sovereign's edict was returned unopened for additional effect in this final
fusal.

Either that day or the next, the Han ministers again memorialized, (d
38) reviewing the whole case: precedents, the faults of Han, auspicious p
tents, sincere urgings. The King's order in response (doc. 39) is a masterpi
of restrained dissimulation:

Anciently, great Shun ate dried rice tailings and slept on straw, and wisl
so to end his days [but became Sovereign instead]. This then was [als
my previous ambition. When [Shun] came to accepting Yao's abdic

ion he put on the rare cloaks and wived his two daughters as if he had always had them. This then was [how he] accorded with Heaven's Mandate. All you ministers sincerely hold that Heaven's Mandate may not be rejected, the hopes of the people may not be violated. How then can I [further] refuse?

On the *keng-wu* day, the 28th, Dec. 10, 220, the fourth edict (doc. 40) ering the Wei King's accession came from the Han Sovereign. Huan Chieh his fellows must have been tremendously relieved that the charade had lly been played out. In their memorial (doc. 41) urging final acceptance y show themselves now almost exultant and at last certain of the result. ir joyous exclamations closed with:

We have[, on our own,] ordered the Prefect of the Grand Astrologer to select an auspicious day and [he has said that] you may mount the platform and accept the Mandate on the 29th day of this moon (*hsin-wei*, Dec. 11, 220). We beg you issue an edict to the kings, dukes, and all ministers to list the [proper] rites and ceremonies in separate memorials.

The King's order (doc. 42) was marvelously brief after all the foregoing biage:

Permitted.

SOME COMMENTS AND CONCLUSIONS

The *Hsien-ti chuan* abdication documents appear at first to represent a r-way correspondence, or at least a correspondence among four entities: Han Sovereign, the Wei King, officials of the Han court, and officials of Wei court. In actuality, only two entities were involved. No Han court ted in reality, since all Han officials owed their appointment and allegiance he King of Wei, and administered the Wei will in the name of Han. Officials the Han court were thus simply additional Wei officials. For the same on, there are no documents in this file actually drafted by or for the Han ereign, although they bear his name. The four edicts (docs. 11, 28, 34, 40) ering the King of Wei to accept the imperial seal and ascend the throne were ally drafted at the order of the Wei King by his own officials. The entire respondence thus may be seen to be a two-way exchange between the Wei g and his own officials.

The situation is not quite so simple however. Most of the documents obviously not an exchange of communication at all, but simply "docu-atary events" produced for effect as propaganda. Most obvious of these are the edicts of the Han Sovereign, which are actually letters from the ¶ King to himself. Similarly, the Wei King's three memorials of refusal (docs. 31, 37), drafted by Wei officials in response to the first three edicts, are a not genuine communications, but were "documentary events."

There being no documents in the file addressed by the Han Sovere to his nominal court, nor any from that nominal court to the Han Soverei and the documents purporting to be an exchange up and down between Han Sovereign and the Wei King shown to be a fraud, there remain only t types of exchange to be examined. They are orders from the Wei King to his o officials, and documents from those officials addressed to the Wei King. Th are seventeen documents addressed upward and eighteen addressed downwa

Of the seventeen documents addressed upward from Wei officials their king, twelve are clearly propagandistic; three (docs. 19, 29, 41), thou couched in floridly persuasive formulaic verbiage, deal also with mechani aspects of the abdication/accession ceremony, and two (docs. 14, 16) se clearly to be office memoranda unselfconsciously dealing with the busines hand. What some of the more sycophantic documents communicate is no much in their bodies as in their signatures, extensive lists of names inde indicating which Wei officials enlisted themselves "on the side of Heaven' its change of Mandate.

Of the eighteen documents addressed downward as orders of the ¶ King, eleven are blatant propaganda rejecting the importunities of the ¶ officials, and five of those (docs. 2, 4, 6, 8, 18) order their own publication the circulation of other propaganda. Six documents (13, 15, 17, 24, 30, . deal clearly with mechanical questions, though two of them (docs. 24, . employ the standard flowery propaganda formulae. The remaining docum (No. 42) is the final order agreeing to the abdication and accession, the sin word *k'o* 可 , "[It is] permitted."

The thirty-five documents representing exchange between the Wei K and his partisans do not constitute a homogeneous corpus. Some are clea elements of the propaganda charade, and these are most easily discerned so much by their content as by the manner in which they interact with ot documents in the chain. Thus, when a memorial to the King is ordered blished and circulated among the officials, we are driven to the interpretat that the document somehow furthers his intentions, and that judgment m stand regardless of any demurrer in the order for publication or any doubt to whether the document in question was compiled under order or not. On other hand, when a memorial to the King is not only uncirculated, but dr an order of rebuff or correction, we must conclude that it somehow does further the King's intentions, and that judgment must stand regardless of h much the style and content of the document in question seem of a piece v

ers. Such a document cannot be taken as part of the charade, and must be
nsidered genuine communication. This is to say, then, that in evaluating
status of any document in this corpus, one must interpret from the point
view of the principals themselves, and that must be done indirectly by
serving how the documents were treated by those principals.

We thus see that the documents form not a chain of sequential communi-
ions, but two parallel chains which have been somehow interfiled. One
in represents the entire propaganda effort, consisting of several stages. There
documents which may be seen as stimuli enabling publishable responses
m the King and further responsive urging from his partisans. Other docu-
nts serve as stimuli of the first type, but are also an integral part of the
ricate ornament of Mandate change; these would be the phony edicts from
Han Sovereign.

The other chain of communication consists of genuine discussion of
tters relating honestly, though naively, to the actual change of ruler. Though
se may be couched in terms which seem identical to the planned propaganda
cuments, they are not seen by the King as contributions to the predeter-
ied sequence; what they propose is dealt with in business-like manner, and
y are rejected as unwarranted intrusions.

The two chains ultimately coalesce in the final documents when, the end
the charade having been accomplished, naive activism once more becomes
propriate.

The remarkable file of the *Hsien-ti chuan* has given us rare insight into
s moment of history. It has enabled us to perceive in significant detail the
plementation of a planned political maneuver. Stripped of the special
nbols and particular jargon of third-century China, that maneuver seems
iost contemporary, so much is it of a piece with the timeless art of poli-
, everywhere.

The reader must now judge the soundness of our original hypothesis.
es such careful and seemingly cynical manipulation of doctrine in practical
itical maneuver raise doubts that the principals themselves were convinced
their own propaganda? Or does the very nature of appeal to this kind of
propaganda constitute a *prima-facie* argument for belief?

I think the answer to the first question is yes, the demonstration of
tle and sophisticated political maneuver displayed in these documents re-
res, at least for Ts'ao P'ei, some presumption of an equally subtle and
histicated world-view.

Ts'ao P'ei's manipulation of the cosmological symbols of state authority
s not, after all, either an original idea or unique effort. A sophisticated lit-
tus, a life-long member of the ruling bureaucracy and the victor in several
portant intrigues, P'ei was anything but a novice at politics. Before him

stood the precedent of Wang Mang's success, while the officialdom throu
which he worked and on which he depended still customarily employed
vocabulary of cosmology in communicating with the throne and cent
administration. This was so much a normal feature of Han administrat
that the record of memorialized phenomena is rather a record of politi
sentiment than of natural events.

What we have been calling the "documentary events" in the *Hsien
chuan* file may now be seen to be something more than mere propaganda, a
even something more than merely symbolic sycophancy. The *Hsien-ti chu*
propaganda documents are, I believe, the record of a kind of nomination a
ratification process carried out through a two-way symbolic communicatin
In this process the thesis of dynastic change was presented to the equival
of an electorate, in this case the principal's own loyal constituency, w
could have responded either affirmatively or negatively. Given an affirmati
the vocabulary of such ratification then itself became a part of the symbo
ornament of change, integrated into, and thereby obscured as part of the ce
mony itself. It is as if the affirmative votes were both the ratification and
proof of change.

The quasi-electorate, each member of which was vitally concerned
his involvement in the fortunes of his lord, was being asked obliquely by t
lord, "Has there occurred a *de facto* change of rule which we may now saf
accord *de jure* recognition?" An affirmative vote both ratified the propc
and by its symbolic jargon provided a portion of the recognition required
effect it. Since such ratification was asked but rarely, and successful dynas
change occurred even more rarely, the record preserved in the *Hsien-ti chu*
file is uniquely valuable and almost unbelievably fortuitous.

The argument that such propaganda documents constituted a cod
communication on an otherwise treasonous topic receives support by adduc
a negative example. Negative votes, denying the Mandate of Heaven to a que
lous aspirant, are also fortuitously recorded. They serve to clarify the essen
importance of the loyal constituency's concurrence in such a fateful step
single example, also from the Three States period, may prove instructive:

From this [time about the year 199, when he had become the ma
power in the northeast, Yüan] Shao's contributions to the [Sovereign
court became slight and dilatory. He privately had his Superintend
of Documents, Keng Pao, make a secret report, saying, "The power
[the] Red [element of Han] has declined to exhaustion. The Yüans
the scions of Yellow [claiming like the Ts'aos descent from the legend
Shun]. It would be proper to accord with Heaven's will." Shao to

the matter secretly reported by Pao and showed it to the generals and staff of his military headquarters. The discussants all considered that Pao had concocted a treasonous lie and should be executed. Shao then killed Pao in order to clear himself [of involvement in the improper suggestion.] [17]

Clearly, in the example cited, the otherwise loyal constituency had not ṇ or could not be convinced that the chance of success justified the risks ṣ claim for their lord at that juncture. In manner similar to the initial ṃments in the *Hsien-ti chuan* file the opinion test was carried out with due ịon and in the well-understood coded form. But since the response was ḍy negative, the attempt to claim the Mandate was never made.

When the "documentary events" of the file are seen thus as meaningfully ẹd two-way communication, they must then be seen as operating politically, ṃ if they also operate functionally in the theocratic ornament of dynastic ṇge. Confusion arises because the functional messages are coded in what ẹars to be a plaintext making sense on other levels. The question of belief ḥose other levels is irrelevant to this discussion.

If we similarly apply our newly acquired perspective to review the ques- concerning appeal to accepted dogma, I would argue that such appeal ọnstrates awareness of the political validity of the dogma but does not re- ẹ literal belief therein.

As stated at the outset of this paper, I hoped to give no more than ạtive support to the views argued above. Perhaps the presentation of this ẹrial will enable others to discern factors which have so far eluded me.[18]

---

[7] *SKCCC* Wei 6:50b, citing *Tien lüeh* 典略 ; also see *HHS* B64A: 12a.

[8] The final sentence of this paper is an example of a message coded in the manner ṛibed above. While the conventions of scholarship, in which I sincerely believe, de- ḍ the inclusion of such a demurrer, I leave the reader to discern the extent of my ḷl belief in the apparent plaintext.

Table I

ABDICATION DOCUMENTS RECORDED IN *HSIEN-TI CHUAN, SKCCC* WEI 2:14b-35b

Doc. No.	Day of 10th moon	Nominal Sender	Addressee	Summary of content	Reference
1	?	Li Fu, Han official	Wei King	Report of old prognostication, portents	14b
2	?	Wei King	Wei officials	Reject suggestion, but order publication	15a
3	?	Eight Wei officials	Wei King	Review, agree with Li Fu's memorial	15a-16a
4	?	Wei King	Wei officials	Reject doc. 3, order publication of this document	16a
5	9th day	Hsü Chih, Han T'ai-shih ch'eng	Wei King	List ch'an-wei prophesies favoring Wei	16a-19a
6	?	Wei King	Wei officials	Demurrer, ordered published	19a-b
7	?	Nine Wei officials	Wei King	Insist on veracity of portents/prophesies	19b-20b
8	11th day	Wei King	All officials	Reject suggestions, proclaimed to all officials	20b-21a
9	?	Han officials	Wei King	Urging by analysis of precedent	21a-b
10	?	Wei King	Wei officials	More rebuttal of urgings	21b-22b
11	13th day	Han Sovereign	Wei King	First abdication edict, sends seal and cord	22b-23b
12	?	Huan Chieh, others	Wei King	Request to build abdication platform	23b
13	?	Wei King	Wei officials	Orders discussion only of intent to refuse	23b
14	?	Huan Chieh, others	Wei King	Discusses mechanics of building platform	23b
15	?	Wei King	Wei officials	"Why are you anticipating matters?"	23b
16	?	Liu I, others	Wei King	Urge haste, selected the 17th for accession	23b-24a
17	?	Wei King	Wei officials	Saw platform being built, ordered stopped	24a-b
18	17th day	Wei King	All officials	Announces intent to refuse Sovereign's order	25a

21	?	120 officials	Wei King	More urgings	25b-26a
22	?	Wei King	Wei officials	Formalistic refusal, order draft of letter	26a-b
23	(18th day)	Liu I, others	Wei King	Protest refusal, but draft letter	26b
24	(18th day)	Wei King	Wei officials	Suggests will refuse three times, per precedent	26b
25	18th day	Wei King	Han Sovereign	First formal refusal, returns seal and cord	26b-27a
26	19th day	Su Lin, Tung Pa	Wei King	Astrological evidence for accession	27a-28b
27	?	Wei King	Wei officials	Admits authenticity of evidence, but refuses	28b
28	20th day	Han Sovereign	Wei King	Second abdication edict	28b-29a
29	?	Huan Chieh, others	Wei King	Again urge building platform, selecting day	29a-b
30	?	Wei King	Wei officials	Will refuse three times, "What's the rush?"	29b
31	22nd day	Wei King	Han Sovereign	Second formal refusal	29b
32	?	Liu I, others	Wei King	Urging by *yin-yang* theories	29b-30a
33	?	Wei King	Wei officials	Wait until after refusal to discuss possibility	30a
34	25th day	Han Sovereign	Wei King	Third abdication edict	30a
35	?	Han officials	Wei King	Reviewed correspondence, urge acceptance	30a-31a
36	?	Wei King	All officials	Florid refusal	31a
37	27th day	Wei King	Han Sovereign	Third formal refusal, edict returned unopened	31a-b
38	?	Han officials	Wei King	Review Han faults, portents, urge acceptance	31b-34a
39	?	Wei King	All officials	"How can I again refuse?"	34b
40	28th day	Han Sovereign	Wei King	Fourth abdication edict	34b-35a
41	(28th day)	Huan Chieh, others	Wei King	Select 29th day, ask edict of announcement	35a-b
42	(28th day)	Wei King	All officials	"Permitted."	35b

APPENDIX

Bibliography of Herrlee Glessner Creel

29 *Sinism, a study of the evolution of the Chinese world-view.* Chicago: Open Court. 127 pp.

31 "Confucius and Hsün-tzu," *Journal of the American Oriental Society*, 51, pp. 23-32.

32 " 彞 *i* as equivalent to 道 *tao*," *Journal of the American Oriental Society*, 52, pp. 22-24.

"Was Confucius agnostic?" *T'oung Pao*, 29, pp. 55-99.

33 "*Yüan tao tzu yü i tzu chih che-hsüeh i-i*" 原道字與彞字之哲學意義 [The philosophical significance of the "tao" and "i"], *Hsüeh Heng* [The Critical Review], 79, 12 pp.

34 "The rediscovery of pre-Confucian China," *Open Court*, 49, pp. 177-86.

35 "Dragon bones," *Asia Magazine*, pp. 176-82.

"Shih t'ien" 釋天 [The origin and development of the concept *t'ien*, "Heaven"] (tr. into Chinese by Liu Chieh), *Yen-ching Hsüeh-pao* [Yenching Journal of Chinese Studies], 18, pp. 59-71.

"On the origins of the manufacture and decoration of bronze in the Shang period," *Monumenta Serica*, 1, pp. 39-69.

"Les récents progrès de l'archéologie en Chine" (tr. into French by Jean Buhot), *Revue des Arts Asiatiques*, 9, pp. 96-107.

"Soldier and scholar in ancient China," *Pacific Affairs*, 8, pp. 336-43.

Obituary of Berthold Laufer in *Monumenta Serica*, 1, pp. 487-88.

36 *The birth of China, a survey of the formative period of Chinese civilization.* London: Jonathan Cape. 395 pp.

"Bronze inscriptions of the Western Chou dynasty as historical documents," *Journal of the American Oriental Society*, 56, pp. 335-49.

"Notes on Professor Karlgren's system for dating Chinese bronze
    Journal of the Royal Asiatic Society, pp. 463-73.
"Notes on Shang bronzes in the Burlington House Exhibition," *Rev
    des Arts Asiatiques*, 10, pp. 17-22.
"On the nature of Chinese ideography," *T'oung Pao*, 32, pp. 85-161

1937 *The birth of China* (American edition). New York: John Day. 402 p
    La Naissance de la Chine (French translation of *The birth of Chin*
        Paris: Payot et Cie. 368 pp.
    Studies in early Chinese culture, first series (American Council
        Learned Societies Studies in Chinese and Related Civilizatio
        no. 3). Baltimore: Waverly Press. 266 pp.
    "Why is a Sinologist?" *University of Chicago Magazine* (January 193
        pp. 6-10.

1938 *Literary Chinese by the inductive method* (with the assistance of Cha
        Tsung-ch'ien and Richard C. Rudolph), Vol. I. Chicago: T
        University of Chicago Press. 188 pp.
    "On the ideographic element in ancient Chinese," *T'oung Pao*, :
        pp. 265-94.

1939 *Literary Chinese by the inductive method* (with the assistance of Cha
        Tsung-ch'ien and Richard C. Rudolph), Vol. II. Chicago: T
        University of Chicago Press. 252 pp.
    "An inductive method for literary Chinese," *Notes on Far Easte
        Studies in America*, 5, pp. 1-7.

1943 *Newspaper Chinese by the inductive method* (with the assistance
        Teng Ssu-yü and others). Chicago: The University of Chicago Pre
        265 pp.
    Chinese writing (American Council on Education, Asiatic Studies
        American Education, no. 2). Washington, D.C. 16 pp.

1948 *Literary Chinese by the inductive method*, Vol. I (revised editio
        213 pp. Vol. II (reprint). Chicago: The University of Chicago Pre

1949 *Confucius, the man and the myth.* New York: John Day. 363 pp.
    "Confucius did *not* say . . . ," *United Nations World* (May 194
        pp. 32-33.
    "The Master who lighted the way in China," *The New York Tim
        Magazine* (August 28, 1949), pp. 15-16, 18.
    "Sinism—a clarification," *Journal of the History of Ideas*, 1
        pp. 135-140.
    "Some notes on *li*," *People*, 4, pp. 3-5.

1950 "Chinese philosophy (Confucianism, Moism, Taoism, Legalism
        Chapter 4, pp. 44-56, of *A history of philosophical systems*, edit

by Vergilius Ferm. New York: The Philosophical Library.
"Must one world be based on one religion?" *Common Cause* (February 1950), pp. 377-83.

1   *Confucius, the man and the myth* (British edition). London: Routledge and Kegan Paul, Ltd. 337 pp.

2   *Literary Chinese by the inductive method* (with the assistance of Chang Tsung-ch'ien and Richard C. Rudolph), Vol. III. Chicago: The University of Chicago Press. 331 pp.

3   *Chinese thought from Confucius to Mao Tse-tung.* Chicago: The University of Chicago Press. 292 pp. New York: Mentor. 240 pp.
    "Chinese philosophy and the Second East-West Philosophers' Conference," *Philosophy East and West*, 3, pp. 73-80.

4   *The birth of China* (third printing). New York: Frederick Ungar Publishing Company. 402 pp.
    Chinese thought from Confucius to Mao Tse-tung (British edition). London: Eyre and Spottiswoode. 301 pp.
    "On two aspects in early Taoism," *Silver Jubilee Volume of Zinbun-Kagaku-Kenkyusyo, Kyoto University*, pp. 43-53.
    "United States policy in Asia and the Chinese mind," *Union League Men and Events* (June 1954), pp. 6-9, 20-22.

5   *La Pensée chinoise de Confucius à Mao Tseu-tong* (French translation of *Chinese thought from Confucius to Mao Tse-tung*). Paris: Payot et Cie. 281 pp.

6   "What is Taoism?" *Journal of the American Oriental Society*, 76, pp. 139-52.

8   *Chinese civilization in liberal education* (editor). Proceedings of a Conference held at the University of Chicago, November 1958. 222 pp.
    "Liberal education and Chinese culture," in the above, pp. 17-26.
    "Filosofia Cinese," in *Le Civiltà dell'Oriente*, Vol. III, edited by Giuseppe Tucci (Rome), pp. 973-1012.

9   "Chinese culture and liberal education," *The Journal of General Education*, 12, pp. 29-38.
    "The Meaning of 刑名 *hsing-ming*," in *Studia Serica Bernhard Karlgren Dedicata* (Copenhagen: Munksgaard), pp. 199-211.
    "On the origins of the Chinese examination system," *Akten des Vierundzwanzigsten Internationalen Orientalisten-Kongresses, München 28, August bis 4, September 1957*(Weisbaden),pp.628-30.

0   *Confucius and the Chinese way* (Harper Torchbooks paperback edition of *Confucius, the man and the myth*). New York: Harper. 363 pp.

Chinese thought from Confucius to Mao Tse-tung (reprint). Chica
The University of Chicago Press. 293 pp. Paperback.

Chinese thought from Confucius to Mao Tse-tung (reprint). New Yo
The New American Library of World Literature, Inc. 240
Paperback.

1961   *Kō-shi* 孔子 (Japanese translation by Tajima Michiji of *Confucius,
man and the myth*). Tokyo: Iwanami Shoten. 462 pp.

"The Fa-chia 法家: 'legalists' or 'administrators'?" *Bulletin of
Institute of History and Philology, Academia Sinica*, extra
no. 4, *Studies Presented to Tung Tso-pin on His 65th Birthc
(Taipei), pp. 607-36.

1962   *Chinese thought from Confucius to Mao Tse-tung* (British paperb
edition). London: Methuen and Co., Inc. 301 pp.

1964   "The beginnings of bureaucracy in China: the origin of the *hsie
Journal of Asian Studies*, 23, pp. 155-84.

1965   "On the origin of *wu-wei* 無為," *Symposium in Honor of Dr. Li
on His Seventieth Birthday* (Taipei: Institute of History
Philology, Academia Sinica), pp. 1-33.

"The role of the horse in Chinese history," *American Histori
Review*, 70, pp. 647-72.

1968   "The great clod: A Taoist conception of the universe," *Wen-
Studies in the Chinese Humanities*, edited by Chow Tse-tsu
(Madison: University of Wisconsin Press), pp. 257-68.

1970   *The origins of statecraft in China*, Vol. I: *The Western Chou Emp
Chicago: The University of Chicago Press. 559 pp.

What is Taoism? and other studies in Chinese cultural history (collec
reprints). Chicago: The University of Chicago Press. 192 pp.

1973   *Il pensiero cinese da Confucio a Mao Tse-tung* (Italian translation
Chinese thought from Confucius to Mao Tse-tung*). Rome: Armor
Armondo. 327 pp.

1974   *Shen Pu-hai: A Chinese political philosopher of the fourth cent
B.C.* Chicago and London: The University of Chicago Press. 446

1976   *El pensamiento chino desde Confucio hasta Mao Tse-Tung* (Span
translation of *Chinese thought from Confucius to Mao Tse-tur
Madrid: Alianza Editorial. 321 pp.

1977   *What is Taoism? and other studies in Chinese cultural history* (reprir
Chicago: The University of Chicago Press. 192 pp. Paperback.

Index

093432